Texts and Monographs in Computer Science

Texts and Monographs in Computer Science

Micha Hofri

Probabilistic Analysis
of Algorithms

On Computing Methodologies for Computer
Algorithms Performance Evaluation

With 14 Illustrations

Springer-Verlag New York Berlin Heidelberg
London Paris Tokyo

Micha Hofri
Department of Computer Science
Technion—IIT
Haifa 32000
Israel

Series Editor
David Gries
Department of Computer Science
Cornell University
Ithaca, New York 14853
USA

Library of Congress Cataloging-in-Publication Data
Hofri, Micha.
    Probabilistic analysis of algorithms.
    (Texts and monographs in computer science)
    Bibliography: p.
    Includes index.
    1. Electronic digital computers—Programming.
2. Algorithms. 3. Probabilities. I. Title. II. Series.
QA76.6.H59   1987   005.1'2   87-16581

Text prepared by the author in camera-ready form on Laser Writer Plus.
Printed and bound by R.R. Donnelley & Sons, Harrisonburg, Virginia.
Printed in the United States of America.

9 8 7 6 5 4 3 2 1

ISBN 0-387-96578-5 Springer-Verlag New York Berlin Heidelberg
ISBN 3-540-96578-5 Springer-Verlag Berlin Heidelberg New York

להורי -
שרה ויצחק חפרי

PREFACE

This book originated from notes used for a course I gave in the Department of Computer Science of the Technion during the Spring term of 1986. The course had the same title as this volume. It was intended for both graduates and undergraduates who are close to finishing their studies and are looking for a suitable area in which to specialize. This was one of the factors that determined the coverage of the course - and consequently of the text as well; the latter contains much material that I had no time to discuss in class, as well as a good deal more exercises than the students could be asked to tackle.

Until quite recently, "analysis of algorithms" was nearly synonymous with determining the "complexity class" of an algorithm. This has the objective, most often, of finding whether in *all* cases the running time (or storage requirements) of the algorithm operation is or is not bounded by some specified function of the size of a suitably devised representation of the problem. It usually boils down to the consideration of some extreme, especially crafted problem instances. The realization that there is more one could say to characterize the cost of using an algorithm is probably due to the influence of Knuth's series on "The Art of Computer Programming", which started out in 1968. There, clearly, the operation of algorithms was shown to be associated with probabilistic concepts and processes.

Random elements, and hence the call for stochastic analysis, may enter algorithms in essentially two ways. On the one hand, we find the so called "probabilistic algorithms", such that choose part of their actions on the basis of random elements, explicitly introduced into the algorithm specification (pseudo-random numbers, simulated coin flipping and the like). Numerous algorithms of this class were recently developed, some showing prowess well beyond anything one has believed hitherto possible (primality testing algorithms provide a good example). On the other hand, we find the operation of deterministic algorithms on input data over which some probability measure can be stipulated. While the sources of the randomness present a true dichotomy, the required analyses turn out typically to be of the same nature in both cases. Among the algorithms for which we provide detailed analyses, the reader will find examples of both varieties. While the analyses proper are similar, we show in Chapter 1 that the second type brings up methodological and conceptual problems that the first case need not entail. The difficulty there may be phrased as lending substance to the notion of two algorithms having the same complexity "on the average", or "in distribution". The problem may also be seen to reside in the attribution of *a priori* probability measures to the input instance space. At the time of writing there is no coherent accepted theory or even taxonomy for these vexing issues, comparable to standard complexity theory; we shall mostly skirt them, using reasonable - sometimes seemingly facile - assumptions, invoking naturalness as our guideline.

The probabilistic analysis of algorithms, as a discipline, draws on a fair number of branches of mathematics. Principally: probability theory (especially as applied to stochastic processes), graph theory, combinatorics, real and complex analysis, and occasionally algebra, number theory, computation theory, operational calculus and more. It was unreasonable to expect the students to have more than a cursory knowledge of most of the techniques we used, so much of the time was given over to introducing and exploring these methods as we went along. Arranging the text so it could be conveniently used both as a text and as a reference posed a problem which was solved by departing in the book version from the order of the class presentation to a large extent, collecting most of the methodological material in Chapter 2.

The prerequisites that *were* assumed are basic courses in discrete mathematics, calculus (including a smattering of differential equations), linear algebra, probability theory, data structures and graph algorithms; all these being required courses in our department. The last two are assumed to impart to the students some algorithmic literacy.

The emphasis throughout is on the analytic and probabilistic aspects of our activity, rather than the algorithmic ones. Good texts for the latter exist and are multiplying satisfactorily; references are scattered throughout the book. For a while I occupied myself with the question whether the text should have some chapter on the needed tools from probability theory, or an introduction to the subject, or at least an appendix - and decided against it. This subject has been royally served in the last decade or two, with very good books, at every level of depth and sophistication. Indeed, since I am not even aware of all the good sources that exist now, the reference section mentions only those recently used in my work, as well as for the preparation of this text. What I *did* include is a section - 2.6 - containing a few results from probability theory that are outside the normal curricula and that I had occasion to witness their usefulness.

Computer algorithms deal with discrete quantities, and estimating their operations is very often reducible to a counting problem, in one guise or another. Hence the above mentioned need of combinatorics. Chapter 2 contains many combinatorial tools and concepts, either in the text proper or in exercises. Further sources for this important area are discussed in Chapter 1.

In addition to Chapter 1, which is used mainly to establish the context of the book, and the methodological Chapter 2 mentioned above, a few sample analyses are collected in the subsequent three chapters. The choice of the particular algorithms to analyze in detail was another non-trivial issue. The quest was easier for the first, simpler ones which are used mainly to introduce the nomenclature and a point of view. Here I could capitalize on ideas found in the so-far rather scanty literature on the subject; but beyond that I was mainly guided by personal preferences and experience, and to some extent by requests of students in the class, inasmuch as they agreed with the types of analysis I were interested in or able to display. The last reservation hints at some of the difficulty in teaching this subject: for some interesting analyses the sheer technical complexity (as distinct from their mathematical profundity) is such that presenting them in class is an unjustifiable harassment of the students (and the teacher too, no doubt). An analysis in which I was involved could serve as an illustration of such an unpleasantness (Fayolle et al., 1986).

The exercises are mostly extensions of the text, and sometimes were used to avoid giving much space to technicalities that tax the endurance of the reader and that the student should anyway gain some proficiency in performing on his own. Occasionally a large exercise presents a complete research problem, broken down to steps, with hints provided on the way to proceed.

Given the course (or book) prerequisites, the text is quite self-contained. There was no effort to keep the level of detail in the presentations uniform, and earlier sections tend to be more detailed. In the later sections a larger part of the derivation devolves to exercises, as mentioned above.

The material I used in class was (in order of presentation): Chapter 1, portions of sections 2.2.1, 2.2.2, 2.6.1, Chapter 3, 2.2.3-4, 2.4 and Chapter 4 (barring section 4.2.3). The teaching assistant, beside doing some of the exercises also covered Section 2.1, most of 2.3, and some of 2.5.

NOTATION

The references are all cited by author(s) and year, as in the above example, (Fayolle et al., 1986), and are collected at the back of the volume. I make no claim there for either completeness or historical fairness; these are simply the sources I actually used in preparing the text.

Equations are numbered separately in each major section (1.2, 3.3 etc.). Equation (7) in section 3.2 will be denoted as (7) throughout 3.2, and by (3.2-7) elsewhere; similar notation applies to exercises. The notation (A.1.7) and (C.3) refers to equations number (1.7) and (3) in appendices A and C, respectively. The mark □ indicates the end of a proof, a theorem which is not followed by a proof, or of a longer example.

Symbols are defined as needed. I tried to follow a few ground rules for uniformity: random variables and processes are denoted by capital italics, realized values by lower-case ones; probability distribution-, density- and mass-functions by F, f, and p, respectively, with suitable subscripts. Generating functions of several varieties by forms of the letter g, or by a letter derived from the name of the generated series or variable. Integer indices by i, j, k, l, m, n (shades of FORTRAN?). Kronecker's delta by δ_{ij}. E and V are reserved for the expectation and variance of random variables. There are a few exceptions. Most of the latter resulted from my trying, when following an analysis developed elsewhere, to adhere to the notation used there, so as to facilitate reference to the original paper. Symbols that are frequently used are collected in the Notation Index, at the back of the volume. Acronyms are expanded in the general index.

Starred exercises are those for which no satisfactory solution has yet been worked out.

ACKNOWLEDGMENTS

The decision to write the book was taken following a conversation with Philippe Flajolet. Alexander H.G. Rinnooy-Kan suggested the chapter on bin-packing. The involvement of Ms Lynn Montz, the Computer Science Editor of Springer-Verlag, New York, in the book production, was of a considerable help and is much appreciated. Mrs. Raya Anavi set an example in typing part of the material. The following colleagues and students read portions of the text and provided comments and corrections that greatly improved the presentation: Eyal Bardavid, John Bruno, Guy Fayolle, Aura Ganz, Zehava Koren, Shay Leshkovitz, Johann Makowsky, Hadas Shachnai and Moshe Sidi. Their contributions are gratefully acknowledged.

Still, their help does not entitle the above to any claim on errors and misrepresentations, which remain wholly mine. Help in further reducing these is avidly solicited, and will be very welcome.

The typesetting was done on equipment of the Department of Computer Science of the Technion. The help of the principal system engineers, Aythan Avior and Shlomo Goldberg, has been invaluable in getting around a myriad trivial obstacles that were as exasperating as they were unexpected.

Haifa, Israel, March 1987.   M. Hofri

ACKNOWLEDGMENTS

Figure 3.4, p. 130 is based on Fig. 11, p.87 of Donald E. Knuth, THE ART OF COMPUTER PROGRAMMING, Vol 3, © 1973 by Addison Wesley Publishing Company, Inc. Reading Massachusetts. Reprinted with permission.

Figures 4.1 and 4.2, p.149, and portions of Tables 1 and 2, p.158, are reproduced from Figures 1 and 2 p.276, and Tables 2 and 3, p.280 of J.C. Lagarias, A.M. Odlyzko and D.B. Zagier: "On the Capacity of Disjointly Shared Networks.", published in Computer Networks, **10,** 275-285, © 1985 by North-Holland Publishing Company, Amsterdam. Reprinted with permission.

Figures 1.1 and 1.2, pp.5, 6 are reprinted from unnumbered figures on pp.2, 3 in Rainer Kemp, FUNDAMENTALS OF THE AVERAGE CASE ANALYSIS OF PARTICULAR ALGORITHMS, © 1984 by John Wiley & Sons Ltd. and B. G. Teubner, Stuttgart. Reprinted with permission.

Contents

CHAPTER 1

Introduction

1.1 Criteria for the Performance and Quality of Algorithms

Algorithms embody methods for the treatment of data so as to meet desired objectives. Normally we specify an algorithm by stating

(a) What is a legal input for the algorithm. This contains typically parameters and data. For example, an integer n followed by n pairs of real numbers.

(b) The transformation that the algorithm should perform on the input. Equivalently, we could provide a description of the output in terms of the input. For example, in (a), when the number pairs are construed as point coordinates in the plane, we could ask for the output to be a sequence of those points that are the convex hull of the entire set.

We shall never concern ourselves with what happens when illegal input is given. Even when the input is legal, however, an algorithm may display highly non-uniform behavior when different input instances are processed. The subject Analysis of Algorithms tries to cope with this non-uniformity and quantify it.

Non-uniformity in algorithm operation arises on two distinct levels, or in two senses. The first concerns the resource requirements of the algorithm. The second concerns the quality of the performance of the algorithm. We shall have opportunity to tackle examples of both of them. Consider first the resource consumption: As we are exclusively concerned with algorithms that operate in a digital computer two resources are significant:

Time - the running time of the algorithm is normally represented by the number of operations the algorithm has to do in order to complete its task. This appears a reasonable approach as long as all the operations require essentially the same time. When this is not the case one may use suitable weighting, to reflect the relative execution durations of the instructions. An extreme example: when the process calls for accessing secondary storage, typically a much longer operation than internal manipulations, we shall content ourselves by just counting these dominating operations, seeing the others as a perturbation of the main term.

Storage - the amount of internal or secondary storage the algorithm requires for temporary storage that is beyond the storage used to keep the input and store the final result.

The second aspect of behavior an algorithm may display arises in the following context: we are considering a difficult problem. This problem *can* be completely solved, but only at a considerable expenditure in computing resources, and thus we would like to make do with a cheaper procedure, even if a suboptimal one - an algorithm that does not necessarily provide the correct, or optimal, answer, but only an approximation thereof. Common examples arise in scheduling theory. The problem of assigning a set of tasks to a group of machines so as to optimize their average waiting time, or the total completion time, is sometimes NP-complete and often NP-hard. We shall say that such a problem is intractable when we do not know an efficient algorithm to obtain the optimal schedule. However, it is common that simple algorithms exist that produce schedules that are "acceptable". Quantifying this property, or more precisely, the difference between the optimal result and the one obtained by the simple algorithm, is the second aspect of the algorithmic behavior we shall consider.

Whichever aspect we consider there are two basic questions one would like to answer:

(1) Can we guarantee the performance of the algorithm? Can we find a function of the parameters common to all possible input instances and state that "for any legal input the running time of the algorithm will not *exceed* this function" (or will be *at least* that function)? Similar questions can be posed, of course, for any other descriptor as well.

(2) What can be said about the *probable* performance of the algorithm? Here we are concerned with statements like "the average temporary storage the algorithm will require is twice the size of the input". Or "the probability that the algorithm will have to scan the input more than k times is at most c/k^2."

Questions of the first type, such that provide bounds on performance, deal with individual executions of the algorithm. In order to find the answers one typically has to consider all possible inputs, and select the set - often containing a single instance - that accounts for the extreme behavior. Only on those instances will the algorithm perform at its best (or worst). Since the worst behavior is usually of more concern, this approach has acquired the unsavory title of "worst-case analysis."

The questions of the second type also involve the entirety of the possible inputs, but from a different point of view. This change of view often raises a preliminary, and sometimes a more difficult, question to answer: since we need to consider probable performance, we must be able to give a statement about the likelihood of the algorithm having to work on different input instances. Put differently: we need a probability measure on the input space. Clearly the probability of the algorithm being assigned various input instances influences its probable performance! Consider a pathological example, when one source of the inputs we use is heavily biased toward producing only samples on which the algorithm performs at close to its best behavior; and another source of legitimate input is biased to produce instances on which the algorithm displays nearly its worst performance. Almost always we would obtain two different, possibly very different, behavior patterns! In a sense, we want the *true* distribution of the input. One could conjure a hypothetical situation where the algorithm is to be performed many times on inputs that are generated by well understood processes, and through knowledge of these processes we can obtain an estimate of the input distribution. This is a highly unlikely scenario. Almost always we have to make do with some alternative. For example: when the number of possible inputs is finite, N, we shall normally assume (again, unless additional information is available) that each input has the same probability, namely $1/N$. When the number of possible inputs is not finite, we shall need some probabilistic assumptions on the generator of the input, and from these we shall derive statements about the relative probabilities of different input instances. A more detailed example will probably clarify both these remarks and the importance of the issue:

On the Average Length of Resolution.

One of the celebrated members of the family of NP-complete problems is the satisfiability problem. We consider its following formulation: the input consists of two sets. One is a set V of r boolean variables, $\{v_j\}$, termed literals in this context. The second is a set of n clauses, each being a disjunction of up to r literals (where a literal may appear as either v_j or its complementary variable $\bar{v}_j$). The problem is to determine whether there exists a "truth assignment" to the r literals, such that *all* n clauses are TRUE. A truth assignment is a function $t: V \rightarrow$ {TRUE, FALSE}. Hence there are 2^r truth assignments. A number of procedures for solving this problem have been fashioned, all having of course worst-case behavior that is exponential in the size of the input, which is essentially a specification of the clauses. Not too much is known about their *probable* behavior. In Goldberg (1979) it is shown that a certain algorithm for this problem, the Davis-Putnam procedure (DPP), has a running time which is almost always (i.e. with probability approaching one, for large sample spaces), approximately quadratic in n, when n is not "too large" compared to r. The assertion had naturally to assume a probability distribution on the inputs, and although for given n and r the number of possible inputs is finite, the chosen measure was not the uniform one mentioned above, but one that envisaged the input as coming from a source generator with the following properties:

A sample problem is generated according to the $g(n, r, p, q)$ measure, when n and r are parameters, with the meaning as defined above, p and q are real positive numbers such that $p + q \leq 1$. Each of the n clauses is generated independently. In each clause a literal v_j appears, independently of all other literals in that clause, with probability p, and its complementary $\bar{v}_j$ with probability q. Thus a clause may contain between zero literals (an empty clause, which cannot be satisfied) and $2r$ literals.

However, in Franco and Paull (1983) it is shown that the distributions $g(n, r, p, q)$ almost always generate problems that are very easily satisfiable (or easy to check that they cannot be satisfied), so much so that the seemingly inane procedure of checking the problem clauses against a fixed, predetermined set of truth assignments will almost always - i.e. with a probability approaching 1 - find a solution within a computable, constant time (under this particular input distribution).

The same two authors then propose another random generator for satisfiability problems. This generator uses a distribution $f(n, a, k)$, where n and k are integers and a is a positive real number. Each instance contains n clauses, each consisting of a subset of size k of literals chosen randomly from the set of $r(n, a) = 2\lfloor an \rfloor$ literals $\{v_1, v_2, \cdots, v_{r(n,a)}, \bar{v}_1, \bar{v}_2, \cdots, \bar{v}_{r(n,a)}\}$. Now they show that on the collection of problems thus generated the above procedure (DPP) will almost always require a running time that is exponentially related to the input size! We find ourselves hard put to say that one of the distributions is "better" in any sense than the other; the only definite conclusion is that the performance of the DPP is sensitive to the probability measure on its sample space, and in a way that equally "typical" or "reasonable" distributions may reveal very different behavior. The moral is that we need robust procedures. Or that we need to know how to tailor an algorithm to a given situation. See also the readable lecture of Karp (1986) for discussions on related topics in a different vein altogether.

A somewhat unexpected fact is that results of worst-case analysis may differ from those of probabilistic analysis in a qualitative sense as well. A simple example will be shown in Section 5.2. A recent, possibly more surprising example concerns the algorithms used to allocate main storage, when the framework is allocation of "variable, static partitions". There are two algorithms that are most often used for this purpose: First Fit (FF) and Best Fit (BF). Now, it has been shown that the worst-case behavior of BF in terms of external fragmentation is by far worse than that of FF (see Robson, 1978), whereas recent work by Coffman et al. (1986) indicates that in terms of essentially the same criterion, under simple but reasonable assumptions, the expected allocation efficiency under BF is much better than under FF. We remark that empirical evidence, from systems in the field, is hard to come by, and not quite conclusive.

In some of the literature probabilistic analysis is called "average-case analysis", to produce the obvious contrast. Often, computing expected values is indeed all that we can accomplish. As every enterprising cook knows, though, nothing of value comes out as expected. Consequently the analyst tries, whenever possible, to obtain more informative results: complete distributional description is the ideal, and relatively rare possibility. The second moment, or more precisely the variance, usually provides decent bounds on the likelihood of deviations from the mean, and in several of the analyses done in detail later we shall make do with it.

1.2 The Analysis of a Very Simple Algorithm

Most of our work will concern general methods, rather than particular algorithms. Still, we shall find it appropriate to consider some special ones, demonstrating these methods. Here is the first such instance, following Kemp (1984).

Consider a one-tape one-head Turing machine entrusted with the task of adding one to a number given in binary representation. The machine recognizes the characters 0, 1, and *. The initial state of the machine and its context may look as given in Fig 1.1(a), and the final position then should appear as in Fig. 1.1(b), where the numbers as written on the tape satisfy

$$\sum_{i=0}^{n} b_i 2^i = \sum_{i=0}^{n-1} a_i 2^i + 1 .$$

An algorithm that performs the task is not complicated: it examines the characters from right to left, continuing left as long as only '1's are encountered, converting them to '0's and keeping a '1' as carry, until a '0' is encountered or the leftmost

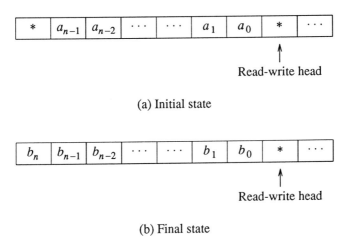

(a) Initial state

(b) Final state

Fig. 1.1: A Turing machine 1-adder (Kemp, 1984).

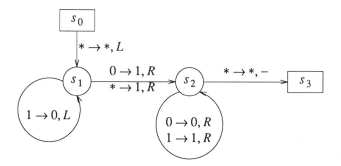

Fig. 1.2: Add one, the Turing way (following Kemp, 1984).

comes first. The addition can then be completed. Since we would like the procedure to be well-formed, the head needs to be left where it started, hence the additional traversal to the right.

This tale is told in Fig 1.2, where an edge carrying $x \rightarrow y, z$ means: if the tape square opposite the head carries the symbol x replace it with a y and move z. The entire addition is actually carried out in state s_1. We shall make the reasonable identification of the cost of the algorithm with the total number of steps the head executes in the process. This number is even, and equals $2(m+1)$ if the input has exactly m trailing '1' digits, for $0 \le m \le n$.

Thus, letting T_n denote the running time of the algorithm, we may write

$$\text{Prob}(T_n = 2m)$$

$$= \text{Prob}(\text{precisely the } m-1 \text{ rightmost digits of the input are } '1's), \quad 1 \le m \le n+1$$

and we face again the question of putting a measure over the input. Taking the uniform approach, we note that n digits make for 2^n distinct numbers, and ascribe to each the probability 2^{-n}. Hence the right-hand side of the equation reads

$$2^{-n} \times (\text{the size of the set of numbers that satisfy the digit condition}).$$

Note that if the above algorithm were a part of a more complex procedure, and for some intrinsic reason only even numbers could be generated at this stage, then the number of moves would be 2, with probability one.

Under the uniformity assumption, once m digits are fixed ($m-1$ '1's and the adjacent '0'), the remaining $n-m$ digits allow for 2^{n-m} distinct numbers. This holds for $1 \le m \le n$, and there is one number for $m = n+1$ as well, hence

$$\text{Prob}(T_n = 2m) = \begin{cases} 2^{-n} \cdot 2^{n-m} & 1 \le m \le n, \\ 2^{-n} & m = n+1. \end{cases} \tag{1}$$

We have obtained the complete distribution of the algorithm running time; we shall rarely be able to come up with such a feat when more complicated algorithms are discussed. For illustration, we shall also evaluate the moments of T_n. Thus its expected value is

$$E(T_n) = \sum_{m=1}^{n} 2^{-m} 2m + 2(n+1)2^{-n}. \tag{2}$$

The sum can be reduced using the familiar formula

$$\sum_{k=1}^{n} kq^k = \frac{q}{(1-q)^2}[1 - (n+1)q^n + nq^{n+1}], \qquad q \neq 1 \tag{3}$$

with $q = \frac{1}{2}$, to get

$$E(T_n) = 4 - 2^{-n+1}. \tag{4}$$

Likewise

$$E(T_n^r) = \sum_{m=1}^{n} (2m)^r 2^{-m} + 2^r (n+1)^r 2^{-n}$$

$$= 2^r \sum_{m \geq 1} m^r 2^{-m} + [(n+1)^r 2^{r-n-1} - 2^r \sum_{m \geq n+2} m^r 2^{-m}]. \tag{5}$$

The expression in brackets is approximately $n^r 2^{-n}$, i.e. exponentially small for large n, and we disregard it. Using the asymptotic notation introduced in Section 2.1.1 it is conventionally written as $O(n^r 2^{-n})$. The first term on the right-hand side is expressible via the Eulerian polynomials, defined through

$$\sum_{k \geq 0} k^r x^k = \frac{A_r(x)}{(1-x)^{r+1}}, \qquad \text{(Eulerian polynomials)}. \tag{6}$$

Some properties of these polynomials and relations they satisfy may be found in Knuth (1973) and Kemp (1984). Thus, for fixed r and sufficiently large n we write

$$E(T_n^r) = 2^{2r+1} A_r(\tfrac{1}{2}) + O(n^r 2^{-n}). \tag{7}$$

Since $A_2(\frac{1}{2})$ is very nearly $\frac{3}{4}$, we get, for example, $E(T_n^2) \approx 24$. Hence the variance of T_n is about 8. In later sections we encounter tools, namely Chebyshev's inequality and the central limit theorem, that use this quantity to provide a measure on the likely variations of T_n from its mean, for large n.

We have analyzed an algorithm. Before more ambitious analyses are attempted, we make a long digression to discuss our main sources, notations and analytical tools. We shall see that while the paradigm of the above analysis will be often repeated, its difficulty is hardly so predictive.

1.3 Comments on Sources and Resources

The nature of the work required in the process of the analyses we contemplate often involves substantial computations. The undesirability of reinventing the wheel (or estimating its circumference) is obvious, and there are a great many wheels one needs in the course of a non-trivial analysis.

In Chapter 2 we bring tools and techniques that we, and others, have found useful. Clearly there are numerous specialized devices and results buried in the literature that we can neither present nor mention, but there exist a few repositories of such concentrated information that should be brought to the reader's attention. The bibliographic data are given fully in the references section.

• Knuth's three volumes (starting in 1968 and hopefully still going on) contain a great variety of complete analyses and isolated results, many of these in exercises, with detailed solutions. They are rather scattered, and accessible usually only through the index. Some of these we use in the sequel (in Sections 2.1.1 and 3.3.2).

• Erdèlyi et al. (1953) bring information about a large number of representations of known functions. Once the analyst discovers that some expression he manufactured in his computations is equal to some such recognized function, the road is open to take advantage of known properties of the function, numerical values, asymptotic behavior, alternative representations, etc. Often these properties are apparent only from such other representations, and the equivalence could be sometimes very hard to deduce.

• Abramowitz and Stegun (1964) is another collection of such information, with many tables and numerical expansions, some asymptotics, less on representations and properties than Erdèlyi et al.

• Gradshtein and Rej'ik (1981) bring an unparalleled collection of integrals, some indefinite, much more definite ones. It also contains more information on special functions, in the spirit of the last two references, but each of the three contains some results the other two do not.

• Sloane (1973) is a unique anthology of sequences of integers; obtaining a prefix of such a sequence in experimentation, or by solving a few stages of a recursion, brings the analyst to a position where the use this book will provide him with pointers to general forms and further literature.

There are many other specialized collections, but for us the above publications have been the main resource for this kind of information.

Books similar to the present one are few yet. The above volumes by Knuth stand foremost, but their coverage is mainly oriented to the algorithms proper, with the analysis given as the need arises.

Greene and Knuth (1982) is a collection of handouts to students in a course like the one on which this text is based. It offers a very elegant presentation, rather tersely, of some of the tools we present, and a few detailed analyses.

Kemp (1984) is rather closer in spirit to the present text, and indeed we borrowed from it the example above and the idea behind Section 2.6.1. It is mainly oriented toward the very detailed analysis of a few algorithms that generate trees and random walks on a plane lattice.

Other sources that should be mentioned include the books by de Bruijn (1981), Comtet (1974), Davies (1978), Feller (especially Vol. I, 1973), Goulden and Jackson (1983), Riordan (1964 and 1968), and the surveys by Bender (1974), Coffman et al. (1984, 1985, 1986) and Flajolet (1984).

Readers interested in more information about algorithms as such could do worse than consult the Knuth volumes mentioned above. Their coverage, in the topics they discuss, is remarkable. Gonnet (1984) is a much more concise summary and specification of basic algorithms over data structures (bringing also known results about their performance characteristics). Texts on algorithms over data structures are aplenty, and lacking experience in using them in the class we have no favorites.

Exercises and Complements

1. Describe real-life situations where the input to a sort routine will *not* be a random permutation.

2. In Franco and Paull (1983) it is stated that the measure $g(n,r,1/3,1/3)$, a special case of the one introduced in Section 1.1, generates all the possible problems with equal probability. This requires that we define precisely when two problems are considered distinct. Under what definition does the above statement hold?

3. Without trying any detailed analysis, can you suggest why the cited authors of analyses of algorithms for the satisfiability problem (as well as others we have not explicitly mentioned), all eschewed the uniform measure over the problem space and adopted generative models? [*Hint*: the key word is 'dependence'].

4. This question deals with the notion of a *random graph*. An introduction to this sometimes surprising topic may be found in Bollobas (1979). We consider only undirected simple graphs (i.e. without loops or multiple edges). Several probability spaces have been used to support such graphs. Here are three examples:

(a) $G(n,p)$ has n nodes, and each pair of nodes has a connecting edge with probability p, independently of all others.

(b) $G(n,d)$ has n nodes, and each node is connected to precisely d others. Each such graph is given the same probability. (How are n and d related?)

(c) $G(n,d)$ has n nodes and is created by first distributing directed arcs, from a node at a time, so that each node has the same outdegree d, with the other end nodes selected at random from the nodes still unattached to that node. Then the direction of the arcs is removed.

[One further makes a distinction between *labeled* and *unlabeled* graphs. Thus the labeled graphs written in the format $G(V,E)$, $G(\{1,2,3\}, \{(1,2)\})$ and $G(\{1,2,3\}, \{(2,3)\})$ are different when considered as labeled graphs, but identical with the labeling removed. The most common probability space on which labeled graphs are grown is formed by considering the graphs $G(n,M)$, with n nodes and M edges, and assigning to each of the $\binom{n(n-1)/2}{M}$ such graphs the same probability.]

With $n=6$, $p=1/3$ and $d=2$, what is the probability under each of the above models of obtaining a connected graph?

5. Use the one-sided Chebyshev inequality (C.3) (see also its use in Section 3.1), to estimate the probability that T_n exceeds $1.5E(T_n)$. Then compare the value you obtained to the correct one, using equation (1).

CHAPTER 2

Tools of the Trade

Tinker, tinker, what is your trade?
A pot, a pan, and a well-honed blade.

A workman is known by his tools - proverb

2.1 Introduction to Asymptotics

It is rare that the analysis of an algorithm produces closed-form expressions in terms of standard functions that are convenient to use. It is even rarer that the results have a form simple enough, to provide an intuitive insight into the dependence of the algorithm properties on the various parameters of the input. More often the analyst nets an unwieldy sum, such an integral, or worse - the result is only available in terms of transforms that are hard to invert; sometimes even this is not available explicitly: one can only determine a recalcitrant equation that the result satisfies.

Barring simulation, the usual recourse is to asymptotic analysis. Generally, an asymptotic expansion is a series, hopefully of a simple structure, that we use to represent a more complicated expression in a certain "limiting sense". We begin with definitions of the asymptotic notation, the purpose of which is to lend precision to this sense. Following that, we present, as examples, two tools used in asymptotic analysis. The first is a method of approximate summation, tailored to the types of sums that tend to crop up in our work: sums that involve volatile functions such as factorials or binomial coefficients. The other is more general - the Euler summation formula - that replaces a sum by an integral and a series of correction terms. Section 2.5 presents a number of results from complex function theory, that allow the analyst to go beyond the methods of this section.

Remark: The mathematical subject of asymptotic analysis is considerably wider than we have the occasion to encompass here and in Section 2.5. A good introduction to the subject is Chapter 11 of Henrici (1977), which also provides further leads.

2.1.1 Asymptotic Notation

The main asymptotic notation we shall use is the "big oh", O. It is defined as follows:

$a_n = O(f(n))$ implies the existence of two (unspecified) integers M and N such that $|a_n| \leq Mf(n)$ for $n \geq N$.

Thus the statement $a_n = O(f(n))$ may be taken as saying that $f(n)$ provides an upper bound, up to a sign and a multiplicative constant, on a_n, when n is large. We shall nearly always consider n as taking integer values only, but all the properties hold for a continuous variable as well.

The merits of this notation are:

1)   it simplifies relations, in letting us concentrate our attention on the dominant terms. Thus, if $f(n)$ is the sum of n and $\sin(g(n))$, where $g(n)$ is a hard-to-determine real-valued function, writing $f(n) = n + O(1)$ captures simply the essential information for large n.

More important is that

2)   it allows us to replace inequalities by "equalities". The double quotes should serve as a warning that not all the manipulations permissible with normal equations are allowed here. The most glaring difference is that it should not be considered reflexive (and is hence intransitive as well). Thus $n+1 = O(n)$ is correct, but $O(n) = n+1$ is rather meaningless. The "rule of thumb" is that the left-hand side of an asymptotic relation should be more detailed, or less crude than the right-hand side.

The *converse* statement - a_n is bound *from below* up to a sign and a constant integer by $f(n)$ - is written $a_n = \Omega(f(n))$. If $g(n) = O(h(n))$ and $g(n) = \Omega(h(n))$ we abbreviate and write $g(n) = \Theta(h(n))$. This then implies $|h(n)/g(n)|$ remains in a bounded interval, away from 0, as n increases.

Remark: The notation $O(n)$ is occasionally used informally to denote a quantity that is *of order n* (rather than, say, its square or its logarithm).

One further notation we shall use rather infrequently is the "small o" symbol. $f(n) = o(g(n))$ means $\lim_{n \to \infty} f(n)/g(n) = 0$. It is less useful, since it is less informative about the rate of convergence, which is often important. The O and o

notations are associated with the name of E.G.H. Landau, as well as the symbol ~, where $f(n) \sim g(n)$ means $\lim_{n \to \infty} f(n)/g(n) = 1$.

The following is a list of the simple manipulations that may be performed with the O symbol.

$$c \cdot O(f(n)) = O(f(n)), \quad \text{(c is a constant)} \qquad (1)$$

$$O(f(n)) + O(f(n)) = O(f(n)) \qquad (2)$$

$$O(O(f(n))) = O(f(n)) \qquad (3)$$

$$g(O(n)) = O(g(n)). \qquad (4)$$

For the last relation to hold, $g(x)$ should be a nondecreasing polynomial, or satisfy $g(n) = O(P(n))$, where $P(n)$ is a polynomial, nondecreasing in the relevant range.

$$O(f(n)) \cdot O(g(n)) = O(f(n)g(n)) = f(n)O(g(n)). \qquad (5)$$

These equalities should be understood as substitution rules. Thus the last one should be read as "the product of two functions, of which one is $O(f(n))$ and the other $O(g(n))$, is $O(f(n)g(n))$", etc.

If $f(z)$ has a power series expansion $\sum_{n \geq 0} f_n z^n$ which is absolutely convergent in the disk $|z| \leq r$, for some $r > 0$, then for any k

$$f(z) = f_0 + f_1 z + \cdots + f_k z^k + O(z^{k+1}), \qquad |z| \leq r. \qquad (6)$$

This must hold, since $f(z) - \sum_{n=0}^{k} f_n z^n = z^{k+1}(f_{k+1} + f_{k+2}z + \cdots)$ and for $|z| \leq r$ the assured convergence of the expansion implies that the term in parentheses is bounded.

For example,

$$n^{a/n} = e^{\frac{a}{n} \log n} = 1 + a\frac{\log n}{n} + O\left(\left(\frac{\log n}{n}\right)^2\right),$$

for *any* fixed a.

2.1.2 Summation Asymptotics

It is common that the analysis of an algorithm produces a sum, usually finite, for which no representation in primitive terms or known functions exists. This is particularly common in problems involving enumeration. Appendices A and B contain results useful in reducing sums that include binomial coefficients or Stirling numbers. The Lagrange expansion theorem (Section 2.2.3) or the Mellin summation formula (Section 2.3.3) sometimes provide a concise representation for obdurate sums, but they all fail at times, rather frequently actually, and we are obliged to resort to asymptotics.

Fortunately we shall find that sums arising from enumerations are often characterized by two properties that help in obtaining usable asymptotic values:

a)   The summands are unimodal in the index of summation (consist of one or two monotone sequences of terms).

b)   Nearly the entire value of the sum comes from the contribution of a small fraction of the summation range.

The following procedure is suggested to take care of such sums (Bender, 1974):

1)   Change the index of summation, so that the maximal term obtains at or near the value 0 of the index. Usually one need not take any special steps when the change of index is fractional, rather than integral. If the maximum is at the boundary of the summation range, the shift will be rounded usually to an integer. (An example will be given below.)

2)   Evaluate the remaining sum; sometimes this can be done directly, often the sum is replaced by an integral. When the peak of the summands is flat enough, this replacement is straightforward. The Euler summation formula (Section 2.1.3) or the Mellin summation formula (Section 2.3.3) can otherwise help.

The so far unique book, de Bruijn (1981), demonstrates a few more devices and derivations worthy of attention.

The following two examples are adapted from Bender (1974), and demonstrate the above procedure.

Example 1: Asymptotic value for the Bell numbers. The n-th Bell number, given by

$$B_n = \frac{1}{e} \sum_{k \geq 1} \frac{k^n}{k!},$$ (7)

will be shown in Section 2.4.2 to be the number of ways to break up a set of n elements to disjoint subsets. We estimate its value, using the above procedure.

The summand $k^n/k!$ is rewritten, with the zero-order Stirling approximation (see relation (A.5.1)), as $b_k = \frac{1}{\sqrt{2\pi}} k^{n-k-\frac{1}{2}} e^k$. To find the value of k that yields its maximum take its logarithm, discarding the first factor,

$$\log b_k = k + (n-k-\tfrac{1}{2})\log k .$$ (8)

Differentiating this expression as if k were continuous, we find that it is maximized at $k = t$, with t determined by

$$t \log t = n - \frac{1}{2} .$$ (9)

Digression: Equation (9) provides an implicit relation for t in terms of n. How can t be determined explicitly? A standard technique borrowed from numerical analysis is to proceed by iteration (numerical analysts refer to it as the *successive approximations method*): pick some initial solution, say $t_0 = n$ and iterate, $t_{i+1} = (n - \frac{1}{2})/log\ t_i$.

   Question: what do you expect would happen if you used instead the iteration $t_{i+1} = \exp((n - \frac{1}{2})/t_i)$? Try a few steps to see that an iteration does not - need not - automatically converge. Consider the generic equation $x = f(x)$; under what conditions on the behavior of $f(x)$ near a solution, and choice of an initial value, will the iteration $x_{i+1} = f(x_i)$ converge? For a comprehensive treatment see Section 5.1 of Blum (1972).

This procedure can be viewed slightly differently, as providing a sequence of asymptotic estimates for t. It is then called (by Knuth) "bootstrapping": On inspection of equation (9) it is obvious that $t = O(n)$. Hence, resubstituting, using equation (4):

$$t_1 = O\left(\frac{n - \frac{1}{2}}{log\ n}\right),\ t_2 = O\left(\frac{n - \frac{1}{2}}{log(n - \frac{1}{2}) - log\ log\ n}\right), \cdots \qquad (10)$$

Already for the second approximation, the ratio $\dfrac{\bar{t}_2 log\bar{t}_2 - (n - \frac{1}{2})}{n}$ (with $\bar{t}_2$ representing the value in parentheses in the above approximation) is quite small. When $log\ n$ is in the range of 2 to 10, the ratio is about 10^{-3}.

End of *digression*.

   Getting back to b_k, we want to translate it into a convenient b_j, with $j = k - t = o(t)$. We use the approximation for small x of $log(1 - x) = x - x^2/2$ and write the following sequence of estimates

$$b_j = \frac{(j+t)^{n-k-\frac{1}{2}}}{\sqrt{2\pi}}\ e^{j+t} = \frac{t^{n-k-\frac{1}{2}}}{\sqrt{2\pi}}\ e^{j+t}\ \left(1+\frac{j}{t}\right)^{(n-\frac{1}{2})-t-j} \qquad (11)$$

$$= \frac{t^{n-t-j}}{\sqrt{2\pi t}}\ e^{j+t}\left(1+\frac{j}{t}\right)^{t\ log\ t-t-j} \equiv \frac{t^{n-t}}{\sqrt{2\pi t}}\ e^{j+t}\cdot\alpha\cdot\beta\cdot\gamma \qquad (12)$$

with $log(1 + j/t) \approx \dfrac{j}{t} - \dfrac{j^2}{2t^2}$, when $j = o(t)$, and we set

$$\alpha \equiv \left(1+\frac{j}{t}\right)^{t\ log\ t} = e^{t\ log\ t \cdot log(1+\frac{j}{t})} \approx e^{log\ t(j-\frac{j^2}{2t})}$$

$$\beta \equiv e^{-t\ log(1+\frac{j}{t})} \approx e^{-j+\frac{j^2}{2t}} \qquad (13)$$

$$\gamma \equiv t^{-j} e^{-j\ log(1+\frac{j}{t})} \approx e^{-j\ log\ t-\frac{j^2}{t}}.$$

Summing all the exponents we obtain

$$b_j \approx \frac{t^{n-t}}{\sqrt{2\pi t}}\ e^t \cdot e^{-(1+log\ t)\frac{j^2}{2t}}. \qquad (14)$$

For the summation on j we note that already at $j = t^{\frac{1}{2}}$ and above the contribution is negligible, so we may sum for $-\infty < j < \infty$ without jeopardizing the above approximations. The functional dependence on j in the summand is the same as in the normal pdf, the integral of which over the entire real line is known; so replacing the sum by an integral (more on this in Section 2.1.3), we obtain

$$\sum_{j \ge -t} e^{-(1+\log t)\frac{j^2}{2t}} \approx \int_{-\infty}^{\infty} e^{-(1+\log t)\frac{j^2}{2t}} dj = \sqrt{\frac{2\pi t}{1+\log t}}. \tag{15}$$

Hence

$$B_n = \frac{1}{e} \frac{t^{n-t}}{\sqrt{2\pi t}} e^t \sqrt{\frac{2\pi t}{1+\log t}} \approx \frac{t^{n-t} e^{t-1}}{\sqrt{\log t}}. \tag{16}$$

The approximations in (10) can be used to write explicit expressions in terms of n.

Example 2: A binomial sum.

We shall consider now the sum

$$A_n = \sum_{0 \le k \le \lambda n} \binom{n}{k}^r \tag{17}$$

for some $0 < \lambda \le 1$, $r > 0$ and large n. The maximum value of the binomial coefficient obtains at $k = n/2$. Note that this value need not be integral. In principle one can use the gamma function to represent values of the factorials called for by a binomial coefficient with nonintegral components, but in practice it will be taken care of automatically by our use of the Stirling approximation. The derivation of the sum proceeds somewhat differently in the three cases: $\lambda = \frac{1}{2}$, $\lambda < \frac{1}{2}$ and $\lambda > \frac{1}{2}$.

First $\lambda = \frac{1}{2}$.

Define $j = \dfrac{n}{2} - k$; then $k = \dfrac{n}{2} - j$, $\dfrac{n}{k} = \dfrac{2n}{n-2j}$, $n - k = \dfrac{n}{2} + j$ and
$\dfrac{n}{n-k} = \dfrac{2n}{n+2j}$.   These, using Stirling's approximation for the binomial coefficient (relation (A.5.2)), give

$$\binom{n}{k} = \frac{\sqrt{n}}{\sqrt{2\pi k(n-k)}} \left(\frac{n}{k}\right)^k \left(\frac{n}{n-k}\right)^{n-k} \left(1 + O\left(\frac{1}{k} + \frac{1}{n-k}\right)\right)$$

$$= \left(\frac{2}{n\pi}\right)^{\frac{1}{2}} 2^n \left(1 + \frac{2j}{n}\right)^{-\frac{n}{2} - j} \left(1 - \frac{2j}{n}\right)^{j - \frac{n}{2}} \left(1 + O\left(\frac{1}{n-2j} + \frac{1}{n+2j}\right)\right). \tag{18}$$

Since the binomial coefficient is quite a "steep" function of its lower argument, and has its maximum at $j = 0$, nearly the entire sum is formed from contributions with $j = o(n)$, and thus the O terms in equation (18) may be safely discarded, as they amount to a factor of $(1 + O(n^{-1}))$ when summed. Using again the above approximation of $\log(1+x)$ for small x we find

$$\log\left[\left(1+\frac{2j}{n}\right)^{-n-\frac{j}{2}}\left(1-\frac{2j}{n}\right)^{j-\frac{n}{2}}\right]$$

$$=-\left(\frac{n}{2}+j\right)\left(\frac{2j}{n}-\frac{4j^2}{2n^2}+O\left(\frac{j^3}{n^3}\right)\right)+\left(j-\frac{n}{2}\right)\left(-\frac{2j}{n}-\frac{4j^2}{2n^2}+O\left(\frac{j^3}{n^3}\right)\right) \quad (19)$$

$$=-\frac{2j^2}{n}+O\left(\frac{j^3}{n^2}\right),$$

and

$$\binom{n}{k}=\left(\frac{2}{n\pi}\right)^{\frac{1}{2}}2^n e^{-\frac{2j^2}{n}+O\left(\frac{j^3}{n^2}\right)}, \qquad k=\frac{n}{2}-j. \quad (20)$$

We have observed that we only have to sum for $0 \le j < n^s = o(n)$, due to the rate of decrease of the binomial coefficient from its maximal value when the index j increases; but what value of s should we pick? It turns out not to matter much, as long as $s < 1$, so that the O term in the exponent can be safely discarded, and we have then

$$A_n \sim \left(\frac{2}{n\pi}\right)^{r/2} 2^{nr} \sum_{j=0}^{n^s} e^{-2rj^2/n}. \quad (21)$$

As argued, the range of summation in (21) may be now extended to $0 \le j \le \infty$ without hurting the asymptotic equivalence, and then the sum may be replaced by the corresponding Riemann integral, to which it converges when n increases (see Exercise 7(b)):

$$A_n \sim \left(\frac{2}{n\pi}\right)^{r/2} 2^{nr} \int_{j=0}^{\infty} e^{-2rj^2/n}\, dj = \left(\frac{2}{n\pi}\right)^{\frac{r}{2}} 2^{nr}\left(\frac{\pi n}{2r}\right)^{\frac{1}{2}} \quad (22)$$

$$= 2^{nr-1}\left(\frac{2}{n\pi}\right)^{(r-1)/2} r^{-\frac{1}{2}}. \quad (23)$$

Note the ratio between this result and the maximal term: it is about $\dfrac{1}{2}\left(\dfrac{n\pi}{2r}\right)^{\frac{1}{2}}$, and is thus quite significant, in spite of the stated "steepness" of the function! The point is that near the maximal term the binomial coefficient is *not* steep at all.

For $\lambda > \frac{1}{2}$ the maximum term occurs well within the range of the summation, and everything would proceed as above, except that now we have to use the integral on both sides of the origin, and might just as well let it cover the entire real axis. The final result is then just twice the value given in equation (23), independently of the precise value of λ!

For $\lambda < \frac{1}{2}$ the maximum is again at the summation boundary, but in this region the function is steep indeed and we should expect the maximal term, $\binom{n}{\lfloor \lambda n\rfloor}$ to dominate the sum. Indeed, let $\alpha = \lambda n$, $j = \alpha - k$, and then using equation (A.5.4) (see Exercise 8) we can write

$$\binom{n}{\alpha-j} \sim \binom{n}{\alpha}\left(\frac{\lambda}{1-\lambda}\right)^j \sim \binom{n}{\lfloor\alpha\rfloor}\left(\frac{\lambda}{1-\lambda}\right)^{j-x}, \quad x = \alpha - \lfloor\alpha\rfloor, \text{ uniformly in } j \text{ (24)}$$

The sum on j reduces now to a sum of a geometric series, which up to a factor $1 + [\lambda/(1-\lambda)]^\alpha$, that we can afford to disregard, yields

$$A_n \sim \sum_{j-x\geq 0} \binom{n}{\lfloor\alpha\rfloor}^r \left[\left(\frac{\lambda}{1-\lambda}\right)^r\right]^{j-x} = \binom{n}{\lfloor\alpha\rfloor}^r \frac{1}{1-[\lambda/(1-\lambda)]^r}. \tag{25}$$

Note that in the final result it is important to use $\lfloor\alpha\rfloor$ in the binomial coefficient, rather than α itself. The difference can be quite substantial. (See Exercise 9.)

In Exercise 12 we present an example that combines several useful devices in the summation of series: the exponential approximation, the use of the gamma function to obtain asymptotics, and the splitting of a summation range in order to prove the asymptotic order of a sum.

2.1.3 Euler's Summation Formula

The standard proof of Riemann's integrability criteria starts with replacing an integral by a sum. Euler's summation formula turns the tables around, approximating a sum by an integral, that is, the sum $\sum_{k=1}^{n-1} f(k)$ by the integral $\int_1^n f(x)dx$. Note the upper limits!

The formula also provides correction terms and a bound on the remaining error.

Following the derivation in Knuth (1968) we define

$$\{x\} = x \text{ modulo } 1 = x - \lfloor x\rfloor,$$

and integrate by parts

$$\int_k^{k+1} (\{x\} - \tfrac{1}{2})f'(x)dx = \frac{1}{2}[f(k+1) + f(k)] - \int_k^{k+1} f(x)dx \tag{26}$$

as $\{x\} = x - k$ in the interval $[k, k+1)$.

Summing equation (26) for $1 \leq k \leq n-1$ we obtain:

$$\int_1^n (\{x\} - \tfrac{1}{2})f'(x)dx = \sum_{k=1}^{n-1} f(k) + \frac{1}{2}[f(n) - f(1)] - \int_1^n f(x)dx. \tag{27}$$

The polynomial $x - \tfrac{1}{2}$ is called $B_1(x)$, the first order Bernoulli polynomial. Evaluating the integral on the left-hand side is usually as difficult as doing $\Sigma f(k)$ in the first place. However, by repeatedly integrating it by parts we often obtain - if $f(k)$ is smooth enough - terms that are values of higher order derivatives of $f(x)$ at $x=1$ and n, and decreasing remainder terms.

The expressions that we get employ the Bernoulli numbers and polynomials of higher order, defined below[1].

$$\sum_{k=1}^{n-1} f(k) = \int_1^n f(x)dx + \sum_{k=1}^m \frac{B_k}{k!} \left[f^{[k-1]}(n) - f^{[k-1]}(1) \right] + R_m \qquad (28)$$

where

$$R_m = \frac{(-1)^{m+1}}{m!} \int_1^n B_m(\{x\}) f^{[m]}(x)dx . \qquad (29)$$

Some bounds on the remainder term can be stated, starting with:

$$B_m(\{x\}) < \frac{4m!}{(2\pi)^m} .$$

Thus, when $f^{[2k+1]}(x) \underset{x \to \infty}{\to} 0$ monotonically,

$$R_{2k} = \theta \frac{B_{2k+2}}{(2k+2)!} \left[f^{[2k+1]}(n) - f^{[2k+1]}(1) \right], \quad 0 < \theta < 1$$

$$B_{2m} \sim (-1)^{m-1} \frac{2(2m)!}{(2\pi)^{2m}} . \qquad (30)$$

Note that it is not the case usually that using (28) and (29) for higher and higher m will yield better and better estimates, as B_m increases rather fast for high m and often $f^{[m]}(x)$ follows suit. So there is usually an optimal value of m.

Bernoulli Numbers and Polynomials

The Bernoulli numbers have the exponential generating function

$$\frac{x}{e^x - 1} = \sum_{k \geq 0} B_k \frac{x^k}{k!} , \qquad (31)$$

$$B_0 = 1, B_1 = -\frac{1}{2}, B_2 = \frac{1}{6}, B_4 = -\frac{1}{30}, B_6 = \frac{1}{42}, B_8 = -\frac{1}{30}, B_{2k+1} = 0, k \geq 1.$$

The Bernoulli polynomials are defined through the numbers:

$$B_m(x) = \sum_{k \geq 0} \binom{m}{k} B_k x^{m-k} . \qquad (32)$$

In Abramowitz and Stegun (1964), Chap. 23, one can find a list of further properties of the Bernoulli numbers and polynomials, as well as the symmetry they display with Euler numbers and polynomials. (*Not* the Eulerian ones.) Note that the definitions of all these combinatorial creatures are not uniform across the literature. We use the same conventions as e.g. Knuth, which differ from those of

---

[1]Naturally enough both the Bernoulli and the Bell numbers, introduced above, are denoted by the symbols B_n. No relation whatsoever.

Whittaker and Watson, Davies and others.

Exercises and Complements

1. (a) Show that $g(n) = O(h(n))$ and $g(n) = \Omega(h(n)) \Rightarrow |h(n)| \sim |g(n)|$, but that the converse need not be true.
(b) Prove the properties claimed in equations (1) through (5).

2. Use equation (31) to show that the Bernoulli numbers of odd index larger than 1 all vanish.
[Hint: If the left-hand side of equation (31) were an even function, *all* the odd-indexed coefficients would vanish.]

3. From equation (32) obtain the first derivative of $B_m(x)$ in terms of a lower order Bernoulli polynomial, and then use this result to obtain equation (28).

4. Use the Euler summation formula to evaluate the following sums:
(a) $\sum_{k=1}^{n} \sqrt{k}$ to order $O(n^{-3/2})$
(b) $\sum_{k=1}^{n} k \log k$ to order $O(n^{-1})$
(c) $\sum_{k=-n}^{n} e^{-k^2\alpha/n}$ to order $O(e^{-bn})$ [see N.G. de Bruijn, 1981, p. 43.]

5. Obtain equation (9) by differentiating (8). Verify it is a maximum point, by an additional differentiation.

6. Programming exercise for Example 1 in Section 2.1.2: evaluate the first ten B_i, $1 \le i \le 10$, explicitly, from the sum in equation (7) and compare with the approximation in equation (16). The value of t needed there is easily obtained via the successive approximations method described following equation (9).

7. (a) Justify the statement made in Example 2 in Section 2.1.2, that $A_n(\lambda > \frac{1}{2}) = 2A_n(\lambda = \frac{1}{2})$, irrespectively of the exact value of λ.
(b) The sum in equation (21) was replaced with no ado by the integral in equation (22). Use equation (28) to evaluate the first correction term to this estimate.

8. Using the development $\log(1+x) = x - x^2/2$ for small x (i.e. $x \ll 1$), show that for large n

$$\binom{n}{s+t} \sim \binom{n}{s}\left(\frac{n-s}{s}\right)^t,$$

with $t^2 = o(s)$, $t^2 = o(n-s)$.

9. Determine, for a given n, the maximum relative error that can be perpetrated if one uses α rather than $\lfloor \alpha \rfloor$ in the binomial coefficient in equation (25).

10. (a) Using the same procedure as in the first Example of Section 2.1.2 for the sum arising in computing $b_n = [z^n]B(z) = [z^n]\sum_{k\ge 0} \dfrac{e^{zk(k-1)/2}}{k!}$, show that

$b_n \sim \left(\frac{t}{2}\right)^n \sqrt{\pi/n}\,/\Gamma(t)$, where t is determined via the equation $t\log t = 2n$.

(b) Following (in part) Example 2 of Section 2.1.2, estimate for large t $\sum_{r=0}^{t}\binom{2t}{r}a^r$, both for a less than or larger than one. Check the quality of your estimate by numerical computation. Use your estimate to give an expression for the expectation and variance of the random variable Z defined as follows: X has the binomial $B(n,p)$ distribution, $Y = n - X$, and $Z = min(X,Y)$. [For $a < 1$ higher order terms must be used than in the above example, and for $a > 1$ use the Euler summation formula.]

11. (de Bruijn)

(a) Show that the equation

$$e^{tf(t)} = f(t) + t + O(1), \qquad 0 < t < \infty$$

is consistent, for large t, with the following asymptotic solution (and improve it by one order in t):

$$f(t) = \frac{\log t}{t} + O(t^{-2}).$$

(b) Using the "bootstrapping" approach that produced equation (10), show that the root, $f(t)$, of the equation $e^{f(t)} + \log f(t) = t$ satisfies the relation

$$f(t) = \log t + \frac{\log\log t}{t}\, P\left(\frac{\log\log t}{t\log t}, \frac{1}{t\log t}, \frac{\log\log t}{t}\right).$$

where $P(u,v,w)$ is a power series in the variables u, v and w, convergent for all small values of $|u|$, $|v|$ and $|w|$.

12. This exercise concerns the expected length of a CRI, as derived in Exercise 2.2-5. The result obtained there is

$$l_n = 1 + \sum_{k=2}^{n}\binom{n}{k}\frac{2(-1)^k(k-1)}{1-p^k-q^k}, \qquad n \geq 0. \tag{12-1}$$

This expression is not satisfactory for the analytical determination of the channel capacity. We need an explicit expression for the dependence of l_n on n, and an asymptotic evaluation would suffice. (The complete derivation may be found in Hofri, 1983.)

(a) Rewrite equation (12-1) as

$$l_{n+1} = 1 + 2\sum_{i\geq 0}\sum_{r=0}^{i}\binom{n}{i}\sum_{k=2}^{n}\binom{n}{k}(k-1)\beta^k$$

$$= 1 + 2\sum_{i\geq 0}\sum_{r=0}^{i}\binom{n}{i}[(1+\beta)^n\,n\beta - (1+\beta)^n+1], \qquad \beta \equiv -p^r q^{i-r}. \tag{12-2}$$

(b) Use the "exponential approximation" to obtain an approximation of l_n, denoted by a_n, that is used below to compute the necessary explicit formula. Writing $x = -n\beta$ approximate, for large n, $(1+\beta)^n = (1-\frac{x}{n})^n$ by e^{-x}. In this part you have to prove $\delta(p,n) \equiv l_{n+1} - a_{n+1} = O(1)$, uniformly in p, asymptotically in n.

[Guidance: Disregarding a factor of 2,

$$\delta(p,n) = \sum_{i \geq 0} \sum_{r=0}^{i} \binom{i}{r}[xe^{-x} + e^{-x} + (1+\beta)^n n\beta - (1+\beta)^n]$$

$$= \sum_{i \geq 0} \sum_{r=0}^{i} \binom{i}{r}(x + 1)[e^{-x} - (1 - \frac{x}{n})^n], \quad x = np^r q^{i-r}. \tag{12-3}$$

Show it is only necessary to prove for the x component of the $(x+1)$ factor (i.e. -
the same proof steps show the required for the second component too). Note that

$e^{-x} - (1 - \frac{x}{n})^n = e^{-x} - e^{n\log(1-\frac{x}{n})}$. Developing the logarithm function as a

Taylor power series to two terms and writing the remainder explicitly,

$$e^{-x} - (1 - \frac{x}{n})^n = e^{-x}(1 - \exp[-\frac{x^2/n}{2(1 - \theta x/n)^2}]), \quad 0 < \theta < 1$$

$$< e^{-x}(1 - e^{-x^2/n}).$$

The last inequality actually only holds for i (there is an i in x) that is 2 or larger;
argue why it still may be taken as "less than ... for our purposes". Note that for
$i > 2$, $2(1 - \theta\frac{x}{n})^2 > 1$, and $1 - e^{-c} < c$ for any positive c. To emphasize the role of
n we write from now on $x = na(i,r)$. The proof consists of splitting the sum over
i into three parts and showing that each is $O(n^{-s})$ for some nonnegative s. The
partial-sum limits one should choose are to some extent arbitrary; one possible
choice is $n_1 \equiv (\log n - \log\log n)/\log(1/q)$ and $n_2 \equiv \log n/\log(1/r_2)$ where
$r_2 = p^2 + q^2$. Remember that the notation was fixed so that $p \geq q$.

For $0 \leq i < n_1$ use the last overestimate to write

$$\delta_1(p,n) = \sum_{i=0}^{n_1-1} \sum_{r=0}^{i} \binom{i}{r}n^2 a^3(i,r)e^{-na(i,r)}, \tag{12-4}$$

and show that for the above range of i, $a_1 \equiv q^{n_1} \leq a(i,r)$, leading to the bound
$e^{-na_1} \geq e^{-na(i,r)}$, and thus $\delta_1(p,n) < n^2 e^{-na_1} \sum_{i=0}^{n_1-1} \sum_{r=0}^{i} \binom{i}{r}a^3(i,r) = n^2 e^{-na_1} \times$
$\sum_{i=0}^{n_1-1}(p^3+q^3)^i = O(e^{2\log n - na_1})$. Show that this is small as required, for the above
choice of n_1.

For the second part of the sum use the same bound as in (12-4), in the range
$n_1 \leq i < n_2$. Adapt the mean value theorem to finite sums, to write a value that is
asymptotically equal to δ_2:

$$\delta_2(p,n) = O((n_2 - n_1)jn^2\binom{j}{k}a^3(j,k)e^{-na(j,k)}) \tag{12-5}$$

for some $n_1 \leq j < n_2$, $0 \leq k \leq j$. For the claim to hold, (12-5) must be $O(n^{-s})$
with nonnegative s for *every* j and k in that range. This can be shown by

replacing the value in (12-5) by a larger value $n^2 n_{2p}{}^{3k} q^{3j-3k} j^{k+1} \exp[-np^k q^{j-k}]$: observing that for $p \geq q$ and $j \geq n_1$ this is an increasing function of k. Then taking $k = j$, the resulting value is an increasing function of j, and taking the value at $j = n_2$ one finally obtains $\exp[2\log n + (2+n_2)\log n_2 - 3n_2 \log(1/p) - np^{n_2}]$; with the above choice of n_2 and[2] $p > \frac{1}{2}$ the exponent is indeed negative.

For the last part, $i \geq n_2$, note that at this range, finally, the natural bound, which holds for any real a, $e^{-na}(1-e^{-na^2}) < a$ is effective. Show that this inequality implies $\delta_3(p,n) < \sum_{i \geq n_2} \sum_r \binom{i}{r} na^2 = \sum_{i \geq n_2} n(p^2+q^2)^i$, that this term is $O(nr_2^{n^2})$, and that by the above choice of n_2 the claim is now satisfied.]

(c) Now the approximation obtained from (12-2) is

$$a_{n+1} = 1 + 2\sum_{i \geq 0} \sum_{r=0}^{i} \binom{n}{i}[1 - xe^{-x} - e^{-x}], \qquad x = np^r q^{i-r}. \qquad (12\text{-}6)$$

Show that from the standard relation for the gamma function[3] $e^{-x} = \int_{(c)} \Gamma(z) x^{-z} dz$ for any $c > 0$, you get, by moving the contour of integration past the poles of $\Gamma(z)$ at $z=0, -1$ that $e^{-x} + x - 1 = \int_{(c)} \Gamma(z) x^{-z} dz$ for $-2 < c < -1$, which is precisely what is needed in order to rewrite (12-6), taking, arbitrarily, the midpoints in the integration strips:

$$a_{n+1} = 1 - 2\sum_{i \geq 0}\sum_r \binom{n}{i}[x(e^{-x}-1)+(e^{-x}+x-1)]$$

$$= 1 - 2\sum_{i\geq 0}\sum_r \binom{n}{i}[\, x\int_{(-\frac{1}{2})} \Gamma(z)x^{-z}dz + \int_{(-3/2)} \Gamma(z)x^{-z}dz\,]. \qquad (12\text{-}7)$$

Why is the special repartition of terms in the first expression necessary? (See below.) The second integral of (12-7) is, by change of variable, equal to $\int_{(-\frac{1}{2})}\Gamma(z-1)x^{1-z}dz = \int_{(-\frac{1}{2})}(z-1)^{-1}\Gamma(z)x^{1-z}dz$, hence

$$a_{n+1} = 1 - 2\sum_{i\geq 0}\int_{(-\frac{1}{2})}\Gamma(z)\frac{z}{z-1}\sum_{r=0}^{i}\binom{n}{i}x^{1-z}dz$$

$$= 1 - 2\sum_{i\geq 0}\int_{(-\frac{1}{2})}\Gamma(z)\frac{zn^{1-z}}{z-1}q^{i(1-z)}\left(1+(\tfrac{p}{q})^{1-z}\right)^i dz$$

Now sum the geometrical series to get

$$a_{n+1} = 1 - 2\int_{(-\frac{1}{2})}\Gamma(z)\frac{z}{z-1}\frac{n^{1-z}}{1-p^{1-z}-q^{1-z}}dz \qquad (12\text{-}8)$$

Show that the last summation converges only if $\text{Re}(z) < 0$; this is why the special representation chosen in equation (12-7) is required. The merit of equation (12-8)

---

[2] For $p = \frac{1}{2}$, $\delta_2 = 0$, since then n_1 and n_2 coincide.

[3] The notation $\int_{(c)}$ stands for $\dfrac{1}{2\pi i}\int_{c-i\infty}^{c+i\infty}$.

over all preceding steps is that n is exposed here "in splendid isolation". The evaluation of the contour integral is routine: one goes from $(-\frac{1}{2},-iN_1)$ to $(-\frac{1}{2},iN_1)$ to (N_2,iN_1) to $(N_2,-iN_1)$ to $(-\frac{1}{2},-iN_1)$, – in a negative sense. Show that $|\Gamma(t+iN)|=O(|t+iN|^{t-\frac{1}{2}}e^{-t-\pi N/2})$, and that this leads to the vanishing of the contribution of the horizontal parts of the contour when N_1 increases, and that the n^{1-z} takes care of the receding vertical component. Hence the required integral is minus the sum of residues of the integrand to the right of $-\frac{1}{2}$. Determining these requires information about the roots of $1-p^s-q^s$. For a few isolated values of p these can be determined[4], but in general all one can say is: a) $\text{Re}(s) \le 1$ and for the most part $-1 < \text{Re}(s)$, with rather rare exceptions. b) The roots are well separated (Prove this!) and thus easy to determine numerically.

The pole at $z = 0$ is the first to consider. Show that it is simple and the residue there contributes $\dfrac{-n}{p\log p + q\log q}$; the rest we list implicitly, yielding:

$$a_n = 1 + 2n\left[\frac{-1}{p\log p + q\log q}\right.$$
$$\left. + 2\text{Re}\{\sum_\zeta \frac{\zeta\Gamma(\zeta)}{\zeta-1} n^{-\zeta}\text{Res}[1-p^{1-z}-q^{1-z}]^{-1}; z = \zeta]\} + O(1),\right. \tag{12-9}$$

where 'Res' denotes the residue of the quantity in brackets at the designated point, and ζ goes over all roots of $1-p^{1-z}-q^{1-z}$ that lie to the right of the contour. The sum in the braces turns out to be extremely small, due to cancellations which are quite hard to estimate analytically. It was found, via numerical computations, to be typically four to seven orders of magnitude below the leading term.

A subsidiary result from the above, which may be unsettling at first is that while a_n is essentially linear in n, the quantity a_n/n does not approach a limit as $n \to \infty$, but oscillates with a minute amplitude and ever increasing period around the value of the leading term above, that is independent of n.

---

[4] For example, for $p = \frac{1}{2}$ the roots are $s = 1+ 2\pi i k/\log 2$, k being any integer; for $p = 2/(1+\sqrt{5}) = \phi^{-1}$, the golden ratio, $s = (-1)^{k+1}+ k\pi i/\log\phi$.

2.2 Generating Functions

Generating functions (gf's) and integral transforms (*it*'s) are certainly the main computational tools of the analyst. They will be treated in this section and 2.3, respectively, with gf's taken up again in Section 2.4. For historical reasons, gf's are sometimes called "z transforms", especially in engineering texts. We shall use the term transform generically to refer to both. We shall observe that gf's appear in several guises, or roles. Rather than deal here with the subject in its full generality we shall proceed through the basic definitions and properties of these artefacts, and demonstrate their use via examples. Two analytical tools are then presented: the Lagrange expansion theorem, and the Poisson transform. A comprehensive and more rigorous treatment of gf's is available in Goulden and Jackson (1983) and in Riordan (1964), and of *it*'s in Davies (1978). In Section 2.4 we further discuss gf's as enumerating tools.

2.2.1 Elementary Properties and Applications

A sequence $\{a_0, a_1, \cdots \}$ is associated with the ordinary generating function

$$a(z) = \sum_{i \geq 0} a_i z^i .$$

If the sequence is finite, $a(z)$ is a polynomial.

Examples

(a) If $a_i = a$, then $a(z) = a/(1-z)$.

(b) If $a_i = \binom{n}{i}$, then $a(z) = (1+z)^n$.

Another type of function that arises naturally in many applications is the exponential gf (egf):

A sequence $\{a_0, a_1, \cdots \}$ is also associated with the egf

$$\hat{a}(z) = \sum_{i \geq 0} a_i \frac{z^i}{i!} .$$

Examples

(a) If $a_i = a$, then $\hat{a}(z) = ae^z$.

(b) If $a_i = i^2$, then $\hat{a}(z) = z(z+1)e^z$.

A related function, which is sometimes more expedient in use, is the Poisson gf, $e^{-z} \hat{a}(z)$. It is used extensively in the analyses in Section 4.2 (see also Exercise 5).

The symbol "z" in the above definitions may be viewed in two distinct aspects: It can be considered an indeterminate symbol. The functions $a(z)$ and $\hat{a}(z)$ are then sometimes called "formal power series". They are elements of Cauchy algebras. From this point of view, one uses these functions merely as a method of encapsulating a (possibly infinite) sequence in a single expression, which may be formally manipulated, under very mild restrictions, just as functions of a continuous variable. Equations in terms of these functions are construed to only represent equalities between coefficients of like powers of z on both sides of the equation. Using the convenient bracket notation of $[z^n]f(z)$ for the coefficient of z^n in the development of $f(z)$ as a power series, we have

$$f(z) = g(z) \iff [z^n]f(z) = [z^n]g(z), \qquad \forall n \geq 0. \tag{1}$$

The qualification $n \geq 0$ in equation (1) is inessential, and merely reflects the convention of denoting in nearly all our sequences the first term with the index zero. The operations of addition, subtraction, multiplication, differentiation and integration are defined in the intuitive way yielding, *inter alia*

$$[z^n]a(z) = a_n = \frac{1}{n!}\frac{d^n}{dz^n}\,a(z)|_{z=0} = \frac{d^n}{dz^n}\,\hat{a}(z)|_{z=0}. \tag{2}$$

An equally valid view holds z to be a variable in the complex plane, and then the question of convergence of the defining series arises. The analytic properties of gf's then frequently yield information that is quite hard to come by otherwise. This is the basis of nearly all the methods to be presented in Section 2.5. There is never the need to choose and settle on an *a priori* interpretation. When gf's are used in the sequel we shall vacillate freely between the two points of view.

Relations between Operations on Sequences and the Corresponding gf's and egf's

Let $a_i = cb_i$, then

$$a(z) = cb(z), \quad \hat{a}(z) = c\hat{b}(z). \tag{3}$$

Let $c_i = a_i \pm b_i$, then

$$c(z) = a(z) \pm b(z), \quad \hat{c}(z) = \hat{a}(z) \pm \hat{b}(z). \tag{4}$$

Let $c_i = a_i b_0 + a_{i-1}b_1 + \cdots + a_0 b_i = \sum_{k=0}^{i} a_{i-k}b_k$ for $i \geq 0$. Then multiplying this relation by z^i, summing over $i \geq 0$ and changing the order of summation provides

$$c(z) = a(z)b(z). \tag{5}$$

Similarly, let $d_i = \sum_{k=0}^{i}\binom{i}{k}a_{i-k}b_k$, then

$$\hat{d}(z) = \hat{a}(z)\hat{b}(z). \tag{6}$$

Equations (5) and (6) can also be directly shown by considering the coefficient of z^i when multiplying $(a_0 + a_1 z + a_2 z^2 + \cdots)(b_0 + b_1 z + b_2 z^2 + \cdots)$, for equation (5), and similarly for equation (6). The $\{c_i\}$ in equation (5) are called a convolution of the sequences $\{a_i\}$ and $\{b_i\}$. This relation is conventionally denoted by $c_i = a * b_i$. The subscript i is carried by the single symbol $a * b$. As we shall see, these combinations turn up very frequently.

If $b_i = 1$, then equation (5) gives the gf for partial sums of the elements of $\{a_i\}$, since then $c_i = \sum_{k=0}^{i} a_k$. Using $b(z)=1/(1-z)$ we obtain $c(z) = a(z)/(1-z)$. This provides an often useful device in the summation of series.

The convolution of more than two sequences may be thus formed, one at a time, as e.g. $d_i = (a*b)*c_i$ etc. Since the gf of $\{d_i\}$ would then be $d(z) = a(z)b(z)c(z)$, we see that the convolution operation is commutative and associative. In particular, if we convolve a sequence with itself a given number of times, we get a sequence which has a gf that is equal to the gf of the original sequence, raised to the power of the same number.

Example

The first example shows the use of gf's in manipulating sums. Let $a_i = i$; find its gf. This can obviously be done directly, but we proceed as follows:

$$\sum_{k=0}^{i} 1 \cdot 1 = i+1 = a_i + 1.$$

Hence a_i is a convolution of $\{1\}$ with itself, up to a difference of 1, and as the gf of $\{1\}$ is $1/(1-z)$, we have from equations (4) and (5) $\left(\dfrac{1}{1-z}\right)^2 = a(z) + \dfrac{1}{1-z}$, or

$$a(z) = \frac{1}{(1-z)^2} - \frac{1}{1-z} = \frac{z}{(1-z)^2}. \tag{7}$$

Now let $b_i = i^2$. Since $i^2 = 2\sum_{k=0}^{i} k - i$, the sum being a convolution of $\{k\}$ and $\{1\}$, we have

$$b(z) = 2\frac{z}{(1-z)^2} \cdot \frac{1}{1-z} - \frac{z}{(1-z)^2} = \frac{z^2+z}{(1-z)^3}. \tag{8}$$

Equation (5) with $b_i = 1$ can thus be iterated, and one obtains sums of sums to any desired degree. Let us use the notation $S^n a_i = S[S^{n-1}a_i]$, that is

$$S^0 a_i = a_i$$
$$S^1 a_i \equiv S a_i = a_0 + a_1 + \cdots + a_i$$
$$S^2 a_i = S(a_0 + a_1 + \cdots + a_i) \tag{9}$$
$$= (i+1)a_0 + ia_1 + \cdots + 2a_{i-1} + a_i = \sum_{k=0}^{i} (k+1)a_{i-k},$$

and so on.

Experimenting with $n = 2, 3$ suggests the following expression for $S^n a_i$, which we prove by mathematical induction:

$$S^n a_i = \sum_{k=0}^{i} \binom{n+k-1}{n-1} a_{i-k}. \tag{10}$$

For $n = 2$ equation (10) reduces to the second line in equation (9). Now

$$S^{n+1}a_i = S[S^n a_i],$$
$$= S^n a_0 + S^n a_1 + \cdots + S^n a_i$$
$$= \sum_{j=0}^{i} S^n a_j,$$

and by the induction hypothesis,

$$= \sum_{j=0}^{i} \sum_{k=0}^{j} \binom{n+k-1}{n-1} a_{j-k}.$$

Perhaps the simplest way to handle this sum is by first introducing $u=j-k$ and eliminating k,

$$S^{n+1}a_i = \sum_{j=0}^{i} \sum_{u=0}^{j} \binom{n+j-u-1}{n-1} a_u,$$

changing the order of summation (always allowed for finite sums) and the range of j to $0 \le j \le i-u$ produces

$$S^{n+1}a_i = \sum_{u=0}^{i} a_u \sum_{j=u}^{i} \binom{n+j-u-1}{n-1} = \sum_{u=0}^{i} a_u \sum_{j=0}^{i-u} \binom{n+j-1}{n-1}.$$

Using the identity (see Exercise 2)

$$\sum_{k=0}^{m} \binom{r+k}{k} = \binom{r+m+1}{m}, \qquad r,m \text{ integers}$$

we obtain

$$S^{n+1}a_i = \sum_{u=0}^{i} a_u \binom{n-1+i-u+1}{i-u} = \sum_{u=0}^{i} a_{i-u} \binom{n+u}{n},$$

in agreement with equation (10).

In accordance with equation (5) the gf for $S^n a_i$ is $\dfrac{a(z)}{(1-z)^n}$. We may view this as having the same content as identity (10) above.

Difference Equations, Mostly Linear

The second example of the use of gf's concerns their application to the solution of linear difference equations. Consider first an example with constant coefficients: $f_n = \sum_i b_i a_{n-i}$, $n \ge 0$, with $\{f_n\}$ and $\{b_n\}$ known sequences that determine the unknown $\{a_i\}$. Since $f = b*a$, the corresponding gf's satisfy $f(z) = b(z)a(z)$ and we have a solution in the form

$$a(z) = \frac{f(z)}{b(z)}. \tag{11}$$

This solution is rarely quite sufficient. In the first place, the extraction of an explicit expression for the $\{a_i\}$ may still be quite tedious. Furthermore, it is rarely the case that the difference equation is of the same form for all values of n: usually the first values are determined by given boundary values or special relations, which rather muddy the simple form of equation (11). We show a specific example, where $\{b_i\}$ has only three nonzero terms and the f_n are all identical:

$$a_{n+2} - \alpha a_{n+1} - \beta a_n = \gamma, \qquad n \geq 0. \tag{12}$$

This relation determines $\{a_n\}$ for $n \geq 2$ only, so we supplement it by the two initial values: a_0 and a_1. Defining $a(z) = \sum_{n \geq 0} a_n z^n$, multiplying equation (12) by z^{n+2} and summing over all n gives

$$a(z)(1 - \alpha z - \beta z^2) = \frac{\gamma z^2}{1 - z} + a_0 + (a_1 - \alpha a_0)z. \tag{13}$$

While this is indeed a solution, we might want an explicit representation for a_i. Let $1 - \alpha z - \beta z^2 = (1 - cz)(1 - dz)$ (i.e. $cd = -\beta$, $c + d = \alpha$). Assume $c \neq d$ and both c and $d \neq 1$ (see Exercise 1 for the case $c = d$). Divide (13) by this product and expand in partial fractions to obtain

$$a(z) = \frac{1}{(1 - cz)(1 - dz)}[\frac{\gamma}{1 - z} + a_0 - \gamma + (a_1 - \gamma - \alpha a_0)z]$$

$$= \frac{\gamma}{(1-c)(1-d)} \cdot \frac{1}{1-z} + \frac{(1-c)(a_1 + ca_0 - \alpha a_0) - \gamma}{(1-c)(1-d)} \cdot \frac{1}{1-cz}$$

$$+ \frac{(1-d)(\alpha a_0 - da_0 - a_1) + \gamma}{(1-d)(c-d)} \cdot \frac{1}{1-dz}. \tag{14}$$

Denoting the three coefficients (not involving z) of the fractions in (14) by A, B and C, respectively, writing $1/(1-cz) = \sum_{i \geq 0}(cz)^i$ etc. and picking out the coefficients of z^n we get

$$a_n = A + Bc^n + Cd^n, \qquad n \geq 0. \tag{15}$$

Substituting $n = 0,1$ in (15) indeed produces identities, which can be used as computational checks. The special case $\gamma = 0$ is important: equation (13) then greatly simplifies to yield

$$a(z) = \frac{1}{c-d}[\frac{a_1 + ca_0 - \alpha a_0}{1 - cz} + \frac{\alpha a_0 - da_0 - a_1}{1 - dz}],$$

and now

$$a_n = \frac{1}{c-d}[(a_1 + ca_0 - \alpha a_0)c^n + (\alpha a_0 - da_0 - a_1)d^n]$$

$$= \frac{1}{c-d}[(a_1 - \alpha a_0)(c^n - d^n) + a_0(c^{n+1} - d^{n+1})]. \tag{16}$$

When the coefficients of a linear difference equation are not constant, we get a linear differential equation for the gf, rather than an algebraic one:

Consider the equation

$$(i+1)x_{i+1} - (i+r)x_i = 0, \qquad i \geq 0, \quad x_0 = x$$

Let $G(z)$ be the gf for the $\{x_i\}$. Multiplying by z^i and summing for $i \geq 0$,

$$\sum_{i \geq 0} (i+1)x_{i+1}z^i - \sum_{i \geq 0} ix_i z^i - r\sum_{i \geq 0} x_i z^i = 0$$

we obtain

$$G'(z) \quad - \quad zG'(z) \quad - \quad rG(z) = 0,$$

or

$$(1-z)G'(z) = rG(z) \quad \Rightarrow \quad G(z) = \frac{A}{(1-z)^r},$$

and the initial value requires $A = x$. Using the binomial expansion of $(1-z)^{-r}$ we immediately find

$$[z^n]G(z) = x\binom{-r}{n}(-1)^n = x\binom{r+n-1}{n}.$$

If the equation is of higher order (e.g. x_{i+2} is expressed in terms of x_{i+1} and x_i), we shall get a higher order differential equation, and the same holds for the case of coefficients that are higher order polynomials in i.

Another kind of a difference equation arises in the following example:

Enumerating Binary Trees

Practically every combinatorial problem that deals with unbounded collections is likely to be best tackled via gf's. We give below a simple example; a more general treatment will occupy us in Section 2.4.

Let b_n denote the number of binary trees with n nodes. We conveniently define $b_0 = 1$, and proceed to obtain b_n for all n. Clearly $b_1 = 1, b_2 = 2$, since we make a distinction between the right and the left subtrees. Noting that every binary tree of size n consists of a root, a left subtree of size r, $0 \leq r \leq n-1$ and a complementary right subtree, one has

$$b_n = \sum_{r=0}^{n-1} b_r b_{n-r-1}, \qquad n \geq 1.$$

Letting $b(z) = \sum_{n \geq 0} b_n z^n$ we have

$$b(z) - 1 = z\sum_{n \geq 1} \sum_{r=0}^{n-1} b_r b_{n-r-1}z^{n-1} = z\sum_{r \geq 0} b_r z^r \sum_{n \geq r+1} b_{n-r-1}z^{n-r-1}$$

$$= zb^2(z),$$

hence $zb^2(z) - b(z) + 1 = 0$. Solving for $b(z)$ gives $b(z) = [1 \pm \sqrt{1-4z}]/2z$. The solution with the minus sign is chosen, so as to satisfy $b(0) = b_0 = 1$. Using the binomial expansion we may write

$$b(z) = \frac{-1}{2z} \sum_{n\geq 1} \binom{\frac{1}{2}}{n}(-4z)^n;$$

hence

$$b_n = -\frac{1}{2}\binom{\frac{1}{2}}{n+1}(-4)^{n+1} = \frac{1}{n+1}\binom{2n}{n}. \tag{17}$$

The last equality is easy to obtain by representing the binomial coefficient explicitly, and introducing the missing factors to obtain in the numerator $(2n)!$. The numbers b_n are known as Catalan numbers. See Example (1) in Section 2.2.3 for a "smoother" treatment.

2.2.2 Probability gf's (pgf), Moment gf's

If a sequence of numbers is construed as a probability mass function (pmf), i.e. probabilities of an integer-valued random variable, we call its gf a pgf. The restriction to integral values is arbitrary, removable and convenient. As a rule we only have to deal with non-negative random variables. The following notation is used: $\text{Prob}(X = i) = p_i$ or $p_X(i)$, $g_X(z) = \sum_{i\geq 0} p_i z^i$. Note that this can also be written as $g_X(z) = E(z^X)$. This view of the pgf, as an expected value, will often be useful. The X subscript will be dropped when there is no danger of confusion. Clearly $g(1) = 1$. From the analytic point of view this equality is important, as it guarantees the convergence of the series for $|z| \leq 1$ and its analyticity for $|z| < 1$. Individual probabilities can in principle be recovered from $g(z)$ as above, by differentiating at $z=0$. The pgf is primarily a convenient vehicle for the evaluation of *moments*. This is accomplished by differentiating $g(z)$ at $z=1$. Note however that the n-th derivative yields the n-th *factorial* moment:

$$E[X(X-1)(X-2)\cdots(X-n+1)] = \frac{d^n}{dz^n}g(z)|_{z=1}. \tag{18}$$

In particular

$$E(X) = g'(1); \quad V(X) = g''(1) + g'(1)[1 - g'(1)],$$

where $V(X)$ is the variance of X.

Denote the cumulative probability mass function (cpmf) of X by q_i: $q_i = \sum_{j\leq i} p_j$. By the discussion following equation (10) we have

$$G(z) \equiv \sum_i q_i z^i = g(z)/(1-z). \tag{19}$$

Convolutions. Frequently we are interested in the sum of independent random variables. Let X and Y be such rv's, then the pmf of their sum is a convolution of those of X and Y:

$$\text{Prob}(X+Y = i) = \sum_{k=0}^{i} \text{Prob}(X=k, Y=i-k),$$

and due to their independence

$$\text{Prob}(X+Y = i) = \sum_{k=0}^{i} p_X(k)p_Y(i-k).$$

Hence

$$g_{X+Y}(z) = g_X(z)g_Y(z). \tag{20}$$

Example

For our next example on the use of gf's we adopt the second point of view mentioned above, gf's as functions over the complex plane. Consider two dice. Assuming the dice are "fair", the probability of rolling each value with each die is the same, $1/6$, and when we consider the sum of two values as both are rolled, we get different probabilities for the several possible values: thus $\text{Prob}(2) = 1/36$, whereas $\text{Prob}(7) = 1/6$. Denote the value rolled with the first die by I and the second value by J. The question is: how to modify the dice ("load" them), so that $I + J$ is uniformly distributed on the values 2 to 12? Let the pmf's of I and J be $\{p_i\}$, $1 \le i \le 6$, and $\{q_i\}$, respectively. Since I and J are independent, we obtain $g_{I+J}(z) = g_I(z)g_J(z)$. To have the sum $I + J$ uniformly distributed requires that

$$\frac{1}{11}(z^2 + z^3 + \cdots + z^{12}) = (p_1 z + p_2 z^2 + \cdots + p_6 z^6)(q_1 z + q_2 z^2 + \cdots + q_6 z^6),$$

or

$$\frac{z^2}{11} \frac{1-z^{11}}{1-z} = z^2(p_1 + p_2 z + \cdots + p_6 z^5)(q_1 + q_2 z + \cdots + q_6 z^5).$$

Discard the z^2 factors on both sides, and consider what remains as functions on the complex plane. Both are polynomials, so they must have the same roots. The left-hand side has five pairs of complex conjugate roots, of the form $\exp(\pm 2\pi k/11)$, $1 \le k \le 5$. The right-hand side is the product of two polynomials of the fifth degree, with real coefficients. Each must have 1, 3 or 5 real roots. Thus the sides cannot agree. Hence the answer is that such dice *do not* exist.

2.2.3 Lagrange Expansion and Applications

We present here one of the more useful tools in extracting the coefficients from the developments of generating functions, for which we do not have an explicit form, but only an implicit equation. It turns out to be expedient also in developing summation formulas that are quite hard to come by otherwise. A detailed presentation is available in Whittaker and Watson (1927), from which the following formulation is taken.

Lagrange Expansion Theorem

Let $f(z)$ and $\phi(z)$ be functions of z, analytic on and inside a contour C surrounding a point u, and let t be a number such that the inequality $|t\phi(z)| < |z-u|$ is satisfied at all points on the contour C; then the equation

$$\zeta = u + t\phi(\zeta), \qquad (21)$$

regarded as an equation in ζ, has one root $\zeta(t)$ in the interior of C[1]. Furthermore, any function satisfying the conditions put on $f(z)$ above can be expanded at ζ as a power series in t:

$$f(\zeta) = f(u) + \sum_{n \geq 1} \frac{t^n}{n!} \frac{d^{n-1}}{dx^{n-1}} [f'(x)\phi^n(x)]_{|x=u}. \qquad (22)$$

An often useful point of view, brought out in the example (2) below, is to regard f and ϕ as defined in two different complex planes, with z and u in one, and t and ζ in the other.

A restatement of equation (22) in terms of coefficients would read

$$[t^n]f(\zeta(t,u)) = \frac{1}{n}[(x-u)^{n-1}]\{f'(x)\phi^n(x)\}, \qquad n \geq 1 \qquad \square \qquad (23)$$

The most common uses of equations (22)-(23) appear to be with $u=0$ and $f(x)=x$.

Examples

1. Consider the equation we obtained for the gf of the number of binary trees of a given size in Section 2.2.1, $b(z) = 1 + zb^2(z)$. This is in the form of equation (21) with $u = 1$ and $\phi(x) = x^2$. Hence, using $f(x) = x$, from equation (23) we get $[z^n]b(z) = (1/n)[(z-1)^{n-1}]z^{2n}$, or $1/n[(z-1)^{n-1}]((z-1)+1)^{2n}$. This leads to

$$[z^n]b(z) = \frac{1}{n}\binom{2n}{n-1} = \frac{(2n)!}{n(n-1)!(n+1)!} = \frac{1}{n+1}\binom{2n}{n},$$

the familiar result. A slightly more convenient way would have been to define $B(z) = b(z) - 1$, then $B(z)$ satisfies equation like (21) with $u=0$. Note that $[z^n]b(z) = [z^n]B(z)$, for $n \geq 1$. In this case we re-solved for the coefficients determined by a quadratic equation. When one counts k-ary trees, where each node may have up to k sons, we get by the same reasoning the equation for the gf of $c_k(n)$, the number of such trees with n nodes: $g_k(z) - 1 = zg_k^k(z)$. Solving such an equation, and then extracting the coefficients from the solution, poses a daunting prospect, even for $k=3$. Proceeding by the above alternative, write $G_k(z) = g_k(z) - 1$, then precisely the same manipulation provides

$$c_k(n) = \frac{1}{n}\binom{kn}{n-1} = \frac{1}{(k-1)n+1}\binom{kn}{n}.$$

---

[1] This is an immediate result of Rouché's Theorem.

2. Picking $\phi(u) = u^r$, we first show

Lemma For an integer $r \geq 2$ and $|z| < (r-1)^{r-1}/r^r$, the equation

$$zx^r = x - 1 \qquad (*)$$

has a unique root $X(z)$ that is

- analytic in z in the open disk $= \{z : |z| < (r-1)^{r-1}/r^r\}$, which we denote by D_1,
- takes the value 1 at $z = 0$.

Moreover, if $f(x)$ is analytic in the open disk $D_2 = \{x : |x - 1| < 1/(r - 1)\}$, then

$$f(X(z)) = f(1) + \sum_{i \geq 1} \frac{z^i}{i!} \frac{d^{i-1}}{du^{i-1}} [u^{ir} f'(u)]_{|u=1}. \qquad (24)$$

Proof: For each z there are r roots of the equation $zx^r = x - 1$. When $|z| < (r-1)^{r-1}/r^r$, the inequality $|zx^r| < |x-1|$ is satisfied for all x on the boundary of the disk D_2. Since the equation $x - 1 = 0$ has a single root in D_2, Rouché's theorem implies that equation $(*)$ has a unique root $X(z)$ in the interior of this disk. Since x^r is analytic in and on D_2, equation (24) follows from equation (22) of the expansion theorem. $\qquad \square$

For $f(z) = z^s$ (with s real), which is analytic in and on D_2, we then obtain the expansion

$$X^s(z) = \sum_{i \geq 0} z^i \frac{s}{ir+s} \binom{ir+s}{i}. \qquad (25)$$

Replacing z by z^r in (25), differentiating and adding (25) yields

$$X^s(z^r) + rz^r X^{s-1}(z^r) \frac{d}{du} X(u)_{|u=z^r} = \sum_{i \geq 0} z^{ir} \binom{ir+s}{i}.$$

Differentiating the defining relation $zX^r(z) = X(z) - 1$ at z^r provides:

$$\frac{d}{du} X(u)_{|u=z^r} = \frac{X^{r+1}(z^r)}{r - (r-1)X(z^r)}, \qquad (26)$$

which with the last expansion gives the very useful relation

$$Q_{r,s}(z) \equiv \sum_{i \geq 0} \binom{ir+s}{i} z^i = \frac{X^{s+1}(z)}{r - (r-1)X(z)}, \qquad zX^r(z) = X(z) - 1. \qquad (27)$$

3. Taking $\phi(x) = e^{-x}$ we observe that the equation $X(z) = ze^{-X(z)}$ has a unique solution for all z, $|z| < e^{-1}$ in the disk $|x| < 1$. Furthermore, $|z| < e^{-1}$ provides $|ze^{-x}| < x$ on $|x| = 1$. Then the choices $u = 0$, $f(z) = z$ will provide the equation

$$X(z) = \sum_{n \geq 1} \frac{z^n}{n!} \frac{d^{n-1}}{du^{n-1}} [e^{-nu}]_{|u=0} = \sum_{n \geq 1} \frac{-(-z)^n n^{n-1}}{n!}. \qquad (28)$$

Hence we obtain the sum formula

$$\sum_{n \geq 1} \frac{z^n n^{n-1}}{n!} = -X(-z), \qquad X(z) = ze^{-X(z)}. \tag{29}$$

Note that $|z| < e^{-1}$ is also the region of convergence of this sum.

A few related sums will be shown now. First, differentiating the defining equation of $X(z)$ we obtain $X'(z) = e^{-X(z)} - zX'(z)e^{-X(z)}$, so

$$X'(z) = \frac{e^{-X(z)}}{1 + ze^{-X(z)}} = \frac{1}{e^{X(z)} + z}.$$

Thus, by differentiating the sum in equation (29) we obtain

$$\sum_{n \geq 1} \frac{z^{n-1} n^n}{n!} = X'(-z) = \frac{1}{e^{X(-z)} - z}, \qquad X(z) = ze^{-X(z)}. \tag{30}$$

Another sum we derive here is $U(z) = \sum_n n^{n+1} z^{n+1}/(n+1)!$. It is not easily obtainable from the above sums, but re-using equation (22) and changing $f(x)$ to e^x, we find

$$e^{X(z)} = 1 + \sum_{n \geq 1} \frac{z^n}{n!} \frac{d^{n-1}}{du^{n-1}} [e^u e^{-nu}]_{|u=0} = 1 - \sum_{n \geq 1} \frac{(-z)^n (n-1)^{n-1}}{n!},$$

hence

$$1 - \sum_{n \geq 0} \frac{n^n z^{n+1}}{(n+1)!} = e^{X(-z)}, \qquad X(z) = ze^{-X(z)}. \tag{31}$$

Now write

$$U(z) = \sum_{n \geq 1} \frac{n^{n+1} z^{n+1}}{(n+1)!} = z^2 \frac{d}{dz} \sum_{n \geq 1} \frac{n^n z^n}{(n+1)!} = z^2 \frac{d}{dz} \frac{1 - e^{X(-z)}}{z},$$

which on using equation (30) and some rearranging, with the defining equation, we find

$$U(z) = \sum_{n \geq 1} \frac{n^{n+1} z^{n+1}}{(n+1)!} = \frac{e^{X(-z)}}{1 + X(-z)} - 1, \qquad X(z) = ze^{-X(z)}. \tag{32}$$

2.2.4 The Poisson Transform (Gonnet and Munro, 1984)

Many combinatorial algorithms - sorting and hashing are particular cases here - can be viewed as the marshaling of n "elements" over an array of m "places", where each element is to be associated with one place, chosen uniformly and independently. This often provides a reasonable probabilistic model for the input to algorithms, the so called "balls into cells" model.

If the operation of the algorithm depends on the occupancies of these places, the analysis usually runs into serious snags, since the occupancies are not independent. Thus, to take an extreme example, if place 1 was chosen by n

elements, we know the others to be all vacant.

An alternative stochastic characterization, devised purposely to get around this dependence is to assume that elements are "generated" for each place independently by a Poisson process with mean α. It is then hoped that picking $\alpha = n/m$ will yield close enough results. This, indeed, is often borne out. But how can we assess the quality of these results? One should be rightly suspicious of results obtained by this method, unless there is some way to control the error it introduces. Normally, estimating this error is no easy matter. In addition, there are cases where the analyst would expect the error to be significant, and in certain cases - such as in the analysis of hashing algorithms under heavy load - even to be dominating.

It is not surprising that assuming different measures over the input provides different results. Note that under the Poisson model the total number of the "balls" is not even a parameter, but an unbounded random variable.

The purpose of the Poisson transform is to formulate a method that recovers from results obtainable via the Poisson model the exact values that analysis under the "balls into cells" model would have obtained, were it possible. The presentation below follows closely that of Gonnet and Munro (1984).

Thus assume that a characteristic of an algorithm, where the input to each cell is independently generated by a Poisson process with mean α, is found to be $g(m,\alpha)$. This can be *any* quantity associated with the algorithm: its mean running time, the rth moment of the number of elements it moves, or the pgf for the distribution of storage it requires, etc. Under the alternative measure over possible inputs, the "balls into cells" model, the corresponding quantity is denoted by $f(m,n)$.

The crucial observation is as follows: Let the number of elements associated with place i be X_i. Under the Poisson model, *given* that $\sum_{i=1}^{m}X_i = n$, the n elements are distributed uniformly over the places.

Thus the contribution of this event to $g(m,\alpha)$ is precisely $f(m,n)$:

$$g(m,\alpha) = \sum_{n \geq 0} f(m,n)\text{Prob}(X_1 + \cdots + X_m = n). \qquad (33)$$

Remark: The phrase "uniformly distributed" above has an important implication; it means we are considering as equiprobable the m^n possible assignments of n distinguishable, or "numbered" balls into m distinct cells. This may appear strange at first glance, since the Poisson process generates indistinguishable balls, as it were; but it merely means that the characteristic $f(m,n)$, to justify this association, must arise out of the statistics of distinguishable items (the so-called Maxwell-Boltzmann statistics). Exercise 11 provides an illustration of this association. Some examples of occupancy problems involving items that are distinguishable or not are given in Section 2.4.1.

The rest is merely mechanical manipulations. We note that the sum of m

independent Poisson variables is a random variable with Poisson distribution, with its parameter the sum of the parameters of the summed random variables; hence $\text{Prob}(X_1 + \cdots + X_m = n) = e^{-m\alpha}(m\alpha)^n/n!$, and so

$$g(m,\alpha) = \sum_{n \geq 0} e^{-m\alpha} \frac{(m\alpha)^n}{n!} f(m,n),$$

and then

$$f(m,n) = \left[\frac{(m\alpha)^n}{n!}\right]\{e^{m\alpha}g(m,\alpha)\} = \frac{n!}{m^n}[\alpha^n]\{e^{m\alpha}g(m,\alpha)\}. \tag{34}$$

In other words, $e^{m\alpha}g(m,\alpha)$ is the egf, over n, of $m^n f(m,n)$. It is as simple as it is ingenious.

Writing explicitly a gf[2] for $g(m,\alpha)$

$$g(m,\alpha) = \sum_{i \geq 0} a_i \alpha^i, \tag{35}$$

we have

$$e^{m\alpha}g(m,\alpha) = \sum_{k \geq 0} c_k \alpha^k, \quad \text{where} \quad c_k = \sum_{l=0}^{k} a_l \frac{m^{k-l}}{(k-l)!}, \tag{36}$$

and equation (34) then yields

$$f(m,n) = c_n \frac{n!}{m^n} = \sum_{l=0}^{n} a_l \frac{n^{\underline{l}}}{m^l}, \tag{37}$$

where $n^{\underline{l}}$ is the descending factorial : $n^{\underline{l}} = n(n-1) \cdots (n-l+1) = n!/(n-l)!$. (In some of the literature this quantity is denoted by $(n)_l$.)

Given $g(m,\alpha)$, equations (35) and (37) provide a complete expansion for $f(m,n)$. This is the purpose of the transform.

In many situations the following elaboration is useful.

Asymptotics

The summation (37) can often be quite arduous and not very illuminating in that form. We can develop, however, a sequence of approximations, that will produce for $f(m,n)$ asymptotic representations, for large m (and n too, naturally, as their ratio α is kept fixed). This will require some regularity conditions on $g(m,\alpha)$ in α, as we shall see.

Using equation (35), rewrite (37) (the upper bound can be removed, as the descending factorial vanishes for $l > n$):

---

[2] We assume that this representation exists. Formally $g(m,\alpha)$ is supposed to be a regular function around $\alpha = 0$. This appears a natural assumption that algorithms behave properly when the loading is very light.

$$f(m,n) = \sum_{l \geq 0} a_l \frac{n^{\underline{l}}}{m^l} = \sum_{l \geq 0} a_l \alpha^l + \sum_{l \geq 0} a_l \left(\frac{n^{\underline{l}}}{m^l} - \alpha^l \right)$$

$$= g(m,\alpha) + \sum_{l \geq 0} a_l \left(\frac{n^{\underline{l}}}{(m\alpha)^l} - 1 \right) \alpha$$

Or, since α is postulated to equal n/m

$$f(m,n) = g(m,\alpha) + \sum_{l \geq 0} a_l \left(\frac{n^{\underline{l}}}{n^l} - 1 \right) \alpha^l . \tag{38}$$

The sum in equation (38) provides the "correction" to $g(m,\alpha)$ as an approximation of $f(m,n)$.

Now, observe the following reduction:

$$\frac{n^{\underline{l}}}{n^l} - 1 = \frac{1}{n^l} \left(n(n-1)(n-2) \cdots (n-l+1) - n^l \right) \tag{39}$$

$$= \frac{1}{n^l} \left[-n^{l-1} \sum_{j=0}^{l-1} j + \frac{1}{2} n^{l-2} \sum_{\substack{i=0 \\ j \neq i}}^{l-1} \sum_{j=0}^{l-1} ij + O(n^{l-3}) \right],$$

where the "O" term in equation (39) reflects our intention of using only a fixed, typically small number of terms from the sum in equation (38). This procedure is suitable unless a_l are fast increasing in l.

Carrying out the summations in equation (39) and substituting into (38) provides

$$f(m,n) = g(m,\alpha) + \sum_{l \geq 0} a_l \left(-\frac{l(l-1)}{2n} + \frac{l(l-1)(3l-1)(l-2)}{24n^2} + O(n^{-3}) \right) \alpha^l . \tag{40}$$

However, we also see by differentiating equation (35) with respect to α,

$$g'_\alpha(m,\alpha) = \sum a_l l \alpha^{l-1},$$

$$g''_\alpha(m,\alpha) = \sum a_l l(l-1) \alpha^{l-2}, \quad \text{etc.}$$

Thus, the first component in the sum in (40) can be represented as follows:

$$-\sum a_l \frac{l(l-1)}{2n} \alpha^l = -\frac{\alpha^2}{2n} g''_\alpha(m,\alpha) = -\frac{\alpha}{2m} g''_\alpha(m,\alpha), \tag{41}$$

where we used again $n = \alpha m$.

Similarly we observe that

$$l(l-1)(3l-1)(l-2) = 3l(l-1)(l-2)(l-3) + 8l(l-1)(l-2),$$

and thus

$$\sum a_l \frac{l(l-1)(3l-1)(l-2)}{24n^2}\alpha^l = \frac{\alpha^4}{24n^2}\cdot 3g_\alpha^{[4]}(m,\alpha) + \frac{\alpha^3}{24n^2}\cdot 8g_\alpha^{[3]}(m,\alpha)$$

$$= \frac{\alpha^2}{24m^2}\cdot 3g_\alpha^{[4]}(m,\alpha) + \frac{\alpha}{24m^2}\cdot 8g_\alpha^{[3]}(m,\alpha),$$

where bracketed superscripts denote the order of differentiation. Doing this for one more term finally provides

$$f(m,n) = g(m,\alpha) - \frac{\alpha}{2m}g_\alpha''(m,\alpha) + \frac{\alpha}{m^2}\Big(\frac{\alpha}{8}\cdot g_\alpha^{[4]}(m,\alpha) + \frac{1}{3}g_\alpha^{[3]}(m,\alpha)\Big)$$

$$- \frac{\alpha}{m^3}\Big(\frac{\alpha^2}{48}g_\alpha^{[6]}(m,\alpha) + \frac{\alpha}{6}g_\alpha^{[5]}(m,\alpha) + \frac{1}{4}g_\alpha^{[4]}(m,\alpha)\Big) + \cdots$$

(42)

This can be carried out to any order (see Exercise 9). Whether equation (42) is a proper asymptotic representation depends on the functional form of the derivatives $g_\alpha^{[r]}(m,\alpha)$. If these derivatives, for increasing r are not of higher order (e.g., as polynomials) in m, then (42) provides a proper asymptotic representation.

Exercises and Complements

1. Complete the solution of the difference equation (12) when $c=d$. (Use equation (2.3-10).)

2. (a) Show the identity

$$\sum_{k=0}^{m}\binom{r+k}{k} = \binom{r+m+1}{m}, \quad r,m \text{ integers.}$$

(b) Show that for integers $u \geq s \geq 0, w \geq 0, r \geq 0$:

$$\sum_{k=0}^{r}\binom{r-k}{w}\binom{s+k}{u} = \binom{r+s+1}{w+u+1}, \quad u \geq s \geq 0, \ w \geq 0, \ r \geq 0.$$

This can be done via identities that the binomial coefficients satisfy, or, seeing the left-hand side as a convolution, with the use of gf's.

3. (Riordan) Using the addition formula of the binomial coefficients (A.1.1), show that

$$f_n = \sum_{k=0}^{n}(-1)^{n-k}2^{2k}\binom{n+k+1}{2k+1} = n+1.$$

In the process you should also obtain

$$g_n = \sum_{k=0}^{n}(-1)^{n-k}2^{2k}\binom{n+k}{2k} = 2n + 1.$$

4. (Greene and Knuth) Consider the difference equation

$$x_n = f_n + \frac{2}{n}\sum_{i=0}^{n-1} x_i , \qquad n \geq 0$$

where $\{f_n\}$ is a given sequence. The $\{x_i\}$ seemingly depend on all their history ...

(a) Show the equation can be reduced to a first order difference equation, with non-constant coefficients.

(b) Derive a differential equation for the gf of the $\{x_i\}$ and solve it, using the formula below, for the cases

(i) $f_n = 1$, (ii) $f_n = n^2$. Extract the $\{x_i\}$ from the final result for the gf.

The general linear differential equation of first order:

$$y'(x) + h(x)y(x) = g(x),$$

with $h(\cdot)$ and $g(\cdot)$ known functions, and a given boundary value $y_0 = y(x_0)$, has the solution

$$y(x) = e^{-\int h dx}\left(C + \int g e^{\int h dx}\, dx\right),$$

where the constant C is determined from the boundary value.

5. The following problem arises in the analysis of the capacity of a random-access channel under the Capetanakis-Tsybakov-Mikhailov tree algorithm with blocked arrivals. The "collision resolution interval (CRI)" durations for n packets, L_n, are random variables that satisfy the recursion

$$L_n = 1 + L_I + L_{n-I} , \qquad n \geq 2, \qquad \text{with } L_0 = L_1 = 1,$$

with I having the binomial distribution $B(n,p)$.

(a) Derive the following equation for the pgf of L_n:

$$g_n(u) \equiv \sum_{k \geq 1} \text{Prob}(L_n = k)u^k = u\sum_{i=0}^{n}\binom{n}{i}p^i q^{n-i} g_i(u)g_{n-i}(u),$$

and obtain a recursion for $E(L_n) \equiv l_n$ by taking the first derivative of the pgf at $u = 1$:

$$l_n = 1 + \sum_{i=0}^{n}\binom{n}{i}p^i q^{n-i}(l_i + l_{n-i}), \qquad n \geq 2, \qquad l_0 = l_1 = 1.$$

(b) Define an egf for l_n by $\hat{a}(z) = \sum_{n \geq 0} l_n z^n/n!$, to obtain

$$\hat{a}(z) = e^z - 2 - 2z + e^{qz}\hat{a}(pz) + e^{pz}\hat{a}(qz).$$

The use of the Poisson gf $\hat{b}(z) = e^{-z}\hat{a}(z)$ yields a more convenient equation:

$$\hat{b}(z) - \hat{b}(pz) - \hat{b}(qz) = 1 - 2(1 + z)e^{-z}, \qquad \hat{b}(0) = 1, \ \hat{b}'(0) = 0.$$

(c) By equating coefficients of z^n on both sides of the last relation obtain

$$b_n = \begin{cases} 1 & n=0 \\ 0 & n=1 \\ \dfrac{2(-1)^n(n-1)}{n!(1-p^n-q^n)} & n\geq 2 \end{cases}$$

and from this

$$l_n = \sum_{k=0}^{n} b_k \frac{n!}{(n-k)!} = 1 + 2\sum_{k=2}^{n} \binom{n}{k}\frac{(k-1)(-1)^k}{1-p^k-q^k}.$$

(d) Show that the l_n are minimized for all n when $p = \frac{1}{2}$. For this value of p obtain a recursive expression for l_n that is better suited for numerical evaluation:

$$l_n = l_{n-1} + 2(n-1)\sum_{k\geq 1} 2^{-k}(1-2^{-k})^{n-2}, \quad n\geq 3.$$

Remark: Exercise 2.1-12 provides a guided derivation of the asymptotic value of l_n, from the expression obtained in part (c) above.

6. Example 1 in Section 2.2.3 considered binary and k-ary trees. Show that the conditions required for the Lagrange expansion to hold are satisfied there, as well as in the cases below. We look now in generalizations.

(a) An ordered tree (also called a plane tree) is similarly created, but there is no constraint on the number of subtrees each node can sprout. The structural properties of such trees are discussed in detail in Knuth (1973) Section 2.3.4.1. and in Zaks (1980).
Show that the gf for the number of ordered trees of a given size satisfies the equation

$$G(z) = \sum_{n\geq 0} p_n z^n = \frac{z}{1 - G(z)},$$

and obtain the representation $p_n = \dfrac{1}{n}\binom{2n-2}{n-1}$. This is a Catalan number! (Can you justify the relation with the number of binary trees, by considering the structure of the ordered trees?)

(b) Show that the number of ordered trees of n nodes, where the root has precisely m nonempty subtrees, is given by

$$p_{n,m} = \frac{m}{n-1}\binom{2n-m-3}{n-m-1}.$$

7. (a) (Whittaker and Watson) Use the Lagrange expansion theorem to obtain for the sum

$$a + \sum_{n\geq 1} \frac{(-1)^{n-1}(2n-2)!}{n!(n-1)!a^{2n-1}}t^n$$

with $|t| < |a/2|$, the value $\zeta_1(t) = \frac{1}{2}a[1 + \sqrt{1 + 4t/a^2}]$.

[Hint: Pick $f(z)=z$, $\phi(z)=1/z$. Consider the curve $|z(z-a)|=|t|$ that surrounds the point $z=a$. Let C be a contour just outside this one, so that on C $|z(z-a)|>|t|$. When t satisfies the above restriction, there is another such curve that surrounds the origin of the z plane, but does not include a, and ζ_1 is the only root of the equation (in ζ) $\zeta^2-a\zeta-t=0$ that is within C. (If t is larger, the two curves coalesce into one, and both roots are inside the "larger" curve).]

(b) (Comtet) Use the Lagrange expansion theorem with $\phi(x)=e^x$ and a an arbitrary complex number to show the sums

$$e^{ay}=1+\sum_{n\geq1}\frac{a(a+n)^{n-1}x^n}{n!}, \qquad \frac{e^{ay}}{1-y}=\sum_{n\geq0}\frac{(a+n)^n x^n}{n!}, \qquad x=ye^{-y}.$$

Establish the conditions for the applicability of the theorem!
[Hint: the second result is obtained by differentiating the first.]

8. Using equation (37) obtain the Poisson transform in the following cases (only in some cases a closed-form expression is available):

(a) $g(m,\alpha)=\alpha^r$
(b) $g(m,\alpha)=(1-m\alpha)^{-1}$
(c) $g(m,\alpha)=(1-c\alpha)^{-r}$
(d) $g(m,\alpha)=e^{a\alpha}$
(e) $g(m,\alpha)=\int_0^\alpha\frac{1-e^{-mt}}{t}dt$ (Use (h) below)
(f) $g(m,\alpha)=e^{-\alpha}\alpha^i/i!$

If $f(m,n)$ is the transform of $g(m,\alpha)$, what are the transforms of $g_1(m,\alpha)$, where

(g) $g_1(m,\alpha)=g'_\alpha(m,\alpha)$
(h) $g_1(m,\alpha)=\int_0^\alpha g(m,t)dt$

9. Complete the development started in equation (42): Show that

$$f(m,n)=g(m,\alpha)+\sum_{p\geq1}n^{-p}\sum_{k=p+1}^{2p}c_{k,p}\alpha^k g_\alpha^{[k]}(m,\alpha),$$

where $c_{0,p}=\delta_{0,p}$, $c_{1,p}=0$, $c_{k,0}=0$, and $(k+1)c_{k+1,p+1}=-kc_{k,p}-c_{k-1,p}$.

10. For the cases $g(m,\alpha)=e^{m\alpha}$ and $g(m,\alpha)=m^\alpha$, obtain $f(m,n)$ from equation (37), evaluate also in equation (42), compare and explain.

11. The following placement problems are simple enough to be tractable directly under both the "balls into cells" model and the Poisson model. Solve under the assumptions of both models, and show that your solutions satisfy equation (34).

(a) Inserting elements (assume they are all distinct) into a table of size m, what is the probability that precisely k certain cells remain empty? [Hint: what is the combinatorial interpretation of the Stirling number $\left\langle{n\atop k}\right\rangle$?]

What is the probability that at least k (unspecified) cells remain empty?

(b) Same experiment; compute the probability that no cell remains empty. For the first model use the inclusion-exclusion method.

(c) Inserting balls into m cells that have a capacity of 1 each. Let Y_i denote the number of balls overflowing from location i (they are not reinserted, but accumulated separately). Let $Y = \Sigma_{i=1}^m Y_i$. Compute $p_k \equiv \mathrm{Prob}(Y=k)$, its pgf and $E(Y^r)$ under both models.

12. (Fibonacci Numbers). This exercise will serve to present one of the most common sequences of integers in combinatorics. The Fibonacci numbers F_n, $n \geq 0$ are defined by

$$F_0 = 0, \quad F_1 = 1, \quad F_n = F_{n-1} + F_{n-2}, \quad n \geq 2.$$

so that the first few values are $0,1,1,2,3,5,8,13,21$. (In some of the literature F_0 is given the value 1, so there would be a shift of 1 in the indices.)

(a) Prove by induction from the above definition the identities

$$F_n F_{n+1} - F_n^2 = (-1)^n. \tag{12-1}$$

$$F_{n+m} = F_m F_{n+1} + F_{m-1} F_n. \tag{12-2}$$

(b) Let $g(z) = \Sigma_{n \geq 0} F_n z^n$. Show that $g(z) = z/(1 - z - z^2)$, and develop $g(z)$ by partial fractions to get $F_n = (\alpha^n - \beta^n)/\sqrt{5}$, where $\alpha = (1 + \sqrt{5})/2$, $\beta = (1 - \sqrt{5})/2$.

(c) Using the representation of part (b), show $\alpha^n = F_{n-1} + F_n \alpha$, $\beta^n = F_{n-1} + F_n \beta$. Use then this result to prove

$$\sum_{k=0}^n F_k F_{n-k} = \frac{n-1}{5} F_n + \frac{2n}{5} F_{n-1}. \tag{12-3}$$

[Hint: the left-hand-side is a convolution, so evaluate $g^2(z)$.]

2.3 Integral Transforms (*it's*)

Gf's are related to sequences in essentially the same way as *it*'s are related to functions of a continuous variable. While this statement holds in general, we shall mainly introduce, and use, transforms of distributions of nonnegative continuous random variables. There is a great variety of such transforms. All our requirements will be met, however, by the Laplace transform, with occasional use of the Mellin transform. The standard reference for the Laplace transform is Doetsch (1974). For a lively survey of several integral transforms and their applications see Davies (1978).

2.3.1 Laplace Transform

This transform when applied to distributions is often called the Laplace-Stieltjes transform (LST), and we shall adhere to this usage. When a rv X has the distribution function (cdf) $F_X(\cdot)$, its LST is the function

$$L_X(s) \equiv E(e^{-sX}) = \int_0^\infty e^{-sx} dF_X(x), \quad s \geq 0, \tag{1}$$

and when $F_X(\cdot)$ has a density $f_X(\cdot)$, then $L_X(s) = \int e^{-sx} f_X(x) dx$. A commonly used name for $L_X(\cdot)$ is the "moment generating function". This appellation clearly results from the following relation:

$$E(X^n) = \int x^n dF_X(x) = (-1)^n \frac{d^n}{ds^n} L_X(s) \big|_{s=0}. \tag{2}$$

While the definition above allows $F_X(\cdot)$ to consist solely of atoms at the integers, yielding an ordinary pgf (with the customary z replaced[1] by e^{-s}) we shall reserve this notation for continuous variables.

The following two properties hold for both varieties:

(1) Distinct pmf's (cdf's) have distinct pgf's (LSTs).
(2) If a sequence of pmf's (cdf's) approaches a limit, so does the sequence of the corresponding transforms, and this limit is the transform of the limit of the first sequence.

When the *it*'s of any functions - not necessarily cdf's - are used, the following properties are of importance:

Linearity: Let $f(x) = ag(x) \pm bh(x)$ where a and b are constants, then $L_f(s) = aL_g(s) \pm bL_h(s)$.

Differentiation and integration: the corresponding formulas depend on the kernel of the transform, and differ for the various *it*'s. Often these relationships are the

---

[1] This formal similarity explains the many common properties of pgf's and LSTs.

reason for the it's being introduced into the calculation in the first place. For the LST we find, through integration by parts,

$$L_{g'}(s) = sL_g(s) - g(0^+),$$ (3)

where $g(0^+) = \lim\limits_{x\to 0} g(x)$, the limit being taken via positive values of x. This is only of importance if $g(\cdot)$ has a discontinuity at $x=0$. Repeating the integration by parts we find:

$$L_{g^{[n]}}(s) = s^n L_g(s) - \sum_{k=1}^{n} s^{n-k} g^{[k-1]}(0^+),$$ (4)

where $g^{[i]}(x)$ is the i'th derivative of $g(x)$. When $G(x) = \int_0^x g(t)dt$, we have by change of order of integration and substitution,

$$L_G(s) = \int_0^\infty e^{-xs} \int_0^x g(t)dtdx = \int_0^\infty g(t) \int_t^\infty e^{-xs} dxdt = \frac{1}{s} \int_0^\infty e^{-ts} g(t)dt$$
$$= \frac{1}{s} L_g(s).$$ (5)

A complementary result can easily be shown as well: if $g(x) = f(x)/x$ then $L_g(s) = \int_{t \geq s} L_f(t)dt$.

Translation: Let $g(x) = f(x-a)$ for $a > 0$, and $f(x) = 0$ for $x < 0$. Then[2] $L_g(s) = e^{-as} L_f(s)$. If $g(x) = f(x+a)$, with $a > 0$ (a translation to the left), we have a more cumbersome relation:

$$L_g(s) = e^{as} L_f(s) - \int_0^a e^{(a-t)s} f(t)dt,$$

where the finite integral obstructs calculations usually, unless $f(x)$ happens to vanish conveniently for $x < a$.

Finally we present a reciprocal relationship between the asymptotic behavior of the LST and a representation of the density near the origin:

Watson's lemma: If $f(t)$ can be represented for $t \to 0$ as a series

$$f(t) \approx \sum_{l \geq 1} a_l t^{\lambda_l}, \qquad -1 < \text{Re}(\lambda_1) < \text{Re}(\lambda_2) < \cdots$$ (6.a)

then

$$L_f(s) \approx \sum_{l \geq 1} \frac{a_l \Gamma(\lambda_l + 1)}{s^{\lambda_l + 1}}, \qquad |s| \to \infty, \quad |\arg(s)| < \pi/2.$$ (6.b)

An important special case which is often adequate arises if $\lambda_1 = 0$; then $f(0) = a_1$

---

[2] The same relation is sometimes found written as $L[f(t-a)] = e^{-as} L[f(t)]$, where the translation, rather than the independent variable has been made explicit, and t is specious.

and $L_f(s) \approx a_1/s$ for $|s| \to \infty$. The uniqueness property of the transform assures us that had we obtained a transform which has an asymptotic representation as given by (6.b), then the primitive function has the asymptotic expansion (6.a). $\square$

Further material concerning such relations is given in Feller (1971 Chap. XIII) and in Copson (1965). We shall expand on these topics in Section 2.5.

Convolutions. The convolution property of the gf's holds for LSTs too and is of paramount importance here as well. Let the cdf $F_C(\cdot)$ be available as the convolution of $F_A(\cdot)$ and $F_B(\cdot)$, then

$$F_C(x) = \int_0^x F_A(x-u)dF_B(u) \iff L_C(s) = L_A(s)L_B(s).$$

If the cdf's have densities (pdf's), then

$$f_C(x) = \int_0^x f_A(x-u)f_B(u)du = \int_0^x f_A(u)f_B(x-u)du.$$

The most important application comes when the rv C is the sum of two (or more) *independent* rv's. For example, a rv Y having the Erlang distribution law, with parameters n and λ may be viewed as the sum of n independent rv's, each having the exponential distribution with parameter λ,

$$f_{X_i}(x) = \lambda e^{-\lambda x}, \quad L_{X_i}(s) = \lambda \int_0^\infty e^{-\lambda x - sx}dx = \frac{\lambda}{\lambda+s},$$

and then

$$L_Y(s) = \left(\frac{\lambda}{\lambda+s}\right)^n.$$

Inversion of the Laplace Transform

We have already mentioned a property common to both gf's and *it*'s: inasmuch as they exist they are unique; equivalently, distinct distributions correspond to distinct transforms, and *vice versa*. Thus deriving a gf or an *it* is tantamount to obtaining 'its' distribution (or more generally, its primitive function). This statement is adequate, even complete, as long as the objective is demonstrating the feasibility of the calculation and uniqueness of the result. While some further information - especially the first few moments - is rather easily obtained, in order to regain the complete distribution one has to invert the transform.

For gf's this may be done by successive differentiation of the gf at $z=0$. This usually laborious process may be quite often supplanted by writing the function in such a form that the coefficients of successive powers of the argument can be 'picked out', as was done in equation (2.2-15). Here is a related situation:

Example. Let $f(z) = C\dfrac{e^{-az}}{z-b}$. When $C = (1-a)e^a$, $f(z)$ is a proper pgf. It may be converted to the product of two series in z:

$$f(z) = -\frac{C}{b} \left[\sum_{i \geq 0} \frac{(-az)^i}{i!} \right] \sum_{j \geq 0} \left(\frac{z}{b} \right)^j .$$

Collecting contributions to the coefficient of z^n in $f(z)$ we have

$$[z^n]f(z) = -\frac{C}{b} \sum_{k=0}^{n} \frac{(-a)^k}{k!} \left(\frac{1}{b} \right)^{n-k} = \frac{-C}{b^{n+1}} \sum_{k=0}^{n} \frac{(-ab)^k}{k!} .$$

For the first few values of n the sum is easy to evaluate, and then it rapidly approaches e^{-ab}. We show below that it's may respond to a similar attack as well.

Generally, inversion of the it's we consider involves contour integration in the complex plane. Specifically, for the LST: if $L(s)$ exists for $\text{Re}(s) > c$, then

$$f(t) = \frac{1}{2\pi i} \int_{\gamma - i\infty}^{\gamma + i\infty} e^{ts} L(s) ds , \qquad \text{for } any \; \gamma > c. \qquad (7)$$

Often (and always so for distributions) $c = 0$ is adequate. Numerous tables exist, some quite extensive (especially Erdélyi, 1954), giving $f(\cdot)$ for a variety of $L(\cdot)$. We shall only exhibit here the important special case where $L(\cdot)$ can be written as a rational function - a ratio of two polynomials, $L(s) = A(s)/B(s)$, where $A(\cdot)$ and $B(\cdot)$ do not have any common factors and the degree of the numerator is lower than that of the denominator (otherwise one does long division, the quotient contributing to the first $deg(A) - deg(B) + 1$ coefficients, and the remainder is handled as follows).

Consider first the case where $B(\cdot)$ has roots $\alpha_1, \alpha_2, \cdots, \alpha_n$ that are all distinct. Then $L(\cdot)$ can be expanded into partial fractions of the simple form

$$L(s) = \sum_{i=1}^{n} \frac{A(\alpha_i)}{B'(\alpha_i)(s - \alpha_i)} , \qquad (8)$$

yielding the inverse

$$f(t) = \sum_{i=1}^{n} \frac{A(\alpha_i)}{B'(\alpha_i)} e^{\alpha_i t} . \qquad (9)$$

When the roots are not all distinct the calculations are somewhat heavier. We shall look at the case where only one root, α, has a multiplicity m that is larger than one. The effect of more such roots is merely additive, and is handled identically. The partial fraction decomposition will now contain the added sum $\sum_{j=1}^{m} \gamma_j / (s - \alpha)^j$, where the γ_j are usually easiest to obtain by equating the ratio $L(\cdot)$ to its expansion, multiplying throughout, to bring to a common denominator, and comparing coefficients of like powers of s.

The coefficients can also be explicitly written as

$$\gamma_{m-j} = \frac{1}{j!}\frac{d^j}{ds^j}[(s-\alpha)^m \frac{A(s)}{B(s)}]_{s=\alpha}, \qquad 0 \le j \le m-1. \qquad (10)$$

When the desired result is the analytic form of the transform of the inverse of an LST, direct evaluation of the integral (7) or table scanning are the only open ways. In the context of analysis of algorithms, however, this is rarely the case. When a random variable is investigated, usually the first few moments (mainly two), give nearly all the practical information, and these are normally not nearly as hard to obtain, through equation (2). The problem of numerical inversion of the LST is treated in detail in Bellman, Kalaba and Locket (1966), and summarized by Davies (1978). When tail probabilities are required, there probably is no other way.

2.3.2 Mellin Transform

This *it* appears to be especially useful in the manipulation of generating functions to obtain information about their expansion coefficients and asymptotic estimates. A rather elaborate application is in the heart of Fayolle et al. (1986). More information on the properties and uses of the Mellin transform than we briefly list below may be found in Davies (1978). The transform is defined for every function as

$$M_f(p) = \int_0^\infty x^{p-1}f(x)dx , \qquad \alpha < \mathrm{Re}(p) < \beta \qquad (11)$$

and normally exists only when p is in some strip as denoted in equation (11). The inverse relationship is

$$f(x) = \int_{(c)} x^{-p}M_f(p)dp , \qquad (12)$$

where $\int_{(c)}$ is the standard short notation for $\frac{1}{2\pi i}\int_{c-i\infty}^{c+i\infty}$, and the real number c in (12) is limited to be in the strip determined in (11), i.e. $\alpha < c < \beta$.

Example. The Mellin transform of the exponential function is the gamma function: Let $f(x) = e^{-ax}$, then

$$M(p) = \int_0^\infty x^{p-1}e^{-ax}dx = a^{-p}\Gamma(p), \quad \mathrm{Re}(p)>0 \qquad (13)$$

and the inverse relation yields a representation important in its own right:

$$e^{-ax} = \int_{(c)} \Gamma(z)(ax)^{-z}dz , \qquad c > 0. \qquad (14)$$

For an application of this representation see Exercise 2.6-5.

To continue with this example, note that the integrand in equation (14) has all its poles to the left of the integration contour, since the exponential part there is entire and the gamma function has only simple poles at zero and the negative integers. Its residues at $z = -n, n \geq 0$ are $(-1)^n/n!$. Completing the integration contour to a rectangle on the left, as in Fig. 2.1, and using the exponential decline of the gamma function for arguments with large imaginary component:

$$\Gamma(t+iN) = O\left(|t+iN|^{t-\frac{1}{2}}e^{-t-\pi N/2}\right), \quad \text{as } N \to \infty, \tag{15}$$

the contribution to the integral from the horizontal portions of the completed contour vanishes as $N_1 \to \infty$. On the left vertical line, the integrand can be evaluated using $\Gamma(z+1) = z\,\Gamma(z)$, yielding $\Gamma(c+iv)\dfrac{(ax)^{N_2+iv}}{(N_2-1)!}$, which also leads to vanishing contribution as $N_2 \to \infty$. Hence the integral in (14) is equal to the sum of the residues of the integrand to the left of the contour,

$$e^{-ax} = \sum_{n \geq 0} \frac{(-1)^n}{n!}(ax)^n, \tag{16}$$

a familiar expansion.

Properties of the Mellin Transform

The Mellin transform of a usual convolution is not as nicely or usefully related to those of the participating functions, as was the case for the LST, but if we have a (weighted) *multiplicative* convolution, such as

$$h(x) = \int_0^\infty y^a f(xy)g(y)dy \;; \quad \text{or,} \quad k(x) = \int_0^\infty y^a f\left(\frac{x}{y}\right)g(y)dy, \tag{17}$$

then

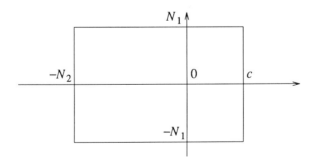

Fig. 2.1: Integration contour for equation (14)

$$M_h(p) = M_f(p)M_g(a-p+1), \quad \text{and} \quad M_k(p) = M_f(p)M_g(a+p+1). \quad (18)$$

Conversely, a Parseval-like relation is easy to compute

$$M_{fg}(p) = \int_{(c)} M_f(s)M_g(p-s)ds. \quad (19)$$

The property most often encountered in applications, and to our mind the main merit of this transform is when

$$h(x) = f(ax) \quad \to \quad M_h(p) = a^{-p}M_f(p). \quad (20)$$

Note that this last relation can be obtained from equations (17) and (18) by substituting a Dirac delta function for $g(\cdot)$ there.

Two further relations that are easy to obtain and often useful in computations are (see Exercise 2):

$$g(x) = x^r f(x) \implies M_g(p) = M_f(p+r), \quad (21)$$

and

$$g(x) = f'(x) \implies M_g(p) = -(p-1)M_f(p-1). \quad (22)$$

2.3.3 Mellin Summation Formula

The basic form of this formula refers to infinite sums, but it may also be used to obtain a representation for finite sums, asymptotic in the upper summation limit. Consider the problem of evaluating the sum

$$S = \sum_{n \geq 1} f(n), \quad (23)$$

where the function $f(\cdot)$, over the reals, has the Mellin transform $M(p)$. Using equation (12) with x replaced by n we substitute in (23) to obtain

$$\begin{aligned} S &= \int_{(c)} M(p) \sum_{n \geq 1} n^{-p}\,dp \\ &= \int_{(c)} M(p)\zeta(p)\,dp, \qquad \text{(Mellin summation formula)} \end{aligned} \quad (24)$$

where $\zeta(p)$ is the Riemann zeta function. It will become obvious from the example below that using it properly requires some familiarity with the properties of the gamma and zeta functions. The best source for these is probably still the encyclopedic coverage of Whittaker and Watson (1927). A list of properties and representations, asymptotic expansions and further references may also be found in Abramowitz and Stegun (1964).

Example. To obtain the sum

$$S = \sum_{n \geq 1} \frac{\cos \beta n}{n^2}, \qquad 0 \leq \beta < 2\pi \tag{25}$$

we need the integral

$$\int_{x=0}^{\infty} \cos \beta x \; x^{p-1} dx = \Gamma(p)\beta^{-p} \cos(\pi p/2), \quad 0 < \mathrm{Re}(p) < 1. \tag{26}$$

The Mellin transform of the summands in equation (25), $n^{-2}\cos\beta n$ is then

$$M(p) = -\Gamma(p-2)\beta^{2-p} \cos(\pi p/2), \quad 2 < \mathrm{Re}(p) < 3. \tag{27}$$

Substituting this into equation (24), and exchanging the order of summation and integration (the sum converges absolutely on the integration contour) we have

$$S = -\int_{(c)} \Gamma(p-2)\beta^{2-p} \cos(\pi p/2) \; \zeta(p)dp, \quad 2 < c = \mathrm{Re}(p) < 3. \tag{28}$$

To evaluate the integral we use Riemann's functional relationship

$$\pi^s \zeta(1-s) = 2^{1-s} \Gamma(p) \cos(\pi s/2)\zeta(s), \tag{29}$$

to bring the integral to the form

$$S = -\tfrac{1}{2}\beta^2 \int_{(c)} \left(\frac{2\pi}{\beta}\right)^p \frac{\zeta(1-p)}{(p-1)(p-2)} \; dp. \tag{30}$$

The integrand has three simple poles, at $p = 2$, 1, and 0. The residues are easy to compute (if you know that $\zeta(0) = -\tfrac{1}{2}$, $\zeta(-1) = -1/12$ and its only singularity is at 1, with a residue of 1), and we get the pleasantly simple result

$$\begin{aligned}
S &= -\tfrac{1}{2}\beta^2\left[\left(\frac{2\pi}{\beta}\right)^2 \zeta(-1) - \frac{2\pi}{\beta}\zeta(0) - \frac{1}{2}\right] \\
&= \frac{\pi^2}{6} - \tfrac{1}{2}\pi\beta + \frac{\beta^2}{4}.
\end{aligned} \tag{31}$$

Further examples may be found in Davies (1978), Section 13.

Exercises and Complements

1. Prove the relations satisfied by the LST, as given in equations (3) and (4).

2. Obtain from the definition of the Mellin transform the properties listed in equations (18) to (22).

3. Evaluate $\displaystyle\sum_{n \geq 1} \frac{\sin \beta n}{n}$.

4. Show the following summations:

$$\sum_{n\geq 1}(-1)^{n+1}n^{-s} = (1-2^{1-s})\zeta(s)$$

and

$$\sum_{n\geq 1}(2n+1)^{-s} = (1-2^{-s})\zeta(s).$$

5. Use the relation $(a+l)^{-1} = \int_0^1 u^{a+l-1}du$, to show the summation

$$\sum_{l=0}^{m}\frac{(-1)^l}{(m-l)!l!(a+l)!} = \frac{(a-1)!}{(m+a)!}.$$

2.4 Combinatorial Calculus (The Symbolic Operator Method)

Generating functions, both ordinary and exponential have been defined in Section 2.2. There they were viewed as compact representations for sequences, though some of the examples in Section 2.2.1 already hint they can be used in some cases rather as operators. In this section the latter view is given prominence. The dual nature of these functions that was mentioned in Section 2.2.1, as members in Cauchy algebras of formal power series as well as functions in C, persists and continues to bear fruit. We remark that those operations performed on the series that define the functions are legitimate within the formalism of Cauchy algebras only so long as the determination of each coefficient involves a *finite* number of operations. It will turn out, in the few instances where this requirement puts constraints on the functions we can use, that these constraints are intuitively reasonable, in the sense that violating them would take us afield of "physically" meaningful operations anyway.

2.4.1 Elementary Examples

We display below some simple definitions and applications, intended to bring out the intuitive flavor behind the more formal treatment presented in Section 2.4.2.

Let S be a countable set of some entities, such as numbers, words, graphs, coins, algorithms ... . The letter σ will designate a typical element of S. Let $w(\sigma)$ be the *weight* of the element σ, a non-negative integer. The function $\phi_S(z)$ is defined as the generating function of S through

$$\phi_S(z) = \sum_{\sigma \in S} z^{w(\sigma)}. \tag{1.a}$$

An obvious equivalent definition proceeds as follows: let a_r be the number of elements in S that satisfy $w(\sigma) = r$, then

$$\phi_S(z) = \sum_{r \geq 0} a_r z^r. \tag{1.b}$$

Two immediate consequences follow from the definition:

$$\phi_S(1) = |s|, \quad \text{the size of } S,$$

$$\phi_S'(1) = \sum_{r \geq 1} r a_r = w(S), \text{ the total weight of the elements of } S.$$

On account of these relations $\phi_S(\cdot)$ is called in texts on combinatorics the *enumerator* of S. In the examples below we show some of its uses for enumeration problems. In the next section we also use egf's, similarly defined through

$$\hat{\phi}_S(z) = \sum_{\sigma \in S} \frac{z^{w(\sigma)}}{w(\sigma)!} = \sum_{\sigma \in S} a_r \frac{z^r}{r!}. \tag{2}$$

Examples (a):

(1) Let S be a set of coins: 3 cents, 1 nickel, 5 dimes and 7 quarters; let the function $w(\cdot)$ be the value of a coin in cents, then

$$\phi_S(z) = 3z + z^5 + 5z^{10} + 7z^{25},$$

$$\phi_S(1) = 3+1+5+7 = 16, \qquad \phi'_S(1) = 3+5+50+175 = \$2.33.$$

Older British coinage afforded a richer variety of powers.

(2) Let S_1 be the set $\{a_1, a_2, \cdots, a_n\}$, and S the set of all subsets of S_1 (including the empty set). Define $w(\sigma)$ as the number of S_1 elements in σ. There are $\binom{n}{r}$ elements in S with weight r, hence

$$\phi_S(z) = \sum_{r \geq 0} \binom{n}{r} z^r = (1+z)^n, \quad \phi_S(1) = 2^n, \quad \phi'_S(1) = n\,2^{n-1}. \tag{3}$$

(3) Consider now an infinite set: all the "words" constructible from the three-letter alphabet $\{a,b,c\}$. Let the weight of an element be its letter count, then a_r, the number of r-letter words is 3^r and

$$\phi_S(z) = \sum_{r \geq 0} 3^r z^r = (1 - 3z)^{-1}. \tag{4}$$

As a function in the complex domain this representation of $\phi_S(z)$ is only valid for $|z| < 1/3$, and indeed $\phi_S(1)$ and $\phi'_S(1)$ do not have the meaning used above. If we limited the word lengths to a finite R, we are back on familiar ground (See Exercise 3.)

The sum and multiplication rules

These are the first two rules providing us with a method of constructing gf's.

Let $S = S_1 \cup S_2$, $S_1 \cap S_2 = \varnothing$, and the *same* weight function $w(\cdot)$ is defined over both S_i. Then

$$\phi_S(z) = \sum_{\sigma \in S} z^{w(\sigma)} = \sum_{\sigma \in S_1} z^{w(\sigma)} + \sum_{\sigma \in S_2} z^{w(\sigma)} = \phi_{S_1}(z) + \phi_{S_2}(z). \tag{5}$$

Let $S = S_1 \times S_2$, the cartesian product of S_1 and S_2 (i.e. each element σ of S is an ordered pair (σ_1, σ_2), $\sigma_i \in S_i$). Define the weight of such a σ as $w(\sigma) = w(\sigma_1) + w(\sigma_2)$. Then

$$\phi_S(z) = \sum_{\sigma \in S} z^{w(\sigma)} = \sum_{\sigma_i \in S_i} z^{w(\sigma_1)+w(\sigma_2)} = \sum_{\sigma_1 \in S_1} z^{w(\sigma_1)} \sum_{\sigma_2 \in S_2} z^{w(\sigma_2)} = \phi_{S_1}(z)\phi_{S_2}(z). \tag{6}$$

The above is entirely analogous to the derivation of the convolution formula, equation (2.2-5) (see Exercise 2).

Examples (b): Compositions and partitions of integers.

(1) The *compositions* of n, with k parts, or components, are the non-negative integer solutions of

$$a_1 + \cdots + a_k = n, \quad a_i \geq 0. \tag{7}$$

We shall consider as different two solutions which consist of different arrangements of the same values: $(0, 2, \cdots)$ and $(2, 0, \cdots)$ are distinct solutions. Order counts.

Denote by I_j the collection of all integers not smaller than j. Clearly every solution of equation (7) is an element of the set of k-dimensional non-negative vectors $S = I_0 \times I_0 \times \cdots \times I_0$ (k factors). From equation (6), with a weight function over the elements of I_0 equal to their numerical value,

$$\phi_S(z) = \phi_{I_0}^k(z) = \left[\sum_{i \geq 0} z^i \right]^k = [(1-z)^{-1}]^k = (1-z)^{-k}. \tag{8}$$

Since we are asking about the number of elements of S with weight n we need $[z^n]\phi_S(z)$, and by the binomial theorem and equation (A.1.2)

$$[z^n]\phi_S(z) = [z^n](1-z)^{-k} = \binom{-k}{n}(-1)^n = \binom{k+n-1}{n}, \tag{9}$$

as one would expect. Writing out in full the relation (8) as

$$\phi_S(z) = (1 + z + \cdots + z^i + \cdots)(1 + z + \cdots + z^j + \cdots) \cdots (1 + z + \cdots + z^r + \cdots),$$

lets one have a more pictorial idea how the coefficient in (9) is "assembled". A variety of special cases and extensions is considered in Exercise 4.

(2) What is the number of compositions of n with up to k components? The above procedure, using equation (A.2.1), leads to:

$$\sum_{i=1}^{k} \binom{n+i-1}{n} = \binom{n+k}{k-1}. \tag{10}$$

(3) What is the number of compositions with *any* k allowed? Clearly the number is unlimited if we allow $a_i \in I_0$. How is this obvious statement reflected in the above mechanism? Formally, we would then have: $S = I_0 + I_0^2 + \cdots$ (these are all the cartesian products of I_0 with itself), i.e.

$$\phi_S(z) = \sum_{k \geq 1} \phi_{I_0}^k(z) = \sum_{k \geq 1} \frac{1}{(1-z)^k} = \frac{1}{1-z} \cdot \frac{1}{1 - 1/(1-z)} = -\frac{1}{z}. \tag{11}$$

Indeed, this will not yield the $[z^n]\phi_S(z)$ term in a finite number of operations. Also, we observe that the series $\Sigma(1-z)^{-k}$ does not define an analytic function for z in any neighborhood of the origin.

If we require however $a_i \in I_1$, the situation is entirely different, since clearly only $k \leq n$ will contribute. Still, the computation of an explicit answer is easier if we leave k unrestricted:

$$\phi_S(z) = \sum_{k \geq 1} \phi_{I_1}^k(z) = \sum_{k \geq 1} \left(\sum_{r \geq 1} z^r \right)^k = \sum_{k \geq 1} \left(\frac{z}{1-z} \right)^k$$

$$= \frac{z}{1-z} \cdot \frac{1}{1 - z/(1-z)} = \frac{z}{1-2z},$$

and, for $n > 0$

$$[z^n]\phi_S(z) = [z^n] \frac{z}{1-2z} = [z^{n-1}] \sum_{i \geq 0} (2z)^i = 2^{n-1}. \tag{12}$$

(4) Consider the set $N_n = \{1, 2, \cdots, n\}$. How many different subsets of size k does the power set 2^{N_n} contain? This number is well known to be $\binom{n}{k}$. The answer is less straightforward when one imposes certain restrictions on the subset composition. We shall consider now a particular restriction, and Exercise 5 asks you to calculate a few related ones.

What is the number of subsets of size k that may not contain successive numbers? Each subset we select has a unique representation when its terms are arranged in increasing order. We shall denote it when thus written by $A_k = \{a_i\}$, $1 \leq i \leq k$, and then $1 \leq a_1 < a_2 < \cdots < a_k \leq n$. The above restriction translates to $a_{i+1} - a_i \geq 2$, $1 \leq i \leq k-1$. A direct approach to the problem of counting these subsets is based on the observation that for each such a subset one may fit the subset $\{a_1, a_2 - 1, a_3 - 2, \cdots, a_k - (k-1)\}$, and this is a subset selected from $N_{n-(k-1)}$ with no restrictions; hence the desired count is given by $\binom{n-k+1}{k}$, from equation (9). The following device not only reproduces this result but also enables the enumeration under more complicated restrictions on successive differences.

Define $a_0 \equiv 0$, $a_{k+1} \equiv n$ and $d_i \equiv a_{i+1} - a_i$ for $0 \leq i \leq k$. Clearly, given these $k+1$ d_i values, A_k is uniquely determined. Moreover, we observe that

$$d_0 \geq 1, \quad d_i \geq 2, \quad 1 \leq i \leq k-1, \quad d_k \geq 0, \quad \text{and} \quad \sum_{i=0}^{k} d_i = n. \tag{13}$$

Thus we have found that the number of desired sets, of "type" A_k, to be denoted by $c_{n,k}$, is equal to the number of $k+1$ part compositions of n, subject to the restrictions in (13). This implies that $c_{n,k}$ is the coefficient of z^n in the gf of the set $I_1 \times I_2^{k-1} \times I_0$:

$$c_{n,k} = [z^n]\phi_{I_1}(z)\phi_{I_2}^{k-1}(z)\phi_{I_0}(z) = [z^n] \frac{z}{1-z} \left(\frac{z^2}{1-z} \right)^{k-1} \frac{1}{1-z}$$

$$= [z^n] z^{2k-1}(1-z)^{-k-1} = [z^{n-2k+1}](1-z)^{-(k+1)} = \binom{-k-1}{n-2k+1}(-1)^{n-2k+1} \tag{14}$$

$$= \binom{n-k+1}{n-2k+1} = \binom{n-k+1}{k}.$$

Just the number we obtained above.

(5) We consider now *partitions* of n, i.e. solutions of the equation $\sum_{j \geq 1} a_j = n$, with an unspecified number of parts $a_j \geq 1$, and with their order not taken into account. Thus $3 + 4 = 4 + 3 = 7$ is just one such partition of the number 7, into two parts. Let p_n denote the number of such solutions. For example, $p_4 = 5$, with the solutions being $\{1,1,1,1\}$, $\{1,1,2\}$, $\{1,3\}$, $\{2,2\}$ and $\{4\}$.

The building blocks we use now are the sets consisting of a single element i, an integer, and its unlimited repetitions, $\{i\}^*$, where

$$\{i\}^* \equiv \{ \; ; i ; i,i ; i,i,i ; \cdots \}. \tag{15}$$

As definition (15) shows, "unlimited repetition" extends to zero repetitions. Assigning to each element in $\{i\}^*$ a weight equal to the sum of its terms, we find for its gf, $\phi_{\{i\}^*}(z)$, the value

$$\phi_{\{i\}^*}(z) = \sum_{k \geq 0} \phi_{\{i\}^k}(z) = \sum_{k \geq 0} z^{ik} = \frac{1}{1-z^i}. \tag{16}$$

Every solution to $\sum a_j = n$ is an element of the set $C = \{1\}^* \times \{2\}^* \times \cdots$, where the term picked from $\{i\}^*$ corresponds to those a_j that satisfy $a_j = i$. Clearly then

$$p_n = [z^n] \phi_C(z) = [z^n] \frac{1}{1-z} \cdot \frac{1}{1-z^2} \cdot \frac{1}{1-z^3} \cdots . \tag{17}$$

For a given n we need only consider the first n factors in the right-hand side of (17), since higher factors will not contribute any suitable powers of z; i.e.

$$p_n = [z^n] \frac{1}{(1-z)(1-z^2)(1-z^3) \cdots (1-z^n)}. \tag{18}$$

Unfortunately, there is no convenient expression for this coefficient other than equation (18) as is. Even in this form, however, it can be used in a number of ways. See Exercises 6, 7 and 8. Part (e) of Exercise 6 shows the gf for k part partitions. Exercise 9 tackles a related problem by a similar method.

Examples (c): Occupancy problems.

Counting the ways of distributing objects into receptacles or cells is a basic combinatorial activity. Detailed expositions are given in Riordan (1958) and Kolchin et al. (1978). We present here a few special cases.

The problem admits several variants, according to whether we consider the objects distinct or not, and similarly for the cells. It is self-referential to observe that we thus have four types of problems. Subvarieties arise when certain limitations are placed on the cell occupancies, as shall be seen below.

(1) Like Objects, Like Cells

Consider the number of ways to distribute n identical objects over m places that are indistinguishable. This is precisely the problem of enumerating partitions of n, having up to m parts. The gf for this count can be obtained from Exercise 6(e), but no simple-to-handle explicit results exist.

Let us go now to another variety that will appear familiar.

(2) *Like Objects, Unlike Cells*
Counting the number of distinct occupancies arising from dropping n identical balls into m ordered places is just the problem we encountered above, of enumerating m part compositions of n. Equations (8) and (9) are the basic results. As shown in example (b.4) and Exercises 4 and 5, associating different gf's with different parts opens the way for a wealth of applications. The general term for such gf's associated with distinct parts is *enumerators*. A general impression from the applications of placement problems is that this is the most frequently encountered placement model, with the next one a close runner-up.

(3) *Distinguishable Objects, Distinct Cells*
Consider m numbered cells, and let n_i denote the number of elements in cell i. Every possible occupancy configuration will then be represented by a so-called *indicator* gf $z_1^{n_1} z_2^{n_2} \cdots z_m^{n_m}$. How are these configurations to be counted? Let us start with a single object. It has the possible gf's $z_1, z_2, \cdots, z_m$, and hence all its configurations are given, according to the sum rule, by the gf, $\sum_{i=1}^{m} z_i$. Taking now n elements, since they are all distinct, the product rule applies, and their configurations are generated by

$$g_n(z_1, \cdots, z_m) = \left(\sum_{i=1}^{m} z_i \right)^n .$$

Note that this provides the indicator $z_1^{n_1} \cdots z_m^{n_m}$ with the multinomial coefficient $\binom{n}{n_1, \cdots, n_m}$.

More interesting results emerge when we construct the egf of these indicators:

$$g(t; z_1, \cdots, z_m) = \sum_{n \geq 0} g_n(z_1, \cdots, z_m) \frac{t^n}{n!} = \exp t(z_1 + \cdots + z_m)$$

$$= e^{t z_1} \cdots e^{t z_i} \cdots e^{t z_m} .$$

(19)

Each cell contributes separately its indicator. If the possible occupancy of cell i must exclude certain values, then the entire series $\exp t z_i = 1 + t z_i + \frac{1}{2}(t z_i)^2 + \cdots$ will not be included, but only the allowed terms. The number of configurations, or occupancy vectors, possible with n objects is given in any such case by $n![t^n] g(t; z_1, \cdots, z_m)|_{z_1 = \cdots = z_m = 1}$.

For example, the number of configurations that leave no cell empty is given by

$$n![t^n]\prod_{i=1}^{m}\left(e^{tz_i}-1\right)|_{z_1=\cdots=z_m=1} = n![t^n](e^t-1)^m$$

$$= n![t^n]m!\sum_k \left\langle{k \atop m}\right\rangle \frac{t^k}{k!} = m!\left\langle{n \atop m}\right\rangle, \tag{20}$$

where $\left\langle{n \atop m}\right\rangle$ is the Stirling number of the second kind – equation (B.1.4).

Similarly, the indicator of an empty cell is 1; hence, again using equation (B.1.4), the number of configurations that leave exactly r cells empty is

$$n![t^n]\binom{m}{r}(e^t-1)^{m-r} = \binom{m}{r}(m-r)!\left\langle{n \atop m-r}\right\rangle = \frac{m!}{r!}\left\langle{n \atop m-r}\right\rangle, \tag{21}$$

and the total number of occupancy vectors, with no restrictions is the obvious m^n. Physical systems that are modeled by a collection of "n balls in m cells", and display a behavior that indicates that all the m^n occupancy configurations are equiprobable are said to obey the "Maxwell-Boltzmann statistics". This is to be contrasted with systems that behave as if it is the configurations counted by equations (8) and (9) that are equiprobable. The latter are said to satisfy the "Bose-Einstein statistics". See Feller (1968, Section II.5a) for exasperated and interesting remarks on this topic.

When the n objects consist of several subsets, p_k subsets containing k *identical* elements, we say the objects have the *specification* $(1^{p_1}2^{p_2}\cdots)$. We have then p_1 singletons, p_2 (identical) twins, p_3 triplets, etc. By implication, elements in different subsets are distinct. When no restrictions on the occupancies exist, the product rule tells us that the entire number of configurations is obtained by multiplying the number of ways to distribute the p_1 singletons by the number of ways to accommodate p_2 distinct pairs and so on, and equation (9) brings this to a total of

$$U([n],m) = m^{p_1}\binom{m+1}{2}^{p_2}\cdots\binom{m+k-1}{k}^{p_k}\cdots \tag{22}$$

with $[n]$ implying the specification.

Let $R([n],m)$ denote the similar count for configurations with the restriction that no cell may be left empty. $U([n],m)$ is easily related to such R's, by breaking down its enumeration according to the number of cells left unoccupied in the counted configurations:

$$U([n],m) = \sum_{k\geq 0}\binom{m}{k}R([n],m-k). \tag{23}$$

With k being the number of empty cells, and $\binom{m}{k}$ the number of such choices, this sum obviously covers all the configurations that make up $U([n],m)$. Now invoke the inverse relation (4.1) of Appendix A, and identify $(-1)^k b_k$ there with $R([n],k)$. We find then

$$R([n], m) = \sum_{k \geq 0} \binom{m}{k}(-1)^k U([n], m-k).$$ (24)

Some further developments of this example, and in particular recurrences for $R([n], m)$ are given in Riordan (1958, p. 94ff).

(4) *Distinct Objects, Like Cells*
For this last variation we note that like the first one above, generally no usable explicit results exist. An exception is the case when only configurations that leave no cell empty are considered, since then the occupying objects provide an ordering of the cells. The number of such configurations would then be just $1/m!$ of the number found under similar restriction in example (3) above, given by equation (20), that is, $\left\langle {n \atop m} \right\rangle$.

2.4.2 Admissible Combinatorial Constructions

In Section 2.4.1 we have displayed several manipulations with gf's that enabled us to obtain rather simply useful results, relying on the intuitive enumeration properties of these functions. In this section we formalize these properties, following Flajolet (1984).

The symbols A, B and C, sometimes subscripted, are used below to denote combinatorial classes, meaning collections of *combinatorial structures*. A structure can be as simple as a single letter or number, or as complex as a graph with a specified list of properties. A collection may be finite or denumerable. A weight function $w(\cdot)$ assigns to each structure a non-negative integer, its weight. We use $A_{(n)}$ to denote the subclass in A consisting of elements (=structures) of weight n. Their number, $|A_{(n)}|$, will be denoted by a_n. A condition which is important to impose, and proves harmless in applications, is that even when $|A|$ is not finite, every $|A_{(n)}|$ must be. This requirement entails some restriction on the classes of structures that can partake in the operations to be discussed below.

A *combinatorial construction* Φ of order k is an operation that associates k combinatorial classes, C_1 to C_k with a class A, $A = \Phi(C_1, C_2, \cdots, C_k)$.

Gf-admissible Constructions

A combinatorial construction is *gf-admissible* if there exists an operator Ψ that allows us to compute the gf of A, $\phi_A(z)$, from the gf's $\phi_{C_i}(z)$ of C_i: $\phi_A(z)$
$= \Psi(\phi_{C_1}(z), \phi_{C_2}(z), \cdots, \phi_{C_k}(z))$.

The essence of this definition is that the information contained in the $\phi_{C_i}(z)$ must suffice to compute $\phi_A(z)$. Note the close similarity with the definition of a random variable, which must be measurable with respect to the supporting probability space. The similarity is not accidental, since computing a gf implies counting the structures of different weights, and these counts can be used to construct a probability space. (An equivalent formulation is that a random variable has to be adapted to the event algebra: the random variable can be *defined* as associating specific values to specific events, just as the gf-admissibility tells us we can find the weight of specific elements of A from the weights associated with its components.)

Table 1 displays several gf-admissible constructions and the corresponding operators.

The definitions of the union and cartesian product constructions were given in Section 2.4.1 and need not be repeated here. Table 1 does not make explicit any restrictions that the classes may have to satisfy in order for the operations on them to be admissible. For example, we have remarked (see Exercise 1) that for the union to be admissible A and B need to be disjoint; other restrictions will be pointed out below.

Substitution. $C = A[B]$ corresponds to associating with each element in $A_{(n)}$ an element of B^n, the n-th cartesian product of B with itself:

Construction	Notation	Operator
Union	$C = A + B$	$\phi_C(z) = \phi_A(z) + \phi_B(z)$
Cartesian product	$C = A \times B$	$\phi_C(z) = \phi_A(z)\phi_B(z)$
Substitution	$C = A[B]$	$\phi_C(z) = \phi_A(\phi_B(z))$
Marking	$C = \mu A$	$\phi_C(z) = z\,\phi'_A(z)$
Diagonalization	$C = \Delta(A \times A)$	$\phi_C(z) = \phi_A(z^2)$
Sequence of	$C = A^*$	$\phi_C(z) = (1 - \phi_A(z))^{-1}$
Power set [1]	$C = 2^A$	$\phi_C(z) = 2^{a_0}\exp\{\sum_{j\geq 1}\frac{(-1)^{j-1}}{j}\tilde{\phi}_A(z^j)\}$
Multiset	$C = M\{A\}$	$\phi_C(z) = \exp\{\sum_{j\geq 1}\frac{1}{j}\phi_A(z^j)\}$

Table 1: Gf-admissible constructions (Source: Flajolet, 1984)

---

[1] $\tilde{\phi}_A(z)$ is defined as $\phi_A(z) - a_0$ (see the proof of this result).

$$C = \sum_{n \geq 0} A_{(n)} \times B^n . \tag{25}$$

This operation is meaningful when the elements of A are composed of atoms (letters in words, nodes in graphs, etc.), and the number of these atoms is the defined weight. Furthermore, the action of the substitution itself must be well defined: this is natural in the case of replacing letters in words, but not so obvious in the case of graphs. (What options do we have for the replacement of a node in a graph by a whole graph? However, the replacement of a node in a graph by a word, is simple.)

How is the number of elements in C to be tallied - that is, its gf computed? One way is to view equation (25) as successive applications of the cartesian product and union operations; since the gf of $A_{(n)}$ is $a_n z^n$, but the weight it contributes to the element of C is zero (it only contributes its structure, as is) we have

$$\phi_C(z) = \sum_{n \geq 0} a_n \phi_B^n(z) = \phi_A(\phi_B(z)).$$

Another tack is to observe that some element σ of C is in $C_{(r)}$ for $r > 0$ iff there is an $n > 0$ such that there exist an element $\sigma_a \in A_{(n)}$, and a collection of n elements σ_i of B (not necessarily distinct), with $w(\sigma) = \Sigma_i w(\sigma_i) = r$, such that substituting the σ_i in σ_a yields σ. Hence

$$c_r = [z^r]\phi_C(z) = \sum_{n \geq 1} a_n [z^r]\phi_B^n(z) = [z^r] \sum_{n \geq 1} a_n \phi_B^n(z) , \qquad r > 0. \tag{26}$$

If we agree to identify $C_{(0)}$ with $A_{(0)}$ we get again the same result. Note that if A is not finite, we must have $b_0 = 0$. Otherwise $C_{(0)}$ will not be well-defined.

Marking. This operation is meaningful for the same types of structures as the class A we used in substitution. It implies distinguishing one component in a structure (like fixing the root, in making a tree out of an undirected connected graph that contains no cycles). Hence marking amounts to taking the cartesian product of each subset $A_{(n)}$ with N_n, and the first two rules can be invoked again to determine the gf of μA (Exercise 10).

Diagonalization This correspond to picking just the "diagonal" of $A \times A$, i.e., pairs of the form (σ, σ) with $\sigma \in A$. The gf is then obvious (Exercise 10).

Sequence-of. This construction assembles $\varnothing, A, A \times A, A \times A \times A \cdots$, and the union and product rule clearly apply - subject to the restriction that A may not have elements of weight 0.

Power set. This amounts to taking each possible subset of A, with the weight of an element in C being the sum of the weights of the chosen elements of A. We use the conventional notation, 2^A, for the set of all subsets of A. Thus

$$\phi_C(z) = \sum_{\sigma \in 2^A} z^{w(\sigma_1)+w(\sigma_2)+\cdots+w(\sigma_k)} \qquad \text{notation: } \sigma = \{\sigma_1, \sigma_2, \cdots, \sigma_k\}$$

$$= \prod_{\sigma_j \in A} \left(1 + z^{w(\sigma_j)}\right), \qquad (27)$$

where each $\sigma \in 2^A$ specifies which of the terms in each factor of the (possibly infinite) product is to be picked. There are exactly a_n factors of the form $(1+z^n)$, hence

$$\phi_C(z) = \prod_{n \geq 0}(1+z^n)^{a_n} = 2^{a_0}\prod_{n \geq 1}(1+z^n)^{a_n}$$

$$\log \phi_C = \log 2^{a_0} + \sum_{n \geq 1} a_n \log(1+z^n) = \log 2^{a_0} + \sum_{n \geq 1} a_n \sum_{j \geq 1} \frac{(-1)^{j-1}}{j} z^{nj}. \qquad (28)$$

Changing the order of summation (this is permissible once we removed, as above, the zero-weight term) we obtain

$$\log \phi_C(z) = \log 2^{a_0} + \sum_{j \geq 1} \frac{(-1)^{j-1}}{j} \sum_{n \geq 1} a_n z^{jn}. \qquad (29)$$

Using the notation $\phi_A(z) = a_0 + \tilde{\phi}_A(z)$ we obtain the result, as shown in Table 1.

Multiset. The multisets of A are the possible sets formed from its elements, with unbounded repetitions allowed. Hence C, the collection of all multisets, may be represented as $\prod_{\sigma \in A} \{\sigma\}^*$, the cartesian product of the sequence operation on all the elements. Using the operator for this construction as given in Table 1, provides

$$\phi_C(z) = \prod_{\sigma \in A}(1 - z^{w(\sigma)})^{-1} = \prod_{n \geq 1}(1-z^n)^{-a_n}. \qquad (30)$$

The rest of the computation is precisely as for the power set operation. Note that the use of the sequence operator requires $a_0 = 0$, which should be obvious. (Why?)

We remark in conclusion that the proof of the admissibility of these operations consists in demonstrating the possibility of the above computations.

Examples. Consider $A = N_m = \{1, 2, \cdots, m\}$ and let $w(j) = 1$, $1 \leq j \leq m$, hence $\phi_A(z) = mz$. Now let $C = 2^A$, the power set of A. The weight of each element of C is then simply the number of elements from A in it. Using the expression given for $\phi_C(z)$ in Table 1 we obtain

$$\phi_C(z) = \exp\left(\sum_{j \geq 1} \frac{(-1)^{j-1}}{j} mz^j\right) = \exp\left(m \log(1+z)\right) = \exp\left(\log(1+z)^m\right)$$

$$= (1+z)^m. \qquad (31)$$

Hence c_r, the number of choices of r elements, equals $[z^r](1+z)^m = \binom{m}{r}$, as expected.

For the same $A = N_m$, let the weight function for each element now be its numerical value, and consider again its power set. This time $\phi_A(z) = \sum_{i=1}^m z^i = z(1-z^m)/(1-z)$, and the gf of 2^A is

$$\log \phi_C(z) = \sum_{j \geq 1} \frac{(-1)^{j-1}}{j} \left(z^j + z^{2j} + \cdots + z^{mj} \right)$$

$$= \log(1+z) + \log(1+z^2) + \cdots + \log(1+z^m), \qquad (32)$$

and exponentiating both sides,

$$\phi_C(z) = (1+z)(1+z^2) \cdots (1+z^m).$$

Hence $[z^r]\phi_C(z)$ is the number of distinct-part partitions of r, with up to m components that do not exceed m.

Egf-admissible constructions

Enumerations where egf's are used rather than gf's will turn up less frequently in the kinds of analyses we shall consider. The paradigm combinatorial object over which operations generate relations that are captured by egf's is the example (C.3) in Section 2.4.1 above, dealing with the association of distinguishable elements with distinct cells. We shall display the properties of these relations through a specific example, namely, the enumeration of labeled (undirected) graphs; here the labels will provide both distinctions - of items and receptacles. Denoting by G_n the class of such graphs with n nodes, we observe that it is obtained from the set of unlabeled graphs by attaching to the nodes labels, exhausting the set $N_n = \{1, \cdots, n\}$.

We shall explore operations over these objects with the intent of answering the question: how many (labeled) *connected* graphs are there with n nodes. This number is denoted by k_n. When counting composite objects one should understand clearly when two of them are to be considered distinct, and when they are merely two ways of looking at the same element. For the elements of G_n this is simple to do: Every possible subset of the $\binom{n}{2}$ node pairs (which carry labels), defines a distinct instance of the graph. Hence, the total number of labeled graphs with n nodes, g_n, is given by

$$g_n = 2^{\binom{n}{2}}. \qquad (33)$$

The union of disjoint collections of labeled graphs holds no surprises, and the same sum rule as for gf's hold here for the egf's as well.

The situation with the analog of the cartesian product is less simple. Suppose we wish to create such a product of two sets of labeled graphs, K_1, K_2. The generic element of such a product, an ordered pair (k_1, k_2), $k_i \in K_i$ is not a proper labeled graph since

- the ordering of components should not be taken into account, when counting such distinct graphs.
- the labeling is improper, since duplicate labels exist.

Thus we need a somewhat more elaborate arrangement, consisting in a disregard of the order of the "factors" and a redistribution of the labels. The first is simply handled, but for the second we need an intermediate operation.

Define a *bipartition* π of a set of label $N_n = \{1, \cdots, n\}$ as a pair of subsets of N_n, denoted by $\pi = (\alpha, \beta)$, $\alpha \cup \beta = N_n$, $\alpha \cap \beta = \varnothing$. The *type* of the bipartition is the integer pair $(|\alpha|, |\beta|)$, and is denoted by $\pi(|\alpha|, |\beta|)$.

The *partitional product* of two elements, k_r and k_s, having r and s components (carrying this many labels) respectively, creates the set of of pairs $(\bar{k}_r, \bar{k}_s)$, where in each pair the labels are replaced by a bipartition of N_{r+s} with a restriction is that the replacement is done in the order of the original labels. Thus one particular bipartition of type $\pi(r,s)$ with $\{a_1, a_2, \cdots, a_r\}$ and $\{b_1, b_2, \cdots, b_s\}$, will define an element $(\bar{k}_r, \bar{k}_s)$ of the partitional product if

$$a_1 < a_2 < \cdots < a_r \; ; \quad b_1 < b_2 \cdots < b_s \, ,$$

and then the component $\bar{k}_r$ is obtained from k_r by replacing each label j by a_j, and likewise the label j in k_s will be replaced by b_j to form $\bar{k}_s$. (Why is this restriction required? Remember: we want the procedure to be egf-*admissible*.)

Thus the operation *partitional product* on the *classes*, or *sets*, K_1 and K_2 will pair elements with r and s labels and reassign to them all the bipartitions of N_{r+s} of type $\pi(r,s)$. Each structure thus created will be said to have weight $r+s$ and belong to $K_1 * K_2$. (See Exercise 16(a).) When the sets K_1 and K_2 are the same class, we shall obtain the *abelian*[2] *partitional product* (app) when we agree to identify the two pairs $(\bar{k}_r, \bar{k}_s)$, and $(\bar{k}_s, \bar{k}_r)$. The number of bipartitions of S_n of type $\pi(l, n-l)$ being $\binom{n}{l}$ (why?) we obtain the

Proposition: The egf of $C = A * B$, where "*" stands for the partitional product is given by the product of the egf's of A and B.

Proof: Clearly, by the above argumentation

$$c_n = \sum_{l=0}^{n} \binom{n}{l} a_l b_{n-l} \, . \tag{34}$$

Then

$$\hat{\phi}_C(z) = \sum_{n \geq 0} \frac{c_n}{n!} z^n = \sum_{n \geq 0} \sum_{l=0}^{n} \frac{a_l}{l!} z^l \frac{b_{n-l}}{(n-l)!} z^{n-l} \, , \tag{35}$$

and changing the order of summation provides the desired result,

---

[2] The adjective abelian is meant to highlight the commutativity of this operation.

$\hat{\phi}_C(z) = \hat{\phi}_A(z)\hat{\phi}_B(z).$ □

The app of a class A with itself will be denoted by $A^{[2]}$, and repeating this $k-1$ times provides $A^{[k]} = A * A^{[k-1]}$, $A^{[1]} \equiv A$. The collection of all $A^{[k]}$, $k \geq 0$, is denoted by $A^{[*]}$, and is called the *abelian partitional complex* of A.

Note that the app operation on two sets will only be admissible if they have either no element in common, or all their elments are common, and then they are identical. Why is this so? [Hint: How would you count the elements of such a product?]

Returning to labeled graphs we observe that they can all be constructed by performing the app operation on classes of *connected* labeled graphs (see Exercise 16). Let $\hat{\phi}^{(c)}(z)$ be the egf of all labeled graphs of c components. Since the graph formed from the components $(k_1, \cdots, k_c)$ will appear c! times, we find

$$\hat{\phi}^{(c)}(z) = \frac{1}{c!}\,\hat{\phi}_K^c(z), \tag{36}$$

and summing over c we finally obtain

$$\hat{\phi}_C(z) = \exp(\hat{\phi}_K(z)). \tag{37}$$

The coefficients of $\hat{\phi}_C(z)$ equal $g_n/n!$, from equation (33), hence

$$\hat{\phi}_K(z) = \log\hat{\phi}_C(z) = \log\Big(1 + \sum_{n \geq 1} 2^{n(n-1)/2}\,\frac{z^n}{n!}\Big), \tag{38}$$

and using the power series development for the log function we can obtain the relation (see Exercise 11),

$$k_n = \sum_{j \geq 1} \frac{(-1)^{j-1}}{j}\sum_{n}\binom{n}{n_1, \cdots, n_j}2^{\sum_{r=1}^{j}\binom{n_r}{2}}, \tag{39}$$

where the summation over n ranges over all j part partitions of n.

Note that though the series in (38) diverges, as a function in C, for all z, the terms k_n can be constructed with a *finite* number of operations, since the contributions of all $j > n$ in equation (39) vanish.

Finally, we remark that the operations of **marking** and (labeled) **substitution** can be carried out here, on labeled structures, to yield relations entirely analogous to those listed in Table 1 (see Exercise 12).

Example: Set partitions and Bell numbers.

Let S_n be a set of n elements; in how many ways can we partition S_n to any number of disjoint and exhaustive subsets? Denote the number of such partitions by B_n. We need to consider combinations of sets of sizes up to n. Then B_n will be just the number of those those combinations that are of size n. Let A be the collection of all N_i, $i \geq 1$

$$A = \{ \{1\}, \{1,2\}, \cdots \}$$

and let $B = A^{[*]}$, the abelian partitional complex of A. Define the weight of each element of A to be the number of components in it, and hence $a_n = 1$. Notice the naturalness of the relabeling when we compute the app of A. Since

$$\hat{\phi}_A(z) = \sum_{n \geq 1} 1 \cdot \frac{z^n}{n!} = e^z - 1, \tag{40}$$

we find

$$\hat{\phi}_B(z) = \exp(e^z - 1).$$

The number of partitions we need is available as

$$B_n = \left[\frac{z^n}{n!}\right]\exp(e^z-1) = \left[\frac{z^n}{n!}\right]\sum_{r \geq 0}\frac{(e^z-1)^r}{r!} = \sum_{r \geq 0}\frac{n!}{r!}\sum_{j=0}^{r}\binom{r}{j}[z^n]e^{jz}(-1)^{r-j}$$

$$= \sum_{r \geq 0}\frac{n!}{r!}\sum_{j=0}^{r}\binom{r}{j}(-1)^{r-j}\frac{j^n}{n!}, \tag{41}$$

and writing $k = r - j$

$$B_n = \sum_{r \geq 0}\frac{1}{r!}\sum_{k=0}^{r}\binom{r}{k}(-1)^k(r-k)^n. \tag{42}$$

Note that the r-th summand is just $\left\langle{n \atop r}\right\rangle$, the Stirling number of the second kind, as given in equation (B.5.5). By exchanging the order of summation we also find

$$B_n = \sum_{k \geq 0}\frac{(-1)^k}{k!}\sum_{r \geq k}\frac{(r-k)^n}{(r-k)!} = \frac{1}{e}\sum_{r \geq 0}\frac{r^n}{r!}. \tag{43}$$

B_n is called the n-th Bell number. Exercise 25 outlines a different method of obtaining their representation.

The identification above of $\left\langle{n \atop r}\right\rangle$ provides us again with the combinatorial interpretation of this number that was obtained in example (C.3) in Section 2.4.1.

2.4.3 Operator Methods

Operator methods in analysis have a rich and variegated history. They have been particularly effective in the investigation of differential equations and control problems that depend on such equations, but are ubiquitous elsewhere. We shall not develop here any of the underlying theory, but only use some examples to demonstrate how they can be used effectively in the types of analysis we do.

Operators transform one function into another, and the word 'function' in this section only refers to such that can be viewed as a gf, i.e. it has a Taylor series development.

The operators we shall use are the following ones:

$$
\begin{array}{lll}
c & \text{constant multiplier} & cf(x) = c \cdot f(x), \\
U & \text{evaluation at } x=1 & Uf(x) = f(1), \\
Z & \text{evaluation at } x=0 & Zf(x) = f(0), \\
D & \text{differentiation} & Df(x) = f'(x).
\end{array}
\tag{44}
$$

In addition to the operator c we shall also use a variable multiplier, x, or even a polynomial in x, $P(x)$, which has the intuitive meaning, $Pf(x) = P(x)f(x)$.

Equality between operators implies identical effect on every admissible function at each point in its domain of regularity: $A = B \Rightarrow Af(x) = Bf(x)$ $\forall f, x$. We follow the convention of using the same symbols $+, -, =$ etc. for operators and for functions, since they have all the properties of these symbols we are used to, even though their semantics in the two cases are rather different: thus $A + B$, for operators A and B, is an operator that associates with $f(x)$ the value $Af(x) + Bf(x)$. The combination AB is construed as successive application, and defined through $(AB)f(x) = A(Bf(x))$, etc. Verify that the distributive law holds here, on both sides: $A(B+C) = AB + AC$, $(A+B)C = AC + BC$.

It is important to remember with respect to the operation of successive application, that we write - possibly somewhat misleadingly - as a multiplication, that the operators do not commute! (In general, that is.) Consider the operator UD. Applying it to a pgf produces the first moment:

$$
UDg_X(x) = Ug_X'(x) = g_X'(1) = E(X),
\tag{45}
$$

but

$$
DUg_X(x) = Dg_X(1) = 0.
\tag{46}
$$

Equation (46) can be represented as $DU = 0$. Now consider the operator Dx^n:

$$
Dx^n f(x) = nx^{n-1}f(x) + x^n Df(x),
\tag{47}
$$

or, when expressed as an equality between operators

$$
Dx^n = x^n D + nx^{n-1}.
\tag{48}
$$

A relation we shall often use. In Exercise 17 you are asked to show another useful relation:

$$
UD^n x = UD^n + nUD^{n-1}.
\tag{49}
$$

We shall discuss now an example designed to bring out some uses of the above operators. We do not claim that the analysis below is always the simplest possible for this problem. The first part of the example is based on Greene and Knuth, (1982) Section 3.1.

Let $\{X_n, n \geq 0\}$ be a process with the initial value $X_0 = 1$ that at each stage n may grow, by 1, with a probability proportional to its current value:

$$\text{Prob}(X_{n+1}=j\mid X_n=i) = \begin{cases} ip & j=i+1 \\ 1-ip & j=i \\ 0 & j\neq i,i+1. \end{cases} \tag{50}$$

The process lives as long as $pX < 1$, and dies when it reaches or exceeds $1/p$.

The questions of interest are: How large is X_n? What is the lifetime, T, of the process?

One way to tackle the problem proceeds via definition of the state probabilities

$$q_{n,i} = \text{Prob}(X_n = i), \tag{51}$$

and writing difference equations that these state probabilities satisfy, directly from equation (50):

$$q_{n,i} = q_{n-1,i}(1-ip) + q_{n-1,i-1}(i-1)p. \tag{52}$$

These can be routinely processed to provide all the results we derive below, by different, non-operational means (see Exercise 18). We shall fry this particular fish differently.

Define the pgf

$$g_n(x) = \sum_{i\geq 1} q_{n,i} x^i, \tag{53}$$

(we shall use x here rather than the customary z to avoid possible confusion with the operator Z).

Now, instead of using (52) to deal with the development of the state probabilities we shall observe the transition of the coefficients in $g_n(x)$ directly: equation (52) tells us that $[x^i]g_{n-1}(x)$ appears in $g_n(x)$ in the coefficient of x^{i+1}, multiplied by ip, and in that of x^i multiplied by $(1-pi)$. Symbolically,

$$x^i \Rightarrow pix^{i+1} + (1-pi)x^i = (pix+1-pi)x^i = (1+p(x-1)i)x^i. \tag{54}$$

Hence, a step in the process life effects the operator $1+p(x-1)i$ on the term x^i in $g_n(x)$, to produce the coefficient $[x^i]g_{n+1}(x)$. The dependence on i precludes the use of this operator on the entire function. There is a way, though, around this difficulty, which is the essence of this approach. Since for any $i \geq 0$ the operators xD and i provide equivalent effect on x^i, we can rewrite relation (54) as the effect of the operator $\Phi \equiv 1+p(x-1)xD$ on x^i, and likewise on the entire function $g_n(x)$:

$$g_n(x) = \Phi g_{n-1}(x) = \Phi^n g_0(x) = \Phi^n x , \qquad \Phi = 1+p(x-1)xD. \tag{55}$$

Thus equation (55) provides an explicit - even if seemingly hermetic - expression for the pgf of X_n. We shall now see how one can use it to extract the information that we normally need: moments and individual probabilities.

Using equation (45) we find $E(X_n) = UD\,\Phi^n x$. What can one say about the operator $UD\,\Phi^n$? Let us examine the simplest case, $n = 1$:

$$UD\,\Phi = UD\,(1 + p\,(x-1)xD\,)$$
$$= UD + pUD\,(x-1)xD.$$
(56)

Using equation (48) we find $D(x-1) = Dx - D = xD + 1 - D = 1 + (x-1)D$, hence

$$UD\,\Phi = UD + pU\,(1 + (x - 1)D\,)xD$$
$$= UD + pUxD + pU\,(x - 1)DxD.$$
(57)

Since for any operator A we have $UxA = UA$, and $U\,(x-1)A = 0$, the right-hand side in equation (57) simplifies to

$$UD\,\Phi = UD + pUD = (1+p\,)UD.$$
(58)

Here is indeed a pleasant surprise - UD is a left "eigenoperator" of Φ, and has the eigenvalue $(1+p\,)$. This can be immediately used to evaluate $E\,(X_n)$:

$$E\,(X_n) = UD\,\Phi^n x = (1+p\,)UD\,\Phi^{n-1}x = (1+p\,)^n\,UDx = (1+p\,)^n\,.$$
(59)

How is the variance of X_n to be computed? Since $V(X_n) = E\,(X_n^2) - E^2(X_n)$, the second moment is required. $E\,(X_n^2)$ is obtained from the second factorial moment, given by $UD^2 g_n = g_n''(1) = E\,(X_n(X_n-1)) = E\,(X_n^2) - E\,(X_n)$. To compute $UD^2 g_n$ we again start with n = 1:

$$UD^2\Phi = UD^2(1 + p\,(x-1)xD\,) = UD^2 + pUD^2(x-1)xD.$$
(60)

Using equation (49), $UD^2(x-1) = UD^2 + 2UD - UD^2$, hence

$$UD^2\Phi = UD^2 + 2pUDxD = UD^2 + 2pUxD^2 + 2pUD\,,$$

where equation (48) has been used again, so that

$$UD^2\Phi = (1+2p\,)UD^2 + 2pUD.$$
(61)

No such luck this time. But a comparison of the right-hand sides of equations (61) and (58) suggests the combination $UD^2 + aUD$ might be an eigenoperator of Φ; and so it is, as a computation similar to the above will show, for $a = 2$. Now $UD^2 + 2UD$ is just $UD^2 x$, by equation (49), and indeed, it is easy to show (Exercise 21) that there is a whole slew of such eigenoperators, of which the two above are but the first two special cases:

$$UD^n x^{n-1}\Phi = (1+np\,)UD^n x^{n-1}.$$
(62)

Let us complete the variance computation:

$$g_n''(1) = UD^2\Phi^n x = (UD^2 + 2UD\,)\Phi^n x - 2UD\,\Phi^n x$$
$$= (1+2p\,)^n\,(UD^2 + 2UD\,)x - 2(1+p\,)^n\,UDx$$
(63)
$$= (1+2p\,)^n\cdot 2 - 2(1+p\,)^n\,.$$

And we finally obtain

$$V(X_n) = g_n''(1) + E(X_n) - E^2(X_n)$$
$$= 2(1+2p)^n - 2(1+p)^n + (1+p)^n - (1+p)^{2n} \qquad (64)$$
$$= 2(1+2p)^n - (1+p)^n(1 + (1+p)^n).$$

The probabilities making up the pgf $g_n(x)$ can be extracted using a similar approach. Since they are required, however, for the evaluation of the distribution of the lifetime of the process, T, we shall consider now the latter in detail.

Denote $\lceil 1/p \rceil$ by N. The event $T=r$ implies $X_{r-1} = N-1$ and $X_r = N$, hence

$$\text{Prob}(T = r) = \text{Prob}(X_{r-1} = N-1 \text{ and } X_r = N) = p\,(N-1)[x^{N-1}]g_{r-1}(x). \quad (65)$$

What is $[x^{N-1}]g_{r-1}(x)$? It is given by the operation $\dfrac{1}{(N-1)!} ZD^{N-1}g_{r-1}$.

To evaluate this we need to consider the operators $ZD^i \Phi^r$. In Exercise 22(a) you are asked to prove

$$ZD^n x^i = n^{\underline{i}} ZD^{n-i} \qquad i \le n, \qquad n^{\underline{i}} \equiv n!/(n-i)! . \qquad (66)$$

This identity provides

$$ZD^n \Phi = (1-pn)ZD^n + pn(n-1)ZD^{n-1}. \qquad (67)$$

So ZD^n is not an eigenoperator of Φ, but using equations (66-67) one can show the convenient relation (Exercise 22(b))

$$A_n \Phi = (1-pn)A_n, \qquad A_n \equiv ZD^n(1-x)^{n-1}. \qquad (68)$$

In particular,

$$A_n g_r(x) = A_n \Phi^r x = (1-pn)^r A_n x = (1-pn)^r ZD^n(1-x)^{n-1}x$$
$$= (1-pn)^r n!(-1)^{n-1}. \qquad (69)$$

In order to evaluate $ZD^n g_r$ we have to express ZD^n in terms of the A_i, and this can be done by a standard inverse relation, from equation (A.4.1):

$$a_n = \sum_k \binom{n}{k}(-1)^k b_k, \qquad b_n = \sum_k \binom{n}{k}(-1)^k a_k. \qquad (70)$$

We show in some detail how this relation can be used here:

$$A_n = ZD^n(1-x)^{n-1} = ZD^n \sum_{i=0}^{n-1}\binom{n-1}{i}(-1)^i x^i = \sum_{i=0}^{n-1}\binom{n-1}{i}(-1)^i ZD^n x^i. \quad (71)$$

Using equation (66) we find

$$A_n = \sum_{i=0}^{n-1}\binom{n-1}{i}(-1)^i \frac{n!}{(n-i)!}ZD^{n-i}.$$

Let $j = n-i-1$, to produce the form

$$A_n = (-1)^{n-1} n! \sum_{j=0}^{n-1} \binom{n-1}{j} (-1)^j \frac{ZD^{j+1}}{(j+1)!}. \tag{72}$$

Define $a_{n-1} \equiv \dfrac{(-1)^{n-1}}{n!} A_n$, $b_j \equiv \dfrac{ZD^{j+1}}{(j+1)!}$, and then equation (72) corresponds to the left part of relation (70), and the right part provides

$$b_n \equiv \frac{ZD^{n+1}}{(n+1)!} = \sum_{k=0}^{n} \binom{n}{k} (-1)^k \frac{(-1)^k}{(k+1)!} A_{k+1}. \tag{73}$$

Hence

$$ZD^n = n! \sum_{k=0}^{n-1} \binom{n-1}{k} \frac{A_{k+1}}{(k+1)!}, \tag{74}$$

and finally, using equation (69),

$$\begin{aligned} ZD^n g_r &= n! \sum_{k=0}^{n-1} \binom{n-1}{k} \frac{1}{(k+1)!} (1-p-pk)^r (k+1)! (-1)^k \\ &= n! \sum_{k=0}^{n-1} \binom{n-1}{k} (-1)^k (1-p-pk)^r. \end{aligned} \tag{75}$$

We do not know a closed form for this sum (see Exercise 24). Adapting it to equation (65) we get

$$\mathrm{Prob}(T=r) = p(N-1) \sum_{k=0}^{N-2} \binom{N-2}{k} (-1)^k (1-p-pk)^{r-1}. \tag{76}$$

Exercises and Complements

1. In the definition of the sum rule, equation (5), what is the significance of the requirement $S_1 \cap S_2 = \varnothing$?

2. Show that equation (6) determines a convolution.

3. Consider the set of all words formed from the three-letter alphabet $\{a,b,c\}$. Use equations (5) and (6) even when you could write the answer outright.
Construct the gf given in equation (4) from the gf's of words over one-letter alphabets. What is the gf's for the sub-collections that contain words that have the letter a
(a) Exactly 3 times?
(b) Exactly k times?
(c) Up to k times?
(d) Each of the three letters the same number of times?
(e) Consider the set of all words of length up to R that can be formed from the three-letter alphabet $\{a,b,c\}$, with the same weight function. Using equations (5) and (6), redo questions (a) to (d) under this constraint.

4. Consider k component compositions of n. What is the number of compositions $(a_1, \cdots, a_k)$ such that

(a) $a_i \geq i$? [Answer: $\binom{n-k(k-1)/2-1}{k-1}$]

(b) n is even and all a_i are even? [Answer: $\binom{k+n/2-1}{k-1}$]

(c) All a_i are odd? [Answer: $\binom{(k+n)/2-1}{(n-k)/2}$]

(d) n is odd and all a_i but one are even? [Answer: $k\binom{k+(n-3)/2}{(n-1)/2}$]

(e) How would you derive equation (9) and the above results from "balls into cells" arguments?

(f) For $m > k$, $a_i \equiv i \pmod{m}$, show that the number of such k part compositions of n is $\binom{k+j-1}{j}$ where j is uniquely determined by the relation $n = \binom{k+1}{2} + mj$.

(g) (bounded components) $0 \leq a_i \leq L$ [Answer: $[z^n](1 + z + z^2 \cdots + z^L)^k$
$= \sum_j \binom{k}{j}(-1)^j \binom{n+k-j(L+1)-1}{k-1}$]

5. Continuing Example b(4) in Section 2.4.1: Consider k-element subsets of $S_n = \{1,2,\cdots,n\}$, subject to the following constraints, and determine their number. Denote by $(a_1, a_2, \cdots, a_k)$ the terms in such a subset when arranged in increasing order:

(a) a_{2i} is even, a_{2i-1} is odd, for $1 \leq i \leq \lceil k/2 \rceil$. [Answer: $\binom{\lfloor(n-k)/2\rfloor +k}{k}$]

(b) $c \leq a_{i+1} - a_i \leq d$. [Answer: $\sum_{i,j}(-1)^j \binom{k+i}{i}\binom{k-1}{j}$, the summation being over all i and j that satisfy the equation $i+(d-c)j = n-c(k-1)-1$]

(c) $a_{i+1} - a_i > i$. [Answer: $\binom{n-k(k-1)/2}{k}$]

(d) $a_{i+1} - a_i \neq q$. [Answer: $\sum_{i=0}^{\lfloor(n-k)/q\rfloor}(-1)^i\binom{k-1}{i}\binom{n-qi}{k-i}$]

(e) (Prodinger, 1983) The pairs $i, i+2$ are forbidden in the subset, for $1 \leq i \leq n-2$. [Answer: $\sum_{i=0}^{k}(-1)^i\binom{n-k-i+2}{k-i}$]

(f) Using the original result in Example b(4), show that the number of *all* subsets of N_n that do not include adjacent members of N_n is the Fibonacci number F_n, introduced in Exercise 2.2-12.
[Show that the requested quantity and the Fibonacci numbers satisfy the same recursion and have the same initial values.]

6. What are the generating functions for the number of partitions of $n > 0$, with the following restrictions on the summands:

(a) All parts are odd (with repetition allowed).

(b) All parts are even and distinct.

(c) All parts are prime (with repetition allowed).

(d) No part is repeated more than r times (also show that this equals the number of partitions where no part may be divisible by $r+1$).

(e) Show that the number of k part partitions of n is given by

$$p_{k,n} = [u^k z^n] \frac{1}{(1 - uz)(1 - uz^2)(1 - uz^3) \cdots (1 - uz^{n-k+1})}.$$

The need for these numbers arises *inter alia* when preparing to use the Faa-di-Bruno formula that provides the derivatives of compound functions:

$$f(g(z))^{[r]} = \sum_{j=1}^{r} f^{[j]}(g(z)) \sum_{\mathbf{k}} F_{j,r}^{\mathbf{k}} \prod_{l=1}^{r} [g^{[l]}(z)]^{k_l},$$

with the coefficients F given by

$$F_{j,r}^{\mathbf{k}} = \frac{r!}{\prod_{i=1}^{r} k_i!(i!)^{k_i}},$$

and the sum over $\mathbf{k}$ ranges on all j part partitions of r.

(f) Consider the storage required for the $p_{k,n}$ partitions counted in (e) above. Each can be represented as $(c_1, c_2, \cdots, c_n)$, where c_j is the number of parts that equal j. If storage is at premium, a more parsimonious representation is $(i; c_1, c_2, \cdots, c_i)$, where $c_j = 0$ for $i < j \le n$. Show that the storage thus required for the $p_{k,n}$ partitions is given by

$$q_{k,n} = [u^k z^n] \sum_{l=1}^{n} \frac{(l+1)uz^l}{(1 - uz)(1 - uz^2) \cdots (1 - uz^l)}.$$

7. (a) Show via partition generating function arguments that each integer has a unique representation in the base r number system ($r \ge 2$).

(b) Similarly, show a unique representation in the form $\sum_{i \ge 1} i! r_i$, $0 \le r_i \le i$.

8. In Israel, 1986, there are two different coins worth one agora (the smallest monetary unit), three kinds of coin worth 5 agorot (the Hebrew plural for agora), three kinds for 10 agorot and two again for 50 agorot. In how many different ways is it possible to make change for one sheqel (worth 100 agorot)?

9. A problem somewhat akin to partitions concerns the decomposition of strings of symbols. For example, let s_1 and s_2 be two {0,1} strings, $s_1 = 010$, $s_2 = 0010$, with $s_1 s_2$ interpreted as their concatenation, $s_1 s_2 = 0100010$. If A_1 and A_2 are sets of strings, then $A_1 A_2$ is the set of all strings $a_1 a_2$ with $a_i \in A_i$. Similarly, $A^* = \{\varepsilon\} \cup A \cup AA \cup \cdots = \{\varepsilon\} \cup A \cup A^2 \cup A^3 \cup \cdots$, where ε is the empty string.

(a) Let A and B be two sets of {0,1} strings. Under what conditions is the number of strings in AB equal to $|A| \cdot |B|$?

(b) With the weight of a string equal to its size, show that the gf of $\{0,1\}^*$ is $(1 - 2z)^{-1}$.

(c) Argue that each {0,1} string is in the form $1^*(00^*11^*)^*0^*$, and show that the set of such strings has the gf you found in (b).

(d) What is the number of {0,1} strings of size n that contain no continuous run of k 0's, for some $k \ge 2$? [Hint: modify the representation given in (c).]

10. Prove the functional operators as given in Table 1 for the constructions μA, $\Delta(A \times A)$, A^*, $M\{A\}$.

11. Complete the derivation of equation (39), using

$$\log(1+x) = \sum_{j \geq 1} \frac{(-x)^{j-1}}{j}.$$

12. (a) Let $C = A^{<*>}$ be the class of labeled structures consisting of the empty set, the set A and all its partitional products with itself. Show $\hat{\phi}_C(z) = (1 - \hat{\phi}_A(z))^{-1}$.
(b) Let $C = \mu A$ be obtained from the labeled class A by marking in each element any of its atomic components (e.g., in an undirected connected cycle-less labeled graph, denoting one node as the root of a tree). Show $\hat{\phi}_C(z) = z\,\hat{\phi}_A{}'(z)$.
(c) Let $C = A[B]$ be obtained from the two labeled classes A and B by substituting in an element of A elements of B for its atomic components, and redistributing the labels appropriately (a generalization of bipartition). Show $\hat{\phi}_C(z) = \hat{\phi}_A(\hat{\phi}_B(z))$.

13. Argue from equation (42) that $\left\langle {n \atop r} \right\rangle$ is the number of partitions of a set of size n into r disjoint blocks.

14. What is the egf of the number of partitions of a set of size n into blocks of size not exceeding r? [Answer: $\exp(e_r(z)-1)$, where $e_r(z)$ is the incomplete exponential function $\sum_{i=0}^{r} \frac{z^i}{i!}$.]

15. Write the (ordinary) gf's for the numbers of compositions and partitions of the integer n into parts not exceeding r.

16. (a) Form the entire set of labeled graphs that are the partitional product of the two sets of such graphs: $K_1 = \{\ k_{11} = (\ \{1\}, \{\ \}\ ),\ k_{12} = (\ \{1,2\}, \{(1,2)\}\ )\ \}$, $K_2 = \{\ k_{21} = (\ \{1,2\}, \{\ (1,2)\}\ ),\ k_{22} = (\ \{1,2,3\}, \{(1,3),(2,3)\}\ )\ \}$.
(b) Why is the app of these two sets not egf-admissible?
(c) Prove the statement that the entire collection of labeled graphs is obtained as the abelian partitional complex of the collection of all connected labeled graphs. [What you have to show is that this complex obtains each such graph, exactly once.]

17. Prove by induction on n the operator identity (over formal power series)

$$UD^n x = UD^n + nUD^{n-1}.$$

18. Starting with equations (52) and (53), obtain $g_n(x)$, $E(X_n)$, $V(X_n)$ and $g_T(x)$. [To obtain $g_n(x)$ define a gf over these functions. Use the solution of the first order ODE presented in Exercise 2.2-4.]

19. Show that the transition displayed in equation (54) is consistent with equation (52). Use the relation $g_n(x) = \Phi^n x$ to obtain $g_2(x)$ and $g_3(x)$ explicitly and compare with their values as obtained via equation (52).

20. Show that the result in equation (59) for $E(X_n)$ follows immediately from writing $X_{n+1} = X_n + \delta_n$, where δ_n gets the values 1 and 0 with probabilities pX_n and $1 - pX_n$, respectively.

21. (a) Prove equation (62), using equations (48) and (49).
(b) Develop an expression for $UD^n x^{n-1}$ as a sum $\sum_{i=1}^{n} a_i UD^i$, and use it to obtain a recursive expression for all $E(X_n^r)$. Note that $UD^r g_n$ gives the r-th *factorial moment* of $X_n: E[(X_n(X_n-1) \cdots (X_n-r+1)]$.

22. (a) Prove equation (66), using equation (48) and induction on n. Apply then equation (66), to obtain equation (67).
(b) Prove equation (68).
[Expand the binom in x and use the identity $n \binom{n-1}{n-r} = r \binom{n}{n-r}$.]

23. Derive an expression for the pgf of T based on the observation that the number of stages the process spends at size i is distributed geometrically with parameter ip. Obtain equation (76) from this expression.
[Answer: $g_T(x) = \prod_{i=1}^{N-1} ipx / (1 - x + ipx)$.]

24. Show that equation (76) defines a probability distribution (i.e. all the terms are nonnegative, and sum to 1). Compute its mean and variance.

25. The egf for the Bell numbers was obtained in equation (40) from a symbolic argument. Show that it can be computed from recurrence considerations as well.
[Show that the number of such set partitions should satisfy the recurrence

$$B_{n+1} = \sum_{i=0}^{n} \binom{n}{i} B_i, \qquad B_0 = 1,$$

and from this that the egf should satisfy the equation $B'(z) = e^z B(z)$.]

2.5 Asymptotics from Generating Functions

Generating functions - and sometimes integral transforms - are our main computational tools. This will be borne out in any analysis we present in this book, and the sample is not biased. Nonetheless, it is not these functions themselves the analyst is after, but rather statements about moments, probabilities, counts, etc. The functions are then merely the vehicle; one finds in the literature picturesque references to the "transform smoke screen", through which the analyst has to grope in order to get usable results from his analysis. The purpose of this section is to provide some techniques and guidelines for this murky terrain.

All the methods we present rely on the consideration of gf's as complex functions, of a complex variable. Hence we begin by listing the definitions and theorems we use in the sequel. No proofs are given. These may be found in any standard text (Henrici (1974,1977), Nehari (1982), Whittaker and Watson (1927) are good choices). The rest of the section lists methods to obtain bounds or asymptotic estimates of terms in gf's. The techniques are arranged by the characteristic of the gf which serves as the basis of the estimate.

2.5.1 Complex Functions – Definitions and Theorems

We start with a few definitions.

(1) The function $f(z)$ is said to be **analytic** at the **point** $z = \theta$ if it is differentiable at the point θ.

remark: the requirement of differentiability with respect to a complex variable is much more demanding than requiring differentiability along a single line - such as the real axis.

(2) The function $f(z)$ is said to be **analytic** in the **domain** D iff it is analytic at every point in D.

If $f(z)$ is analytic and **single-valued** throughout D it is said to be **regular** in D.

A completely equivalent line of definitions starts by defining $f(z)$ to be regular at the point θ if there is a power series development $\sum_{i \geq 0} f_i (z - \theta)^i$ that converges to $f(z)$ in some open neighborhood of θ.

(3) If $f(z)$ is regular for all z in the plane, except the point $z = \infty$ it is said to be an **entire** function.

(4) If $f(z)$ is not regular at θ but there is an integer $m > 0$ such that $(z - \theta)^m f(z)$ is, then $f(z)$ is said to have a **pole** at θ. The smallest m that makes $(z - \theta)^m f(z)$ regular at θ is called the **order** of the pole.
When $m = 1$, the pole is called **simple**.

(5) If $f(z)$ has a pole of order m at θ, then it may be represented in some open neighborhood of θ by a power series $\Sigma_{i \geq -m} f_i (z-\theta)^i$. The coefficient f_{-1} is called the **residue** of $f(z)$ at θ.

(6) If $f(z)$ is analytic in a region except for a finite number of points where it has poles, it is called **meromorphic**.

(7) Let $f(z) \equiv \Sigma_{n \geq 0} f_n z^n$ converge absolutely for all $|z| < r$. The largest r for which this holds, R, is called the **radius of convergence** of this series, and there is at least one singularity of $f(z)$ on $|z| = R$.

Now for a list of the theorems we shall find useful later on:

Theorem 1: (Cauchy integral theorem). If $f(z)$ is regular in a simply connected domain D, and C_1 and C_2 are two paths in D, say from point P to point Q, then

$$\int_{C_1} f(z) dz = \int_{C_2} f(z) dz . \tag{1}$$

The theorem remains true also when D is not simply connected, but C_1 can be continuously deformed into C_2 without passing outside D.

Theorem 2: (Cauchy integral formula) If $f(z)$ is regular in D and the closed curve (also called contour) C passes entirely inside D and encloses the point θ, then

$$f(\theta) = \oint_C \frac{f(z)}{z - \theta} dz \equiv \frac{1}{2\pi i} \int_{(C)} \frac{f(z)}{z - \theta} dz , \tag{2}$$

where the integral is taken along C in the positive (counterclockwise) sense.

This formula displays explicitly what rigid a structure a regular function is: its values on a contour determine uniquely its values in the interior, which is of course of a higher dimension. Herein lies its great attraction to applied mathematicians.

Theorem 3: (The residue theorem) If $f(z)$ is meromorphic in a domain D, with poles at α_j, $1 \leq j \leq m$, and C is a closed contour in D, then

$$\oint_C f(z) dz = \sum_j \text{Res}(f; \alpha_j), \tag{3}$$

where the summation is carried out on all the poles that are within the contour, and $\text{Res}(f; \alpha_j)$ is the residue of $f(z)$ at $z = \alpha_j$.

The determination of residues is often of importance. Since at a pole θ of order m the function $(z - \theta)^m f(z)$ is analytic, it is simple to find, as a special case of equation (2.3-10):

$$\text{Res}(f; \theta) = \frac{1}{(m-1)!} \frac{d^{m-1}}{dz^{m-1}} [(z - \theta)^m f(z)]_{z=\theta}. \tag{4}$$

Computing the right-hand side of equation (4) is not always the easiest route to find the residue - see Section 2.3.1. For a simple pole it is indeed simpler to evaluate directly

$$\text{Res}(f;\theta) = \lim_{z \to \theta} (z - \theta)f(z), \qquad \text{at a simple pole.} \qquad (5)$$

An immediate result of the residue theorem has already been used, without being so identified:

$$[(z - a)^n]f(z) = \oint_C f(z)\frac{dz}{(z - a)^{n+1}}, \qquad (6)$$

where the contour C must enclose the point $z = a$, and be entirely within a regularity domain of $f(z)$. Another result of Cauchy integral formula:

Theorem 4: (The maximum principle) If $f(z)$ is regular in D and on its boundary, $\max_{z \in D} |f(z)|$ is attained at a point on the boundary of D.

As a result of this, the only entire function that can be bounded (for all z) is a constant (Liouville's theorem).

Example 1: (Diagonalization of series) We conclude with an example of the use of the residue theorem. Given a two-variable function that has the power series development $F(w,u) \equiv \sum_{m,n} a_{mn} w^m u^n$, determine an explicit expression for its "diagonal sum" $G(z) \equiv \sum_n a_{nn} z^n$.

A result we shall need for this is an immediate consequence of the Residue Theorem above: $\oint_C z^i dz = \delta_{i,-1}$, when C encloses the origin. An integral of the function $\frac{1}{t}F(t, \frac{z}{t})$ on such a contour will provide what we require:

$$\oint_C \frac{1}{t}F(t, \frac{z}{t})dt = \oint_C \sum_{m,n} a_{mn} t^{m-n-1} z^n \, dt = \sum_{m,n} a_{mn} z^n \delta_{m-n-1,-1}$$

$$= \sum_n a_{nn} z^n = G(z). \qquad (7)$$

The exchange of the order of summation and integration in the first line of equation (7) is allowed when the sum converges absolutely at each point on the contour.

In particular, to evaluate $\sum_{n \geq 0} \binom{2n}{n} z^n$, observe that

$$F(w,u) \equiv \sum_{m,n \geq 0} \binom{m+n}{n} w^m u^n = \sum_{m,n \geq 0} w^m \binom{-m-1}{n}(-u)^n = \sum_{m \geq 0} \frac{w^m}{(1-u)^{m+1}} \qquad (8)$$

$$= \frac{1}{1-u}\frac{1}{1 - \dfrac{w}{1-u}} = \frac{1}{1-u-w}. \qquad (9)$$

The sums evaluated in equation (8) converge for $|u| < 1$ and $|w| < |1-u|$ only. Substituting into equation (7),

$$\oint_C F(t,\frac{z}{t})\frac{dt}{t} = \oint_C \frac{dt}{t(1 - t - \frac{z}{t})} = \frac{1}{\sqrt{1 - 4z}} . \tag{10}$$

Explanation: The convergence conditions of equation (8) require that $|t| > |z|$ and $|t^2| < |t - z|$, and then the contour C encloses only the pole at $t = (1 - \sqrt{1 - 4z})/2$, as we keep within the regularity region of $F(w,u)$. The residue there for the above integrand is immediately available, by equation (5), as $\frac{1}{\frac{1}{2}(1+\sqrt{1-4z}) - \frac{1}{2}(1-\sqrt{1-4z})}$. See Exercise 2 for an application of this procedure.

2.5.2 Expansions at Singularities

We begin now our examination of methods for the extraction of asymptotic information about the coefficients of generating functions. One cannot really talk about any unifying theory in this area, or for this activity, save for the theory of functions of complex variables. Thus what we present has the appearance of a bag of tricks, rather than an orderly discipline. We find it also quite hard to perceive any structure in this collection of results, though some guidance may be had from the analytic properties "in the large" of the gf's we consider.

The prime distinction is between functions that have no singularities at all (entire functions), and those that do. We relegate the former to Section 2.5.3. When a gf is blessed with one or more singularities, its behavior in the proximity of these points is the main source of information we use. We start with a crude estimate.

2.5.2.1 Radius of Convergence Bounds

Directly from the alternative definition we gave for regularity in Section 2.5.1 we obtain our first (and roughest) asymptotic estimate.

Theorem 1: Let the gf $f(z)$ have the power series development $\Sigma f_n z^n$, absolutely convergent for $|z| < R$ at most; then for every $\varepsilon > 0$

$$(\frac{1-\varepsilon}{R})^n \underset{i.o.}{\leq} |f_n| \underset{a.e.}{<} (\frac{1+\varepsilon}{R})^n . \qquad \Box \tag{11}$$

The notation *i.o.* stands for "infinitely often", that is, the inequality holds for an infinite number of coefficients f_n. The notation *a.e.* stands for "almost everywhere", that is, this inequality is satisfied for all but a finite number of coefficients. This number is possibly zero, and typically, it may depend on ε. $\Box$

An alternative phrasing of the right-hand side is $f_n = O(R^{-n})$. As we shall see, one can almost always obtain better estimates than these.

2.5.2.2 Meromorphic Functions

Theorem 2: Let $f(z)$ be meromorphic for $|z| < R$, analytic on $|z| = R$, and have in $|z| < R$ the poles $\theta_1, \theta_2, \cdots, \theta_r$, where the pole at θ_j is of order m_j. Then

$$f_n = \sum_{j=1}^{r} \theta_j^{-n} P_j(n) + O(R^{-n}), \tag{12}$$

where $P_j(n)$ is a polynomial in n of degree $m_j - 1$.

In particular, when $m_j = 1$, that is, θ_j is a simple pole, $P_j(n)$ is a constant (in n) and is given by

$$P_j(n) = -\frac{1}{\theta_j} \operatorname{Res}(f; \theta_j), \qquad m_j = 1. \qquad \square \tag{13}$$

Regardless of the order of the poles, the one closest to the origin determines the exponential growth rate of f_n. This property will persist also for singularities of different types.

An important special case arises when $f(z)$ is a rational function, $f(z) = N(z)/D(z)$, where $N(z)$ and $D(z)$ are both polynomials, and $D(0) \neq 0$. In this case $f(z)$ is meromorphic in the entire plane and the error term in equation (12) can be scuttled.

How can the polynomials $P_j(n)$ be determined? When the poles are simple, equation (13), with equation (5), is all one needs to complete the evaluation of the coefficients. When the poles are multiple, and when the numerator is not a polynomial, it is heavier going. One can still write expressions that provide the *exact* answers, not just asymptotics (see e.g. Exercise 6), but we should expect to derive little comfort (or benefit) from them; just one of the reasons why one wants asymptotics in the first place.

Example 1. In equation (12) we observe that the size of the region in which we sum over the contributions of the singularities determines the exponential error term.

Remark: Asymptotic expressions with *exponential* error terms turn out to be the privilege of functions with polar singularities. When the dominating singularity is of a different type (e.g. a branch point, or essential singularity), we will not be so fortunate.

Consider a function that has an infinite number of poles: $f(z) = (2 - e^z)^{-1}$. Every root of the equation $e^z = 2$ is a simple pole. These roots are summarized by

$$\theta_k = \log 2 + 2\pi i k, \qquad k = 0, \pm 1, \pm 2, \cdots. \tag{14}$$

Choosing regions $|z| \leq R$ with increasing R will capture more poles, give more accurate expressions for f_n and smaller error terms. In this particular case it is even a simple matter to let $R \to \infty$ and have an *exact* rather than an asymptotic value; even though equation (12) gives rise to a sum for which we do not have a closed form, its numerical behavior is very congenial.

First compute the residues, using equation (5):

$$\text{Res}(f\,;\,\theta_j) = \lim_{z \to \theta_j} \frac{z - \theta_j}{2 - e^z} = \frac{1}{-e^{\theta_j}} = -\frac{1}{2}\,, \tag{15}$$

where we have used L'Hopital's rule. By equations (12) and (13) then

$$f_n = \sum_j \theta_j^{-n} \frac{-1}{\theta_j} \cdot (-\frac{1}{2}) = \frac{1}{2}\sum_j \theta_j^{-n-1}$$

$$= \frac{1}{2}\Big[\frac{1}{\log^{n+1}2} + \sum_{j \geq 1}\Big(\frac{1}{(\log 2 + 2\pi ij)^{n+1}} + \frac{1}{(\log 2 - 2\pi ij)^{n+1}}\Big)\Big] \tag{16}$$

$$= \frac{1}{2\log^{n+1}2}\Big[1 + 2\sum_{j \geq 1}\text{Re}\Big(1 + \frac{2\pi ij}{\log 2}\Big)^{-n-1}\Big].$$

Even for moderate n the sum in equation (16) converges very rapidly. For $n = 10$ the $j = 0$ term alone provides the first 10 decimals correctly, and the $j = 1$ term adds three more! We should expect this, as the first singularity is the only one for $|z| \leq 6.33$, then $6.33^{-10} < 10^{-8}$ and the f_n are larger than 1.

2.5.2.3 Sympathetic Asymptotics

We say a function allows us to obtain its asymptotics sympathetically when the properties of these estimates are largely determined by one part, or one factor in the function (when it is a sum or a product of several terms, respectively).

In one way or another, most of the estimates we propose can be thus viewed. Equation (12), for example, expresses the coefficients f_n largely in terms of the poles of $f(z)$. In other words, only the prefix with negative powers of its Laurent series development plays a role in the estimate. Usually we shall reserve the term for situations like those displayed below.

Theorem 3: (Bender, 1974) Let $f(z) = A(z)B(z)$; the power series expansions of $A(z)$ and $B(z)$ are $\sum a_n z^n$ and $\sum b_n z^n$, and their radii of convergence are $\alpha > \beta \geq 0$ respectively. Assume also that the limit $b_{n-1}/b_n \to b$ exists, and that $A(b) \neq 0$. Then

$$f_n \sim A(b)b_n\,. \qquad \Box \tag{17}$$

When the radii of convergence are *equal*, this theorem cannot be used; a partial palliative will be given in Theorem 8 below. This theorem is useful as a tool for the derivation of properties of estimates in general setups, but one can also use it directly:

Example 2: Let $f(z) = e^{\cos z}(z - 2)^{-2}$, and define

$$f(z) = A(z)B(z), \quad A(z) = e^{\cos z}, \quad B(z) = \frac{1}{(z - 2)^2}\,. \tag{18}$$

$A(z)$ is entire, with $\alpha = \infty$, and $\beta = 2$. Furthermore,

$$B(z) = \frac{1}{4\left(1 - \frac{z}{2}\right)^2} = \frac{1}{2}\sum_{i \geq 1} i \frac{z^{i-1}}{2^i} = \sum_{i \geq 0} \frac{i+1}{2^{i+2}} z^i, \tag{19}$$

hence $b_n = (n+1)2^{-(n+2)}$ and $b = \lim_{n \to \infty} b_{n-1}/b_n = 2$. Since $A(b) \neq 0$ all the conditions necessary for Theorem 3 hold and we obtain

$$f_n \sim e^{\cos 2}(n+1)2^{-(n+2)}. \qquad \square \tag{20}$$

Later we shall be able to improve on this estimate. See also Exercise 7.

The following theorem, also to be found in Bender (1974), is useful when $f(z) = g(A(z))$, and the growth of the coefficients a_n is the determinant factor in the dependence of f_n on n.

Theorem 4: Let $f(z) = F(z, A(z))$, with $A(\cdot)$ and $F(\cdot, \cdot)$ having the known expansions

$$A(z) = \sum_{n \geq 1} a_n z^n, \quad F(x, y) = \sum_{i,k \geq 0} f_{i,k} x^i y^k, \tag{21}$$

and define

$$D(z) = \frac{\partial}{\partial y} F(z, y)|_{y=A(z)} = \sum_{k \geq 0} d_k z^k.$$

When the coefficients satisfy the following three conditions:

(i) $a_{n-1} = o(a_n)$, implying rapid increase of a_n with n,

(ii) $\sum_{k=r}^{n-r} |a_k a_{n-k}| = O(a_{n-r})$ for some $r > 0$,

(iii) for every $\delta > 0$, there exist numbers $M(\delta), K(\delta)$ such that $|f_{i,k} a_{n-i-k+1}| \leq K(\delta) \delta^{i+k} |a_{n-r}|$ for all $n \geq M(\delta)$ and $i+k > r+1$ (the r generated by condition (ii)), then

$$f_n = \sum_{k=0}^{r-1} d_k a_{n-k} + O(a_{n-r}). \qquad \square \tag{22}$$

An important particular case in which condition (iii) holds is when $F(x, y)$ is analytic at $(0,0)$. The condition can be difficult to ascertain otherwise.

We consider a partial example (partial in that it does not use the full generality of the theorem):

Example 3: We wish to obtain asymptotic representation for the coefficients f_n where $f(z) = (\sum_{n \geq 0} n! z^n)^{-1}$. Using $F(z, y) = (1+y)^{-1}$, which is clearly analytic at $(0,0)$, we examine whether $A(z) = \sum_{n \geq 1} n! z^n$ satisfies the first two conditions. Condition (i) is obvious, as $(n-1)! = o(n!)$. Since a_n is real and positive, in order to show property (ii) we need to show that $\sum_{k=r}^{n-r} a_k a_{n-k}/a_{n-r}$ is bounded for some r. Thus we consider the sum $\sum_{k=r}^{n-r} k!(n-k)!/(n-r)!$. Since the sum is symmetric about $n/2$, and the terms are monotonically decreasing in the range $r \leq k \leq n/2$ we obtain

$$\sum_{k=r}^{n-r} \frac{k!(n-k)!}{(n-r)!} \le 2\sum_{k=r}^{n/2} \frac{k!(n-k)!}{(n-r)!} = 2r! + 2\sum_{k=r+1}^{n/2} \frac{k!(n-k)!}{(n-r)!}$$

$$\le 2r! + 2(\frac{n}{2} - r) \frac{(r+1)!(n-r-1)!}{(n-r)!} .$$

(23)

Rearranging, the last expression equals

$$= 2r! + \frac{(r+1)!(n-2r)}{n-r} = r!(2 + \frac{(r+1)(n-2r)}{n-r}) < r!(r+3),$$

so that (ii) is satisfied for *any* $r \ge 0$. Since $D(z) = -(1 + A(z))^{-2}$, substitution in equation (22) produces

$$f_n = -\sum_{k=0}^{r-1} (n-k)![z^k](1 + A(z))^{-2} .$$

(24)

Writing $(1 + A(z))^{-2}$ as $(1 + z + 2z^2 + 6z^3 + 24z^4 + \cdots)^{-2} = (1 + 2z + 5z^2 + 16z^3 + 64z^4 + \cdots)^{-1}$, the necessary coefficients are easy to find, e.g. by writing

$$(1 + 2z + 5z^2 + 16z^3 + 64z^4 + \cdots)(a + bz + cz^2 + dz^3 + ez^4 + \cdots) = 1 ,$$ (25)

and equating successively the coefficients of like powers of z. Thus, taking $r = 3$ we need a, b and c, which are 1, -2 and -1; hence

$$f_n = -(n! - 2(n-1)! - (n-2)!) + O((n-3)!)$$

$$= -(n-2)!(n^2 - 3n + 1) + O((n-3)!) = -(n-2)!(n^2 - 3n + 1)(1 + O(n^{-3})).$$

(26)

This can be continued of course for higher values of r, obtaining smaller error terms (see Exercise 15).   □

In Wright (1970) there is a detailed discussion of functional relationships of the type $1 + a(z) = \exp(b(z))$, where $a(\cdot)$ and $b(\cdot)$ are either ordinary gf's or egf's. Given a_n he provides complete and asymptotic developments for b_n, and *vice versa*.

2.5.2.4 Singularity Improvement

This is one of the important methods we describe, and in a sense it is the source of all singularity based asymptotic estimation methods.

Let $f(z) = \Sigma f_n z^n$ be absolutely convergent (and hence regular) for $|z| < R$. We want a better estimate for f_n than the raw $O(R^{-n})$, which the convergence information supplies. Let $g(z)$ be another function, with a *known* development $\Sigma g_n z^n$ that has the same radius of convergence. If we choose well, $h(z) \equiv f(z) - g(z)$ will be regular on $|z| = R$, so it would have, by the maximum principle, a larger radius of convergence, and we would obtain $f_n = g_n + O(S^{-n})$, where $S > R$. In this sense we have improved the singularity; or at least its value for us. When the singularity is polar, we can always improve the exponential error term. When the singularity is of a different sort, the improvement will be milder. Examples for these two possibilities follow.

We consider a function with one polar singularity. The effect of several poles is merely additive, as equation (12) indicates.

Example 4: Let $f(z) = (z - \theta)^{-m} v(z)$, with $v(z)$ regular at $z = \theta$. Define

$$g(z) = \frac{q(z)}{(z - \theta)^m}, \qquad h(z) = f(z) - g(z) \tag{27}$$

$$q(z) = \sum_{r=0}^{m-1} \frac{1}{r!} v^{[r]}(\theta)(z - \theta)^r, \tag{28}$$

so that the difference $h(z)$ is indeed regular at $z = \theta$. As a specific case we reconsider the function treated above, in Example 2, and obtain, via equations (27) and (28)

$$f(z) = e^{\cos z}(z - 2)^{-2}, \quad v(z) = e^{\cos z}, \quad q(z) = e^{\cos 2} - (z-2)\sin 2 e^{\cos 2}$$

$$h(z) = \frac{e^{\cos z} + (z-2)\sin 2 e^{\cos 2} - e^{\cos 2}}{(z - 2)^2}. \tag{29}$$

Thus $h(z)$ is regular at $z = 2$. Moreover, it is an entire function, and its coefficients must then decrease superexponentially fast. So the equality $f(z) = g(z) + h(z)$, when we only consider the coefficients of $g(z)$ provides

$$f_n \sim [z^n]g(z) = [z^n]\left\{ \frac{e^{\cos 2}}{(z-2)^2} - \frac{\sin 2 e^{\cos 2}}{z - 2} \right\}$$

$$= e^{\cos 2}\left[\frac{n+1}{2^{n+2}} + \frac{\sin 2}{2^{n+1}} \right], \tag{30}$$

which is quite an improvement over the estimate given in equation (20). As $h(z)$ is entire the methods of this section are powerless to improve the estimate of f_n any further. We deal with this issue in Section 2.5.3.   □

Consider now a different type of singularity, a branch point.

Example 5: The function $f(z)$ is defined as the solution of the equation $f = z(1 + f + f^2)$ that is analytic at $z = 0$. This last requirement could stem from our knowing $f(z)$ to some extent, at least sufficiently to expect that it has a valid power series development around the origin. From the pair

$$f_{1,2}(z) = \frac{1}{2z}(1 - z \pm \sqrt{(1-z)^2 - 4z^2}), \tag{31}$$

we pick therefore the one with the minus sign in front of the radical,

$$f(z) = \frac{1}{2z}(1 - z - \sqrt{(1+z)(1-3z)}). \tag{32}$$

This $f(z)$ displays two branch points, at $z = \frac{1}{3}$ and at $z = -1$. As the first is closer to the origin it dominates, and we shall use it only. We want however, more detailed information than the simple estimate $f_n = O((\frac{1}{3})^{-n}) = O(3^n)$ it provides immediately. The initial $1-z$ terms in $f(z)$ contribute to the first two coefficients only; since it is f_n for large n we are after, we disregard these terms. Consider then the remaining part

$$F(z) \equiv -\frac{1}{2z}\sqrt{1+z}\sqrt{1-3z} \ . \tag{33}$$

As $\dfrac{-1}{2z}\sqrt{1+z}$ is regular at $z = \frac{1}{3}$, it admits there a Taylor series development

$$F(z) = -\frac{1}{2z}\sqrt{1-3z}\ \big(a + b(1-3z) + c(1-3z)^2 + \cdots \big), \tag{34}$$

where

$$a = \sqrt{1+z}\ |_{z=\frac{1}{3}} = \frac{2}{3}\sqrt{3}, \quad b = -\frac{1}{3}\frac{d}{dz}\sqrt{1+z}\ |_{z=\frac{1}{3}} = -\frac{\sqrt{3}}{12} \quad \text{etc.}$$

We consider now a first order estimate only (see Exercise 9). Write

$$F(z) = -\frac{1}{2z}\big(a(1-3z)^{\frac{1}{2}} + O(1-3z)^{3/2}\big), \tag{35}$$

hence

$$f_n = [z^n]F(z) = -\frac{\sqrt{3}}{3}[z^{n+1}](1-3z)^{\frac{1}{2}} + O\big([z^n](1-3z)^{3/2}\big). \tag{36}$$

Now $[z^{n+1}](1-3z)^{\frac{1}{2}} = [z^{n+1}]\sum_{i\geq 0}\binom{\frac{1}{2}}{i}(-3z)^i = \binom{\frac{1}{2}}{n+1}(-3)^{n+1} = \binom{n-\frac{1}{2}}{n+1}3^{n+1}$, and
$\binom{n-\frac{1}{2}}{n+1} = \dfrac{(n-\frac{1}{2})!}{(n+1)!(-3/2)!}$, where $r!$ for a fractional r should be interpreted as
$\Gamma(r+1)$. Since $\Gamma(\frac{1}{2})$ is known to be $\sqrt{\pi}$, we obtain $(-3/2)! = \Gamma(-\frac{1}{2}) = \Gamma(\frac{1}{2})/(-\frac{1}{2})$
$= -2\sqrt{\pi}$, and using Stirling approximation for the other factorials, some cancellations produce

$$\binom{n-\frac{1}{2}}{n+1} \approx -\frac{1}{2\sqrt{\pi n^3}}, \quad \text{so that} \quad [z^{n+1}](1-3z)^{\frac{1}{2}} \approx -\frac{3^{n+1}}{2\sqrt{\pi n^3}} \ . \tag{37}$$

Similarly, $[z^n](1-3z)^{3/2} = O(3^n n^{-5/2})$. Note that at a branch point we could only improve (reduce) the power of n in the error term, while the exponential factor remained the same.

2.5.2.5 Algebraic Singularities

The following theorem is a generalization of Theorem 2 in that we do not limit the singularities of the examined function to poles, but allow any *algebraic* singularity.

Definition: A function $f(z)$ is said to have an *algebraic singularity* at θ, if for z near θ it can be represented as a sum of two terms, one of which may be analytic at θ and the other has the form

$$\big(1 - \frac{z}{\theta}\big)^{-w}g(z), \qquad z \text{ near } \theta, \tag{38}$$

where $g(z)$ is analytic around θ with $g(\theta) \neq 0$, and each w is a complex number which may not be zero or a negative integer. The real part of w is called the *weight* of the singularity.

Theorem 5: (Darboux theorem) Let $f(z) = \Sigma f_n z^n$ be analytic near $z = 0$ and have only algebraic singularities on its circle of convergence $|z| = R$. Near the singularity θ_k suppose $f(z) \sim (1 - \frac{z}{\theta_k})^{-w_k} g_k(z)$, and define $W = \max_k \mathrm{Re}(w_k)$, then

$$f_n = \frac{1}{n} \sum_k \frac{g_k(\theta_k) n^{w_k}}{\theta_k^n \Gamma(w_k)} + o(R^{-n} n^{W-1}). \qquad \square \qquad (39)$$

Example 6: *Bernoulli numbers*. These numbers, together with their egf, were presented in Section 2.1.3,

$$\sum_{k \geq 0} B_k \frac{z^k}{k!} = \frac{z}{e^z - 1}. \qquad (40)$$

Clearly this is of the same type as the function investigated in Example 1. (See Exercise 11.) Using Theorem 5, we observe that the circle of convergence of the series contains two simple poles, $\theta_{1,2} = \pm 2\pi i$. For simple poles $W = 1$. Then

$$g_1(\theta_1) = \lim_{z \to \theta_1} (1 - \frac{z}{\theta_1}) B(z) = \lim_{z \to \theta_1} z \frac{1 - z/\theta_1}{e^z - 1} = \theta_1 \frac{-1/\theta_1}{e^{\theta_1}} = -1, \qquad (41)$$

and the same holds at the other pole, for $g_2(\theta_2)$. Hence

$$\frac{B_n}{n!} = \frac{1}{n} \left[\frac{-1 \cdot n}{\Gamma(1)(2\pi i)^n} + \frac{-1 \cdot n}{\Gamma(1)(-2\pi i)^n} \right] + o((2\pi)^{-n}). \qquad (42)$$

For B_{2n} this provides the known asymptotic value

$$B_{2n} = -2(2n)!(-4\pi^2)^{-n} + o((2n)!(2\pi)^{-2n}), \qquad (43)$$

whereas for B_{2n+1} we only get $o((2n+1)!(2\pi)^{-(2n+1)})$, rather than the correct value, 0. This phenomenon, that occasionally cancellations in the main term of equation (39) render the theorem rather useless, is a characteristic of Theorem 5.

Partition-like generating functions

Darboux's theorem can only be used when the number of algebraic singularities on the circle of convergence is finite. This excludes cases where the number is infinite, or where the *weight* is unbounded. One speaks in such cases of the circle of convergence being the "natural boundary" of the function, since it is not possible to construct for it an analytic continuation across the circle. A useful result for certain such cases is found in Brigham (1950):

Theorem 6: Let the gf $f(z)$ be given in the form

$$f(z) = \prod_{i \geq 1} \frac{1}{(1 - z^i)^{b_i}}, \qquad (44)$$

and let the parameters b_i in it satisfy the conditions:

(i) $b_1 \geq 1$, $b_i \geq 0$. The condition on b_1 can be replaced by:

($i1$) $b_i \neq 0 \Rightarrow b_i \geq 1$, $\quad i \geq 1$,

($i2$) Every sufficiently large integer has a partition such that if j is a part in it, $b_j \neq 0$.

(ii) There is an asymptotic "density" for the b_i:

$$\sum_{i \leq x} b_i \sim Kx^u (\log x)^v , \qquad u > 0 . \tag{45}$$

then

$$\log f_n \sim C [n^u (\log n)^v]^{\frac{1}{u+1}} , \quad C = \frac{1}{u}[Ku(u+1)^{u-v}\Gamma(u+2)\zeta(u+1)]^{\frac{1}{u+1}} . \quad \square \tag{46}$$

This theorem is "tailored" for gf's of partitions of integers. The discussion leading to equation (2.4-18) can be generalized to apply to the enumeration of partitions over *any* set of integers S, $p_n(S)$, and we find

$$p_S(z) = \prod_{i \in S} \frac{1}{1 - z^i} , \qquad p_n(S) = [z^n]p_S(z) . \tag{47}$$

This corresponds to having all the b_i equal to 1 or 0, according to whether i is in S or not. When S is finite, Darboux's theorem can be directly used, but when this is not the case the above theorem helps:

Consider first the enumeration of standard partitions, when S contains all natural numbers. In this case all b_i are 1, and from equation (45) we get $K = 1$, $u = 1$ and $v = 0$. Then $C = \pi\sqrt{2/3}$ and $\log f_n \sim \pi\sqrt{2n/3}$.

Another example is when S contains only the set of all *primes*. The prime number theorem provides that the relative density of primes among the natural numbers up to n is $1/\log n$, and equation (45) will give accordingly $K = 1$, $u = 1$ and $v = -1$. The same procedure as above provides that $\log f_n \sim 2\pi\sqrt{n/3\log n}$, which appears to be surprisingly large compared with the preceding result. See Exercise 16.

We shall conclude this section with a few theorems found in the literature. They are all rather specialized, and come with quite a troop of conditions. Thus one would expect them only rarely to fit a specific need as is; one would be wrong, at least with standard enumerations, using recursive derivations. Still we should consider them as models for further development, rather than an end of the road.

Theorem 7: (Bender, 1974). Let the gf $f(z)$ be determined implicitly by the equation $F(z, f(z)) = 0$. Let $r > 0$, $s > f_0$ be real numbers, and

(i) $\exists \delta > 0$, with $F(z,w)$ analytic in the region $|z| < r + \delta$, $|w| < s + \delta$;

(ii) $F(r,s) = F_w(r,s) = 0$;

(iii) $F_z(r,s) \neq 0$, $F_{ww}(r,s) \neq 0$;

(iv) The point (r,s) is the unique solution of the set of equations

$F(z,w) = F_w(z,w) = 0$ in $|z| \le r$, $|w| \le s$.

[A condition which is stricter than (iv) and implies it, but sometimes easier to verify is the conjunction of (v) and (vi) below:

(v) For all n sufficiently large $a_n > 0$.

(vi) There is a function $\phi(z,w)$, analytic in the region $|z| \le r + \delta$, $|w| \le s + \delta$, that satisfies

1) $F(z,w) = F_w(z,w) = 0$ implies $\phi(z,w) = c$ for some fixed positive c.

2) In the development $\phi(z,w) = \Sigma \phi_{i,k} z^i w^k$ all the coefficients $\phi_{i,k}$ are non-negative.

3) If $\phi(z,w)$ does not depend on w, i.e. $\phi_{i,k} = 0$ for $k \ne 0$, then the gcd for all i for which $\phi_{i,0} \ne 0$ is 1.]

$$\text{Then} \quad f_n ~ \sim~ \sqrt{\frac{rF_z(r,s)}{2\pi F_{ww}(r,s)}} \; n^{-3/2} r^{-n}. \qquad \square \qquad (48)$$

The proof of the theorem combines the implicit function theorem and Theorem 5. Bender (1974) brings some applications of this theorem. See Exercises 13, 14.

Theorem 8: (Odlyzko, 1982). Let $P(z)$ and $Q(z)$ be nonzero polynomials with real non-negative coefficients satisfying $P(0) = Q(0) = Q'(0) = 0$. Assume $Q(z)$ has the form $Q(z) = \Sigma_{j=0}^{N} q_j z^{i_j}$, $N \ge 1$, $2 \le i_j < i_{j+1}$, $(q_j > 0)$, and the gcd of the differences $i_j - i_0$, for $1 \le j \le N$ is 1. (This is similar to condition $(i2)$ in Theorem 6.) If the gf $f(z)$ satisfies $f(z) = P(z) + f(Q(z))$, then

$$f_n = n^{-1} \alpha^{-n} u(\log n) + O(n^{-2} \alpha^{-n}). \qquad (49)$$

where α is the (unique) real non-zero root of the equation $z = Q(z)$, and $u(z)$ is a continuous non-constant positive function with a period of $\log(Q'(\alpha))$. $\square$

And finally a theorem that may be used when Theorem 3 does not hold because of the equality of the radii of convergence:

Theorem 9: (Meir and Moon, 1978) Let $f(z) = A(z)B(z)$; the power series expansions of $A(z)$ and $B(z)$ are $\Sigma a_n z^n$ and $\Sigma b_n z^n$. Let the coefficients have the asymptotic representations $a_n ~ \sim~ aR^{-n} n^{-\alpha}$, $b_n ~ \sim~ bR^{-n} n^{-\beta}$, for $a,b,R > 0$, then

$$\alpha=0, \; \beta=1/2 \; \Rightarrow \; c_n ~ \sim~ 2abR^{-n}\sqrt{n}$$

$$\alpha = \beta = 1/2 \; \Rightarrow \; c_n ~ \sim~ \pi abR^{-n}$$

$$\alpha = \beta = 3/2 \; \Rightarrow \; c_n ~ \sim~ A(R)b_n + B(R)a_n \qquad (50)$$

$$\alpha = 3/2, \; \beta = 1/2 \; \Rightarrow \; c_n ~ \sim~ A(R)b_n . \qquad \square$$

The last case can be proved also when the condition on a_n is relaxed to $a_n = O(R^{-n} n^{-3/2})$, or even that $A(z)$ is regular in a somewhat larger circle than $B(z)$ (whence we revert to Theorem 3).

2.5.3 Entire Functions

We have seen in Section 2.5.2 that singularities are good leverage points for a variety of asymptotics generating methods. How do we handle those cases where a gf is obtained that is entire, has no singularities whatever in the whole complex plane?

In principle, the only recourse is to fall back on equation (6), which for a power series developed at the origin reads

$$f_n = \oint_C f(z) \frac{dz}{z^{n+1}} . \tag{51}$$

All the methods mentioned in this section are designed to estimate the contour integral in equation (51). Since equation (51) holds not only for entire functions, but is valid whenever C is within the regularity domain of $f(z)$, these methods could also be used for non-entire functions. Often we shall assume that $f(z)$ is a gf of non-negative quantities - i.e. that $f_n \geq 0$ for all n. This does not hold for the gf of the Bernoulli numbers examined above; *all* the methods assume, however, that $f(z)$ is real for real z.

We show first a simple upper bound on the coefficients of $f(z)$ when
(i) All the coefficients are non-negative.
(ii) $f(z)$ is entire but not a polynomial (i.e. for any m there is an $f_n > 0$, for some $n > m$.)

Let C be the circle $|z| = R$. From condition (i), $f(R) = \max \{ |f(z)| : |z| = R \}$. Using this in equation (51) directly

$$f_n \leq \frac{1}{2\pi} \frac{f(R)}{R^{n+1}} 2\pi R = \frac{f(R)}{R^n} . \tag{52}$$

This inequality holds for all $R > 0$; in particular it holds for that value of R, r_n, where the function $f(R)/R^n$ attains its minimum value.

Observe that $f(R)/R^n$ is infinite both at $R=0$ and $R=\infty$ (see Exercise 17). It need not be unimodal in general, although in most of the applications we encountered it is. A local minimum point needs to satisfy the condition $\frac{d}{dR}(\frac{f(R)}{R^n})|_{R=r_n} = 0$, which leads to $a_n(R) \equiv Rf(R) - nf'(R) = 0$ and at that point we would have

$$f_n \leq \frac{f(r_n)}{r_n^n} . \tag{53}$$

If the equation $a_n(R) = 0$ has several solutions (it will always have a finite number) they should be all examined to determine the global minimum. The bound is good inasmuch as $f(z)$ does not vary much on $|z| = r_n$. The Saddle Point method, outlined later in this section. shows how to handle situations where the converse is the case.

Example 7: We pick a simple case. Consider $f(z) = e^z$, then the equation $a_n(R) = 0$ is $e^R(R-n) = 0$, hence $r_n = n$, and

$$f_n \le \frac{e^n}{n^n}, \tag{54}$$

which is reminiscent of Stirling's approximation for $n!^{-1}$.

This result has been considerably strengthened and refined. In particular, it has been extended to a larger class of functions than those satisfying the conditions (i) and (ii) above, and it can provide now asymptotic expansions, not just bounds. As above, we just quote results and provide references for the proofs.

2.5.3.1 H-Admissibility and HS-Admissibility

A substantial improvement over the bound (53) was provided by Hayman (1956). He defined a class of functions which he called "admissible". For specificity we shall denote them by H-admissible, following Odlyzko and Richmond (1984). The first definition is daunting, but there is a second one:

Definition: Let $f(z)$ be analytic for $|z| < R \le \infty$ and real for real z. Define $w(u) = uf'(u)/f(u)$, $b(u) = uw'(u)$; then $f(z)$ is *H-admissible* if there exist $R_0 < R$ and a function $\delta(r)$ such that for $R_0 < r < R$ $\delta(r)$ has values in $(0,\pi)$ and the following three conditions hold:

> (i) $f(re^{i\theta}) \sim f(r)e^{i\theta w(r) - \theta^2 b(r)/2}$,   as $r \to R$
>
> uniformly for $|\theta| \le \delta(r)$
>
> (ii) $f(re^{i\theta}) = o(f(r)/b(r))$,   as $r \to R$ (55)
>
> uniformly for $\delta(r) \le |\theta| \le \pi$
>
> (iii) $b(r) \to \infty$,   as $\to R$ □

This quite heavy definition can be replaced for most purposes with the following recursive one, which may now be given the status of a

Proposition: If $f(z)$ and $g(z)$ are H-admissible in $|z| < R$, $h(z)$ regular for $|z| < R$ and real for real z, and $p(z)$ is a polynomial with real coefficients, then:

1) If $[z^n]e^{p(z)}$ for large enough n are all positive, then $e^{p(z)}$ is H-admissible in $|z| < \infty$.

2) The functions $e^{f(z)}$ and $f(z)g(z)$ are H-admissible for $|z| < R$.

3) If a positive ε exists, such that $\max_{|z|=r<R} |h(z)| = O(f(r)^{1-\varepsilon})$, then $f(z) + h(z)$ is H-admissible in $|z| < R$. Special cases here are $f(z) + p(z)$, and if the leading coefficient in $p(z)$ is positive, also $p(f(x))$.   □

This may be all worth going through because of the following result:

Theorem 10: (Hayman) If $f(z)$ is H-admissible in $|z| < R$, then

$$f_n \sim \frac{f(r_n)}{r_n^n} \frac{1}{(2\pi b(r_n))^{\frac{1}{2}}}, \tag{56}$$

when r_n is the root of $w(r) = n$ in $R_0 < r < R$. See Exercise 19. □

In Harris and Schoenfeld (1968) it is shown that under a stricter set of conditions, of the same flavor as above, one may do better than equation (56) and obtain a *complete* asymptotic expansion.

Definition: A function $f(z)$ which is analytic for $|z| < R$, $0 < R \le \infty$ and real for real z is called *HS-admissible* if the following four conditions hold:

(i) There exist an $R_0 \in (0,R)$ and a function $d(r)$ defined on $r \in (R_0, R)$ that satisfy

$$0 < d(r) < 1, \quad r[1+d(r)] < R, \tag{57}$$

and

$$|z - r| < rd(r) \Rightarrow f(z) \ne 0. \tag{58}$$

(ii) Defining for $k \ge 1$

$$A(z) = \frac{f'(z)}{f(z)}, \quad B_k(z) = \frac{z^k}{k!} A^{[k-1]}(z), \quad B(z) = z B_1'(z)/2, \tag{59}$$

the following hold

$$B(r) > 0, \text{ for } R_0 < r < R, \text{ and } B_1(r) \to \infty \text{ as } r \to R. \tag{60}$$

(iii) The equations $B_1(r) = n+1$ for sufficiently large n have unique roots u_n if we restrict their range to be $R_1 < r < R$, by selecting a suitable R_1. Defining for $j \in I_1$

$$C_j(z,r) \equiv -[B_{j+2}(z) + \frac{(-1)^j}{j+2} B_1(r)]/B(r), \tag{61}$$

there exist a non-negative n_0, and for each $n \ge n_0$, two numbers E_n and D_n such that

$$|C_j(u_n,u_n)| \le E_n D_n^j, \quad j \in I_1. \tag{62}$$

(iv) As $n \to \infty$,

$$B(u_n)d^2(u_n) \to \infty, \quad D_n E_n B(u_n)d^3(u_n) \to 0, \quad D_n d(u_n) \to 0. \tag{63}$$

Based on this definition (which is later shown to be related to H-admissibility), we have Theorem 11:

Theorem 11: (Harris and Schoenfeld). Let $f(z)$ be HS-admissible; assuming the availability of the apparatus used in the definition above we further define the following:

$$\beta_n \equiv B(u_n), \quad \gamma_j(n) \equiv C_j(u_n,u_n), \tag{64}$$

$$F_k(n) \equiv \frac{(-1)^k}{\sqrt{\pi}} \sum_{m=1}^{2k} \frac{\Gamma(m+k+\frac{1}{2})}{m!} \sum_{\substack{j_1,\cdots,j_m \geq 1 \\ \Sigma j_i = 2k}} \gamma_{j_1}(n) \cdots \gamma_{j_m}(n). \tag{65}$$

Let $Q(r)$ be an oriented path in the z-plane, consisting of the line segment $r+ird(r)$ to $r\sqrt{1-d^2(r)}+ird(r)$, and a circular arc passing through the last point, through ir and $-r$, and define

$$\lambda(r;d) \equiv \max_{z \in Q(r)} |f(z)/f(r)|, \tag{66}$$

$$\mu(r;d) \equiv \max\{\lambda(r;d)B(r), \frac{\exp(-B(r)d^2(r))}{d(r)\sqrt{B(r)}}\}, \tag{67}$$

$$E_n' \equiv \min(1,E_n), \quad E_n'' \equiv \max(1,E_n), \tag{68}$$

$$\phi_N(n;d) \equiv \max\{\mu(u_n;d), E_n'(D_n E_n'' \beta_n^{-\frac{1}{2}})^{2N+2}\}. \tag{69}$$

With all of these, for any $N \geq 0$ we may choose,

$$f_n = \frac{f(u_n)}{2u_n^n\sqrt{\pi\beta_n}} \{1 + \sum_{k=1}^{N} F_k(n)\beta_n^{-k} + O(\phi_N(n;d))\}. \quad \square \tag{70}$$

While the result is attractive, the route is less so; a significant saving there accrues from the following result, due to Odlyzko and Richmond:

Theorem 12: If $f(x)$ is H-admissible, then $e^{f(x)}$ is HS-admissible. Also, the term $\phi_N(n;d)$, defined in equation (69), is then $O(\beta_n^{-N})$ for every fixed $N \geq 0$.

2.5.3.2 Saddle Point Estimates

The Saddle Point (SP) method is a well known integral estimation procedure that can be applied to equations like (51). The method uses the idea that when the integrand is rather volatile, there might be a small portion of the integration path where the integrand is much larger than at other parts, and hence that fraction accounts for nearly the entire value of the integral. In particular, when the integrand depends on a parameter, as n in equation (51), and we are interested in values for large value of the parameter, this eventuality is quite common. We naturally obtain then an asymptotic estimate.

The best source for reading on the geometric context of the SP method is de Bruijn (1981). It brings a detailed, picturesque (there is some on mountaineering) account of the SP method as well as several applications. As will transpire from the presentation below, this method is not a good candidate for a cook-book like recipe, as one should check rather carefully that it is indeed applicable for the case at hand. The key word is mentioned above - volatility.

In the discussion of the SP method we represent the integral to be evaluated, following de Bruijn, in the form

$$I = \oint_C e^{h_n(z)} dz \ . \tag{71}$$

To adapt this to equation (51) we have to take

$$h_n(z) = \log f(z) - (n+1)\log z \ . \tag{72}$$

We are free to select whichever contour that encloses the origin, and we pick a circle, $|z| = R$, such that $h'_n(z)|_{z=R} = 0$, expecting that the neighborhood of this point, or more precisely - a relatively short segment of the circle passing through this point - will provide the hoped-for critical contribution. In terms of the estimate of equation (53) we determine $R_n = r_{n+1}$.

The integral along the circle $|z| = R_n$ can be well estimated by the SP method if the contribution from the points $z = R_n e^{i\theta}$ is significant only when $|\theta| < \theta_0$, for some small θ_0.

Referring to Fig. 2.2, we intend to replace the integral on the circle by an integral along the line $z = R_n + it$, $-\infty < t < \infty$, again hoping that only the part of this line which is close to the circle, specifically those points with $\arg(z) < \theta_0$, give rise to a tangible contribution.

For z on this "small" segment we may write

$$h_n(z) = h_n(R_n) + \frac{1}{2} h''_n(R_n)(z - R_n)^2 \quad [\text{The first derivative vanishes at } R_n \, !] \tag{73}$$

and then we have the estimate, writing $z = R_n + it$,

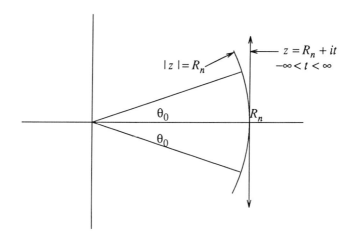

Fig. 2.2: Integration contour containing a saddle point.

$$I \sim e^{h_n(R_n)} \frac{1}{2\pi} \int_{-\infty}^{\infty} e^{\frac{1}{2}h_n''(R_n)(it)^2} dt = e^{h_n(R_n)} \frac{1}{2\pi} \int_{-\infty}^{\infty} e^{-t^2 h_n''(R_n)/2} dt. \quad (74)$$

Recollecting the integral over the normal density

$$\frac{1}{\sigma\sqrt{2\pi}} \int_{-\infty}^{\infty} e^{-x^2/2\sigma^2} = 1,$$

we obtain

$$I \sim \frac{e^{h_n(R_n)}}{\sqrt{2\pi h_n''(R_n)}}. \quad (75)$$

How can we estimate the quality of this estimate? Or rather, the likelihood of a significant error, in equation (75)? It is not easy to find a rule that will be uniformly valid in all cases, but we can point out the following: most of the contribution in (74) comes from $|t| < t_o \equiv [h_n''(R_n)]^{-\frac{1}{2}}$, and thus we should require that the development (73) is a good approximation in $|z - R_n| < t_o$, and that the next few terms, which are bounded by $\frac{t_o^k}{k!} h_n^{[k]}(R_n)$, should tend to be much smaller than 1 for increasing n.

Exercises and Complements

1. Show how equation (6) follows from the residue theorem. What conditions should $f(z)$, C and a satisfy for the derivation to hold?

2. In this problem you have to count the number of vectors $\mathbf{r}(n)$ generated by the following recursive relation

$$\{\mathbf{r}(n+1)\} = \bigcup_{j=1}^{I_n} (0, \mathbf{r}_j(n)) \bigcup_{c=1}^{n} \bigcup_{j=1}^{I_n} (0, \mathbf{r}_j(n) + \mathbf{1}_c).$$

The vector $\mathbf{1}_c$ is a vector of n components that are all 0 except the c'th which is 1. Call this number d_n. Starting at $n = 1$, d_1 is 1, and the corresponding vector is (0).

(a) If the sum of the first i components of a vector is denoted by r_i, show that an equivalent definition of the set of vectors $\mathbf{r}(n)$ is given by $r_i \leq i$, when the components are numbered from 0 to $n-1$.

(b) Define $d_{n,r}$ as the number of such vectors with the sum of their components equal to r. Show that these quantities satisfy the recurrence $d_{n+1,r} = d_{n,r} + d_{n+1,r-1}$, and that $d_n = d_{n,n-1}$.
[Use the above relation $r_i \leq i$].

(c) Define the gf's $D(w,z)$ and $D(z)$ for $d_{n,r}$ and d_n respectively and show the relation $D(w,z) = (z - wzD(wz))/(1-w-z)$. Use the procedure of Example 1 of Section 2.5.1 to obtain $D(z) = (1-\sqrt{1-4z})/2z$, the gf of the Catalan numbers.

Can you show that d_n should be the Catalan number by an analogy to a different structure?

(d) Obtain $d_{n,r}$ from $D(w,z)$ and estimate it asymptotically for large n.

3. Prove equation (11), using for the left-hand inequality the maximality of R, and for the right-hand one use Cauchy integral formula with $C = \{z; |z| = R(1+\varepsilon)^{-1}\}$.

4. Show how equation (13) follows from the residue theorem.

5. Prove equations (13) and (14), for the value of the residue at a pole of a meromorphic function.

6. For $f(z) = N(z)/D(z)$, $N(z) = \sum_{i=0}^{r} n_i z^i$, $D(z) = \prod_{j=1}^{d}(z-\theta_j)^{m_j}$, $\sum m_j > r$, develop an explicit expression for $[z^n] f(z)$.

Use your result to derive a representation for $P_j(n)$ as defined via equation (12), in this special case.

[Hint: use the binomial theorem to develop the denominator as a power series, using the expansion given in equation (2.3-10).]

7. (Bender) The number of ways to create subsets of a set S_n, $|S_n| = n$, so that no subset is repeated and each element is in exactly two subsets has the egf

$$C(z) = \exp(-1-\tfrac{1}{2}(e^z - 1)) \cdot \sum_{k \geq 0} \exp\!\left(z \binom{k}{2}\right)/k! \equiv A(z)B(z).$$

Determine c_n, using equation (17). Establish the conditions for the suitability of this equation. In the process you shall need an estimate of b_n. [Answer: See Exercise 2.1-10; write for the t there an expression in n to order $O(n^{-1})$, $c_n \sim e^{-1} n! b_n$.]

8. Show that the function $h(z)$ defined by equation (27) is regular at $z = \theta$.

9. Use equation (34) and the subsequent development there to extend the asymptotic representation for $f(z)$ of equation (32) by one term (to order $O(3^n n^{-7/2})$).

10. Show that when a gf has only a single (algebraic) singularity on its circle of convergence, Theorem 5 follows from Theorem 3.

11. Handle the egf of example 6 (equation (40)) in the same way as example 1 was done, to produce an exact expression for the Bernoulli numbers [Answer: $B_{2k} = -2(2k)! \sum_{j \geq 1} (-1)^j / (2\pi j)^{2k}$.]

12. Use Darboux's theorem (Theorem 5) to derive asymptotic expressions for the terms belonging to the generating functions:

(a) $f(z) = e^{-z/2} \sqrt{1-z}$

(b) $f(z) = e^{-z + z^2/2} \sqrt{1-z^2}$

13. (Meir and Moon, 1978) Show that the following claim is a special case of Theorem 7:

Let $G(y) = 1 + \sum_{i \geq 1} c_i y^i$ with all $c_i \geq 0$, have the radius of convergence R (which may be infinite), and let $f(z) = z + \sum_{n \geq 2} f_n z^n$ be the solution which is regular at the origin of the equation $f(z) = zG(f(z))$. Also assume

(i) $c_1 > 0$, $c_j > 0$ for some $j > 1$,

(ii) $rG'(r) = G(r)$ for some r, $0 < r < R$,

then $f_n \sim \sqrt{\dfrac{G(r)}{2\pi G''(r)}} n^{-3/2} (G(r)/r)^n$.

14. Use the theorem of Exercise 13 to obtain asymptotic expressions:

(a) For the Catalan numbers, the gf of which we have shown to satisfy the equation $zB^2(z) - B(z) + 1 = 0$. [Answer: $b_n \sim 4^n n^{-3/2}/\sqrt{\pi}$.]

(b) The number of (unordered) labeled trees of n nodes, a_n, with an egf $A(z) = \sum_{n \geq 1} a_n z^n/(n-1)!$ that satisfies the equation $A(z) = z\exp(A(z))$. [Answer: $a_n \sim n! n^{-3/2} e^n /\sqrt{2\pi} \approx n^{n-2}$, by Stirling's approximation; show, by substitution, that this is, however, the exact result!]

15. Improve the error term in equation (23) to $O(n^{-5})$, by choosing $r=5$ and completing the calculations.

16. Use Theorem 6 to obtain asymptotic estimate of the number of ways a large integer n can be partitioned over members of the following sets:

(a) $S = \{4i, 5j\}$, i, j are all the natural numbers.

(b) $S = \{10^i\}$, $i = 0, 1, \cdots$.

17. Prove that when $f(z)$ is entire and non-polynomial $f(R)/R^n$ assumes infinite values for $R=0$ and $R=\infty$ for all large positive integers n.

18. Consider the application of the bound in equation (53) to $i(n)$, the number of involutions in $S(N_n)$, that have the egf $e^{z+z^2/2}$ (see Exercise 3.2-4). Show that r_n is given by $r_n = \frac{1}{2}(\sqrt{4n+1} - 1)$. Compute a sequence of improving estimates of this r_n in terms of n (i.e. $r_n = \sqrt{n}, r_n = \sqrt{n} - \frac{1}{2}, \cdots$) and the resulting sequence of bounds on $i(n)$.

19. Show that the following numbers can be estimated via Theorem 10 (i.e., verify that their gf's are H-admissible) and obtain an estimate from equation (56).

(a) $i(n)$ in $S(N_n)$ (see Exercise 18)

(b) The Bell numbers (use their egf, $\exp(e^z - 1)$.)

20. Show that the value of f_n given in equation (56) is precisely that given by the $N=0$ approximation in equation (70).

21. Use Theorem 11 to improve the estimates obtained in Exercise 19. (Determine first whether Theorem 12 is applicable.)

2.6 Selected Results from Probability Theory

The purpose of this eclectic section is to present some results and computational methods that belong to the body of Applied Probability, such that could be handy tools when taking on problems like those we sample in the following chapters. We limit ourselves to results that are frequently outside the scope of courses in probability theory, or stochastic processes. Specifically, we consider absorption times in transient Markov chains, stochastic inequalities and a discrete version of Wald's identity.

In the analyses to be later presented the reader will also find numerous applications of standard results, which will not be repeated here. I would like to draw the reader's attention however to a few of those: Chebyshev's inequality in §3.1; cycle counting in permutations in §3.2.1 (related to Feller's "observer paradox"); the estimate of means over a regenerative process, in Theorem 2 of §4.2.3 (which is related to Wald's identity proved in this section); the methods of computing the distribution $F_T(x)$ in §5.1.3, and the related moments in §5.1.4; the Central Limit Theorem in §5.2.1.

2.6.1 The Representation of an Algorithm by a Markov Chain

Frequently, when the analysis of an algorithm is undertaken, it is found that the main difficulty in the analysis stems from the following fact: the algorithm performs a sequence of steps. In each step some of the input data are transformed, with the transformation depending both on the data examined in this step and on the execution path of the algorithm up (or down) to that stage. When we want to formulate the probabilistic properties of the algorithm, we find that this dependence complicates our computations intractably. Even if the original underlying distribution of the input is easy to handle, the simplicity is rarely preserved under the (partial) operation of the algorithm. This phenomenon is not unique to analysis of algorithms, but bedevils applied probabilists wherever they ply their trade. The probabilistic model where computations can still often be carried out with manageable complexity arises when the dependence on past operation has a very short memory; put more precisely - when a Markov chain provides an adequate representation of the algorithm environment and evolution. The purpose of this section is to exhibit the principal properties of such a representation. The presentation below is based, in part, on Kemp (1984).

It is often the case that the entire operation of an algorithm may be represented as follows:

The algorithm starts at a well defined initial "state". According to the input it goes through a sequence of "states". A "state" in this context reflects the values of the variables which the algorithm employs to record the processing that has been performed so far. This sequence of transitions terminates when the entire processing is done. We represent this operation by a traversal of a directed graph. Nodes represent states of the algorithm, edges represent possible transitions. The crucial step in the model formulation is the assignment of probabilities to the edges. For consistency, this must be done so that the sum of probabilities for each node, taken over all edges leaving it, is 1.

We shall say that this representation is valid (or *proper*) if, when the algorithm is at a certain state i, the probability that it will next go into a certain other state, j, does not depend on the history of the algorithm execution up to its reaching state i, and is equal to the probability assigned to the edge (i,j). This is equivalent to saying that the above set of states supports a first-order Markov chain, and provides a Markovian description of the algorithm.

Referring to the algorithm described in Section 1.2, we see that it can be represented in such a way. Note though that we cannot use the simple 4-state diagram of Fig. 1.2, because the number of times the head may find '1' is bounded. We can do it, however, with $2(n+1)$ states (see Exercise 2).

By convention we shall only use this description when the algorithm has a single possible initial state and a single possible final state. Obviously, there is no difficulty in rectifying a graph not thus blessed: just manufacture a single source

$$P = \begin{bmatrix} 0 & 1/3 & 2/3 & 0 & 0 & 0 \\ 0 & 0 & 1/2 & 1/2 & 0 & 0 \\ 0 & 0 & 0 & 1 & 0 & 0 \\ 0 & 1/3 & 0 & 0 & 2/3 & 0 \\ 0 & 0 & 0 & 0 & 1/2 & 1/2 \\ 0 & 0 & 0 & 0 & 0 & 1 \end{bmatrix}$$

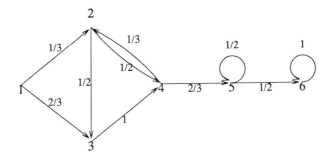

Fig. 2.3: A Markov chain representation for a random algorithm

and a single sink, and link them to the sets of initial and final states of the graph, respectively. The edges leading to originally initial states will carry the probabilities of starting in each such state, and the terminating edges will carry the probability one.

Example: The graph and transition matrix in Fig. 2.3 provide equivalent descriptions.

The state v_6 in Fig. 2.3 has a loop which is not part of the corresponding algorithm formulation, but is necessary in order to make P stochastic. In common terminology the state v_6 is called an absorbing state. In the rest of the discussion we shall assume the algorithm has n possible states, denoted by v_1 to v_n, with v_1 being the initial state, and v_n the terminating (or absorbing) one. A matrix P with structure as in Fig. 2.3 is adjoined to the graph. The matrix entries P_{ij} provide the probabilities of "one step transitions". These are the probabilities carried on the edges. Accordingly, P is called the *transition probability matrix* of the chain.

Remark: We have not stipulated how these probabilities arise. Indeed, they can arise in two distinct ways. One is induced by the input, as in the example cited above, that refers to Fig. 1.2. Another arises when the algorithm itself contains a random element. The collision-resolution-algorithm mentioned in Exercise 2.2-5 is an example of such an algorithm, that is paced by a random number generator.

Reservation: For algorithms that operate on finite input, it would be rather the exception that a Markovian description can be found, which is compact enough to be useful as a computational tool.

The probability of the algorithm taking a path $(v_{i_1}, v_{i_2}, \cdots, v_{i_r})$ is given by the product $P_{i_1 i_2} P_{i_2 i_3} \cdots P_{i_{r-1} i_r}$. The probability of passing from state v_i to v_j in r steps (without specifying the intermediate states) is given by the corresponding element of P raised to the power r, P^r_{ij}.

The general theory of Markov chains provides the following important result

Theorem 1: $P^n \rightarrow \hat{P}$ when $n \rightarrow \infty$, where $\hat{P}$ is a matrix with all its rows identical, and equal to $(0, 0, \cdots, 0, 1)$. The convergence is geometrically fast. $\square$

Note that this $\hat{P}$ satisfies $P\hat{P} = \hat{P}P = \hat{P}\hat{P} = \hat{P}$, hence the following sum exists:

$$\sum_{i \geq 0} (P - \hat{P})^i = \sum_{i \geq 0} P^i (I - \hat{P})^i = \sum_{i \geq 0} P^i (I - \hat{P}) = \sum_{i \geq 0} (P^i - \hat{P}) < \infty .$$

Clearly P, $I - P$ and $\hat{P}$ are all singular, but the existence of the above sum implies

Theorem 2: The *principal matrix* of the chain, $\tilde{P} = I - P + \hat{P}$ is nonsingular.

Proof: Observe that since the above sum converges geometrically, it converges absolutely, and $(P - \hat{P})^i \rightarrow 0$ when $i \rightarrow \infty$, thus

$$\sum_{i=0}^{m}(P-\hat{P})^i(I-P+\hat{P}) = \sum_{i=0}^{m}((P-\hat{P})^i - (P-\hat{P})^{i+1})$$

$$= I - (P-\hat{P})^{m+1} \qquad (1)$$

$$\to I .$$

Hence $(I-P+\hat{P})^{-1} = \Sigma_{i\geq0}(P-\hat{P})^i$. This representation for the inverse of the principal matrix is rarely helpful computationally, but its existence is useful in formal derivations.   □

Let E be the $n\times n$ matrix which is all zero except the (n,n) element, $E_{nn} = 1$. $P-E$ is then a matrix identical to P in its first $n-1$ rows, but it has a last row of zeroes. This matrix will be denoted by π. It is called the *fundamental matrix* of the algorithm. Note that for $1\leq i,j<n, \pi^r_{ij} = P^r_{ij}$. The following claim has an appealing probabilistic proof:

Theorem 3: $\pi^m \underset{m\to\infty}{\longrightarrow} 0$, geometrically fast.

Proof: Since the graph is finite there is an integer r, such that from every node there is a path to v_n which is no longer than r. (Clearly $r < n$ suffices.) Consider the probabilities of all these $n-1$ paths and let ω be the smallest among them. Then the probability of reaching the absorbing state, independently of the initial state, in no more than r transitions, is at least $\omega > 0$. Conversely, the probability of not being absorbed within r transitions is at most $1 - \omega$. And the probability of not being absorbed in kr transitions is at most $(1 - \omega)^k$. Since $(1 - \omega)^k \underset{k\to\infty}{\longrightarrow} 0$, the above partial identification of P with π provides $\pi^{kr} \underset{k\to\infty}{\longrightarrow} 0$.   □

Since this convergence is geometrical, $\Sigma_{i\geq0}\pi^i$ exists. The same procedure that served to show the inverse of the principal matrix will provide

$$\sum_{i\geq0}\pi^i = (I-\pi)^{-1} . \qquad (2)$$

This matrix has a probabilistic interpretation. Define

$R_{ij} \equiv$ The number of times that the algorithm passes through state v_j till absorption, given that it starts in state i.

If $i=j$, the initial sojourn is already counted as one visit.

Theorem 4: $r_{ij} \equiv E(R_{ij}) = (I-\pi)^{-1}_{ij}$.

Proof: We show two proofs. The first is straightforward. Since π^k_{ij} is the probability that the path from v_i will be in v_j in step k (using the fact that $\pi^0 = I$)

$$r_{ij} = \sum_{k\geq0}1\cdot\pi^k_{ij} = (I-\pi)^{-1}_{ij} , \qquad (3)$$

where we simply add up the contributions of all steps.

The second proof furnishes an example of one of the main computational methods useful for Markov chains: randomization on next transition:

$$r_{ij} = \delta_{ij} + \sum_{l=1}^{n} \pi_{il} r_{lj} , \tag{4}$$

where δ_{ij} is Kronecker's delta that vanishes unless $i = j$. Equation (4) holds if we agree to define the reasonable assignment $R_{nj} = 0, j \neq n, R_{in} = 1$, for all i, with probability one, i.e. deterministically.

The last equation is rendered in matrix notation as $r = I + \pi r$, whence we again get $r = (I - \pi)^{-1}$.   □

In Exercise 3 you are asked to evaluate the variance of R_{ij}. The simplest way to do this is through the following results:

Define the following probabilities:

$$w_{ij} \equiv \text{Prob}(R_{ij} > 0), \quad i \neq j, \qquad q_j \equiv \text{Prob}(R_{jj} = 1). \tag{5}$$

These are, respectively, the probabilities that starting at state v_i the chain visits state v_j before absorption, and that starting from state v_j, this state is *not* revisited before absorption.

Theorem 5:

(i) $$q_j = \frac{1}{r_{jj}} ,$$

$$\tag{6}$$

(ii) $$w_{ij} = \frac{r_{ij}}{r_{jj}} .$$

Proof: We need an auxiliary matrix (or rather an infinite set of matrices) that are frequently useful in computations. Also, we shall have the occasion to demonstrate the second important computational method over Markov chains: randomizing on first entry time.

Define:

$$f_{ij}(m) \equiv \text{Prob (starting in } v_i, v_j \text{ is visited for the } first \text{ time at step } m), \quad m \geq 1.$$

For consistency with the definition of R_{ij} we should say that for $i = j$ it is the second visit we observe. Furthermore, the definition could be complemented with $f_{ij}(0) = \delta_{ij}$, but this is not ordinarily needed.

Using the mentioned randomization, the $f(m)$ matrices and P are clearly related through

$$P^k{}_{ij} = \sum_{m=1}^{k} f_{ij}(m) P^{k-m}{}_{jj} , \qquad k \geq 1. \tag{7}$$

Define the generating functions

$$a_{ij}(z) \equiv \sum_{m \geq 0} z^m P^m{}_{ij} , \qquad b_{ij}(z) \equiv \sum_{m \geq 1} z^m f_{ij}(m). \tag{8}$$

Multiplying equation (7) by z^k and summing over $k \geq 1$ immediately gives

$$a_{ij}(z) - \delta_{ij} = \sum_{k \geq 1} z^k \sum_{m=1}^{k} f_{ij}(m) P^{k-m}{}_{jj}$$

$$= \sum_{m \geq 1} f_{ij}(m) z^m \sum_{k \geq m} z^{k-m} P^{k-m}{}_{jj} .$$

Hence,

$$a_{ij}(z) = \delta_{ij} + b_{ij}(z) a_{jj}(z). \tag{9}$$

The definition of w_{ij} implies that it equals $b_{ij}(1)$, and an expression for $a_{ij}(1)$ has already been computed: by the comment following the definition of the matrix π,

$$a_{ij}(1) = \sum_{k \geq 0} P^k{}_{ij} = \sum_{k \geq 0} \pi^k{}_{ij} , \qquad 1 \leq i,j < n$$

$$= (I - \pi)^{-1}{}_{ij}$$

$$= r_{ij} .$$

Hence, for $i \neq j$,

$$w_{ij} = b_{ij}(1) = \frac{r_{ij}}{r_{jj}} ,$$

and when $i = j$,

$$q_j = 1 - b_{jj}(1) = 1 - \frac{r_{jj} - 1}{r_{jj}} = \frac{1}{r_{jj}} .$$

as claimed.   □

Remark: Theorems 2 and 5 made no use of the special structure of P, and are thus valid for any Markov chain.

2.6.2 Inequalities for Sums of Bounded Random Variables (Hoeffding, 1963)

We present a rather general method of deriving probabilistic bounds on values of random variables, and its application to the proof of inequality (C.6). The underpinning idea runs as follows:

Let Y be a random variable. The value of $\mathrm{Prob}[Y - E(Y) \geq nt]$ is equal to the expected value of a random variable that is 1 when $Y - E(Y) \geq nt$, and zero otherwise. Also, for any positive constant h, this expected value is bounded from above by $E\{\exp[h(Y - E(Y) - nt)]\}$, (See Exercise 10). The above reference also provides some of the history of this approach and pointers to earlier usage. Now for our special case:

Let X_i, $1 \leq i \leq n$ be independent random variables. Denote their sum by S

and by $\bar{X}$ their mean: $\bar{X} = S/n = (X_1 + X_2 + \cdots + X_n)/n$. Also denote $E(\bar{X})$ by μ, and then

$$\text{Prob}[\bar{X} - \mu \geq t] = \text{Prob}[S - E(S) \geq nt] \leq E \ e^{h(S-E(S)-nt)}$$

$$= e^{-hnt} \prod_{i=1}^{n} E \ e^{h[X_i - E(X_i)]}. \qquad (10)$$

This is all simple enough. Obtaining useful inequalities consists in obtaining a tight bound on the ultimate right-hand side in (10), and finding an h that minimizes it. We now state and prove

Theorem 6: If $X_1, X_2, \cdots, X_n$ are independent, $\mu = E(\bar{X})$, and they all satisfy $0 \leq X_i \leq 1$, then for $0 < t < 1 - \mu$

$$\text{Prob}[\bar{X} - \mu \geq t] \leq \left[\left(\frac{\mu}{\mu + t} \right)^{\mu+t} \left(\frac{1-\mu}{1-\mu-t} \right)^{1-\mu-t} \right]^n \qquad (11)$$

$$\leq \exp[-nt^2 g(\mu)] \qquad (12)$$

$$\leq \exp[-2nt^2], \qquad (13)$$

where

$$g(\mu) \equiv \begin{cases} \dfrac{1}{1-2\mu} \log\left(\dfrac{1-\mu}{\mu} \right), & 0 < \mu < \dfrac{1}{2} \\[2mm] \dfrac{1}{2\mu(1-\mu)}, & \dfrac{1}{2} \leq \mu < 1. \end{cases} \qquad g(\mu) \geq 2, \ \forall \mu \qquad (14)$$

Note that the X_i need not be identically distributed. If the bounds on X_i are not 0 and 1, but rather $a \leq X_i \leq b$, then the theorem holds with μ and t replaced by $(\mu - a)/(b - a)$ and $t/(b - a)$, respectively. When the X_i have non-uniform bounds, then one may use global bounds of course, but the bound (13) can be adapted to this eventuality:

Theorem 7: If $X_1, \cdots, X_n$ are independent, and $a_i \leq X_i \leq b_i$, then for $t > 0$

$$\text{Prob}[\bar{X} - \mu > t] \leq \exp[-2n^2 t^2 / \Sigma_{i=1}^{n}(b_i - a_i)^2]. \qquad (15)$$

Proofs: The proofs follow Hoeffding (1963) and rely on the convexity of the exponential function. This property implies that for $u \leq x \leq v$ and real h

$$e^{hx} \leq \frac{v-x}{v-u} e^{hu} + \frac{x-u}{v-u} e^{hv}, \qquad u \leq x \leq v. \qquad (16)$$

Similarly, for a random variable X, bounded by u and v, we get the corresponding inequality, upon taking the expectation of both sides of relation (16)

$$E\left(e^{hX}\right) \leq \frac{v-E(X)}{v-u} e^{hu} + \frac{E(X)-u}{v-u} e^{hv}. \qquad (17)$$

Note that h need not be positive here. Apply now this bound to equation (10). Let $\mu_i = E(X_i)$, so that $\mu = \Sigma \mu_i / n$, and then the relation (17) with $u = 0$, $v = 1$ provides

$$\prod_{i=1}^{n} E\,[\exp(hX_i)] \leq \prod_{i=1}^{n} (1 - \mu_i + \mu_i e^h). \qquad (18)$$

The right-hand side of relation (18) in turn can be bounded from above by the known inequality between geometric and arithmetic means (relation C.11)

$$\left[\prod_{i=1}^{n} (1 - \mu_i + \mu_i e^h) \right]^{1/n} \leq \frac{1}{n} \sum_{i=1}^{n} (1 - \mu_i + \mu_i e^h) = 1 - \mu + \mu e^h. \qquad (19)$$

Returning to equation (10), we have shown so far

$$\mathrm{Prob}[\overline{X} - \mu \geq nt\,] \leq e^{-hnt} \prod_{i=1}^{n} E\, \exp[h\,(X_i - \mu_i)]$$

$$= e^{-hnt} \prod_{i=1}^{n} E\,[\exp(hX_i)] \prod_{i=1}^{n} \exp[-h\,\mu_i]$$

$$= e^{-hnt - hn\mu} \prod_{i=1}^{n} E\,[\exp(hX_i)] \qquad (20)$$

$$\leq [e^{-ht - h\mu}(1 - \mu + \mu e^h)]^n.$$

It remains to find the $h = h_o$ that minimizes the last bound in (20), and differentiation provides the suggestion

$$h_o = \log \frac{(1 - \mu)(\mu + t)}{(1 - \mu - t)\mu}. \qquad (21)$$

The interest is when t is in $0 < t < 1 - \mu$, and for this range h_o is positive, so the above chain of bounds holds for it. Inserting $h = h_o$ into the last bound in (20) we establish inequality (11). (See Exercise 7, where the above suggestion is converted to a certainty.)

To show inequality (12) one simply writes the right-hand side of (11) as $\exp[-nt^2 h\,(t,\mu)]$, which results in

$$h(t,\mu) = \frac{\mu + t}{t^2} \log \frac{\mu + t}{\mu} + \frac{1 - \mu - t}{t^2} \log \frac{1 - \mu - t}{1 - \mu}. \qquad (22)$$

It turns out, when we minimize $h(t,\mu)$, for a fixed μ, with respect to t in the range $0 < t < 1 - \mu$, that $h(t^*, \mu) = g(\mu)$ of equation (14) is precisely that minimum. The proof is detailed in Exercise 8. Hence the bound (12) holds for all t there. The bound (13), finally, is an immediate result from Exercise 6(a).

To prove Theorem 7 we proceed in a similar way, except that the heterogeneity of the bounds on X_i brings on a heavier notation. Using equation (17), for X_i, with $u = a_i$, $v = b_i$, we find:

$$E[e^{hX_i} \cdot e^{-h\mu_i}] \le e^{-h\mu_i} \left[\frac{b_i - \mu_i}{b_i - a_i} e^{ha_i} + \frac{\mu_i - a_i}{b_i - a_i} e^{hb_i} \right] = \exp L(h_i), \qquad (23)$$

where

$$h_i = h(b_i - a_i), \quad p_i = \frac{\mu_i - a_i}{b_i - a_i}, \qquad L(h_i) = -h_i p_i + \log(1 - p_i + p_i e^{h_i}). \quad (24)$$

Some algebra provides $L(h_i) \le h^2 (b_i - a_i)^2/8$ (see Exercise 9), hence

$$E[\exp h(X_i - \mu_i)] \le \exp[h^2(b_i - a_i)^2/8]. \qquad (25)$$

Substituting relation (25) into (10) we find

$$\text{Prob}[\overline{X} - \mu \ge t] \le \exp[-hnt + \frac{h^2}{8} \sum_{i=1}^{n} (b_i - a_i)^2]. \qquad (26)$$

It remains to minimize this bound, by choosing the best h, and the value $h_o = 4nt / \Sigma (b_i - a_i)^2$ is trivially shown to be this optimum. Using it in (26) provides the required relation (15). $\square$

The bounds (11) and (12) are reproduced in Appendix C. Relation (13) is used in Section 5.2.1.

The above reference, Hoeffding (1963), also contains a few results where the X_i themselves, as they appear in Theorems 6 and 7 above, are not independent, but result from simple operations over independent variables.

2.6.3 Wald's Identity (Geihs and Kobayashi, 1982)

The identity proved below appears to have been rediscovered several times (including by Turing during WW II), but became widely known when it served for the key results in Abraham Wald's *Sequential Analysis* (J. Wiley, 1947). Its original and most common formulation is for continuous random variables. We bring a version adapted to discrete ones, a version which is likelier to be of use in our analyses, when we consider an algorithm diachronically. An application of the identity in a similar spirit (with continuous rv's), for random walks, is given in Cox and Miller, 1965 Section 2.3(v, vi). The derivation below is based on Geihs and Kobayashi.

Let $X_1, X_2, \cdots$ be i.i.d. integer-valued random variables and let $\{S_k, k \ge 1\}$ denote their partial sums. Define the stopping time J with respect to an interval $[a,b]$ as the first "time" the sum of the X_i falls outside this interval:

$$J = \min\{k : S_k \notin [a,b]\}. \qquad (27)$$

Hence J depends on $X_1, X_2, \cdots, X_J$, and is independent of X_{J+1}, X_{J+2}, etc.

Theorem 8: (Wald's identity). Let X_i, S_k and J be defined as above, and assume the distribution of X satisfies the following conditions:

i) $E(X_i) < \infty, \quad 0 < V(X_i) < \infty,$

ii) $\text{Prob}(X_i > 0) > 0, \quad \text{Prob}(X_i < 0) > 0,$

iii) The (common) pgf of the X_i, $g_X(\cdot)$ exists in a circle of radius $r > 1$.

Then, for such z that $g(z) \geq 1$

$$E\left[z^{S_J} g^{-J}(z)\right] = 1, \qquad \text{(Wald's identity.)} \qquad (28)$$

Remarks: 1) The last condition, on $g_X(\cdot)$ (which we denote below simply by g), is for technical reasons that will become evident.

2) Note that for any *fixed* k, $E(z^{S_k}) = g^k(z)$, so that equation (28) would hold for it at any z. Since J depends on S_J the identity is not trivial.

Proof: Let i be a positive integer constant. Define

$$p_i \equiv \text{Prob}(J \leq i),$$

$$E_i(U) \equiv E(U \mid J \leq i), \qquad \text{for any random variable } U \qquad (29)$$

$$\bar{E}_i(U) \equiv E(U \mid J > i).$$

We always have, for any fixed i,

$$g^i(z) = E(z^{S_i}) = E(z^{S_J + (S_i - S_J)}) \qquad\qquad\qquad (30)$$
$$= p_i E_i(z^{S_J + (S_i - S_J)}) + (1-p_i)\bar{E}_i(z^{S_i}).$$

Given that $J \leq i$, the difference $S_i - S_J$ is independent of S_J, so the conditional pgf of $S_J + (S_i - S_J)$, conditioned on this event can be split:

$$E_i\left[z^{S_J + (S_i - S_J)}\right] = E_i\left[z^{S_J} \cdot z^{S_i - S_J}\right] = E_i\left[z^{S_J} g^{i-J}(z)\right]. \qquad (31)$$

Divide equation (30) throughout by $g^i(z)$ to obtain

$$p_i E_i\left[z^{S_J} g^{-J}(z)\right] + (1 - p_i)\frac{\bar{E}_i(z^{S_i})}{g^i(z)} = 1. \qquad (32)$$

Now let i be increased. $1-p_i$ is bounded, (and under condition *(ii)* goes necessarily to zero). When $g(z) \geq 1$, as required in the theorem, $z \geq 1$. We show that the numerator in equation (32) is then bounded as well: $J > i$ implies $a \leq S_i \leq b$, and thus $z^a \leq z^{S_i} \leq z^b$, for $z \geq 1$, and hence

$$\lim_{i \to \infty} (1 - p_i)\frac{\bar{E}_i(z^{S_i})}{g^i(z)} = 0. \qquad (33)$$

Thus finally, using again $p_i \to 1$ as $i \to \infty$, $E_i(U) \to E(U)$ and equation (32) reduces in the limit to (28).   □

Note that we ordered in the proof functions of z; so the proof as given holds only for real z. It turns out that this is what is needed, when applying the identity, as in Exercise 11.

Exercises and Complements

1. For the Markov chain model of Section 2.6.1, show that d_i, defined as the expected time till absorption since the algorithm is in state v_i, satisfy the system of equations

$$d_i = 1 + \sum_{j=1}^{n-1} P_{ij} d_j, \qquad 1 \le i < n. \tag{*}$$

Show that equation (3) implies $d_i = \sum_{k \ge 1} (\pi^k e)_i$, where e is a vector with all its components 1, and that this is a solution of the system of equations (*).

2. Write a transition matrix to represent the Turing machine addition algorithm analyzed in Section 1.2 as a random algorithm (using the Markov chain model). Why is it impossible to stay with the four s_i states of Fig. 1.2? How general is your answer? Rederive the expression for the average number of moves required. Use the result of Exercise 3(b) below to compute the variance of T_n.
[$\text{Var}(T_n) = 8 - (16n + 15)2^{-n} - 4^{-(n-1)} = 8 + O(n2^{-n})$.]

3. Let (G, P) be a simple random algorithm with the fundamental matrix π, and let R_{ij} be the (random) number of times node v_j is visited in a path from node v_i till absorption in the final state v_n.
(a) Compute the probability $\text{Prob}(R_{ij} = k)$. (Use Theorem 5.)
[$\text{Prob}(R_{ij} = k) = r_{ij}(r_{jj} - 1)^{k-1} r_{jj}^{-k}$, $k \ge 1$, and $\text{Prob}(R_{ij} = 0) = 1 - r_{ij}/r_{jj}$.]
(b) The mean of R_{ij} was computed in Theorem 4. Use the above result to show that the variance of this random variable is given by

$$A_{ij}(2A_{jj} - 1) - A_{ij}^2, \qquad \text{where } A = (I - \pi)^{-1}.$$

4. For the matrix given in Fig. 2.3, write down: $\hat{P}$, $I - P - \hat{P}$, $(I - P + \hat{P})^{-1}$, π, $r_{ij} = (I - \pi)^{-1}$, $\text{Var}(R_{ij})$ and d_i, defined in Exercise 1 above.

5. (Hofri, 1987) In a certain radio communications network comprising of n transmitters, a feedback-less broadcast protocol is used. The time axis is evenly split into slots; the transmitters are all synchronized with respect to the slot boundaries. r slots make up one *phase*, and s phases comprise a *step*. Suitable values for r and s will become apparent below. We only consider a single step, in which one particular node is to be reached by (i.e., receive a message from) an unknown number of its neighbors (those nodes it can hear), who have already received the message. This number is known to be bounded by m, the maximum indegree in the connectivity graph of the network, when viewed as a *directed* graph. At the first slot of a phase all m transmitters are *active*. The following action is repeated by each active transmitter, up to r times:

Transmit the message and flip a coin; with probability p remain active, and with probability $q = 1 - p$ cease activity for this phase.

If at any slot only a *single* source transmits, the phase succeeds (but the transmitters are not aware of this happy eventuality).

(a) Formulate a model of a single phase of the protocol as a Markov chain, the states being the number of active transmitters, initially m.

(b) Compute the probability f_i that a phase succeeds at slot i: that is, the chain enters state "1" for the first time, at that slot. Compute also F_r, the probability that a phase of r slots succeeds.

[Answers: for $m = 1$, $f_1 = 1$; for $m > 1$, $f_i = mp^i\left((1 - p^i)^{m-1} - (1 - p^{i-1})^{m-1}\right)$.

$F_r = m\left(q\sum_{j=1}^{r}p^j (1 - p^j)^{m-1} + p^{r+1}(1 - p^r)^{m-1}\right)$.]

(c) Use the method developed in Exercise 2.1-12 to estimate F_r for m large enough (say, in excess of 30); show that a reasonable choice for r is a small product of $\log m/\log p$. Develop also a recursion for the probability of the number of active transmitters reaching the state "1" at *any* number of steps, without the limit r. Show that these probabilities are equal to F_r, for values of r as suggested above, up to a difference which is approximately m^{-1}, at most.

[The main term of F_r is $-(1+1/(m-1))q/\log p$. Additional terms are $mp^r(1 - p^r)^{m-1}$ and $-q\sum_{i \geq r}mp^i(1 - p^i)^{m-1}$, which for r in excess of $2\log m/\log p$ are smaller than m^{-1}. The recursion for $d_m \equiv$ Prob (the number of active transmitters passes at some stage through 1) - on its way to the absorbing state "0", is given by $d_m = \sum_{i=1}^{m}\binom{m}{i}p^i q^{m-i}d_i$. The same method used in Exercise 2.2-5 produces, through the Poisson gf for the d_i the result $d_m = \sum_{i=1}^{m}\binom{m}{i}qi(-1)^{i-1}/(1 - p^i)$ $= mq\sum_{j\geq 0}p^j(1 - p^j)^{m-1}$, which for large m equals the above "main term".]

(d) The purpose of the algorithm is for a step to succeed with probability π, where π is typically chosen *very* close to 1. If $\pi > F_r$, the algorithm performs s phases to improve its chances. Use the estimate obtained in (c) to compute the required value for s.

[s should be $\lceil \log(1 - \pi)/\log(1 - F_r) \rceil$.]

(e) The duration of the protocol step is rs. Using the asymptotics above, compute a value of p, for given values of m and π that will minimize the duration. Explain, algorithmically, why one should expect a local optimal value to exist.

[Considering only the main contribution in F_r, rs is minimized for $p* \approx 0.0696350$, (independently of m and π!), this being the solution of the equation

$$\frac{1}{p}\log\left(1 + \frac{q}{\log p}\right) - \frac{\log p + q/p}{q + \log p} = 0.$$

For $p = \frac{1}{2}$, the resulting value for rs is nearly 30% higher.]

(f) Use the results of (b) and (d) above to show directly that when m is known, the best values to choose are $p = 1/m$ and $r = 1$, even for large m. How does this reconcile with the result of (e)? If we are provided not only with an upper bound but also with a lower bound on the indegree d of each node, $m_0 \leq d \leq m_1$, what is the best value of p?

6. (a) Show that $g(\mu)$, as defined in equation (14), satisfies $g(\mu) \geq 2$, for $0 < \mu < 1$.

(b) Show that as $t \to 1 - \mu$, the right-hand side of equation (11) goes to μ^n. For this value of t, find X_i such that the *equality* in relation (11) is realized.

7. (a) Show that h_o as defined in equation (21) is a local minimum (with respect to h) of the right-hand side of equation (20).

[Replace in the last line of equation (20) e^{-h} (which is a monotonic function in h) by z, and differentiate the right-hand side there twice with respect to z.]

(b) Show that h_o is a global minimum as well.

[Prove monotonicity on both sides of h_o.]

8. Show that $g(\mu) \leq h(t,\mu)$, when these functions are defined in equations (14) and (22), respectively.

[This can be shown by brute force but is quite tedious then. The proof offered by Hoeffding is more elegant: we shall consider the sign of $\partial h(t,\mu)/\partial t$. Differentiating in (22) we get $t^2 \partial h(t,\mu)/\partial t = H(t/(1-\mu)) - H(t/(\mu+t))$, where $H(x)$ is defined as $(1 - 2/x)\log(1-x)$. We only need $H(x)$ for $0 < x < 1$, and in this range $H(x)$ is monotonic increasing, since it is the product of two such functions of the same sign. Hence $\partial h(t,\mu)/\partial t$ is negative when $t < 1 - 2\mu$, and positive when $t > 1 - 2\mu$, as determined by the order of the two arguments of $H(\cdot)$ in the derivative. Thus when $1 - 2\mu < 0$ we have to take the value of $G(t,\mu)$ at $t = 0$, and when $1 - 2\mu > 0$ the value $t = 1 - 2\mu$ provides the minimum. This is the result in equation (14).]

9. Using the definitions given in equation (24), show $L(h_i) \leq h^2(b_i - a_i)^2/8$.

[For small positive h, expand the Taylor series of $L(h_i)$ around 0, and show $L(0) = L'(0) = 0$, $L''(0) \leq 1/4$. For large h show this directly from the definition, by approximating the logarithm.]

10. With the definitions of Theorem 6, let X_i be i.i.d. Show that if $L(s)$ is the LST of X_1 then $P[\overline{X} - \mu \geq nt] \leq \left(\exp[-h(\mu+t)]L(-h)\right)^n$, where h is the solution of the equation $L'(h)/L(h) = -(\mu + t)$.

11. (Geihs and Kobayashi, 1982). This reference shows a way to compute a bound for the probability of an input stream overflowing (or exceeding a stated level of) a reservoir (such as a computer buffer, a dammed lake ...). The time axis is slotted; at slot k the input is A_k, and an amount B_k is drawn from the reservoir. Define $C_k = A_k - B_k$, with the pgf $H(z) = E(z^{C_k})$. Let its capacity be L, then its contents at the end on slot k, S_k, satisfies

$$S_k = \begin{cases} 0 & S_k - 1 + C_k \leq 0, \\ S_{k-1} + C_k & 0 \leq S_{k-1} + C_k \leq L, \\ L & S_{k-1} + C_k \geq L. \end{cases}$$

You have to consider only the case of infinite capacity. The above reference also shows a way to proceed with when L is finite. Define

$$\bar{F}_\infty(n) = \lim_{k \to \infty} \text{Prob}[S_k > n \mid L = \infty].$$

It is given that $\text{Prob}(C_k > 0) > 0$ (otherwise S_k would always be zero), and $E(C) < 0$.

(a) Show that the equation $H(z) = 1$ has a unique root, ζ, of modulus larger than 1. [Use the Markov inequality (C.1), with X there replaced by z^C to show $z \, \text{Prob}(z^C \geq z) \leq H(z)$; $z > 0$, pick then $z \geq 1$, so that $\text{Prob}(z^C \geq z) = \text{Prob}(C \geq 1)$. Show from this that $H(z) \xrightarrow[z \to \infty]{} \infty$. From the existence of negative values for C deduce $H(0) = \infty$. This limit, the facts that all the coefficients of $H(z)$ are non-negative and $H''(z) > 0$ for all real $z > 0$ (why?), establish the existence of a unique minimum for $H(z)$ over $(0, \infty)$. This conclusion and $H'(1) = E(C)$ result in the minimum being larger than 1, and Weierstrass theorem implies the existence of $\zeta > 1$, as claimed.]

(b) Using Wald's identity, show that $A \zeta^{-n} \leq \bar{F}_\infty(n) \leq B \zeta^{-n}$, where

$$A = \inf_{m \geq 0} 1/E[\zeta^{C-m} \mid C > m],$$

$$B = \sup_{m \geq 0} 1/E[\zeta^{C-m} \mid C > m].$$

[Use Wald's identity with respect to the interval $(-\infty, m]$, at $z = \zeta$, and the fact that for $S_J > n$ to hold, there needs to be an integer m so that $S_J - n = C_J - m$.]

Chapter 3

Algorithms over Permutations

However often the Red Hen
Inspected and ordered her brood,
Chicken Little was found straggling at the end.

In this chapter we concentrate on a simple data structure: a linear array, containing numbers. The basic properties of this structure are its length and the order of the numbers in it. The numbers are considered unrelated, although most of the discussion will assume they are all distinct. Since the actual values of the numbers are immaterial, we may assume - and shall do so through most this chapter, excepting Section 3.3.3 - that they are integers. When an array of size n is considered, the numbers in it are assumed to be 1 through n. Such an array is a "linear representation of a permutation". Simple as it all appears, and even Chicken Little would agree with that, this structure shall furnish us with opportunities for interesting mathematics. We start meekly enough with MAX.

3.1: MAX - Locating the Largest Term in a Permutation

This is the second algorithm we analyze, after the one embedded in the Turing machine of Section 1.2. This algorithm, however, will be assumed to operate in a digital computer of common design.

Algorithm MAX

Input: n, a positive integer; $A_1, \cdots, A_n$ - n distinct numbers.
Output: $\max_{1 \le i \le n} A_i$

The algorithm we propose - and analyze - to locate the maximum of a sequence of numbers is quite simple: we scan the sequence once, retaining the largest number found so far.

Fig. 3.1 lists a proposed realization of the algorithm, in an anonymous programming language.

The numbers in parentheses, on the left, record the number of times each instruction is executed. The ability to make a statement about these numbers determines the level of detail of the operations used in our "programming language". M_n is the number of times the branch in line 7 is taken after the comparison in 6. Clearly Fig. 3.1 indicates that the running time of MAX is of the form $T_n = \alpha + n\beta + \gamma M_n$.

The values α, β, γ depend on the equipment, but neither on the input size nor on the particular permutation encountered. See Exercise 3.

With accumulated experience one can often satisfactorily break down an algorithm specified in a higher level (procedural) language into the parts that display different dependencies on the size parameters, as n here.

Thus it is only M_n that we should know better in order to completely characterize T_n. This M_n is the number of maxima encountered when the permutation is traversed "from left to right" and is accordingly called the number of left-to-right maxima. In our interpretation of this term we do not count the first term as a maximum. Some authors do. In the future, when we need to include the first term as well, we shall simply say it equals M_n+1. This random variable is popular among statisticians (who call it the maximum ladder value index) as a basis for tests of randomness. Obviously, the extreme values of M_n are 0, when $A_1 = n$ and $n-1$ when $A_k = k$.

In order to make probabilistic statements about M_n we must postulate a measure over the input space. We take the uniform approach: n is a parameter, and all $n!$ permutations are equally likely to serve as input (see Exercise 5 for other possibilities).

Define C_{ni} as the number of permutations of n elements for which the value of M_n is i. Then the above probability assignment implies

(1)	1. Read n
(1)	2. $1 \to k$
(M_n+1)	3. $A_k \to m$
(n)	4. $k+1 \to k$
(n)	5. if $k > n \Rightarrow 8$
(n)	6. if $m > A_k \Rightarrow 4$
(M_n)	7. else $\Rightarrow 3$
(1)	8. output m.

Figure 3.1: The algorithm MAX.

$$p_{ni} \equiv \text{Prob}(M_n = i) = \frac{C_{ni}}{n!} . \tag{1}$$

To estimate C_{ni} observe that a permutation with $A_n = n$ provides an M_n which is higher by one than the number of left-to-right maxima generated by A_1 through A_{n-1}. If $A_n \neq n$, it will not produce a branch to line 3 when it is examined in statement 6 when $k = n$. The number of permutations with $A_n = n$ is $(n-1)!$, and there are $n! - (n-1)! = (n-1)(n-1)!$ of the others; hence, conditioning on the event $\{A_n = n\}$ we have

$$C_{ni} = (n-1)! p_{n-1,i-1} + (n-1)(n-1)! p_{n-1,i} , \qquad n \geq 2, \quad i \geq 1. \tag{2}$$

The appearance of the components $p_{n-1,j}$ $j = i, i-1$, in equation (2), uses the fact that when the permutations are uniformly distributed, so are portions thereof (see Exercise 1).

Dividing equation (2) by $n!$ we get an equation involving the probabilities only,

$$p_{ni} = \frac{1}{n} p_{n-1,i-1} + \frac{n-1}{n} p_{n-1,i} , \qquad n \geq 2, \quad i \geq 1. \tag{3}$$

This needs to be supplemented by boundary (or initial) values:

$$p_{1i} = \delta_{i0}, \qquad p_{n0} = 1/n , \tag{4}$$

where the statement $p_{n0} = 1/n$ reflects the probability of having $A_1 = n$.

Define the pgf $G_n(z) \equiv \sum_{i \geq 0} p_{ni} z^i$, which is a polynomial in z of degree $n-1$. Multiplying (3) by z^i and summing for $i \geq 1$ produces

$$G_n(z) - \frac{1}{n} = \frac{z}{n} G_{n-1}(z) + \frac{n-1}{n} \left(G_{n-1}(z) - \frac{1}{n-1} \right), \tag{5}$$

or

$$G_n(z) = \frac{z+n-1}{n} G_{n-1}(z). \tag{6}$$

Reeling off the recursion (6) we find, using $G_1(z) = 1$ from equation (4), that

$$G_n(z) = \frac{1}{z+n} \binom{z+n}{n} = \frac{1}{z} \binom{z+n-1}{n}, \tag{7}$$

which is "essentially" a binomial coefficient.

Explicit Form for p_{ni}: Stirling Numbers

Equation (7) is compact enough a representation to be adequate for most uses - except if we want to extract from it the values of p_{ni}. There are, however, combinatorial artefacts - the Stirling numbers of the first kind, that will do for this purpose. They are defined to satisfy

$$n!\binom{x}{n} = \sum_{k=0}^{n} (-1)^{n-k} \left[\begin{matrix}n\\k\end{matrix}\right] x^k , \tag{8}$$

relating binomial coefficients to powers. Note that this equation may be regarded as defining the gf of $\left[\begin{matrix}n\\k\end{matrix}\right]$, which is then $(-1)^n n!\binom{-x}{n}$. The reverse relation is also a standard combinatorial construction, and is accomplished by the Stirling numbers of the second kind:

$$x^n = \sum_{k=0}^{n} k!\binom{x}{k} \left\langle\begin{matrix}n\\k\end{matrix}\right\rangle . \tag{9}$$

Equation (9) may be considered as a "factorial gf" for the $\left\langle\begin{matrix}n\\k\end{matrix}\right\rangle$, since $k!\binom{x}{k} = x(x-1)\cdots(x-k+1)$. More conventionally, an egf is available, when summing over the *upper* index. It is found with other identities satisfied by these numbers in Appendix B.

Equation (8) is precisely what we need. Using it, the second expression for $G_n(z)$ in equation (7) is seen to have the expansion (using the identity (A.1.2))

$$G_n(z) = \frac{1}{z}\binom{z+n-1}{n} = \frac{(-1)^n}{n!z} \cdot n!\binom{-z}{n} = \frac{1}{n!}\sum_{i=0}^{n} \left[\begin{matrix}n\\i\end{matrix}\right] z^{i-1}. \tag{10}$$

We have found

$$p_{n,i} = \frac{1}{n!}\left[\begin{matrix}n\\i+1\end{matrix}\right], \text{ and } C_{ni} = \left[\begin{matrix}n\\i+1\end{matrix}\right]. \tag{11}$$

This provides a combinatorial interpretation for the Stirling numbers of the first kind. (The numbers of the second kind also have an interpretation: $\left\langle\begin{matrix}n\\k\end{matrix}\right\rangle$ is the number of ways to partition n elements into k nonempty sets. See the related discussion in Section 2.4.1.)

Moments of M_n

Although we have an explicit expression for the probabilities of M_n, the moments are more easily obtained from the gf. This is often the case.

For the first moment, equal to $G_n'(1)$, we start from equation (6) to obtain

$$G_n'(z) = \frac{1}{n}G_{n-1}(z) + \frac{z+n-1}{n}G_{n-1}'(z),$$

and at $z=1$:

$$G_n'(1) = \frac{1}{n} + G_{n-1}'(1). \tag{12}$$

Unraveling equation (12) we have

$$G'_n(1) = \frac{1}{n} + \frac{1}{n-1} + \cdots + \frac{1}{2} + (G'_1(1) = 0),$$

leading to

$$E(M_n) = G'_n(1) = H_n - 1. \tag{13}$$

For large n, the harmonic number H_n is asymptotically $\log n + \gamma + O(n^{-1})$ where γ is Euler's constant, equaling ≈ 0.57716.

For the variance we adopt another tack, viewing the right-hand side of equation (6) as the product of two pgf's. $G_{n-1}(z)$ is obvious, being the pgf of M_{n-1}. The factor $\dfrac{z+n-1}{n}$ is the pgf of the random variable X_n that we used for the randomization in equation (2). It has the two-atom distribution

$$\text{Prob}(X_n = i) = \begin{cases} \dfrac{n-1}{n} & i = 0, \\[2mm] \dfrac{1}{n} & i = 1. \end{cases}$$

Equation (6) then provides $M_n = X_n + M_{n-1}$, with these two being independent (since the pgf of the sum is the product of the pgf's of the components). When such is the case, $V(M_n) = V(X_n) + V(M_{n-1})$. $V(X_n)$ is clearly

$$E(X_n^2) - E^2(X_n) = \frac{1}{n} - \frac{1}{n^2} = \frac{n-1}{n^2}.$$

Again unraveling,

$$V(M_n) = \frac{1}{n} - \frac{1}{n^2} + V(M_{n-1}) = H_n - 1 - (H_n^{(2)} - 1), \tag{14}$$

where $H_n^{(2)} = \sum_{k=1}^{n} \frac{1}{k^2} \xrightarrow[n\to\infty]{} \zeta(2) = \frac{\pi^2}{6}$.

Thus $V(M_n)$ is asymptotically equal to $\log n$ as well.

The latter statement implies that M_n is not well localized near its expected value: one has to consider extremely large values of n before the mean becomes significantly larger than σ_n, the standard deviation of M_n, which is nearly $\sqrt{\log n}$. Thus, to have $E(M_n) > 5\sigma_n$ we need $\log n > 5\sqrt{\log n}$ or $n > e^{25} \approx 7.2 \cdot 10^{10}$.

Chebyshev's Inequality

A rough and ready bound on the probabilities of large deviations of random variables is available from the Chebyshev-Bienaymé inequality (equation (C.2), commonly called simply Chebyshev's inequality):

$$\text{Prob}(|X| > t) \le \frac{E(X^2)}{t^2}. \tag{15}$$

If we "centralize" X, and consider the variable $X - E(X)$, we find

$$\text{Prob}(|X - E(X)| > t) \le \frac{V(X)}{t^2}. \tag{16}$$

Let us use inequality (15) to estimate the probability that M_n exceeds twice its mean:

$$\text{Prob}(M_n > 2(H_n - 1)) \le \frac{H_n - H_n^{(2)} + H_n^2}{[2(H_n - 1)]^2} \approx \frac{\log^2 n}{4\log^2 n} = \frac{1}{4}. \tag{17}$$

The roughness of this bound is evident even for moderate values of n. Consider $n = 8$ and $0 \le k \le 7$:

$$\text{Prob}(M_8 = k) = \frac{\left[^8_{k+1}\right]}{8!} = \frac{1}{8!}(5040, 13068, 13132, 6769, 1960, 322, 28, 1),$$

with $E(M_8) = H_8 - 1 \approx 1.71$, and

$$\text{Prob}(M_8 > 3.42) = \text{Prob}(M_8 \ge 4) = \frac{1960 + 322 + 28 + 1}{8!} \approx 0.0573.$$

For higher n inequality (17) will provide even poorer bounds. The one-sided Chebyshev's inequality (C.3) is better here, but still very rough (Exercise 2(b)).

Exercises and Complements

1. Show that a uniform distribution of permutations of a given set of n distinct elements implies the uniformity of each sub-permutation (e.g., elements A_i to A_{i+j-1} will contain all $j!\binom{n}{j}$ possible arrangements of j out of the n elements with equal probability). Can a similar statement be made when the original distribution is nonuniform?

2. (a) Use inequality (16) to bound $\text{Prob}(|M_{10} - E(M_{10})| \ge 2\sigma_{10}$ and compare this with the exact value.
(b) Use the one-sided Chebyshev-Cantelli inequality (C.3) to estimate $\text{Prob}(M_8 > 2E(M_8))$, and compare this with the exact value.

3. If you have access to a computer system that provides a timing service for program segments, write a simulation program to execute MAX for a range of n values, and use the timing information to estimate α, β and γ of T_n.
[To have an efficient estimator for γ, use the obvious correlated random variable M_n. Information on the use of correlated random variables in simulation (also called control variables), for variance reduction, is available in most modern books on digital simulation. See e.g., (Fishman, 1978).]

4. Obtain the first two moments of M_n from the explicit representation of its distribution, given in equation (11). [Use identities (B.5.1) and (B.4.3).]

5. The algorithm MAX was analyzed under the assumption that the input consisted

of n distinct numbers, and all permutations of the input were equally likely. In this problem you have to consider other possibilities, and to repeat the relevant parts of the analysis for each.

(a) (Knuth) The n numbers contain precisely m different values, but are otherwise arbitrary.

(b) The n numbers are integers, selected *with replacement* from the set $\{1, 2, \cdots, N\}$. Hence they need not be all different (they could even be all equal!). Use the results of part (a). Specialize the result for $n = N$.

(c) The numbers are real and positive. The first number is uniformly distributed in $[0,1]$, and thereafter A_i has the exponential distribution with parameter A_{i-1}, $2 \leq i \leq n$.

6. Use the addition property of the Stirling numbers of the second kind, given in equation (B.2.2), to show their "explicit" representation, (B.5.5). Use the latter to obtain the gf given in (B.1.4).

7. The Stirling numbers of the second kind are closely related to the so called Eulerian numbers. (These numbers are not to be confused with Euler numbers; the latter are closely related to the Bernoulli numbers, which we considered in Section 2.1. See also Comtet (1974), Section I.14.)

In this problem you are led to investigate this relationship, and determine some of the properties of the Eulerian numbers. Their combinatorial significance is treated in Knuth (1973), Section 5.1.3.

The Eulerian numbers $A(n,k)$ satisfy the recurrence

$$A(n,k) = kA(n-1,k) + (n-k+1)A(n-1,k-1), \qquad n \geq k \geq 1$$
$$A(0,k) = \delta_{1,k}, \qquad A(n,0) = 0. \tag{18}$$

(a) Show directly from the recurrence the relations

$$A(n,k) = A(n,n-k+1), \quad n \geq 1, k \geq 0; \qquad A(n,k) = 0, \quad n < k.$$

Show by induction over n that the recurrence (18) implies

$$\sum_k A(n,k)\binom{m+k-1}{n} = m^n, \qquad n \geq 0, \ m \geq 1. \tag{19}$$

Knuth (1973) brings an interesting, though tricky combinatorial proof of equation (19), based on the identification of $A(n,k)$ with the number of permutations in $S(N_n)$ that have exactly k ascending runs. Note the similarity between equations (19) and (9).

Prove that equation (19) is an identity in m, and hence that it holds for nonintegral m as well.

(b) Show the relation

$$\sum_{k=1}^{n} A(n,k)\binom{k}{m} = \left\langle \begin{matrix} n+1 \\ n+1-m \end{matrix} \right\rangle (n-m)!, \qquad n \geq m. \tag{20}$$

[Use relation (18) and equation (B.2.2), with induction on n.]

(c) Define the gf $g_n(z) = \sum_k A(n,k)z^k$. Note that $g_0(z) = z$.
Use equation (20) to show that

$$g_n^{[r]}(z)|_{z=1} = n!\left\langle \begin{matrix} n+1 \\ n+1-r \end{matrix} \right\rangle / \binom{n}{r}, \tag{21}$$

and hence

$$g_n(z) = \sum_{r=0}^{n} \left\langle \begin{matrix} n+1 \\ r+1 \end{matrix} \right\rangle r!(z-1)^{n-r}, \qquad n \geq 1. \tag{22}$$

Use equation (21) to show

$$\sum_{k=1}^{n} kA(n,k) = \tfrac{1}{2}(n+1)! \tag{23}$$

Use equation (22) to show the left part of equation (B.5.8).

(d) Define $h(t,z) = \sum_{n \geq 0} g_n(z)\dfrac{t^n}{n!}$. Show through (B.1.4) that

$$h(t,z) = \frac{z(z-1)}{z - e^{t(z-1)}}. \tag{24}$$

(e) Obtain the following explicit representation for the Eulerian numbers, by directly extracting the coefficients from the gf obtained in (d):

$$A(n,k) = \sum_{j=0}^{k-1} (-1)^j \binom{n+1}{j}(k-j)^n. \tag{25}$$

8. The "factorial gf" of the Stirling numbers of the second kind provides a useful device in reducing finite sums. Thus, show the following sum

$$\sum_{k=0}^{m-1} \binom{m}{k} (-1)^k \sum_{j=0}^{m-k-1} (j+1)^m = \frac{1}{2}(m+1)!$$

by replacing $(j+1)^m$ with the appropriate right-hand side of equation (9), and using further the identity (A.3.6).

The following sums succumb to precisely the same treatment; we collect them here as they will be of use later, in Section 3.3:

$$\sum_{k=0}^{m-1} \binom{m}{k} (-1)^k \sum_{j=0}^{m-k-1} (j+1)^{m+1} = \frac{1}{24}(3m+1)(m+2)!$$

$$\sum_{k=0}^{m-1} \binom{m+1}{k} (-1)^k \sum_{j=0}^{m-k-1} (j+1)^{m+1} = \frac{1}{2}m(m+1)!$$

$$\sum_{k=0}^{m-1} \binom{m+1}{k} (-1)^k \sum_{j=0}^{m-k-1} (j+1)^{m+2} = \frac{1}{24}(3m+1)m(m+2)!$$

3.2 Representations of Permutations

The running time of the algorithm MAX was found in Section 3.1 to depend on M_n, the number of left-to-right maxima, or ladder values in the input permutation. This is but one example of a random variable, defined over a permutation, the likes of which we shall encounter in the sequel. This section is devoted to a brief examination of two such variables - cycles and inversions counts. A more detailed investigation is available in Kemp (1984, Chapter 3) and Comtet (1974, chapter VI).

3.2.1 Cycles in a Permutation

Permutations can be described in several ways. For a permutation of the set N_n, consisting of the integers 1 through n, a common description method is to define a mapping, represented pictorially as two rows, the upper one is the numbers in their natural order, the lower is the subject permutation, as in

$$\sigma = \begin{pmatrix} 1 & 2 & 3 & 4 & 5 & 6 & 7 \\ 7 & 4 & 5 & 3 & 2 & 6 & 1 \end{pmatrix}. \tag{1}$$

The entire set of permutations of the above set N_n is denoted by $S(N_n)$. A permutation $(i_1 \cdots i_n)$ is said to be generated by the mapping $\sigma \in S(N_n)$ when $i_j = \sigma(j)$. In the example (1) above, $7 = \sigma(1)$, $4 = \sigma(2)$, etc. The letter S in this notation is derived from the name given to these permutations when considered as a group. This is the "symmetric group" of n elements. (Its operation is successive application of the mappings σ.)

Picking an element of the permutation, j_1, we now form the sequence $j_k = \sigma(j_{k-1})$, which will repeat j_1 after p_1 terms. The sequence $j_1, \cdots, j_{p_1-1}$ is called the cycle generated by j_1. A number not in this sequence will likewise generate another, disjoint cycle. The entire set N_n can be thus exhausted. Example (1) gives rise to the cycles 7 1, 4 3 5 2 and 6, and it may then be represented as 7 1 | 4 3 5 2 | 6. This representation is not unique - since 6 | 1 7 | 3 5 2 4 represents the same permutation.

The *canonical* cycle representation is obtained when each cycle is rotated until led by its largest member, and the cycles ordered with these members in ascending sequence. Again for the permutation in (1): 5 2 4 3 | 6 | 7 1. Moreover, we can now drop the vertical bars with no fear of ambiguity: a left-to-right scan for maxima will locate all cycle beginnings, if we agree to call the first number the first maximum.

Put another way: the number of cycles in a permutation is larger by one than the number of ladder values in its canonical cycle representation. Since the correspondence between these representations and permutations is bijective, or one-to-one, we have obtained cheaply a proof for

Proposition 1:

$$\text{Prob}(\sigma \in S(N_n) \text{ has } k \text{ cycles}) = \text{Prob}(M_n + 1 = k) = \frac{1}{n!}\begin{bmatrix} n \\ k \end{bmatrix}. \qquad (2)$$

The average number of cycles in a permutation of N_n is then H_n, and its variance $H_n - H_n^{(2)}$. □

Length of a Cycle

Denote the length of a cycle in a permutation of N_n by L_n. The mean of L_n is readily obtained: a permutation has an average of H_n cycles; the entire set $S(N_n)$ then contains (exactly) $n!H_n$ cycles. Since the total length of all these is $n \cdot n!$, we must have an average of

$$E(L_n) = \frac{n \cdot n!}{n! H_n} = \frac{n}{H_n}. \qquad (3)$$

When n is large, so is the average cycle!

What is the distribution of L_n? This question allows two approaches that lead to different answers. Properly speaking the *questions* are different. It will serve as an illustration of an important consideration.

First, we consider the totality of $H_n n!$ cycles, ascribe to each the same probability and ask about the length distribution of a cycle thus picked at random. If there are a_{nl} cycles of length l, we shall define

$$p_{1,n}(l) \equiv \text{Prob (The length of a random cycle is } l) = \frac{a_{nl}}{H_n n!}. \qquad (4)$$

The number of distinct, ordered, l-long sequences out of n elements is $l!\binom{n}{l}$, which up to l cyclic rotations define different cycles of length l. Each appears in $S(N_n)$ in $(n-l)!$ distinct permutations, hence $a_{nl} = (l-1)!(n-l)!\binom{n}{l} = \frac{n!}{l}$, and

$$p_{1,n}(l) = \frac{n!}{lH_n n!} = \frac{1}{lH_n}. \qquad (5)$$

Next, we ask what is the probability that an element, picked randomly from a random member of $S(N_n)$ is in a cycle of length l. Now a cycle of length l is l times as likely to be chosen as a size one cycle. The number of elements in l-length cycles is la_{nl}, and since there are in all $n \cdot n!$ possible choices - all assumed above equi-probable - we get

$$p_{2,n}(l) \equiv \text{Prob (a random element is in a cycle of length } l)$$

$$= \frac{l\, a_{nl}}{n \cdot n!} = \frac{n!}{n \cdot n!} = \frac{1}{n}. \qquad (6)$$

It does not depend on l. We again observe the nonsurprising consequences of changing a point of view of what is a "random choice".

Exercise 3 below provides a number of additional results about cycle structure, as well as a tool, the cycle indicator, which is quite powerful in these investigations.

3.2.2 Inversions

Inversions are pairs of elements in a permutation that are out of their natural (or original) order. Thus, assuming as before that the natural order of N_n is $1, 2, \cdots, n$ we shall say that in $\sigma = (a_1, \cdots, a_n)$, if $i < j$ and $a_i > a_j$, the pair (a_i, a_j) is an inversion. Thus in (2 4 3 1) we find the inversions (2,1), (4,3), (4,1), (3,1).

Inversions are clearly of interest when one considers sorting algorithms, as it is precisely the inversions that these algorithms need to deal with.

Inversion Tables - This is a convenient format to record the structure of a permutation $\sigma \in S(N_n)$ in terms of the inversion counts of its elements. Specifically, the array $I_n = (i_1, \cdots, i_n)$ is the inversion table of such a permutation, when i_j is the number of elements, to the left of j in σ, that are larger than j. Thus for the permutation (7 4 5 3 2 6 1) introduced in Section 3.2.1 the inversion table is (6,4,3,1,1,1,0).

Proposition 2: Inversion tables and permutations determine each other uniquely.

One direction is implied by the definition above. For the other direction see Exercise 6. $\square$

Consider the values $i_j \in I_n$ may get. Clearly $i_n = 0$, i_{n-1} is 0 or 1, according to the position of $n-1$ relative to n, and only $n-j$ numbers can be to the left of j and exceed it:

Proposition 3: The elements of an inversion table satisfy

$$0 \le i_j \le n-j, \quad 1 \le j \le n. \tag{7}$$

They need to satisfy no other constraints, or as one often puts it: they assume their values independently. The elements of the corresponding permutation, a_j, are not independent: they must all be different (see Exercise 8). $\square$

This last property makes the inversion table a much easier to handle a structure than the permutation itself. Proposition 2 assures us, however, that we should get equivalent results.

Examples of applications:

1. The number of different permutations in $S(N_n)$ is obtained by multiplying the ranges of the terms in the inversion table, which are n to 1, yielding the familiar $n!$.

2. $M_n + 1$, the number of left-to-right maxima in a permutation, when the leftmost number is considered the first maximum, is precisely the number of elements in the table I_n that are 0. If all permutations are equally likely, i_j will be 0 with a probability that is $\dfrac{1}{n-j+1}$, since $n-j+1$ is the number of values it can assume. Thus, for example,

$$E(M_n+1) = \sum_{j=1}^{n} 1 \cdot \frac{1}{n-j+1} = \sum_{k=1}^{n} \frac{1}{k} = H_n \;.$$

in conformity with the result in equation (3.1-13) obtained at considerably more labor.

A final remark will be phrased as:

Proposition 4: Exchanging two neighboring elements in a permutation results in a change of the total number of inversions in the permutation by ± 1.

The claim results from the fact that only one term in the inversion table will be affected, and the change cannot be but 1 in absolute value. $\qquad \square$

The Number of Inversions in a Permutation

The variable we investigate here is $I_{n,\sigma}$, the number of inversions in a permutation $\sigma \in S(N_n)$. It is given by the sum of the terms of the corresponding inversion table, and ranges from 0 to $\binom{n}{2}$.

Let $I_n(k)$ be the number of members of $S(N_n)$ for which $I_{n,\sigma} = k$. Assuming all permutations equally likely we define the pgf of $I_{n,\sigma}$ as

$$G_n(z) \equiv \frac{1}{n!} \sum_{k \geq 0} I_n(k) z^k = \frac{1}{n!} \sum_{\sigma \in S(N_n)} z^{I_{n,\sigma}} \,. \tag{8}$$

To compute $G_n(z)$ note that when adding the element n to a permutation $\sigma \in S(N_{n-1})$ it can be placed in n different positions, increasing $I_{n-1,\sigma}$ by any value between 0 and $n-1$. The assumption that all permutations are equi-probable implies that all these increments are equally likely, hence

$$I_{n,\sigma} = I_{n-1,\sigma} + X_n \,, \tag{9}$$

where X_n is uniformly distributed over the integers 0 to $n-1$, and is independent of $I_{n-1,\sigma}$. The pgf of X_n is

$$g_{X_n}(z) = 1 + z + \cdots + z^{n-1} = \frac{1-z^n}{1-z} \,. \tag{10}$$

Thus, recursively

$$G_n(z) = G_{n-1}(z) \frac{1-z^n}{1-z}$$
$$= \frac{(1-z)(1-z^2)\cdots(1-z^n)}{(1-z)^n}. \tag{11}$$

The recursion can be used to show the following properties (Exercise 7):

$$I_n(k) = I_n(k-1) + I_{n-1}(k), \quad k < n \text{ only!} \tag{12}$$

$$\sum_{k=0}^{\binom{n}{2}} I_n(k) = n!, \qquad \sum_{k=0}^{\binom{n}{2}} (-1)^k I_n(k) = 0, \quad n > 1, \tag{13}$$

$$I_n(k) = I_n\left(\binom{n}{2} - k\right). \tag{14}$$

Note that the recurrence (12) holds for a limited range of k only.

There is no simple explicit representation for $I_n(k)$. The moments of $I_{n,\sigma}$ are easy to obtain through the representation in equation (9), which we rewrite as

$$I_{n,\sigma} = \sum_{j=1}^{n} X_j.$$

From (10) we get $E(X_j) = \frac{j-1}{2}$, $V(X_j) = \frac{j^2-1}{12}$, and since they are all independent

$$E(I_{n,\sigma}) = \frac{1}{2} \sum_{j=1}^{n} (j-1) = \frac{n(n-1)}{4} = \frac{1}{2}\binom{n}{2}. \tag{15}$$

$$V(I_{n,\sigma}) = \frac{1}{12} \sum_{j=1}^{n} (j^2-1) = \frac{(n-1)n(2n+5)}{72}. \tag{16}$$

Note that the value for $E(I_{n,\sigma})$ could be inferred from a symmetry argument: pair with each permutation $\{a_j\}$ the reverse one, $\{a_j'\}$, where $a_j' = a_{n-j+1}$. Clearly, if (a_i, a_j) is an inversion, (a_i', a_j') is not, and *vice versa*. Thus in both permutations we find a total of $\binom{n}{2}$ inversions, and all $n!$ permutations can thus be paired off.

Note also that the standard deviation of $I_{n,\sigma}$ is approximately $n^{3/2}/6$, which implies a substantial dispersion of $I_{n,\sigma}$ around its mean.

Exercises and Complements

1. Write a program that reads n, and a permutation of the first n integers, and constructs the permutation $\sigma \in S(N_n)$ for which the input serves as a canonical cycle representation. Show that its runing time has the same functional dependence on n as that of the algorithm MAX in Section 3.1.

2. Use equation (5) to rederive equation (3) and the standard deviation of L_n, under $p_{1,n}$.

3. (Kemp) Consider the number of permutations that have a specified cycle structure. We say a permutation $\sigma \in S(N_n)$ is of type $<c_1, c_2, \cdots, c_n>$ if it consists of c_i cycles of length i, $1 \le i \le n$.

(a) Show, by straightforward construction, that the total number of permutations of the above type is given by $n!/\prod_{i=1}^{n}(i^{c_i}c_i!)$.

(b) Define the *cycle indicator* of $S(N_n)$ as a polynomial in n variables

$$Z(S(N_n);t_1, \cdots, t_n) \equiv \frac{1}{n!} \sum_{\sigma \in S(N_n)} \prod_{i=1}^{n} t_i^{c_i(\sigma)}.$$

Write the cycle indicator of $S(N_3)$.

Express the result you derived in (a) in terms of the cycle indicator.

The rest of this problem can be done by direct enumeration as well, but is easier through the use of the gf of the cycle indicators,

$$f_{S(N)}(u;t_1,t_2,\cdots) \equiv \sum_{n \ge 0} u^n Z(S(N_n);t_1, \cdots, t_n).$$

Show that this gf equals $\exp\left(\sum_{i \ge 1} u^i t_i/i\right)$. [Suggestion: use the result in (a) above, represent u^n as $u^{\sum i c_i}$ and transform the sum over the $\{c_i\}$ from a sum over "equi-n" hyperplanes to a sum along the axes.]

(c) Show that the total number of cycles appearing in all permutations of $S(N_n)$ is given by $n! \times \frac{d}{dt} Z(S(N_n);t, \cdots, t)|_{t=1}$, and obtain the value shown above, $n!H_n$.

(d) Show that the number of cycles of length l appearing in all permutations of $S(N_n)$ is given by $n! \times \frac{d}{dt} Z(S(N_n);1,1,\cdots,t,1,\cdots,1)|_{t=1}$, when the t appears in the $l+1\,st$ position. This value was denoted by a_{nl}, and shown to be $n!/l$.

Hence, the the expected number of cycles of length l appearing in a permutation randomly picked, $\sigma \in S(N_n)$, is l^{-1}. Show that this is also the variance of that random variable.

(e) Show that the number of all permutations in $S(N_n)$ which consist of exactly k cycles is given by $[t^k] n! \times Z(S(N_n);t,t,\cdots,t)$.

(f) Show that the number of all permutations in $S(N_n)$ which contain exactly k cycles of length l (with possibly more cycles, but of different length) is given by $[t^k] n! \times Z(S(N_n);1,1,\cdots,t,1,\cdots,1)$, when the t appears in the $l+1\,st$ position. Furthermore, show that this value is

$$\frac{n!}{l^k k!} \sum_{i=0}^{r} \frac{(-1)^i}{l^i i!}, \qquad \text{where } r = \left\lfloor \frac{n}{l} \right\rfloor - k.$$

4. A derangement is a permutation that leaves no element in its natural position. Denote the number of derangements in $S(N_n)$ by $d(n)$. Obtain the following

results for the derangement count:
(a) The generating function is $d(z) = 1/[e^t(1-t)]$.
(b) The numbers $d(n)$ satisfy the recurrences

$$d(n) = nd(n-1) + (-1)^n , \quad d(n+1) = n[d(n) + d(n-1)] .$$

Prove the recurrences both from the gf and from counting arguments.
(c) An explicit expression for $d(n)$ is easily obtainable either from the recurrences or the gf above: $d(n) = n! \Sigma_{k=0}^{n} (-1)^k / k!$

5. An involution is a member $\sigma \in S(N_n)$ such that applying the mapping twice yields the identity mapping.
(a) Show that an involution can consist of no cycle longer than 2.
(b) Let $i(n)$ the the number of such members in $S(N_n)$. Prove

$$\sum_{n \geq 0} i(n) \frac{z^n}{n!} = e^{z + z^2/2} .$$

(c) Obtain the explicit representation

$$i(n) = n! \sum_{k=0}^{\lfloor n/2 \rfloor} \frac{2^{-k}}{k!(n-2k)!} .$$

(d) Using the methods of Section 2.1.2, obtain an asymptotic estimate for $i(n)$.

6. (a) Design a simple algorithm that accepts as input an inversion table and outputs the corresponding permutation.
(b) The average running time of a straightforward algorithm for this purpose is $O(n^2)$. Can you do better?
(c) The algorithm you designed in (a) probably requires $O(n)$ locations to construct the permutation. What would be the running time of an algorithm that does not use storage beyond the given inversion table and $O(1)$ locations for auxiliary variables (and outputs the permutation one term at a time)?

7. (a) Show from equation (11) that $G_n(z) = z^{\binom{n}{2}} G_n(z^{-1})$. This is the simplest route to showing equation (14).
(b) Use the recurrence in equation (11) to prove the properties listed in equations (12) to (14).

8. If all $\sigma \in S(N_n)$ are equally likely, prove that the terms in the corresponding inversion table are independently and uniformly distributed. [Compute their joint pgf, by construction.]

9. Let (a_i, a_j) be an inversion in a permutation $\sigma \in S(N_n)$. Exchanging a_i and a_j, and obtaining σ', can we find $I_{n,\sigma} \leq I_{n,\sigma'}$?

3.3 Analysis of Sorting Algorithms

Sorting algorithms, as a class, are among the most useful and best investigated algorithms. Vol. III of Knuth's "The Art of Computer Programming" contains a wealth of material on the subject, and is the recommended reference for all aspects algorithmic. The discussion in our Sections 3.3.1 and 3.3.2 is based on Section 5.2.1 there, which also reports on extensive experimentation with the Shell sort algorithm described below. Later references are Gonnet (1984) and part 3 of Mehlhorn (1984). Our presentation is limited to the principal stages of the analysis of a few sorting algorithms; these stages are the identification of the random variables that determine the performance characteristics of the algorithms, and presentation of the crucial computational steps.

In all our discussions of sorting algorithms we visualize the desired result as being in increasing order from left to right, as are the indices in a linear array.

3.3.1 Insertion Sort

This is a straightforward sorting method: given a permutation $(a_1, \cdots, a_n)$, move left each element, starting with a_2 and ending with a_n, until it is in its proper position. After a_j has been thus placed, the leftmost j numbers are correctly sorted. If we move right an element with each such "unsuccessful" comparison, we obtain the algorithm as written in Fig. 3.2(a). Note that the operation can be thus done also when not all the elements are available initially, but are provided one at a time. The usual term for such algorithms is "on-line " algorithms. In Fig. 3.2(b) the procedure is given in a more detailed form, so that we can count each operation.

The letters in the leftmost column in Fig. 3.2(b) give the order in which the entries in the second column, the operation counts, were determined. The a entries are immediate. Line 9 can be reached in two ways, but it will be reached once for every value of j. Then we have to define two variables: X is the number of comparisons, or the number of times line 4 is done. Y is the number of times the branch in line 8 is not taken, and thus is equal to the number of items placed in location 1. With these definitions the rest of the second column can be filled up. For example, line 7 is reached once for every time a comparison is done, except when the "else" part (line 6) is selected.

Thus, once the distributions of X and Y are known, the entire running time of INSERT can be estimated. Consider first Y. This is the number of left-to-right minima in the permutation, and has the same distribution as M_N, determined in Section 3.1 (see Exercise 1). If we adopt the same measure on the input used there – all $n!$ permutations being equally likely – we can, and shall, use the results obtained therein.

INSERT($\{K_k\}$, $1 \le k \le n$)

{for $j = 2$ to N

    for $i = j-1$ by -1 to 0

    $\{K = K_j$; if $K < K_i$

             move K_i to location $i+1$;

             else

             put K in location $i+1$; break;

    }

}

(a)

a.	1	1.	$2 \to j$
a.	$N-1$	2.	$K_j \to K$
a.	$N-1$	3.	$j-1 \to i$
c.	X	4.	if $K < K_i$
e.	$X-(N-1-Y)$	5.	$K_i \to \mathrm{loc}(i+1)$
d.	$N-1-Y$	6.	else $\Rightarrow 9$.
f.	$X-(N-1-Y)$	7.	$i-1 \to i$
f.	$X-(N-1-Y)$	8.	if $i > 0 \Rightarrow 4$.
b.	$N-1$	9.	$K \to \mathrm{loc}(i+1)$
a.	$N-1$	10.	$j+1 \to j$
a.	$N-1$	11.	if $j < N+1 \Rightarrow 2$.
a.	1	12.	end

(b)

Fig. 3.2: INSERT sort procedure

The value of X is determined by the observation that we move a key left as long as we discover for it inversions, and there is one extra comparison to end the move; except when we reached the leftmost position - i.e., except for Y cases. Hence $X = I_{N,\sigma} + N - Y$. The distribution of $I_{N,\sigma}$ was discussed in Section 3.2.2 (see Exercise 2).

3.3.2 Shell Sort

The number of operations in the Insertion sort is roughly proportional to I_N, and thus has a mean of $O(N^2)$. This is inherent in the fact that we use an operation (or, rather, several) to undo each inversion, which in turn results from the fact that at each stage adjacent elements are compared (see proposition 4 in Section 3.2.2).

To improve the running time we must, at some stages of the sorting process, compare elements that are further separated.

The direct application of this idea begat the Shell sort, published in 1959 by Donald L. Shell. Generically, the sorting is done in t phases, with increments h_s, $1 \le s \le t$. The increments are counted "backwards", starting with h_t and ending with $h_1 = 1$. At stage s, $h = h_s$ separate lists are sorted, where list i consists of the elements that are in locations $i+jh$, $0 \le j \le \lfloor(N-i+1)/h\rfloor$, $1 \le i \le h$ (Exercise 3).

The sorting of each list may be done by any desired method. To make use of the results we obtained above we shall assume INSERT is used for each such list, and we obtain the algorithm as in Fig. 3.3 (see Exercise 4).

Clearly, practically all the work is done within INSERT. The running time of this procedure has been shown to depend on the relative arrangement of minima in each list, and on the number of inversions in it - with the last variable dominating. Consequently, the rest of the analysis will only concern the number of inversions (see Exercise 5).

At every stage, for each increment value h, we have h lists, of lengths $q = \lfloor N/h \rfloor$ and $q+1$. The number of lists of the two lengths are $h-r$ and r respectively, where $r = N-qh$. Only at the first stage, however, when $h = h_t$, we can immediately compute the expected number of inversions within these list, as given by

$$(h-r)\frac{q(q-1)}{4} + r\frac{q(q+1)}{4} = q[2r+h(q-1)]/4 . \tag{1}$$

This result holds, at the first stage, when we assume all possible inputs (elements of the $S(N_n)$ group) to be equi-probable, since then each of the lists may be taken as representing a random permutation of the corresponding size (see Exercise 3.1-1; a proof is also available as Lemma 0 in Yao, 1980). In all subsequent stages the permutations do not have the same distributional properties as the original - some rearrangement has taken place. The task of estimating the number of inversions still remaining is what we have to tackle now.

We shall call a permutation, once it has been sorted with an increment h, an

Given: $\{K_j\}$ $1 \le j \le N$, $1 = h_1, \cdots, h_t$
for $s = t$ by -1 to 1
  $\{ h = h_s$; for $i = 1$ to h

    INSERT $(\{K_r\}, r = i+jh, 0 \le j \le \left\lfloor \dfrac{N-i+1}{h} \right\rfloor)$

  $\}$

Fig. 3.3: Shell sort

h-sorted permutation or list.

2-stage Shell Sort, $h_2 = 2$, $h_1 = 1$

We start, following Knuth (1973), with the simplest case: $t = 2, h_2 = 2, h_1 = 1$. It will turn out that the result of this case is immediately applicable as the building block of the results for the more complex cases as well.

For the first stage equation (1) holds with $h = 2$. We are left with computing the number of inversions in a 2-sorted permutation, since this will determine the running time of the second stage.

In such a permutation all the numbers in the odd positions, a_{2j+1}, $0 \leq j \leq \lfloor N/2 \rfloor$, are in increasing order, as well as all of those located in even positions.

The permutation is then determined uniquely once we know which keys are in (say) the odd-numbered locations. We identify, therefore, each 2-sorted permutation with a path of N steps in a plane grid, from the origin $(0,0)$ to $(\lceil N/2 \rceil, \lfloor N/2 \rfloor)$, where step k is up or to the right according to whether the number k, from $1 \leq k \leq N$, is in an even- or odd-numbered location in the permutation. Thus the 2-sorted permutation (1 3 2 6 4 8 5 9 7 11 10) corresponds to the path shown in Fig. 3.4. The diagram can also be used to count inversions. Since each inversion is between an odd- and an even-located element, we follow Knuth and "assign" all inversions to the odd-placed ones. Thus a segment from (i,j) to $(i+1,j)$ implies a placement involved in precisely $|i-j|$ inversions (the

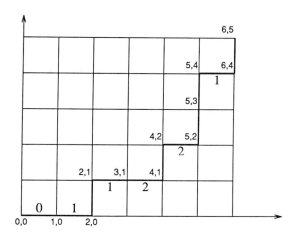

Fig. 3.4: Plane grid representation of a 2-sorted permutation (Knuth, 1973).

corresponding number, $i+j+1$ is placed in a_{2i+1}; think of the numbers to its left, when $i>j$, or to its right, when $j>i$, to justify the last statement).

We shall only proceed here to obtain the *mean* number of inversions in a 2-sorted permutation. (See Exercise 7 for the distribution.) As argued above, the earlier assumption that all possible input permutations are equiprobable translates into equal probability for each 2-sorted one. Hence it suffices to sum over all the paths, representing all 2-sorted lists, collecting the number of inversions associated with each path, and divide by their number, $\binom{N}{\lfloor N/2 \rfloor}$; except that instead of summing over paths directly it is easier to sum over the number of inversions contributed by every horizontal segment of length one in the grid, multiplying each by the number of paths that incorporate it. The number of paths through the segment (i,j) to $(i+1,j)$ is the number of paths from $(0,0)$ to (i,j) times the number of paths from $(i+1,j)$ to $(\lceil N/2 \rceil, \lfloor N/2 \rfloor)$. Since from (k,l) to (u,v) there are $\binom{u-k+v-l}{u-k}$ paths, we get for the total number of inversions, in all possible permutations, the double sum

$$A_N = \sum_{i=0}^{\lceil N/2 \rceil - 1} \sum_{j=0}^{\lfloor N/2 \rfloor} |i - j| \binom{i+j}{i}\binom{N-i-j-1}{\lfloor N/2 \rfloor -j}. \tag{2}$$

This unpleasant looking expression can be simplified in two ways: by considering separately even and odd N, and by splitting the sum to dispose of the absolute value. Thus

$$A_{2n} = \sum_{i=1}^{n} \sum_{j=0}^{i} (i - j)\binom{i+j}{i}\binom{2n-i-j-1}{n-j} + \sum_{i=0}^{n} \sum_{j=i}^{n} (j-i)\binom{i+j}{i}\binom{2n-i-j-1}{n-j}. \tag{3}$$

(The value $j = i$ is repeated for convenience; clearly its contribution vanishes.) Changing the order of summation in the second part of (3), interchanging the indices i and j and then using equation (A.1.1) provides

$$A_{2n} = \sum_{i=0}^{n} \sum_{j=0}^{i}(i - j)\binom{i+j}{i}\left[\binom{2n-i-j-1}{n-j} + \binom{2n-i-j-1}{n-j-1}\right]$$

$$= \sum_{i=0}^{n} \sum_{j=0}^{i}(i - j)\binom{i+j}{i}\binom{2n-i-j}{n-j}. \tag{4}$$

There is no obvious way to handle such a sum, except to evaluate its gf, hoping to get an expression amenable to coefficient extraction. The fruit of this approach is quite remarkable here. (For a rather different way see Exercise 8.) Define

$$A(z) = \sum_{n \geq 0} A_{2n} z^n,$$

insert the right-hand side of equation (4) and exchange the order of summation on n and i, getting

$$A(z) = \sum_{i \geq 0} \sum_{j=0}^{i} (i-j)\binom{i+j}{i}z^i \sum_{n-i \geq 0} \binom{2n-i-j}{n-i}z^{n-i}.$$ (5)

Using the familiar sum from (A.2.5)

$$\sum_{k \geq 0} \binom{r-tk}{k}z^k = \frac{X^{r+1}(z)}{(t+1)X(z)-t},$$ (6)

where $X(z)$ is the solution of $z = X^{t+1}(z) - X^t(z)$ (see example (2) in Section 2.2.3), we find that the rightmost sum is $\frac{1}{s}(\frac{1-s}{2z})^{i-j}$, where $s = s(z) \equiv \sqrt{1-4z}$. Rearranging this result by writing $k = i-j$, exchanging the order of summation and reapplying the same sum formula provide successively

$$A(z) = \sum_{i \geq 0} \sum_{j=0}^{i} (i-j)\binom{i+j}{i}\frac{z^i}{s}(\frac{1-s}{2z})^{i-j} = \sum_{i \geq 0} z^i \sum_{k=0}^{i} \frac{k}{s}\binom{2i-k}{i}(\frac{1-s}{2z})^k$$

$$= \sum_{k \geq 0} \frac{k}{s}(\frac{1-s}{2})^k \sum_{i \geq 0} \binom{2i+k}{i}z^i = \sum_{k \geq 0} \frac{k}{s^2}(\frac{(1-s)^2}{4z})^k.$$ (7)

This is a differentiated geometrical series. Summing it and using the explicit form of $s(z)$ we get

$$A(z) = \frac{z}{s^4} = \frac{z}{(1-4z)^2} = \frac{1}{4}\sum_{n \geq 0} n(4z)^n.$$

Providing the surprisingly concise result

$$A_{2n} = n \, 4^{n-1}.$$ (8)

For A_{2n+1}, rewriting it in the form of equation (3) and doing the same manipulations yields directly twice the right-hand side of equation (4). Thus $A_{2n+1} = 2A_{2n}$, and $A_N = \lfloor N/2 \rfloor 2^{N-2}$ for all N, odd or even. (See Exercise 9.) Hence we find for the mean number of inversions in a 2-sorted permutation

$$f(N,2) = \frac{\lfloor N/2 \rfloor 2^{N-2}}{\binom{N}{\lfloor N/2 \rfloor}} \approx 0.157N^{3/2}.$$ (9)

The last value was obtained via the Stirling approximation.

2-stage Shell Sort, $h_2 = h, h_1 = 1$

So much for a two-stage Shell sort with $h_2 = 2, h_1 = 1$. Now let us compute the corresponding figures for $h_2 = h$, with h any integer larger than 1, still only using $t = 2$. Equation (1) holds here as well, but at stage 2 we have an h-sorted list, rather than a 2-sorted one. More precisely, using the definitions of r and q (preceding equation (1)) we find we have r lists of length $q+1$, and $h-r$ of length q. Now observe the following:

− every inversion is between elements belonging to two lists; thus by picking all $\binom{h}{2}$ pairs of lists, counting the inversions for each such pair and summing the counts, we obtain the total number of inversions.

– Consider any pair of lists; if merged, they would form a 2-*sorted* list, of length $2q$, $2q+1$ or $2q+2$, according to the lengths of the pair members. The mean number of inversions for each such pair is given by the properly adapted equation (9) and we find

Proposition: The mean number of inversions in an h-sorted list of length N is given by

$$
\begin{aligned}
f(N,h) &= \binom{r}{2}\frac{A_{2q+2}}{\binom{2q+2}{q+1}} + r(h-r)\frac{A_{2q+1}}{\binom{2q+1}{q}} + \binom{h-r}{2}\frac{A_{2q}}{\binom{2q}{q}}\\
&= \frac{(2^q\,q\,!)^2}{2(2q+1)!}\left[\binom{r}{2}(q+1)^2 + r(h-r)q(q+1) + \frac{1}{2}\binom{h-r}{2}q(2q+1)\right].
\end{aligned}
\tag{10}
$$

Let us see what improvement over straight Insertion sort is possible with a two-stage Shell sort. We shall only keep track of the main contributions to the running time - i.e., the leading terms in the expressions for the number of inversions in the two stages. For the first we obtain from equation (1) the value $N^2/4h + O(N)$, and for the second stage, from equation (10), one finds the value $\sqrt{\pi h}\,N^{3/2}/8$ (see Exercise 10). Hence

$$
I(N,h) = \frac{N^2}{4h} + \frac{1}{8}\sqrt{\pi N^3}\,h^{1/2} + O(N).
\tag{11}
$$

Disregarding the $O(N)$ term we find that $I(N,h)$ is minimized (taking h as a "continuous" variable) for $h = \left(\frac{16}{\pi}N\right)^{1/3} = cN^{1/3}$ with $c \approx 1.7205$. Substituting this back to equation (11) we find

$$
I(N, h_{opt}) = O(N^{5/3}).
\tag{12}
$$

This is the improvement obtainable by the two-stage Shell sort, over the $O(N^2)$-behavior of the original Insertion algorithm. Can one do better? One can, in two ways: adding more stages and finding a good combination of increments.

t-stage Shell Sort with Divisibility Constraints

It turns out that the above computation is sufficient to estimate the total number of inversions encountered in a t-stage Shell sort when h_s divides h_{s+1}, $1 \le s \le t-1$. Define v_s as h_{s+1}/h_s. At stage $s-1$ the h_{s+1}-sorting is "forgotten", since stage s refined it. Thus, if we use $h = (8,4,2,1)$, once the 4-sorting is done, the number of inversions resolved during the 2-sorting will not depend on the fact that the lists had been previously 8-sorted, etc. Hence at each stage, following the first, we have the same number of inversions as in the second stage of a 2-stage sort with increments $(v_s, 1)$ (justify this statement!), but we still have to add together the contributions from all the h_s lists we have at that stage. Thus, we obtain that under the above divisibility constraint, using the function $f(\cdot,\cdot)$ defined by equation (10)

$$I(N,h_t,\cdots,h_1) = \sum_{s=1}^{t} [r_s f(q_s+1,v_s) + (h_s-r_s)f(q_s,v_s)], \tag{13}$$

where

$$q_s = \lfloor N/h_s \rfloor, \quad r_s = N-h_s q_s, \quad v_s = h_{s+1}/h_s.$$

The computational convenience that led to equation (13) also indicates that one could do better than obey the divisibility constraints. Note that when the increments are related via these constraints, the last stage is the processing of an h_2-sorted list, and by itself would require the undoing of at least the number of inversions quoted preceding equation (11), $O(N^{3/2})$.

Knuth (1973), Section 5.2.1, reports on numerous experiments, with differing sets of increments that provide a substantially better performance. A reasonable choice appears to be

$$h_1 = 1, \quad h_{s+1} = 3h_s+1, \quad 1 \le s \le t \text{ such that } h_{t+2} \ge N. \tag{14}$$

Using this and similar sets of increments, the running times appear to be $O(N^\alpha)$ with $\alpha \approx 1.25$, or $O(N \log^2 N)$; both expressions provide good fit for the data.

For the increments $h_s = 2^s-1$, $1 \le s \le \log_2 N$, it is possible to show that the *maximum* running time (again, counting inversions only) is $O(N^{3/2})$. Experiments show that the average time, with these increments, is $O(N^{1.26})$.

Yao (1980) provides an analysis for the three-stage Shell sort. It is of a similar flavor to the above analysis but considerably more complicated, serving *inter alia* as a demonstration of what we should expect if we wanted to examine higher order versions. We shall cite one result, and that is that the number of inversions in a list which is both 2-sorted and 3-sorted has the mean $N/4 + O(1)$, rather than $O(N^{3/2})$ for a 2-sorted list.

A number of additional results and insights can be found in Pratt (1972).

3.3.3 Linear Probing Sort (Gonnet and Munro, 1984)

We present now a sorting scheme that differs from those that have been presented so far in an essential detail: the values of the keys to be sorted are used not merely for comparison purposes but also arithmetically. From an algorithmic point of view this is important: a comparison produces one bit of information, and since n numbers are in sorted order when in one of their $n!$ possible permutations only (assuming they are all different), we need $O(n \log n)$ comparisons, i.e., one-bit operations, to determine the sorted order. An arithmetic operation over the keys produces typically $\log n$ bits of information (we need as many digits to record the

key values when they are all different), and thus we could hope to make do with
$O(n)$ operations. The Linear Probing sort does realize this goal (as do several
varieties of interpolation sort, radix sort and others. See Gonnet (1984), Chapter
4).

Assume then that we are given the keys K_1 to K_n and the information that
they have been generated independently from the distribution $F(\cdot)$. If $F(\cdot)$ is not
given, we can compute the empirical cdf in two passes over the keys, to the
desired accuracy, and use it instead.

Note that if $K \sim F(\cdot)$, then the transformed random variable $F(K) \sim U(0,1)$
(see Exercise 12).

The algorithm proceeds in two phases: first, each key is inserted into a table
of m positions $(m \geq n)$, in such a way that all the keys in the table are in the
correct order. The key K_i is destined for the location $\lceil mF(K_i) \rceil$ (the first location
is numbered 1). If this location is not empty (it is already occupied by a key), the
locations from this place to the right are examined until a free location is
encountered, which will be filled. During this "probing" sequence we locate K_i
correctly in relation to the other keys (see Exercise 13). When this is done, the
table may contain unfilled positions, and one more pass collects all the keys in the
first n locations. See Fig. 3.5, where the table is called A.

One of the difficulties with this algorithm is that in the process of probing, it
may overflow location m. Indeed, we shall only bring here the analysis needed to
determine the size of the "overflow" area that has to be reserved beyond location

```
for i = 1 to n   (* first phase - insertion *)
{j = ⌈mF (Kᵢ)⌉ ; x = Kᵢ;
    while location j in A is occupied
    { if x < A (j) exchange (x ,A (j));
        j = j+1;
    }
    A (j) = x;
}   (* first phase done *)


i = 1; for j = 1 to n    (* second phase - compaction *)
{ if location i is occupied {A (j) = A (i);   j = j+1}
    i = i+1;
}
```
                    Fig. 3.5: Linear Probing sort

m, so that it will suffice with a suitably high probability.

In Exercise 24 the analysis required to estimate the running time of the algorithm is outlined.

The analysis below relies on the Poisson transform presented in Section 2.2.4. This transform is actually developed in the same paper we refer to in the title of this section. This transform permits us to regard the events {location j is the original target of k keys} as *independent*, and assign to them probabilities which we denote by r_k:

$$r_k \equiv \text{Prob}(R_j = k) = e^{-\alpha}\,\frac{\alpha^k}{k!}\,, \quad k \geq 0,\ 1 \leq j \leq m,\ \alpha \equiv n/m\,. \tag{15}$$

The pgf of $\{r_k\}$ is $R(z) = e^{\alpha(z-1)}$.

Analysis of the Overflow Area

Denote by W_i the number of keys that in the first phase overflow past location i. The quantities of interest here are

$$p_{i,j} \equiv \text{Prob}(W_i = j) = \text{the probability that in the insertion phase exactly } j \text{ keys} \tag{16}$$
$$\text{overflow location } i,\ \ 0 \leq i \leq m, 0 \leq j$$

where the $p_{0,j}$ are defined to simplify our equations at $p_{0,j} = \delta_{0,j}$. Later we also determine the expected value of W_i and its variance.

Note that under the assumption of the Poisson model the number of keys is not bounded!

It is easy to observe successively

$$p_{1,0} = r_0 + r_1$$

$$p_{i,0} = p_{i-1,0}r_0 + p_{i-1,0}r_1 + p_{i-1,1}r_0$$

$$p_{i,1} = p_{i-1,0}r_2 + p_{i-1,1}r_1 + p_{i-1,2}r_0$$

and finally

$$p_{i,j} = \sum_{k=0}^{j+1} p_{i-1,k}\, r_{j-k+1}, \quad j > 0,\ \ i \geq 1\,. \tag{17}$$

Define for each location i the pgf

$$P_i(z) = \sum_{j \geq 0} p_{i,j} z^j\,. \tag{18}$$

Then equation (17) can be used, multiplying it by z^j and summing for $j \geq 0$ to deduce the relation

$$P_i(z) = \frac{1}{z}[(z-1)p_{i-1,0}r_0 + P_{i-1}(z)R(z)], \quad P_0(z) = 1. \tag{19}$$

Equation (19), viewed as a difference equation with variable coefficients (the $p_{i-1,0}$), has the immediate solution

$$P_i(z) = \gamma^i(z) + \beta(z)\sum_{j=0}^{i-1}p_{i-j-1,0}\gamma^j(z), \quad \beta(z) \equiv r_0\frac{z-1}{z}, \quad \gamma(z) \equiv \frac{R(z)}{z} \tag{20}$$

as can be verified by substitution.

The solution given in equation (20) depends explicitly on the entire sequence of $\{p_{i,0}\}$. We have yet to evaluate these quantities. Their calculation is the key to the entire analysis of the distribution of the W_i.

We obtain an equation involving only the $p_{i,0}$, unlike the system above, by extracting the free (from z) term in equation (20). Since

$$[1]z^{-i}e^{\alpha(z-1)} = [z^i]e^{\alpha(z-1)} = e^{-\alpha}\frac{\alpha^i}{i!},$$

we get from equation (20), with similar manipulations, the equations

$$p_{i,0} = e^{-\alpha i}\frac{(i\alpha)^i}{i!} + e^{-\alpha}\sum_{j=0}^{i-1}e^{-j\alpha}[\frac{(j\alpha)^j}{j!} - \frac{(j\alpha)^{j+1}}{(j+1)!}]p_{i-j-1,0}, \quad i > 1. \tag{21}$$

supplemented by $p_{1,0} = r_0 + r_1 = (1+\alpha)e^{-\alpha}$.

Ungainly as the equations (21) may look, they do have an explicit solution. Define the "incomplete exponential function"

$$e_i(x) = \sum_{j=0}^{i}\frac{x^j}{j!}. \tag{22}$$

Proposition: The solution to equations (21) is given by

$$p_{i,0} = e^{-i\alpha}[e_{i+1}((i+1)\alpha) - \alpha e_i((i+1)\alpha)]. \tag{23}$$

The proof is by induction, though anything but straightforward. It is easy to verify for $i = 0,1$. Assume for $j < i$, substitute in (21) (only $p_{j,0}$ with $j < i$ appear on the right-hand side), and it remains to show

$$e_{i+1}((i+1)\alpha) - \alpha e_i((i+1)\alpha) \overset{?}{=}$$
$$= \frac{(i\alpha)^i}{i!} + \sum_{j=0}^{i-1}\frac{(j\alpha)^j}{j!}(1 - \frac{j\alpha}{j+1})[e_{i-j}((i-j)\alpha) - \alpha e_{i-j-1}((i-j)\alpha)]. \tag{24}$$

Now observe that both sides are polynomials in α of degree i precisely (Exercise 15). We shall employ the following device: to simplify the explicit form of (24), add on both sides quantities that contain only powers of α higher than i; not necessarily the *same*, though. If thereby we obtain a relation that is manifestly correct for powers up to i, we have obtained the required proof. Actually, in order to ease the verification, we shall do better - we shall obtain a true equation (i.e., an identity for all powers of α).

Observe first that

$$e_i(x) = e^x + \{x^{i+1}\}, \tag{25}$$

where $\{x^k\}$ denotes[1] "terms that only contain powers of x not less than k". Thus the left-hand side of equation (24) is $e^{(i+1)\alpha}(1-\alpha) + \{\alpha^{i+2}\}$.

In the right-hand side we first do a similar substitution, obtaining

$$\frac{(i\alpha)^i}{i!} + \sum_{j=0}^{i-1} \frac{(j\alpha)^j}{j!} \left(1 - \frac{j\alpha}{j+1}\right) \left[e^{(i-j)\alpha} - \alpha e^{(i-j)\alpha}\right] + \{\alpha^{i+1}\}. \tag{26}$$

Then, the first term is rewritten as

$$\frac{(i\alpha)^i}{i!} = \frac{(i\alpha)^i}{i!}\left(1 - \frac{i\alpha}{i+1}\right) + \{\alpha^{i+1}\},$$

so that it can be lumped with the sum, as the $j = i$ term. Extend then the sum on the right-hand side to infinity (again adding only $\{\alpha^{i+1}\}$), and it remains to verify

$$(1-\alpha)e^{(i+1)\alpha} \overset{?}{=} (1-\alpha)e^{i\alpha} \sum_{j\geq 0} \frac{(j\alpha)}{j!}\left(1 - \frac{j\alpha}{j+1}\right)e^{-j\alpha} + \{\alpha^{i+1}\}. \tag{27}$$

This, however is an identity, *without* the $\{\alpha^{i+1}\}$ part! To show this cancel $(1-\alpha)e^{i\alpha}$ on both sides, and rearrange the right-hand side, to find

$$e^{\alpha} \overset{?}{=} \sum_{j\geq 0} \frac{1}{j!}\left(\frac{j\alpha}{e^{\alpha}}\right)^j \left(1 - \frac{j\alpha}{j+1}\right). \tag{28}$$

Now recall equations (2.2-30,32), slightly rearranged

$$\sum_{j\geq 1} \frac{(jz)^j}{j!} = \frac{z}{e^{x(-z)} - z}, \qquad \sum_{j\geq 1} \frac{(jz)^{j+1}}{(j+1)!} = \frac{e^{x(-z)}}{1 + x(-z)} - 1, \tag{29}$$

where $x(z)$ is the solution of the equation $x(z)e^{x(z)} = z$. These sums are needed in equation (28) with $z \equiv \alpha e^{-\alpha}$, and clearly $x(-z) = -\alpha$ is a solution, by substitution. Inserting the sum formulas in the right-hand side of equation (28) we find (having 1 for the $j=0$ term)

$$1 + \frac{\alpha e^{-\alpha}}{e^{-\alpha} - \alpha e^{-\alpha}} - e^{\alpha}\left(\frac{e^{-\alpha}}{1-\alpha} - 1\right) = e^{\alpha}, \tag{30}$$

as indeed is required, proving the proposition of equation (23). $\qquad\square$

We can use equation (23) to derive an asymptotic estimate of $p_{i,0}$. Consider first the "boundary case" of $\alpha = 1$ where one would expect $p_{i,0}$ to decrease with i:

$$(\alpha = 1) \quad p_{i,0} = e^{-i}\left(e_{i+1}(i+1) - e_i(i+1)\right) = e^{-i}\frac{(i+1)^{i+1}}{(i+1)!},$$

---

[1] This notation is akin to $O(x^k)$ in its disregard of sign, coefficient and higher order terms, but it does not imply a size relation, since x could be less than 1 or larger.

and Stirling's approximation for the denominator provides

$$(\alpha = 1) \quad p_{i,0} \approx \frac{e}{\sqrt{2\pi}} \frac{1}{\sqrt{i}} \left(1 + O\left(i^{-1}\right)\right). \tag{31}$$

For $\alpha < 1$ one would expect the interactions caused by overflowing keys to be more localized. We want to replace $e_{i+1}((i+1)\alpha)$ in equation (23) by $e^{(i+1)\alpha}$, and to examine the error thus introduced:

$$
\begin{aligned}
e^{-i\alpha}[e^{(i+1)\alpha} - e_{i+1}((i+1)\alpha)] &= e^{-i\alpha} \sum_{j \geq i+2} \frac{[(i+1)\alpha]^j}{j!} \\
&= e^{-i\alpha} \frac{[(i+1)\alpha]^{i+2}}{(i+2)!} \sum_{j \geq 0} [(i+1)\alpha]^j \frac{(i+2)!}{(j+i+2)!}.
\end{aligned}
\tag{32}
$$

Since each term in the sum is bounded by $\left(\frac{(i+1)\alpha}{i+3}\right)^j$, the sum is bounded by $1/\left(1 - \alpha\frac{i+1}{i+3}\right)$. As far as bounding the above error is concerned, this is simply $O(1)$. Thus the right-hand side of equation (32) is bounded by (Stirling's approximation again)

$$e^{-i\alpha} \frac{(i+1)^{i+2}\alpha^{i+2}}{(i+2)^{i+2}e^{-i-2}\sqrt{2\pi(i+2)}} = O\left(e^{-i\alpha} \frac{\alpha^i}{e^{-i}\sqrt{i}}\right) = O\left(e^{i(1-\alpha+\log\alpha)}i^{-\frac{1}{2}}\right).$$

Rewriting, $e^{-i\alpha}e_{i+1}((i+1)\alpha) = e^\alpha + O\left(e^{i(1-\alpha+\log\alpha)}i^{-\frac{1}{2}}\right)$. The same holds for $e^{-i\alpha}e_i((i+1)\alpha)$, and we obtain

$$p_{i,0} = (1-\alpha)e^\alpha + O\left(e^{i(1-\alpha+\log\alpha)}i^{-\frac{1}{2}}\right). \tag{33}$$

For most practical purposes a form simpler than equation (33) is convenient. For $0 < \alpha < 1$, define $\beta \equiv \alpha e^{1-\alpha}$ that satisfies $0 < \alpha < \beta < 1$, and then

$$p_{i,0} = (1-\alpha)e^\alpha + O(\beta^i), \tag{34}$$

where we have given up the factor $i^{-\frac{1}{2}}$.

Having obtained an explicit expression and an asymptotic estimate for the boundary probabilities, we return to consider the pgf's $P_i(z)$. Recall equations (19) and (20). The latter is the convenient vehicle for the question of convergence of $P_i(z)$ to a limiting function as $i \to \infty$ (see Exercise 16).

When $P_i(z)$ do converge, equations (19) and (34) imply that the limiting function must satisfy the equation

$$P(z) = \frac{1}{z}[(z-1)(1-\alpha)e^\alpha r_0 + P(z)R(z)], \tag{35}$$

and since $r_0 = e^{-\alpha}$ we obtain

$$P(z) \equiv E(z^W) = \frac{(z-1)(1-\alpha)}{z - R(z)}. \tag{36}$$

Differentiation at $z = 1$ yields the moments of W, in particular (Exercise 17),

$$E(W) = \frac{\alpha^2}{2(1-\alpha)}.$$ (37)

$$V(W) = \frac{6\alpha^2 - 2\alpha^3 - \alpha^4}{12(1-\alpha)^2}.$$ (38)

Moreover, differentiating equation (19) at $z=1$:

$$\begin{aligned}
P_i{}'(1) &= -1 + p_{i-1,0}r_0 + P_{i-1}'(1) + R'(1) \\
&= -1 + e^{-\alpha}p_{i-1,0} + P_{i-1}'(1) + \alpha \\
&= P_{i-1}'(1) + \alpha - 1 + e^{-\alpha}[(1-\alpha)e^\alpha + O(\beta^i)] \\
&= P_{i-1}'(1) + O(\beta^i),
\end{aligned}$$ (39)

and for any $j < i$

$$P_i{}'(1) = E(W_i) = E(W_j) + \sum_{k=j+1}^{i} O(\beta^k).$$ (40)

Since $0 < \beta < 1$, $\sum_{k \geq j+1} O(\beta^k) = O(\beta^{j+1})$, and letting i increase indefinitely in (40) we find, using (37)

$$E(W_j) = E(W) - \sum_{k \geq j+1} O(\beta^k) = \frac{\alpha^2}{2(1-\alpha)} + O(\beta^{j+1}).$$ (41)

Algorithmically, a noteworthy feature of the Linear Probing sort, as shown by equation (41), is that for a fixed loading factor α less than one, $E(W_m) = O(1)$, essentially independent of the table size.

Continuing now to obtain results for the "real" model, with n given keys, one could choose between either using the asymptotic expansion given by equation (2.2-42) with $g(m,\alpha) = \alpha^2/2(1-\alpha)$, or, since this expression is simple enough, computing the exact transform. We select the second (see Exercise 19). From equation (2.2-37) we see that the transform is additive, and from Exercise 2.2-8(a) we find that to $\alpha^2/2(1-\alpha) = \frac{1}{2}\sum_{k \geq 2}\alpha^j$ corresponds

$$E(W_{m,n}) = f(m,n) = \frac{1}{2}\sum_{j \geq 2} \frac{n^{\underline{j}}}{m^j}.$$ (42)

Note that we have quite neglected the $O(\beta^m)$ term from equation (41). This is reasonable, since we shall make do with asymptotic estimates that are only accurate to $O(m^{-2})$ anyway.

The last result can be expressed with the incomplete exponential function we encountered:

$$E(W_{m,n}) = \frac{1}{2} \sum_{j=2}^{n} \frac{n!}{(n-j)!} m^{-j} = \frac{n!}{2} \sum_{i=0}^{n-2} \frac{m^{i-n}}{i!} = \frac{n!m^{-n}}{2} \sum_{i=0}^{n-2} \frac{m^i}{i!}$$

$$= \frac{n!m^{-n}}{2} e_{n-2}(m).$$

(43)

The $e(\cdot)$ function has a known asymptotic expansion (see Exercise 18), from which we obtain

$$e_{n-2}\left(\frac{n}{\alpha}\right) = \frac{(n/\alpha)^{n-1}}{(n-1)!} \left(\frac{\alpha}{1-\alpha} - \frac{\alpha}{n(1-\alpha)^3} + O(n^{-2}) \right), \qquad \alpha < 1.$$ (44)

Using this result in equation (43) we find

$$E(W_{m,n}) = \frac{1}{2} n! m^{-n} \frac{m^{n-1}}{(n-1)!} \left(\frac{\alpha}{1-\alpha} - \frac{1}{m(1-\alpha)^3} + O(m^{-2}) \right)$$

$$= \frac{n^2}{2m(m-n)} - \frac{nm}{2(m-n)^3} + O(m^{-2}).$$

(45)

The above expansion, equation (44), does not hold for $\alpha = 1$ (i.e. $n = m$). Indeed, under the Poisson model $P_i(z)$ do not even converge when $\alpha = 1$ (see Exercise 16). One can, however, use equation (39) for any finite i. We shall be content with simply extending the range of equation (42). We then need:

$$E(W_{m,m}) = \frac{1}{2} \sum_{j=2}^{m} \frac{m^j}{m^j} = \frac{m!m^{-m}}{2} e_{m-2}(m).$$ (46)

The value of $e_{m-2}(m)$ is also available in Knuth (1973), as

$$e_{m-2}(m) = \frac{m^{m-1}}{(m-1)!} \left(\sqrt{\frac{\pi m}{2}} - \frac{4}{3} + \frac{1}{12} \sqrt{\frac{\pi}{2m}} + O(m^{-1}) \right).$$ (47)

Thus

$$E(W_{m,m}) = \frac{1}{2} \frac{m!}{m^m} \frac{m^{m-1}}{(m-1)!} \left(\sqrt{\frac{\pi m}{2}} - \frac{4}{3} + \frac{1}{12} \sqrt{\frac{\pi}{2m}} + O(m^{-1}) \right)$$

$$= \sqrt{\frac{\pi m}{8}} - \frac{2}{3} + \frac{1}{24} \sqrt{\frac{\pi}{2m}} + O(m^{-1}).$$

(48)

Now the overflow is $O(\sqrt{m})$, rather than $O(1)$.

The variance of the overflow can be computed using precisely the same techniques (Exercises 20, 21). Moreover, we can use the limiting function $P(z)$ (for $\alpha < 1$, which is the realistic case, for actual applications of the Linear Probing sort) to compute a direct bound on the probabilities of overflow by the Cauchy integral theorem (see Section 2.5.1).

$$p_j = \text{Prob}(W = j) = \oint_C \frac{P(z)}{z^{j+1}} \, dz,$$ (49)

and thus

$k \backslash \alpha$	0.5	0.7	0.8	0.9	0.95	0.99
6	0.00010013	0.0070643	0.042455	0.21892	0.47427	0.86316
9	0.23099×10^{-5}	0.00093113	0.011657	0.11760	0.34954	0.81273
12	0.53285×10^{-7}	0.00012273	0.0032008	0.063170	0.25761	0.76524
15	0.12292×10^{-8}	0.000016177	0.00087885	0.033933	0.18985	0.72053
18	0.28356×10^{-10}	0.21322×10^{-5}	0.00024131	0.018228	0.13992	0.67844
21	0.65412×10^{-12}	0.28103×10^{-6}	0.000066259	0.0097914	0.10312	0.63880
24	0.15089×10^{-13}	0.37043×10^{-7}	0.000018193	0.0052597	0.076001	0.60148
27	0.34809×10^{-15}	0.48825×10^{-8}	0.49954×10^{-5}	0.0028253	0.056012	0.56634
30	0.80298×10^{-17}	0.64355×10^{-9}	0.13716×10^{-5}	0.0015177	0.041281	0.53325
33	0.18523×10^{-18}	0.84825×10^{-10}	0.37661×10^{-6}	0.00081526	0.030424	0.50209
36	0.42735×10^{-20}	0.11181×10^{-10}	0.10341×10^{-6}	0.00043793	0.022422	0.47276

The large-table limit of the probability of exceeding a specified overflow buffer of size k, as given by equation (52).

$$\text{Prob}(W > k) = \sum_{j > k} \oint_C \frac{P(z)}{z^{j+1}} dz = \oint_C \frac{P(z)}{z^{k+1}(z-1)} dz . \qquad (50)$$

Substituting $P(z)$

$$\text{Prob}(W > k) = \oint_C \frac{(1-\alpha)dz}{z^{k+1}(z-R(z))} = (1-\alpha) \oint_C \sum_{j \geq 0} \left(\frac{e^{\alpha(z-1)}}{z}\right)^j \frac{dz}{z^{k+2}}$$

$$= (1-\alpha) \sum_{j \geq 0} e^{-\alpha j} \oint_C \frac{e^{\alpha z j}}{z^{k+j+2}} dz = (1-\alpha) \sum_{j \geq 0} e^{-\alpha j} [z^{-1}] \frac{e^{\alpha j z}}{z^{k+j+2}} , \qquad (51)$$

where the last equality results from the residue theorem,

$$\text{Prob}(W > k) = (1-\alpha) \sum_{j \geq 0} e^{-j\alpha} [z^{k+j+1}] e^{\alpha j z} = (1-\alpha) \sum_{j \geq 0} e^{-j\alpha} \frac{(\alpha j)^{k+j+1}}{(k+j+1)!}$$

$$= (1-\alpha) e^{(k+1)\alpha} \sum_{j \geq 0} \frac{(j \alpha e^{-\alpha})^{k+j+1}}{(k+j+1)!} . \qquad (52)$$

The sum in equation (52) does not appear to have a closed form, but direct numerical evaluation turns out to be not hard, for α up to approximately 0.9, even though it converges very slowly. The sum mentioned in Exercise 2.2-7 can be used to reduce it to a finite sum and then the computation is much more efficient (for all α). (See Exercise 22.) The appended table was produced using this reduction. Note the pronounced increase of the probabilities with α. Indeed, for $\alpha = 0.99$ k has to be increased to 330 before the probability of overflow drops to an acceptable level of less than 0.001.

Exercises and Complements

1. Prove by a symmetry argument that Y, as defined in Fig. 3.2(b) has the distribution of M_N of Section 3.1.

2. With Fig. 3.2(b) and the discussion of X and Y, write expressions for the expectation and variance of T_N, the running time of the procedure INSERT, as functions of N. Note, for the variance computation, that X and Y (or, for that matter, M_N and I_N) are *not* independent. Use the inversion table (see Section 3.2.2) of the permutation.
$[E(T_N) = N^2 + 6N - 2H_N + 1.]$

3. Produce a random member of $S(N_{20})$. Perform manually a Shell sort on it, with the increments 8, 4, 2, 1. Observe the gradual decrease in the number of inversions.

4. For the Shell sort as presented in Fig. 3.3, prepare a detailed equivalent, in the format of Fig. 3.2(b). Note that the h lists can be sorted in parallel.

5. What is the distribution of Y, the left-to-right minima, in a permutation that is h-sorted?

6. (a)* Can you characterize a 2-sorted permutation through its inversion table? Consider also a different inversion table, $\{k_j\}$, where $k_j = i_{a_j}$. Can you use this table for the task?
(b) Consider permutations of n elements that are both 2- and 3-sorted. How many such permutations exist?
[Consider the possible positions of the numbers n and $n-1$ to show a recurrence satisfied by the Fibonacci numbers - see Exercise 2.2-12.]

7. (Knuth) The same rectangular grid used to obtain the mean of $I_n^{(2)}$, the number of inversions in a 2-sorted permutation, can also be used to evaluate its pgf. This requires however counting not just the total number of inversions, but the number of paths with any given inversion count.
Consider for simplicity $N = 2n$ only. Define the counting functions: $h_n(k)$ - the number of paths with k inversions (k-paths). $g_n(k)$ - the number of k-paths that only visit points (i,j) in the region $i \leq j$. Corresponding to these two define also $\bar{h}_n(k)$ and $\bar{g}_n(k)$, that count the same species with the limitation that they only consider k-paths that avoid all points on the diagonal $i=j$, except $(0,0)$ and (n,n) naturally.

(a) Define the gf's $h_n(z) = \sum_{k \geq 0} h_n(k) z^k$ etc. Compute by inspection the first few instances of these functions.
[You should get, for the first few functions, the values $g_0(z) = 1$, $g_1(z) = z$, $g_2(z) = z^2 + z^3$, $h_0(z) = 1$, $h_1(z) = 1 + z$, $h_2(z) = 1 + 3z + z^2 + z^3$, $\bar{h}_0(z) = 0$, $\bar{h}_1(z) = 1 + z$, $\bar{h}_2(z) = z + z^3$, $\bar{g}_0(z) = 0$, $\bar{g}_1(z) = z$, $\bar{g}_2(z) = z^3$ etc.]

(b) Derive recurrence relations between these functions.
[Each function is related to its barred version by a 'first hitting time'

consideration, yielding

$$g_n(z) = \sum_{k=1}^{n} \bar{g}_k(z) g_{n-k}(z), \qquad h_n(z) = \sum_{k=1}^{n} \bar{h}_k(z) h_{n-k}(z).$$

Also, $\bar{g}_n(z) = z^n g_{n-1}(z)$, and by considering the grid as rotated by 180^0 you should get $\bar{h}_n(z) = \bar{g}_n(z) + z^{-n} \bar{g}_n(z)$.]

(c) Obtain the following equations for the generating functions over n: $G(w,z) = \sum_{n\geq 0} g_n(z) w^n$ and $H(w,z) = \sum_{n\geq 0} h_n(z) w^n$:

$$G(w,z) = 1 + wzG(w,z)G(wz,z),$$

$$H(w,z) = 1 + H(w,z)[wG(w,z) + wzG(wz,z)].$$

(d) Show how the moments of $I_n^{(2)}$ are related to the coefficients of z^n in the derivatives of $H(w,z)$ with respect to z, and derive the first moment and variance of $I_n^{(2)}$. This is best done by using a program (in a symbolic manipulation language, such as MACSYMA or MAPLE) to compute the partial derivatives, but the first moment can still be done reasonably by hand.

8. (Sedgewick, 1983) Show the following combinatorial identity: if $f(i,j)$ is "constant along the diagonals", i.e. satisfies

$$f(i,i-j) = f(j,0), \qquad f(i,i+j) = f(0,j);$$

then

$$\sum_{i=0}^{n-1} \sum_{j=0}^{n} f(i,j)\binom{i+j}{i}\binom{2n-i-j-1}{n-j} = \sum_{k\geq 1} \binom{2n}{n-k} \sum_{j=0}^{k-1} [f(j,0) + f(0,j+1)]. \quad (*)$$

Reduce equation (3) to a form amenable for representation as in (*), and show, using the identity that

$$A_{2n} = \sum_{k\geq 1} \binom{2n}{n-k} k^2.$$

Then, by writing k^2 as $n^2 - (n-k)(n+k)$ obtain equation (8).

9. Following equation (8) we show how to obtain $A_{2n+1} = 2A_n$. Obtain this relation from a direct examination of 2-sorted lists.

10. Show that equation (10) provides $f(N,h) = \sqrt{\pi h} N^{3/2}/8 + O(N)$ using Stirling approximation for the factorials.

11. Use equation (13) to obtain the leading term (in N) for $I(N,\alpha)$, the total number of inversions in a t-stage Shell sort with increments $h_s = \alpha^{s-1}$, $1 \leq s \leq t$, where t is determined by $\alpha^{t+1} \geq N$. What is the optimal value of α? What are then the values of t and $I(N,\alpha_{opt})$?

12. Show that if the random variable X has the cdf $F(\cdot)$, then $F(X)$ is uniformly distributed on $[0,1]$. What if $F(\cdot)$ has atoms, i.e., jumps?

13. Prove that when the first pass of the Linear Probing sort is done all the keys are in the correct order.

14. Obtain equation (19) from (17) and (18). (Careful when exchanging the order of summation!)
Show inductively from equation (19) that all $P_i(z)$ are regular at $z = 0$.

15. Prove by examining coefficients that both sides of equation (24) are polynomials in α of degree i.

16*. Use equation (19) to determine the region, in z, in which $P_i(z) \to P(z)$ for $\alpha < 1$. Gonnet and Munro (1984) claim it converges at least for $z \in [1,1/\alpha]$. What is the meaning of the statement that $P_i(z)$ do not converge when $\alpha = 1$? (what is then the interpretation of equation (36)?).

17. Obtain the values given in equations (37) and (38) (use l'Hopital's rule).

18. Knuth (1973, Section 1.2.11.3) discusses the following functions (quoting Carlitz, 1965):

$$Q_x(n) \equiv 1 + \frac{n-1}{n/x} + \frac{n-1}{n/x} \cdot \frac{n-2}{n/x} + \cdots, \quad R_x(n) \equiv 1 + \frac{nx}{n+1} + \frac{nx}{n+1} \cdot \frac{nx}{n+2} + \cdots$$

(a) Find a simple relation between $Q_x(n)$ and $R_x(n)$.

(b) Define $S_x(n) \equiv \dfrac{1}{1-x} - \dfrac{x}{n(1-x)^3} + O(n^{-2})$. Then, for $|x| < 1$ show

$$Q_x(n) = S_x(n); \qquad R_x(n) = S_x(n)$$

(Remember that the 'O' operator is not transitive!)
(c) For $|x| > 1$ obtain

$$Q_x(n) = \frac{n!}{x}\left(\frac{x}{n}\right)^n e^{nx} + S_x(n)$$

$$R_x(n) = n!\left(\frac{x}{n}\right)^n e^{nx} + S_x(n)$$

(d) Verify equation (44).

19. Obtain equation (45) starting with equation (37) and using the asymptotic expansion given in equation (2.2-42).

20. Handle equation (38) in the fashion equation (37) was used to produce equation (45), and get $V(W_{m,n})$ to $O(m^{-2})$.

21. Obtain $V(W_{m,m})$, to order $O(m^{-1})$, using the same approach that provides the results in equation (48).

22. (a) Show that the sum in equation (52) has a geometrical tail with the factor $\beta = \alpha e^{1-\alpha}$. Estimate this factor for the values of α in the table given there.
(b) Using the sum in Exercise 2.2-7 reduce the above sum to a finite one. Estimate its numerical properties (there is no question obviously of convergence, but how about the required number of digits to guarantee a specified precision?)
[It is bad, very very bad, and one must use a multiple-precision package to compute it.]
(c) Compare terms from the Table on p.142 with the bounds that are provided by

the one-sided Chebyshev inequality.

23. For $n = 4$, $m = 5$, compute explicit expressions (by direct counting) for all the characteristics of the overflow process and compare them with the corresponding values from the asymptotic estimates.

24. This problem concerns the running time of the Linear Probing sort algorithm. First under the Poisson model. Let $C(m, \alpha)$ denote the expected number of times a location in the table is examined in the first phase of the algorithm, as given in Fig. 3.5 (we count as one access the entire sequence of testing whether the location is free, comparing its key with the currently inserted one if it is not and the exchange of keys, if necessary).

(a) Prove that $C(m, \alpha)$ is invariant, for a given set of keys, under any change of the order in which they are processed.

(b) Show

$$C(m,\alpha) = m\alpha + \sum_{i=1}^{m} P_i'(1) + \frac{1}{2} E[W_{m,\alpha}(W_{m,\alpha}-1)]$$

(c) From the analysis of $W_{m,\alpha}$ obtain

$$\frac{1}{2} E[W_{m,\alpha}(W_{m,\alpha}-1)] = \frac{P_m''(1)}{2} = \frac{\alpha^4}{4(1-\alpha)^2} + \frac{\alpha^3}{6(1-\alpha)} + O(\beta^{m+1})$$

where $\beta = \alpha e^{1-\alpha}$. Now obtain the following expression for $S = \Sigma P_i'(1)$

$$\sum_{i=1}^{m} P_i'(1) = \frac{m\alpha^2}{2(1-\alpha)} - \frac{(8-5\alpha)\alpha^3}{12(1-\alpha)^3} + O(\beta^{m+2})$$

by doing steps (d) through (g):

(d) Proceed by first writing S explicitly, from equation (20) and substituting from equation (23).

(e) Prove

$$[\alpha^{j+1}]P_i'(1) = \frac{1}{2}, \quad j < i$$

[Hint: this is immediate using equation (41), but can also be done by direct computation, which is later needed anyway, using the summations shown in Exercise 3.1-8.]

(f) From the sum in (d) show

$$[\alpha^{j+1}]\sum_{i=1}^{m} P_i'(1) = \frac{-3j^2+5j+10}{24} + \frac{m-j}{2}$$

where you could use the summations shown in Exercise 3.1-8.

(g) Use standard summation formulas and the result of (f) to get the result for S above.

(h) Combining previous results obtain finally

$$C(m,\alpha) = \frac{m}{2}\left(\frac{1}{1-\alpha} + \alpha - 1\right) - \frac{\alpha^3(\alpha^2 - 4\alpha + 6)}{12(1-\alpha)^3} + O(\beta^{m+1})$$

(i) Now for the "balls in cells" model, use results from Exercise 2.2-7 to obtain the transform of $C(m,\alpha)$:

$$C(m,n) = \frac{m}{2}\left(\sum_{k\geq 0} q_k(m,n) - \frac{m-n}{m}\right) - \frac{n(m-n+1)}{12m^2} - \sum_{k\geq 0}\frac{(3k-5)k}{24}q_k(m,n)$$

where $q_k(m,n) = \dfrac{n^k}{m^k}$.

(j) Obtain asymptotic expansion for $C(m,n)$ to order $O(m^{-2})$, either from $C(m,\alpha)$ and equation (2.2-42), or from the expression in (i) and equations (43, 44).

(k) So far for the first phase. What is the contribution of the second phase to the number of accesses?

(l) We have defined above $C(m,\alpha)$ (and hence $C(m,n)$ as well) in a rather cavalier way, counting one access for sometimes differing activities. Define now $C_1(m,\alpha)$, $C_2(m,\alpha)$ and $C_3(m,\alpha)$ as the number of tests for occupancy, comparisons between keys and exchanges between keys, respectively. Note that when probing, once a key is placed in its correct location no more key comparisons are needed for that insertion, though occupancy tests and exchanges may still be needed. Outline the computation of these quantities (for the two phases).

Chapter 4

Algorithms for Communications Networks

In this chapter we present analyses of communications-related algorithms and protocols. The criteria I used for selection of the presented algorithms concern the type of analysis and varieties of mathematics involved in computing their operational characteristics, rather than their engineering merits. Indeed, some of the presented protocols must be considered quite unacceptable, on practical grounds. One hopes, nevertheless, that the analysis proper will prove interesting and useful in other circumstances as well. Virtually no previous knowledge of communications techniques and terminology is required, beyond what one assimilates from day-to-day life.

4.1 The Efficiency of Multiple Connections (Lagarias et al., 1985)

Consider a number of users with access to a single broadcast channel. This is a convenient medium for one user to convey a message to all others simultaneously. It is quite common, however, that users wish to communicate pair-wise, and then the universal accessibility of the channel has a serious inhibiting effect, since any two different concurrent broadcasts interfere destructively. In other words, the capacity of the channel is one message at a time. This is the type of channel most frequently encountered in applications. There are numerous technologies that are used to implement such a channel: bus, twisted pair, wideband radio (both terrestrial and satellite links), coaxial cable and more. They all have, however, this sorry capacity in common. Can one do better, while staying within available technology? Indeed it is possible, and we present one such method.

4.1.1 Disjointly Shared Channels - Capacity Considerations

In order to increase the capacity of the network to more than "one message at a time" we must use a medium which is less easily disrupted, which can carry several messages concurrently, or as the above authors call it - a disjointly sharable channel. We are thus led to consider a channel that can be pictorially represented as in Fig. 4.1(a), and which would allow communications to take place within the pairs (1,2), (3,4), (5,6) concurrently. However, if the pairs (1,6) or (2,5) were "talking", all others would be blocked. Let the segment connecting node i to $i+1$ be referred to as segment i. The type of channel considered below is completely characterized by stating that when the pair (i,j) with $i<j$, communicates, segments i to $j-1$ are captured. The effectiveness of this channel depends therefore on the traffic pattern (who wishes to speak with whom, and how often). It also depends on the connection topology and switching capabilities of the nodes. For example, consider a star network, as shown in Fig. 4.1(b). Minimal assumptions imply that only a single pair could use it at any time; more generous assumptions on the switching capacity of node 2 would allow any two disjoint pairs out of the possible 10 to communicate concurrently.

Following the above reference we consider a k-cable network connecting in parallel $2N$ users, with full availability, as represented in Fig. 4.2. We remark that technically such a topology is quite feasible, the full availability being the expensive part. Cost in implementing it could probably be traded off against the

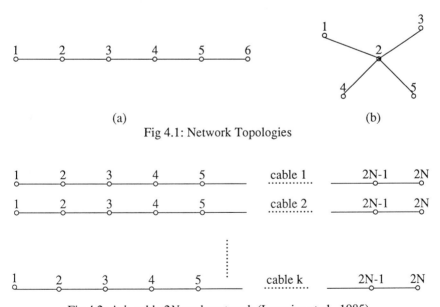

(a)   (b)

Fig 4.1: Network Topologies

Fig 4.2: A k-cable $2N$ node network (Lagarias et al., 1985)

time required to set up a call.

Capacity is defined as the maximal number of useful messages the network can carry simultaneously with no conflict; more precisely, capacity is defined below as this number averaged on the modes of operation of the network that are allowed by the communication protocols used in it. Clearly, if $k \geq N$ no calls would ever be blocked, since each pair could capture an entire cable for itself; the situation is less simple when $k < N$, which is the case of interest, and we propose to study the capacity of the network under this assumption. In particular, we are interested in the dependence of the capacity on the parameters N and k, and especially what happens to the capacity when more nodes are added to an existing network (i.e. N is increased, but k is not).

Protocol Considerations

When asked about the *load* carried on a network, one must know in addition to the network topology which we have defined, also the characterization of the offered traffic and the communication protocol. When the focus is on *capacity* only, the offered traffic is irrelevant, or may be assumed infinitely large (or inexhaustible), and only the protocol has to be further specified. Without going into technical details we shall assume the protocol operates on a "slotted" time schedule; time is viewed as a succession of *sessions* of fixed duration. Each session a number of pairs is allowed to communicate. The set of permitted calls is such that enough cable segments are available so that they can all be set up concurrently. We shall say that each slot, or session, a *realizable configuration of pairs* is enabled.

Consider Fig. 4.2 with $k=2, N=4$. The permission $\{(1,5),(4,6)\}$ is clearly realizable, and we may add to it the pairs (2,3) and (7,8), but not (2,7), as it requires segments that are already completely utilized. In order to compute the capacity of the network we shall need a few definitions:

configuration - a set of pairs $\{(i,j), 1 \leq i < j \leq 2N\}$, such that no node is repeated.

k−realizable configuration - a configuration where all the pairs can communicate concurrently on a k-cable network. We shall often drop the k prefix when it is implied by the context.

k−maximal configuration - a configuration which is k-realizable but is not $(k-1)$-realizable.

full configuration - a configuration of N pairs (i.e., all the nodes are paired off).

k−complete configuration - a configuration to which no pair can be added retaining realizability, either because it is full or because it is maximal.

A formal definition of the *capacity* of the network is given below, in equation (1).

Example. When $k = 2$, $N = 4$:
 $\{(1,2),(3,4),(5,6),(7,8)\}$ is full, and therefore complete but not 2-maximal.
 $\{(1,5),(4,6)\}$ is 2-maximal, but not 2-complete.

A general statement that it is possible to make about network capacity under such "pair enabling" protocols runs as follows:

Let the protocol pick for every session one realizable configuration out of a collection C of such configurations. Assume that these successive decisions (choices) are determined by an independent process. For example, a configuration $c_s \in C$ is picked for each session with a probability p_s. Let the number of pairs enabled in c_s be n_s, then the load capacity of the network, in calls per session, under this protocol is

$$A = \sum_{c_s \in C} p_s n_s \, . \tag{1}$$

One could alternatively reason as follows: Let p_{ij} be the probability that the pair (i,j) is enabled in such a random configuration, i.e.

$$p_{ij} = \sum_{c_s \in C} p_s \chi_{(i,j) \text{ is enabled in } c_s} \, , \tag{2}$$

where the indicator function χ_E is 1 or 0 when the event E does or does not happen, respectively. Then we also have $A = \sum_{i,j} p_{ij}$.

An interesting characterization of a protocol uses the number of segments it utilizes: we can define the mean number of cable segments used by one call during a session

$$\bar{d} = \frac{1}{A} \sum_{i,j} p_{ij} (j-i), \tag{3}$$

where we have made explicit our convention of writing a pair (i,j) so that $i < j$. Since a k-cable $2N$ node network has altogether $k(2N-1)$ segments, its capacity, A, under that protocol, is bounded by $k(2N-1)/\bar{d}$.

Suppose all p_{ij} are equal to some fixed value p, then some computation leads to

$$\bar{d} = \frac{1}{\binom{2N}{2}} \sum_{i=1}^{2N-1} \sum_{j=i+1}^{2N} (j-i) = \frac{2N-1}{3} \, . \tag{4}$$

Thus the mean number of possible calls is bounded by $3k$, independently of N, a manifestly poor behavior. (This result could be viewed as a bound on the value of the probability p defined above, but see Exercise 1(b) for a discussion of a more fundamental difficulty with it.)

Typically k is a small number, even when N could be quite large; in such circumstances the above bound is unacceptable. Rather, we would like protocols that satisfy the following requirements:

a)   Each pair is allowed calls. The time between successive permissions must have two first moments that are finite.

b)   The protocol generates an acceptably low value for $\bar{d}$. In particular, we would like A to be *linear* in N.

Writing the last requirement as $A \sim aN$ we see that it requires $\bar{d}$ to be essentially independent of N. Obviously this means that unlike the egalitarian protocol that led to equation (4) we are interested in protocols that discriminate against expensive calls (i.e. calls that require a large number of cable segments). This should cause no hardship in actual applications *if* the position of nodes on the network could be juggled according to their traffic requirements (see Exercise 11).

Devising algorithms that satisfy the above requirements is no mean undertaking, and our mission here being to demonstrate their analysis, rather than invent them, we pick the next simplest one. It turns out to be acceptable, in the sense that it meets the above criteria.

Definition (The Realizable Configurations protocol) For each session, the protocol draws a configuration at random, independently of previous assignments and equiprobably from all the members of C, the collection of all k-realizable configurations.

The pairs specified by the drawn configuration are enabled. Thus $p_s = 1/|C|$.

Remarks 1. Obviously, this need not the best possible protocol. A conceivably cleverer one may only choose complete configurations; still another might keep only full configurations on the active list, making thus sure that every node can take part in communications at any given slot.

2. Other algorithmic questions of interest (presumably leading to protocols that are better or more efficient in some suitable sense, or easier to implement), could be asked. For example: a) What is the minimal set C_m of realizable configurations that enables all pairs? b) Find, among *all* sets C of realizable configurations that enable all pairs, with a given upper bound on the "inter-permission" interval, the one that minimizes $\bar{d}$. Then there are the questions that concern adapting the protocol to the demand (i.e. the traffic pattern, or the load) on the network, to a given priority assignment on the nodes, to delay bounds and more, which we shall not consider any further, partly because they are not of an analytic nature, and partly because they are very hard indeed.

3. The assumption that the successive operations of the protocol are randomly generated from a feasible assignment list is inessential. The same capacity would be achieved if the successive permissions were generated by going through this list cyclically, similar to a TDMA scheme used in a broadcast network. It follows from well-known results in queueing theory that the delay experienced by messages could be made shorter when such a deterministic assignment is used than when a random assignment is employed.

4.1.2 Counting Realizable Configurations

We proceed now to evaluate the capacity of the above simple protocol. Every set of pair permissions defines an involution over $\{1, 2, \cdots, 2N\}$, that is, a permutation with cycles of length 1 (the unpaired nodes) and length 2 (the enabled pairs) only. The counting of these configurations is tackled now in a few steps. We define first *crossing numbers* vectors. An involution σ is said to assign to segment i a non-negative integer, equal to the number of pairs enabled by σ that must use a segment between i and $i+1$ to communicate. Denoting this number by c_i we have

$$c_i(\sigma) = |\{j : j \leq i < \sigma(j)\}|, \quad 1 \leq i \leq 2N-1 \tag{5}$$

These numbers give us a convenient way to define a realizable configuration: σ is realizable iff $c_i(\sigma) \leq k$, $1 \leq i \leq 2N-1$. It is maximal if there is an i such that $c_i(\sigma) = k$. The first step in the counting procedure is to consider only *full maximal* configurations. These will provide easy access to the number of *full realizable* configurations, and from these we shall finally construct the count of all the k-realizable ones.

Counting Full Realizable Configurations

Full maximal configurations are complete. There may be other complete maximal configurations that are not full. They are not considered in this subsection. A full configuration induces an involution with no fixed point, or no cycles of length 1.

Definition: $i_k(N)$ - the number of k-realizable full configurations (not necessarily maximal) over $2N$ nodes.

Corollary: The number of k-maximal full configurations over $2N$ nodes is $i_k(N) - i_{k-1}(N)$.

Further we define:

$$I_k(z) \equiv \sum_{N \geq 0} i_k(N) z^N, \quad i_k(0) \equiv 1, \quad k \geq 1; \quad i_0(N) = 0, \ N > 0. \tag{6}$$

A characterization of all such configurations in terms of the crossing numbers they induce follows:

Lemma: Let the crossing numbers $(c_1, \cdots, c_{2N-1})$ correspond to a realizable configuration σ.

The necessary and sufficient conditions for σ to be a full configuration are:

a) $c_1 = c_{2N-1} = 1$

b) $c_i \geq 0$, $1 < i < 2N-1$ (7)

c) $c_{i+1} = c_i \pm 1$, $1 \leq i < 2N-1$

Proof: The necessity is obvious, on inspection. For sufficiency, note that $c_1 = 1$ ensures that node 1 is in some pair. Consider the nodes i, $1 \leq i \leq 2N-1$, in increasing order: $c_{i+1} = c_i+1$ means that node $i+1$ is paired with a higher numbered node to be later selected. When $c_i = j$, exactly j among the nodes 1 to i are still free to select a partner from nodes $i+1$ to $2N$. When $c_{i+1} = c_i-1$, node $i+1$ is paired with one of the nodes 1 to i, and there are exactly c_i distinct ways of

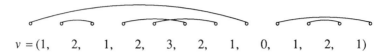

$$v = (1, \quad 2, \quad 1, \quad 2, \quad 3, \quad 2, \quad 1, \quad 0, \quad 1, \quad 2, \quad 1)$$

Fig. 4.3: An example of a "full" crossing-number vector
and a possible corresponding configuration.

doing this. See Fig. 4.3.   □

Let $N(v)$ be the number of configurations that correspond to a vector of crossing numbers $v = (c_j)$, satisfying the constraints (7). The above proof then shows that

$$N(v) = \prod_{i:c_i > c_{i+1}} c_i . \tag{8}$$

A standard way to count such vectors is to consider the paths they prescribe on a plane grid. A very elegant and rather complete treatment may be found in Flajolet (1980); as we need a very special case we compute it directly.

The natural way to proceed would be either one of the following two:

a) Derive an equation (typically a recursion) for $I_k(z)$, from which an explicit representation of $i_k(N)$, or an asymptotic approximation thereof, could be determined. Or

b) Construct the collection of k-realizable full configurations from simpler building blocks we can directly count, as was done several times in Section 2.4.

Neither of these appears doable, so we proceed in a more circuitous manner.

Definition: Let $C_{k,t,N}$ be the set of involutions corresponding to the vector of crossing numbers v that satisfy conditions (7), and in addition

a) $c_i \le k$, $1 \le i \le 2N-1$,

b) $c_i = k$ for exactly t values of i ,   (9)

c) if $t = 0$, there exist such i that $c_i = k-1$.

Also define $f_{k,t}(N) \equiv |C_{k,t,N}|$.

This is admittedly a strange looking construction, but observe that $f_{k+1,0}(N)$ is precisely the number of k-maximal full configurations.

We now prove the recursion

$$f_{k,t}(N) = \sum_{s \ge 0} f_{k-1,s}(N-t)k^t \binom{t+s-1}{t}, \quad t \ge 0. \tag{10}$$

Proof: Consider vectors v that satisfy (7) and (9). Each has exactly t pairs of terms $k, k-1$ in it. Deleting these pairs transforms a vector v into a $2(N-t)$-dimensional vector $v*$ that generates involutions in $C_{k-1, s, N-t}$ for some $s \geq 0$.

Example: $k = 3$, $v = (1\ 2\ \underline{3\ 2}\ \underline{3\ 2}\ 1\ 0\ 1\ 2\ \underline{3\ 2}\ 1)$, $\qquad v* = (1\ 2\ 1\ 0\ 1\ 2\ 1)$.

The converse transformation leads to the

Question: considering a vector $v*$ that corresponds to involutions in $C_{k-1, s, N-t}$, in how many ways can it be augmented to a vector v that corresponds to $C_{k, t, N}$?

Answer: the same as the number of ways to distribute t identical objects (the pairs $k, k-1$) in s distinct cells (adjacent to the right of the s values $k-1$ already in $v*$). This number comes to $\binom{t+s-1}{t}$. According to equation (8), each augmented vector v corresponding to $v*$ will give rise to $k^t N(v*)$ configurations in $C_{k, t, N}$. Hence the ratio between the configuration counts is k^t. Summing on s produces equation (10). $\qquad \square$

The time has come to proceed via gf's; define

$$F_{k,t}(z) \equiv \sum_{N \geq 0} f_{k,t}(N) z^N, \quad F_{1,0}(0) \equiv 1, \ F_{k,t}(0) = 0, \ t > 0. \tag{11}$$

Since as observed above $f_{k+1,0}(N) = i_k(N) - i_{k-1}(N)$, we also have

$$F_{k+1,0}(z) = I_k(z) - I_{k-1}(z). \tag{12}$$

Consider using (10) to evaluate $F_{k,t}(z)$. Since $f_{1,t}(N) = \delta_{t,N}$ (Exercise 3), $F_{1,t}(z) = z^t$. Equations (10) and (A.2.4) then lead to

$$F_{2,t}(z) = \frac{z}{1-z} \left(\frac{2z}{1-z}\right)^t, \ F_{3,t}(z) = \frac{2z^2}{(1-z)(1-3z)} \left(\frac{3z(1-z)}{1-3z}\right)^t. \tag{13}$$

This computation suggests a general form

$$F_{k,t}(z) = A_k(z) B_k^t(z). \tag{14}$$

Substitution of equation (14) into (10) provides

$$F_{k+1,t}(z) = A_k(z) \frac{B_k(z)}{1-B_k(z)} \left(\frac{(k+1)z}{1-B_k(z)}\right)^t$$

When one views t as a parameter, this leads to the following possible scheme

$$A_k(z) = A_{k-1}(z) \frac{B_{k-1}(z)}{1-B_{k-1}(z)}, \ A_1(z) = 1,$$

$$B_k(z) = \frac{kz}{1-B_{k-1}(z)}, \ B_1(z) = z. \tag{15}$$

This scheme also provides a representation for $A_k(z)$

$$A_k(z) = \prod_{i=1}^{k-1} \frac{B_i(z)}{1-B_i(z)}, \tag{16}$$

and the second equation in (15) implies that $B_k(z)$ can be represented as a rational function

$$B_{k+1}(z) = \frac{P_k(z)}{Q_k(z)}, \tag{17}$$

where $P_k(z)$ and $Q_k(z)$ are defined to be relatively prime polynomials, the first few of which can be inferred from equation (15): $Q_{-1}(z) = Q_0(z) = 1$, $P_0(z) = z$, $P_{-1}(z) = 0$. Equation (15) also gives, on substitution (and the primality requirement)

$$P_k(z) = (k+1)zQ_{k-1}(z),$$
$$Q_k(z) = Q_{k-1}(z) - P_{k-1}(z) = Q_{k-1}(z) - kzQ_{k-2}(z). \tag{18}$$

The reason for this roundabout procedure will soon be evident, although we are not yet done.

From equation (14) $F_{k+1,0}(z) = A_{k+1}(z)$, and from equation (12) then

$$I_k(z) = I_0(z) + \sum_{j=2}^{k+1} A_j(z). \tag{19}$$

Substituting the recurrences (18) in equations (15) and (17) gives:

$$B_k(z) = \frac{kzQ_{k-2}(z)}{Q_{k-1}(z)}, \quad 1 - B_k(z) = \frac{Q_k(z)}{Q_{k-1}(z)}, \tag{20}$$

and on substituting this into equation (16) the product "telescopes" into

$$A_{k+1}(z) = \frac{k!z^k}{Q_k(z)Q_{k-1}(z)}. \tag{21}$$

These functions need to be summed, in equation (19), and it would be useful if we found a representation such that the sum telescoped conveniently as well. A natural attempt is to decompose $A_{k+1}(z)$ into partial fractions, that is, into the form

$$A_{k+1}(z) = \frac{R_k(z)}{Q_k(z)} - \frac{R_{k-1}(z)}{Q_{k-1}(z)}. \tag{22}$$

Note that it is not obvious *a priori* that the numerators would prove to be the k and $k-1$ versions of the same function. The derivation below justifies the choice (or the notation) *a posteriori*.

Since $A_1(z) = 1$, $A_2(z) = z/(1-z)$, consistent choices would be $R_{-1}(z) = 0$, $R_0 = 1$, and trying successively for a few higher values we observe that it appears that $R_k(z)$ satisfies the same recursion as $Q_k(z)$, in equation (18). We use this suggestion and shall verify it. The right-hand side of equation (22) suggests a 2×2 determinant, so we represent the common recurrence relations for $Q_k(z)$ and $R_k(z)$ in a matricial form

$$\begin{bmatrix} R_k(z) & R_{k-1}(z) \\ Q_k(z) & Q_{k-1}(z) \end{bmatrix} = \begin{bmatrix} R_{k-1}(z) & R_{k-2}(z) \\ Q_{k-1}(z) & Q_{k-2}(z) \end{bmatrix} \begin{bmatrix} 1 & 1 \\ -kz & 0 \end{bmatrix}, \quad k \geq 1$$

$$\cdot$$
$$\cdot$$
$$\cdot$$

$$= \begin{bmatrix} R_0(z) & R_{-1}(z) \\ Q_0(z) & Q_{-1}(z) \end{bmatrix} \begin{bmatrix} 1 & 1 \\ -z & 0 \end{bmatrix} \begin{bmatrix} 1 & 1 \\ -2z & 0 \end{bmatrix} \cdots \begin{bmatrix} 1 & 1 \\ -kz & 0 \end{bmatrix}.$$

Evaluating the determinant of both sides yields

$$R_k(z)Q_{k-1}(z) - Q_k(z)R_{k-1}(z) = k! z^k, \tag{23}$$

which precisely fits equations (21) and (22).

The expression for $I_k(z)$ in equation (19) then telescopes to provide (using $I_0(z) = 1$)

$$I_k(z) = 1 + \frac{R_k(z)}{Q_k(z)} - \frac{R_0(z)}{Q_0(z)} = \frac{R_k(z)}{Q_k(z)}. \tag{24}$$

From equation (24) we can extract coefficients and compute $i_k(N)$ directly, for not too large k and N. Thus one obtains the appended Tables 1 and 2 (produced by a MAPLE program).

The enumeration of all k-realizable configurations is now simple: any choice of $2m$ out of the $2N$ points provides $i_k(m)$ full configurations. All the realizable configurations are captured when we allow m to range over 0 to N. Thus the total number of configurations this protocol uses is:

$$t_k(N) = \sum_{m=0}^{N} \binom{2N}{2m} i_k(m). \tag{25}$$

Estimating the capacity this protocol affords is now straightforward. Picking a configuration based on a $2m$ full configuration allows m connections, and thus the mean number of pairs enabled by this protocol in each slot is

$$E_k^{(2)}(N) \equiv u_k(N)/t_k(N) = \sum_{m=0}^{N} m \binom{2N}{2m} i_k(m)/t_k(N). \tag{26}$$

(See Exercise 6.) Below we compute an asymptotic estimate (in N) for $E_k^{(2)}(N)$.

4.1.3 Asymptotic Capacity Estimates

We wish now to have an asymptotic estimate of A as defined in equation (1) for this particular protocol, through equation (26). In particular, its dependence on N, for large N, is of interest. The road is much simplified by the following identification:

$k \setminus N$	1	2	3	4	5	6	7	8	9
1	1	1	1	1	1	1	1	1	1
	2	8	32	128	512	2048	8192	32768	131072
2	1	3	9	27	81	243	729	2187	6561
	2	10	70	518	3862	28822	215126	1605718	11985238
3	1	3	15	81	441	2403	13095	71361	388881
	2	10	76	740	7912	87016	964592	10715920	119116576
4	1	3	15	105	825	6675	54375	443625	3620625
	2	10	76	764	9376	128512	1851080	27200776	402780184
5	1	3	15	105	945	9675	104175	1141425	12578625
	2	10	76	764	9496	139432	2294000	40295536	731832544
6	1	3	15	105	945	10395	130095	1739745	23966145
	2	10	76	764	9496	140152	2385440	45314656	927444304
7	1	3	15	105	945	10395	135135	1986705	31516065
	2	10	76	764	9496	140152	2390480	46166416	988201504
8	1	3	15	105	945	10395	135135	2027025	34096545
	2	10	76	764	9496	140152	2390480	46206736	996950944
9	1	3	15	105	945	10395	135135	2027025	34459425
	2	10	76	764	9496	140152	2390480	46206736	997313824

Table 1: Values of $i_k(N)$ (top) and $t_k(N)$ (bottom)
(from Lagarias et al. 1985, in part)

k	$Q_k(x)$	$R_k(x)$
0	1	1
1	$1-x$	1
2	$1-3x$	$1-2x$
3	$1-6x+3x^2$	$1-5x$
4	$1-10x+15x^2$	$1-9x+8x^2$
5	$1-15x+45x^2-15x^3$	$1-14x+33x^2$
6	$1-21x+105x^2-105x^3$	$1-20x+8x^2-48x^3$

Table 2: Values for $Q_k(x)$ and $R_k(z)$ (from Lagarias et al. 1985, in part)

Lemma

$$Q_k(z) = \left(\frac{z}{2}\right)^{(k+1)/2} H_{k+1}[(1/2z)^{1/2}],\qquad (27)$$

where $H_i(z)$ is the Hermite polynomial of order i.

The **proof** consists simply in showing that initial values of Q and H fit equation (27), and by examining the recurrences they satisfy. Now, standard references for orthogonal polynomials (e.g. Abramowitz and Stegun (1964) or Szegö (1967)) provide the information

$$H_1(z) = 2z, \qquad H_2(z) = 4z^2-2, \qquad H_{k+1}(z) = 2zH_k(z) - 2kH_{k-1}(z),\qquad (28)$$

and this is identical with the first few $Q_i(z)$ and equation (18) (Exercise 7).   □

Since $I_k(z) = R_k(z)/Q_k(z)$, the asymptotic properties of $I_k(z)$ depend on the zero of $Q_k(z)$ which is closest to the origin, and in view of equation (27), this requires the knowledge of the *largest* root of $H_{k+1}(z)$. Szegö (1967) provides the information that the roots of $H_r(u)$ are simple, real and positive, and the largest, $\theta_1^{(r)}$, is given by

$$\theta_1^{(r)} = \sqrt{2r+1} - (2r+1)^{1/6}(c_0 + o(1)), \quad c_0 = \frac{i_o}{3\sqrt{6}} \approx 1.85575. \quad (29)$$

Let $\phi_i^{(k)}$ be the roots of $Q_k(z)$. Since we constructed $R_k(z)$ and $Q_k(z)$ as relatively prime, there exist for each integer k real numbers $d_i^{(k)}$, such that

$$I_k(z) = d_0^{(k)} + \sum_{i=1}^{\lceil k/2 \rceil} \frac{d_i^{(k)}}{z - \phi_i^{(k)}}, \quad (30)$$

and when the smallest root is $\phi_1^{(k)}$, $i_k(N) \sim c_1^{(k)}\left(\phi_1^{(k)}\right)^{-N}$, with some real $c_1^{(k)}$. The relative primality of $Q_k(z)$ and $R_k(z)$, evident in equation (23), assures us that $c_1^{(k)} \neq 0$. However, equation (27) implies that

$$\frac{1}{\sqrt{2\phi_1^{(k)}}} = \theta_1^{(k)} \Rightarrow i_k(N) \sim c_1^{(k)}\left[2\left(\theta_1^{(k+1)}\right)^2\right]^N = c_1^{(k)} r_k^{2N}, \quad (31)$$

where $r_k \equiv \sqrt{2}\,\theta_1^{(k+1)}$. From equation (29) then $i_k(N) \sim c_1^{(k)}(4k)^N$.

Substituting in equation (25):

$$t_k(N) \sim \sum_{m=0}^{N} \binom{2N}{2m} c_1^{(k)} r_k^{2m} \sim \frac{1}{2} c_1^{(k)} (1+r_k)^{2N}, \quad (32)$$

(See Exercise 8) and

$$u_k(N) = \sum_{m=0}^{N} \binom{2N}{2m} m\, i_k(m) \sim \frac{1}{2} r_k N\, c_1^{(k)} (1+r_k)^{2N-1}, \quad (33)$$

So that

$$E_k^{(2)}(N) \sim N \frac{r_k}{1+r_k}. \quad (34)$$

Linear in N, as desired. The coefficient is simply available from equation (29).

Exercises and Complements

1. (a) Complete the computations leading to equation (4).
(b) Consider the set-up of Fig. 4.2 with $k = 2, N = 4$. Under what random selection protocol as described there is it possible to obtain $p_{ij} = p$, for all pairs (i,j)? Could you generalize?

2. What is the relation between the crossing numbers of an involution and its inversion table?

3. Show that $f_{1,t}(N) = \delta_{t,N}$ (remember that only full configurations need to be considered), prove equation (12) and compute $F_{3,t}(z)$.

4. Prove equation (21), as outlined in the text.

5. Obtain the first few polynomials and numbers of those given in Tables 1 and 2.

6. Using equation (26) and Table 2 find $E_3^{(2)}(N)$ for $N = 1,2,3$.

7. Show that equations (28) and (27) are in agreement with the recursion of $Q_k(z)$ in equation (18).

8. Complete the computations leading to equations (32)-(34). Note that they are all asymptotic estimates only. Compute the coefficient in equation (34) for $5 \le k \le 10$. Then, use the recursion (28) to produce the corresponding Hermite polynomials and determine $\theta_1^{(k)}$ numerically, to evaluate and compare $E_k^{(2)}(N)$.

9*. As indicated in remark 1 of Section 4.1.1, the protocol analyzed here selects quite often incomplete configurations. How would you proceed to evaluate the efficiency of a protocol that only picks complete configurations?

10*. Under the protocol analyzed in Section 4.1.2, what is the probability that the pair (i,j) is enabled during a random slot?

11*. In this problem you are asked to consider the optimal placement of nodes in a network with the topology of Fig. 4.2, under the assumption that communication permissions are granted on the basis of the algorithm analyzed in Section 4.1.2. Consider the following two different situations that can arise with respect to the information provided about the offered traffic:
(a) Node i generates calls at rate λ_i, with the destinations uniformly distributed over the other $2N-1$ nodes.
(b) The node pair (i,j) is offered traffic at the rate λ_{ij}.
(Remark: while case (a) has a simple and intuitive solution, the case (b) is qualitatively different, and is a variant of the so-called "bookshelf problem".)

12*. Section 4.1.2 and Exercise 9 consider two permission assignment schemes that necessarily have efficiencies which are less than 1. A protocol using only *full* configurations would do better in this respect. Use the results obtained in Section 4.1.2 to determine the traffic possible under such a protocol (this calls for the evaluation of the permission probabilities p_{ij}).

4.2 Collision Resolution Stack Algorithms

In this section we consider an algorithm that is rather different from those we have considered so far, both in the type of input it handles and in the methods that will be required to analyze its operation. We shall present and analyze a collision resolution protocol followed by transmitters in a communications network that will be specified below. The points worth noting at this stage are:

a) The protocol is "non terminating" in the sense that the network is assumed to exist for an unbounded time; data, messages in this context, arrive according to a stochastic process, stay for a while at the transmitting nodes, and when broadcast successfully "depart" - exit the system.

b) The protocol we consider employs a random element; this, added to the arrival process provides us with *two* sources of randomness.

c) Although the system appears to behave as a service system with one server (the broadcast channel), none of the standard techniques developed for analyzing service systems (telephony, queueing theory ...) is useful here. The service mechanism is sufficiently different to make them quite irrelevant.

We shall now describe the network and then specify the protocol to be analyzed.

The reader is not assumed to be familiar with the concepts that underlie computer communications or packet-switching. We shall briefly summarize the system characteristics which describe a rather large variety of types of networks that are the descendants of the ALOHA network, the forerunner of them all. Sometimes we shall specialize to the environment we intend to analyze:

The Network Model

1) An infinite number of users (nodes, transmitters ...) wish to communicate.

2) A single, error-free channel is available. Each user can receive any other on this channel. Alternatively, all the users may be viewed as transmitting to some central location. No other means exist for a user to know about the communications activity, past or intended, of the other users.

3) Communications are performed by transmitting "packets". The time axis is "slotted" into equal sized slots, a slot being the time needed to transmit one packet; propagation delay is negligible and may be taken as zero (whatever delay there is could be considered part of the packet duration). All the users are always synchronized with respect to these slots and transmit packets at slot-start only.

4) The number of new packets created throughout the network during each slot has a Poisson distribution with parameter λ, independently of past events in the network and the current state. This is consistent with the assumption of a multitude of users, each of which only rather rarely needs to transmit. A user that has a packet to transmit is an *active user*.

5) The users are algorithmically and statistically identical, follow the same communications protocol and are not ordered in any sense. They are adamant: in the face of channel over-commitment each active user will keep its packet indefinitely, until it is successfully transmitted.

6) Only active users need to monitor the channel. At the end of each slot each such user can determine whether during the slot a *collision* occurred, arising from the

simultaneous transmission by two or more users, or not (binary feedback). The corresponding channel responses are denoted by *nack* and *ack* (short for acknowledgment). Messages involved in a collision cannot be correctly received, are assumed lost, and need to be retransmitted.

7) The protocol used by transmitters to resolve collisions - that is, to retransmit messages that have been destroyed by a collision, is derived from Collision Resolution Algorithms (CRAs) suggested independently by Capetanakis (1979, 1979a), Tsybakov and Mikhailov (1978) and later elaborated by Tsybakov and Vvedenskaya (1980), and are then called the CTM CRA's.

Protocol Specification

We shall now describe the particular CTM - CRA we analyze below in terms that are different from the original presentation, but are probably simpler to visualize:

8) Each active user maintains a conceptual stack; at each slot-end it determines its position in the stack according to the following procedure identical to all users, who are unable however to communicate their stack states (referring to Fig. 4.4):

8.1) Once a user becomes active, it enters level 0 in its stack and will transmit at the nearest slot beginning. All and only users at stack level 0 transmit.

Remark: Item 8.1 is usually referred to as the "access protocol" followed by the nodes. Exercises 2.2-5 and 2.1-12 outline the analysis and related asymptotics, respectively, of another, cognate access protocol. It differs in the following details: all the users monitor the channel continuously, so they are aware whether a CRA is taking place or not. During a CRA new active users defer transmission till the collision is resolved, and then transmit.

8.2) At slot end, if it was not a collision slot, a user in stack level 0 (there can be at

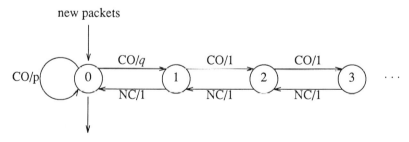

Fig. 4.4: State diagram for a user stack evolution. In xx/t, xx is CO for collision, NC for no collision feedback, t - probability of the transition.

most one such user, system-wide) becomes inactive, and all other users *decrease* their stack level by 1.

8.3) At slot end, if it was a collision slot, all users at stack level i, $i \geq 1$ *increase* their stack position to level $i+1$. The users at level 0 are split into two groups, one remains at level 0, while the other pushes itself into level 1. This partition is assumed to be made on the basis of a random variable (much like the flipping of a coin, but there are other possibilities that we shall not consider any further). We assume that each user, independently of the other active users, has the probability p of staying at level 0 (and the probability $q = 1-p$ of having to wait at level 1), and these probabilities are common to all users and constant over time.

8.4) This algorithm is effected at each successive slot end, and is instantaneous in our time scale.

The period required under this algorithm to dispose of a group of n colliding users, as well as of the other users that will join in before it is through, is called a Collision Resolution Interval (CRI) of type n, or n-CRI, and its duration is a rv denoted by L_n. This includes the slot of the initial collision and subsequent slots, until all the users that monitor the stack depth via the channel responses know it is empty. (The last phrase is perforce somewhat vague. See Exercise 1.)

For uniformity we also define the degenerate CRI durations L_i for $i = 0, 1$ as the time required to dispose of the consequences of zero or one packet at level 0; these two are clearly of size 1. The symbol L is used to denote the duration of a random, unconditional CRI. It will turn out that this variable, L, is of paramount importance in understanding and quantifying the performance of this protocol. The next subsection deals with it.

4.2.1 Channel Capacity Analysis

The capacity of the channel is the highest value of λ, the new packets generation rate, for which the CRI duration L is finite with probability 1. This is equivalent to requiring that L has finite moments of any order, or that its pgf is analytic in the unit disk. In Section 4.2.2 we shall observe how the packet waiting time ties-in with this requirement. Thus we are led to investigate the variable L, or its conditioned versions, L_n. Most of the material of this section is derived from Fayolle et al. (1985, 1986).

The protocol specification provides the recursion

$$L_n = \begin{cases} 1 & n = 0, 1 \\ 1 + L_{I+X_1} + L_{n-I+X_2} & n > 1. \end{cases} \tag{1}$$

In the second line of equation (1), the 1 is the collision slot; I - the number of colliding transmitters that elected to stay at level 0, and hence it has the distribution $B(n,p)$; X_1 - the number of new packets generated during the collision slot, and X_2 - the number of new packets generated during the last slot of the $(I+X_1)$'th CRI. Both X_i have $Poisson(\lambda)$ distribution and all three random variables are independent, as well as the two parts of the CRI duration. For the distribution of X_i we may then write

$$\text{Prob}(X = x) \equiv a(x) = e^{-\lambda}\frac{\lambda^x}{x!}, \quad x = 0, 1, 2, \cdots \quad (2)$$

In preparation for the evaluation of these L_n define the generating functions

(a) $\alpha_n(z) = \sum_{i \geq 1}\text{Prob}(L_n = i)z^i \qquad \alpha_0(z) = \alpha_1(z) = z, \qquad \alpha_n(1) = 1,$

(b) $\alpha(z,u) = \sum_{n \geq 0}\alpha_n(z)\frac{u^n}{n!} \qquad \alpha(1,u) = e^u, \ \alpha(z,0) = z,$ \hfill (3)

(c) $\beta(z,u) = e^{-u}\alpha(z,u) \qquad \beta(1,u) = 1, \ \ \beta(z,0) = z.$

We now do a computation the like of which we need several times in the sequel. So we do it in detail, for once. From equation (1) we have, for $n \geq 2$, by removing the three randomizations (X_1 at x, X_2 at y and I at j):

$$\text{Prob}(L_n = i) = \sum_{x \geq 0}a(x)\sum_{y \geq 0}a(y)\sum_{j=0}^{n}\binom{n}{j}p^jq^{n-j}$$

$$\times \text{Prob}(L_{j+x} + L_{n-j+y} = i-1) \ i \geq 1, \qquad n \geq 2. \quad (4)$$

Multiplying by z^i and summing over $i \geq 1$ yields

$$\alpha_n(z) = z\sum_{x \geq 0}a(x)\sum_{y \geq 0}a(y)\sum_{j=0}^{n}\binom{n}{j}p^jq^{n-j}$$

$$\times \sum_{i \geq 1}\text{Prob}(L_{j+x} + L_{n-j+y} = i-1)z^{i-1}, \quad n \geq 2.$$

Since the two partial L's are independent, the sum over i is a complete convolution, and we get

$$\alpha_n(z) = z\sum_{x \geq 0}a(x)\sum_{y \geq 0}a(y)\sum_{j=0}^{n}\binom{n}{j}p^nq^{n-j}\alpha_{j+x}(z)\alpha_{n-j+y}(z), \qquad n \geq 2. \quad (5)$$

Multiplying both sides of equation (5) by $u^n/n!$ and summing for $n \geq 2$, canceling $n!$ within the binomial coefficient,

$$\alpha(z,u) - \alpha_0(z) - u\alpha_1(z)$$

$$= z\sum_{x \geq 0}a(x)\sum_{y \geq 0}a(y)\sum_{n \geq 2}\sum_{j=0}^{n}\frac{(pu)^j}{j!}\frac{(qu)^{n-j}}{(n-j)!}\alpha_{j+x}(z)\alpha_{n-j+y}(z).$$

Completing the range of n to $n \geq 0$ to change the order of summation of n and j, and subtracting those additions:

$$\alpha(z,u) - z - uz = z \sum_{x \geq 0} a(x) \sum_{j \geq 0} \frac{(pu)^j}{j!} \alpha_{j+x}(z) \sum_{y \geq 0} a(y) \sum_{n \geq j} \frac{(qu)^{n-j}}{(n-j)!} \alpha_{n-j+y}(z)$$

$$- (n=0)z \sum_{x \geq 0} a(x)\alpha_x(z) \sum_{y \geq 0} a(y)\alpha_y(z)$$

$$- (n=1)z \Big[(j=0) \sum_{x \geq 0} a(x)\alpha_x(z)qu \sum_{y \geq 0} a(y)\alpha_{y+1}(z)$$

$$+ (j=1)pu \sum_{x \geq 0} a(x)\alpha_{x+1}(z) \sum_{y \geq 0} a(y)\alpha_y(z) \Big] .$$

(6)

We compute the right-hand side of equation (6) part-by-part. In the first line $n - j$ is replaced by n. Then we compute the factor $\sum_{x \geq 0} a(x) \sum_{j \geq 0} \frac{(pu)^j}{j!} \alpha_{j+x}(z)$. Replace $j+x$ by k, eliminate the sum on x and use equation (2) to get

$$e^{-\lambda} \sum_{k \geq 0} \alpha_k(z) \sum_{j=0}^{k} \frac{(pu)^j}{j!} \frac{\lambda^{k-j}}{(k-j)!} = e^{-\lambda} \sum_{k \geq 0} \frac{\alpha_k(z)}{k!} \sum_{j=0}^{k} \binom{k}{j}(pu)^j \lambda^{k-j}$$

$$= e^{-\lambda} \sum_{k \geq 0} \frac{(\lambda+pu)^k}{k!} \alpha_k(z) = e^{-\lambda} \alpha(z, \lambda+pu).$$

(7)

Similarly, the sum over n and y produces $e^{-\lambda}\alpha(z,\lambda+qu)$. The $(n=0)$ term provides

$$e^{-2\lambda} \sum_{x \geq 0} \alpha_x(z) \frac{\lambda^x}{x!} \sum_{y \geq 0} \frac{\lambda^y}{y!} \alpha_y(z) = e^{-2\lambda} \alpha^2(z,\lambda).$$

(8)

Then the $(n=1, j=0)$ term has the factor

$$\sum_{x \geq 0} a(x)\alpha_{x+1}(z) = e^{-\lambda} \frac{\partial}{\partial \lambda} \sum_{x \geq 0} \frac{\lambda^{x+1}}{(x+1)!} \alpha_{x+1}(z) = e^{-\lambda}\alpha_u(z,\lambda),$$

and using this in the last line of equation (6) it will produce

$$z[e^{-\lambda}\alpha(z,\lambda)que^{-\lambda}\alpha_u(z,\lambda) + pue^{-\lambda}\alpha_u(z,\lambda)e^{-\lambda}\alpha(z,\lambda)]$$

$$= uze^{-2\lambda}\alpha(z,\lambda)\alpha_u(z,\lambda).$$

(9)

Collecting it all together we obtain:

$$\alpha(z,u) - z(u+1)$$

$$= ze^{-2\lambda}\alpha(z,\lambda+pu)\alpha(z,\lambda+qu) - ze^{-2\lambda}\alpha(z,\lambda)[\alpha(z,\lambda) + u\,\alpha_u(z,\lambda)].$$

(10)

By equation (3.c) $\alpha(z,u) = e^u \beta(z,u)$, $\alpha_u(z,u) = e^u \beta(z,u) + e^u \beta_u(z,u)$; replacing all α's in equation (10) by β's we obtain:

$$\frac{1}{z}\beta(z,u) = \beta(z,\lambda+pu)\beta(z,\lambda+qu) + e^{-u}(1+u)$$

$$- e^{-u}\beta(z,\lambda)[(1+u)\beta(z,\lambda) + \beta_u(z,\lambda)]. \tag{11}$$

Equation (11) is the starting point for evaluating moments of L_n. We consider here the first moment. See Exercise 11 for the variance. Let $l_n = E(L_n)$, and write

$$\phi(u) \equiv e^{-u} \sum_{n \geq 0} l_n \frac{u^n}{n!} = \beta_z(1,u). \tag{12}$$

Differentiate equation (11) with respect to z, and substitute from (12) to obtain at $z = 1$:

$$\phi(u) = 1 + \phi(\lambda+pu) + \phi(\lambda+qu) - e^{-u}[2\phi(\lambda)(1+u) + u\phi'(\lambda)]. \tag{13}$$

We introduce now notation that is used much in the computations to follow:

$$\sigma_1(u) \equiv \lambda + pu; \quad \sigma_2(u) \equiv \lambda + qu.$$
$$Rf(u) \equiv f(u) - f(\sigma_1(u)) - f(\sigma_2(u)). \tag{14}$$

Note that since $p + q = 1$, $Rf(\frac{\lambda}{p}) = Rf(\frac{\lambda}{q}) = -f(2\lambda)$. Rewriting equation (13) as

$$R\phi(u) = 1 - e^{-u}[2\phi(\lambda)(1+u) + u\phi'(\lambda)], \tag{15}$$

instantiating it twice, at the values $z = \lambda/p, \lambda/q$, and eliminating $\phi(2\lambda)$, we are provided with a relation between $\phi(\lambda)$ and $\phi'(\lambda)$, which on simplification yields

$$\phi'(\lambda) = 2\phi(\lambda)(K-1),$$

$$K = -\frac{e^{-\lambda/p} - e^{-\lambda/q}}{(\lambda/p)e^{-\lambda/p} - (\lambda/q)e^{-\lambda/q}}, \quad K(p = \frac{1}{2}) = \frac{1}{1-2\lambda}. \tag{16}$$

Substituting this in equation (15) we obtain:

$$R\phi(u) = 1 - 2\phi(\lambda)(1 + Ku)e^{-u}. \tag{17}$$

How does one solve such an equation? We digress to present a general scheme.

Solution by Iteration

Let H be the set of all the mappings created by composing σ_i, as defined in equation (14), in any order:

$$H \equiv \{\sigma: \sigma = \sigma_{i_1}\sigma_{i_2}\cdots\sigma_{i_k}, \ i_j \in \{1,2\} \ \}, \quad k \geq 0, \tag{18}$$

where the composition is the usual functional one, e.g.

$$\sigma_1\sigma_2(u) = \sigma_1(\sigma_2(u)) = \lambda + p(\lambda + qu) = \lambda + p\lambda + pqu.$$

The $k = 0$ term in definition (18) corresponds to the identity mapping $\varepsilon(u) = u$. Under the operation of composition H is a non-commutative semi-group. Further notation we shall use:

$|\sigma|$ - the number of components in σ (called its length),

$|\sigma|_i$ - the number of components of σ that are of the variety σ_i. Note that the length of σ satisfies $|\sigma| = |\sigma|_1 + |\sigma|_2$.

$H_n \equiv \{\sigma : |\sigma| = n\}$.

H may be represented as the following union, with obvious notation

$$H = \{\varepsilon\} \cup \{\sigma_1 H\} \cup \{\sigma_2 H\},$$

$$H = \{\varepsilon\} \cup \{H\sigma_1\} \cup \{H\sigma_2\}. \tag{19}$$

Finally for any two numbers a and b we define

$$(a;b)^\sigma \equiv a^{|\sigma|_1} b^{|\sigma|_2}.$$

Theorem 1: The equation

$$f(u) - \alpha f(\sigma_1(u)) - \beta f(\sigma_2(u)) = t(u), \tag{20}$$

where α and β satisfy the *contraction condition*

$$|\alpha| + |\beta| < 1, \tag{21}$$

and $t(u)$ is entire, has the unique analytic solution

$$f(u) = \sum_{\sigma \in H} (\alpha;\beta)^\sigma t(\sigma(u)). \tag{22}$$

Remark: Equation (22) represents the natural approach to solving an equation such as (20). The point of the theorem is that the sum in equation (22) converges to an analytic function, and that it is the *unique* analytic solution.

Proof: In order to show that the sum (22) exists as an analytic function, observe that (Exercise 4)

$$|\sigma(z)| \le \max(|z|, \lambda/q), \quad \forall\ \sigma \in H,\ z \in C,\ p \ge q. \tag{23}$$

This implies the existence of a t-modulus function $\mu_t(z)$, with respect to H (Exercise 4):

$$\mu_t(z) \equiv \sup\{|t(u)|, u \in C : |u| \le \max(|z|, \lambda/q)\}$$

$$\le \max_{\sigma \in H} |t(\sigma(z))|. \tag{24}$$

Hence

$$|\sum_{\sigma \in H} t(\sigma(z))(\alpha;\beta)^\sigma| \le \mu_t(z) \sum_{\sigma \in H} (|\alpha|;|\beta|)^\sigma = \frac{\mu_t(z)}{1 - |\alpha| - |\beta|}, \tag{25}$$

where the equality in (25) results from there being 2^n σ's in H_n, $\binom{n}{i}$ of which have $|\sigma|_1 = i$.

Since $t(\cdot)$ is entire, $|t(u)|$ has a finite upper bound when u is in any given region that excludes $u = \infty$. Thus in any such region the convergence of the sum is uniform and hence it converges to an entire function.

Showing that $f(u)$ as given by equation (22) solves equation (20) is immediate by using the decomposition (19):

$$\sum_{\sigma \in H} t(\sigma(u))(\alpha;\beta)^{\sigma}$$

$$= t(u)(\alpha;\beta)^{\varepsilon} + \sum_{\sigma \in H\sigma_1} t(\sigma(u))(\alpha;\beta)^{\sigma} + \sum_{\sigma \in H\sigma_2} t(\sigma(u))(\alpha;\beta)^{\sigma}, \qquad (26)$$

and re-using the same representation of H,

$$\sum_{\sigma \in H} t(\sigma(u))(\alpha;\beta)^{\sigma} = t(u) + \sum_{\tau \in H} t(\tau\sigma_1(u))\alpha(\alpha;\beta)^{\tau} + \sum_{\tau \in H} t(\tau\sigma_2(u))\beta(\alpha;\beta)^{\tau} \qquad (27)$$

$$= t(u) + \alpha f(\sigma_1(u)) + \beta f(\sigma_2(u)).$$

So this is indeed a solution.

Uniqueness: This follows the usual route of assuming the existence of two *analytic* solutions and showing that their difference must vanish.

In order to do it we use the following properties of H (Fig. 4.5); without loss of generality we assume $p \geq q$:

1) Given z, all $\sigma(z)$ are on, or in the triangle with vertices at z, $\dfrac{\lambda}{p}$ and $\dfrac{\lambda}{q}$.

2) The interval $[\dfrac{\lambda}{p}, \dfrac{\lambda}{q}]$ is the locus of $\lim_{|\sigma| \to \infty} \sigma(z)$ for all finite $z \in C$. $\qquad$ (28)

3) For any z there exists an n_0 such that $|\sigma(z)| \leq 2\lambda/q$ for all $\sigma \in H_n$, $n \geq n_0$.

Now, assume the existence of two distinct solutions $f_1(u), f_2(u)$, analytic in some region containing the above limit interval. Define

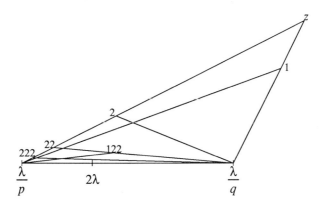

Fig. 4.5: An illustration of the effect of the transformations σ_1 and σ_2, when $p = \frac{2}{3}$. The notations 1, 22 etc. are for the points $\sigma_1(z)$, $\sigma_2(\sigma_2(z))$ etc.

$$\delta(u) = f_1(u) - f_2(u), \tag{29}$$

then from equation (20):

$$\delta(u) - \alpha\delta(\sigma_1(u)) - \beta\delta(\sigma_2(u)) = 0. \tag{30}$$

Remark: Clearly $\delta = 0$ is a solution of equation (30), also by substitution in (22), but we have not yet shown that this is the *only* solution.

For any given z find a suitable n, as provided by property 3 above, and iterate equation (30) n times to obtain:

$$\delta(z) = \sum_{\sigma \in H_n} \delta(\sigma(z))(\alpha;\beta)^\sigma. \tag{31}$$

Since these σ satisfy $|\sigma(z)| \le 2\lambda/q$, define

$$M = \max\{|\delta(u)| : |u| \le 2\lambda/q\}. \tag{32}$$

Hence

$$|\delta(z)| \le M \sum_{\sigma \in H_n} (|\alpha|;|\beta|)^\sigma = M(|\alpha|+|\beta|)^n < M, \tag{33}$$

so that the entire function $\delta(\cdot)$ has a uniform bound for all z, so it must be a constant (by Liouville's theorem), and the only constant compatible with equations (30) and (21) is 0, as required. □

Now, equation (17) cannot be solved directly via Theorem 1, since it does not satisfy the contraction condition. A double differentiation rectifies this readily and we obtain the following

Corollary: The equation

$$\mathbf{R}f(z) \equiv f(z) - f(\sigma_1(z)) - f(\sigma_2(z)) = t(z),$$

with specified values for $f(0)$ and $f'(0)$, given that $t(z)$ is an an entire function that satisfies the consistency condition $t(\lambda/p) = t(\lambda/q)$, has the solution

$$f(z) = f(0) + zf'(0) + \sum_{\sigma \in H} [t(\sigma(z)) - t(\sigma(0)) - (p;q)^\sigma zt'(\sigma(0))]. \tag{34}$$

The detailed proof is asked for in Exercise 8, and relies on the fact, proved above, that the sums here converge uniformly, so that differentiation and integration may be done term by term.

It will be convenient to introduce a symbol for the sum in the right-hand side of equation (34):

$$S(t(\cdot); z) \equiv \sum_{\sigma \in H} \left[t(\sigma(z)) - t(\sigma(0)) - (p;q)^\sigma zt'(\sigma(0))\right]. \tag{35}$$

End of the digression on solution by iteration. □

We have obtained a formal solution for equation (17):

$$\phi(u) = 1 + S(1 - 2\phi(\lambda)e^{-z}(1 + Kz); u) = 1 - 2\phi(\lambda)S(e^{-z}(1 + Kz); u), \tag{36}$$

where the last equality is due to the identity (see Exercise 9)

$$S(af(\cdot)+b; z) = a\, S(f(\cdot); z),$$ (37)

that holds for any entire function $f(\cdot)$. Section 4.2.4 brings some details concerning the actual computations for the operator S. The value of $\phi(\lambda)$ follows from (36):

$$\phi(\lambda) = \frac{1}{1+2S(e^{-z}(1+Kz); \lambda)}.$$ (38)

From the definition of $\phi(u)$, equation (12), and the fact that each CRI starts off with N transmissions, N having the pmf $a(n)$, we obtain that $\phi(\lambda) = E(L)$, the mean length of an unconditional CRI. The finiteness of $\phi(\lambda)$ determines then the stability of the channels. In Fayolle et al. (1986) it is shown that the necessary and sufficient condition for the channel to be stable is that $\lambda < \lambda_{max}$, where λ_{max} is the smallest root of the equation $S(e^{-z}(1+Kz); \lambda) = -\frac{1}{2}$ (and that it is unstable for higher values of λ). The value of λ_{max} depends on p, and is maximized for $p = \frac{1}{2}$, at $\lambda_{max}(p=\frac{1}{2}) = 0.360177147+$. The above reference also contains a rather elaborate asymptotic analysis of the l_n. A strange looking fact discovered in that analysis is that the condition for the ratio l_n/n to converge, as n increases, is that the ratio $\log p/\log q$ must be irrational; otherwise, l_n/n oscillates around a value that depends on p. A rather complicated characterization is given there for this value. Only for $p = \frac{1}{2}$ a compact representation was found, as $2A\,\phi(\lambda)$, with A given by

$$A(p=\frac{1}{2}) = \frac{e^{-2\lambda}}{1-2\lambda}\left[\frac{1}{\log 2} + 2\lambda\sum_{i\geq 0} 2^{-i}e^{2\lambda/2i}\right].$$ (39)

An outline of an efficient procedure to compute $\phi(\lambda)$ is given in Exercise 10 and another is described in Section 4.2.4.

4.2.2 Top of Stack Probabilities and Message Delay

The interest in this subsection and the following one is focused on the delay experienced by an individual packet, which is defined as the number of slots it spends in the transmission process, counting both its initial and successful (and hence final) broadcasts, which may coincide. The essential point to notice is that regardless of the state of the system-wide stack (i.e. the union of all virtual stacks maintained by the active users), an arriving packet only interacts with those that are initially with it at level 0, and with subsequent arrivals, if its first transmission involved a collision. It leaves those packets that were at lower stack levels on its arrival behind; in fact, it is not even aware of their existence. Also, from the description of the CRA followed by the transmitters it is apparent that most of the "action" is at the top of the stack - its level 0. As implied by the above discussion and shown below, the statistics of this level occupancy provide access to the moments of message delay. Thus, we would like to compute the top-of-stack occupancy probabilities. Since the number of messages (or transmitters) at level 0 is not a Markov process we cannot do it directly. We use the fact, mentioned above, that every CRI starts off with a slot in which the number of messages has the $Poisson(\lambda)$ distribution, independently of past history. In other words: the CRIs form a renewal process. All the other processes we consider - specifically, top-of-stack occupancy and message delay - inherit this basic structure. Note that the vector of *all* stack level occupancies is a Markov chain, but its behavior is much too complex for any compact presentation.

Top-of-Stack Occupancy at a Random Slot

Let Q denote the top-of-stack occupancy. More precisely, this is the occupancy at a random slot; later we also present a different randomization. Define $q_k = \text{Prob}(Q = k)$. This may be interpreted as the pmf for the number of transmissions attempted at a random slot. We compute it as follows:

Consider a long sequence of CRIs. Say N CRIs. Note that by taking the degenerate CRIs, which handle no packets or one packet, together with the proper ones, where an actual collision needs to be resolved, the entire time axis is covered by CRIs. We already know that the expected CRI duration (including the degenerate ones), is $\phi(\lambda)$, and the expected length (in number of slots) of the above sequence is $N\phi(\lambda)$. Also, the probability of an n-type CRI is $a(n)$, so the expected number of such CRIs is $Na(n)$. A slot in which $Q = k$ will be called a k-slot, and we finally define

η_n^k - the expected number of k-slots during an n-CRI.

Thus $N\Sigma_{n \geq 0} a(n)\eta_n^k$ is the expected number of k-slots during the above N CRIs. The Law of Large Numbers (LLN) assures us that because of the independence of successive CRIs the following relation holds

$$q_k = \text{Prob}(Q = k) = \lim_{N \to \infty} \frac{N\sum_{n \geq 0} a(n)\eta_n^k}{N\phi(\lambda)} = \frac{1}{\phi(\lambda)} \sum_{n \geq 0} a(n)\eta_n^k . \qquad (40)$$

The $a(n)$ and $\phi(\lambda)$ are known, so we proceed to compute the missing element, η_n^k.

Computing the pmf of Q

At the first slot of an n-type CRI Q is n; thereafter it is described by the following relation, which is *very* similar to the one satisfied by l_n (see Exercise 2(b)):

$$\eta_n^k = \begin{cases} \delta_{n,k} & n = 0,1 \\ \delta_{n,k} + \sum_{j=0}^{n} \binom{n}{j} p^j q^{n-j} \sum_{x \geq 0} a(x) \sum_{y \geq 0} a(y)[\eta_{j+x}^k + \eta_{n-j+y}^k], & n \geq 2 . \end{cases} \qquad (41)$$

Defining

$$P_n(u) \equiv \sum_{k \geq 0} \eta_n^k u^k , \qquad\qquad P_0(u) = 1, \ P_1(u) = u ,$$

$$P(z,u) \equiv e^{-z} \sum_{n \geq 0} P_n(u) \frac{z^n}{n!} , \qquad P(0,u) = 1, \ P_z(0,u) = u-1 , \qquad (42)$$

we obtain successively

$$P_n(u) = u^n + \sum_{j=0}^{n} \binom{n}{j} p^j q^{n-j} \sum_{x \geq 0} a(x)[P_{j+x}(u) + P_{n-j+x}(u)] , \ n \geq 2 \quad (43)$$

and

$$P(z,u) - P(\lambda+pz,u) - P(\lambda+qz,u)$$
$$= e^{(u-1)z} - e^{-z} \left[zP(\lambda,u)(1+u) + zP_z(\lambda,u) \right]. \qquad (44)$$

We shall write the left-hand side here too as $\mathbf{R}P(z,u)$, with the $\mathbf{R}$ operator implicitly operating on the first argument only. Precisely the same reduction as that of equation (15) to (17) yields now (details are asked for in Exercise 13):

$$\mathbf{R}P(z,u) = t(z,u) - 2P(\lambda,u)e^{-z}(1+Kz),$$

$$t(z,u) \equiv e^{(u-1)z} - ze^{-z} \frac{e^{\lambda(u-1)/q} - e^{-\lambda(u-1)/p}}{(\lambda/q)e^{-\lambda/q} - (\lambda/p)e^{-\lambda/p}} , \qquad (45)$$

$$t(z,u) \ (p = \tfrac{1}{2}) = e^{(u-1)z} - ze^{-z} \frac{(u-1)e^{2\lambda u}}{(1-2\lambda)} .$$

The pgf of Q, $\Sigma q_k u^k$ is given, through equation (40) as

$$q(u) = \frac{1}{\phi(\lambda)} e^{-\lambda} \sum_{k \geq 0} u^k \sum_{n \geq 0} \frac{\lambda^n}{n!} \eta_n^k = \frac{P(\lambda,u)}{\phi(\lambda)} . \qquad (46)$$

Using the Corollary (34) and the boundary values of $P(z,u)$ given in (42) we can write

$$P(z,u) = 1 + z(u-1) + \mathrm{S}\big(t(v,u) - 2P(\lambda,u)e^{-v}(1+Kv); v=z \big). \qquad (47)$$

We already know, from equation (38), that $\mathrm{S}(e^{-v}(1+Kv); \lambda)$ equals $(1 - \phi(\lambda))/2\phi(\lambda)$, hence substituting $z = \lambda$ in (47) we find

$$P(\lambda,u) = 1 + \lambda(u-1) - P(\lambda,u)(1 - \phi(\lambda))/\phi(\lambda) + \mathrm{S}(t(z,u); z = \lambda),$$

or

$$P(\lambda,u) = \phi(\lambda)[1 + \lambda(u-1) + \mathrm{S}(t(z,u); z=\lambda)] . \qquad (48)$$

So that the pgf $q(u)$ is given, via equation (46), as

$$q(u) = 1 + \lambda(u-1) + \mathrm{S}(t(z,u); z= \lambda) \qquad (49)$$

At first look equation (49) may appear an unpromising source for simple expressions for the individual q_k. Nevertheless, using the commutativity proved in Exercise 14, and the fact that $t(z,u)$ is (doubly) entire we immediately find:

$$q_0 = 1 - \lambda + S(t(z,0); z = \lambda) = 1 - \lambda + S(e^{-z}(1 + Kz); \lambda)$$

$$= 1 - \lambda + \frac{1 - \phi(\lambda)}{2\phi(\lambda)} = \frac{1}{2} - \lambda + \frac{1}{2\phi(\lambda)} . \tag{50}$$

Even simpler is

$$q_1 = \lambda, \quad \text{since } t_u(z,0) = 0, \tag{51}$$

rather non-surprisingly, and in general

$$q_k = \frac{1}{k!} S(e^{-z}(z^k - zK_k); \lambda), \tag{52a}$$

where

$$K_k = \frac{(\lambda/q)^k e^{-\lambda/q} - (\lambda/p)^k e^{-\lambda/p}}{(\lambda/q)e^{-\lambda/q} - (\lambda/p)e^{-\lambda/p}}, \qquad K_k(p = \tfrac{1}{2}) = \frac{(2\lambda)^{k-1}(k - 2\lambda)}{1 - 2\lambda} . \tag{52b}$$

Top-of-Stack Observed States

We have found the distribution of the number of packets at stack level 0 at a random slot. We shall need however a slightly different random variable, which is to be denoted by R:

$$r_k \equiv \text{Prob}(R = k)$$

$$\equiv \text{Prob(A random packet is first transmitted during a } k\text{-slot)}. \tag{53}$$

One way to obtain the distribution of R is suggested in Exercise 16. Another is more complicated, but displays an argument which is sometimes indispensable:

The Q packets at level 0 in a random slot come from two sources: the first is the arrival of newly generated ones (their number is the random variable X, with *Poisson*(λ) distribution). The second consists of packets that either remained at level 0 following a collision, or popped from level 1 following a no-collision slot. We denote the second component by Q_0. Since the two components are independent, $q(u) = q_0(u)e^{\lambda(u-1)}$, or

$$q_0(u) = q(u)e^{\lambda(1-u)} . \tag{54}$$

A random packet arrives in a group with size distributed as $\overline{X}$, where $\text{Prob}(\overline{X} = j) = ja(j)/\lambda$. (A similar argument was used to obtain equation (3.2-6).) Thus the pgf of $\overline{X}$ is $g_{\overline{X}}(u) = ue^{\lambda(u-1)}$. Since $R = \overline{X} + Q_0$, and independence of the two components can be invoked once more, we obtain, via equation (54)

$$g_R(u) = q_0(u)g_{\overline{X}}(u) = uq(u). \tag{55}$$

This leads immediately to

$$r_k = q_{k-1}. \tag{56}$$

We remark that this result is formally very similar to ones that concern standard queueing systems.

The Packet Delay Process

While the evaluations of Q and R were of interest per se, we arrive now at the root cause: they provide a handle on the delay process. Let $W(n)$ be the delay experienced by a packet that was first transmitted in an n-slot. Then $W(1) = 1$, and for $n > 1$ we have two possible outcomes:

$$W(n) = \begin{cases} 1 + W(I + 1 + X_1) & \text{with probability } p \text{ ,} \\ \\ 1 + L_{I+X_2} + W(n - I + X_3) & \text{with probability } q \text{ ,} \end{cases} \quad n \geq 2 \quad (57)$$

where $I \sim B(n-1, p)$, the X_i are independent Poisson random variables with parameter λ, and n is subject to the measure of R.

It does not appear possible to mix the distributions of $W(n)$ and R and come up with an equation for the distribution of the unconditional delay W, $\text{Prob}(W = i) = \Sigma r_n \text{Prob}(W(n) = i)$. What can be done, however, is to determine from (57) all the *moments* of each $W(n)$, construct from them the pgf of W, and from the latter extract the individual probabilities. This is also too arduous, and we shall be content with the first two moments only. The mechanics of this procedure will be quite familiar, so much of the detail is relegated to exercises. In Section 4.2.3 below we present an alternative route to the evaluation of these quantities.

Define

$$w(z;n) \equiv \sum_{i \geq 1} \text{Prob}(W(n) = i) z^i \text{ ,}$$

$$h(z,u) \equiv e^{-u} \sum_{n \geq 1} w(z;n) \frac{u^{n-1}}{(n-1)!} \text{ .} \quad (58)$$

And routine (well, by now) manipulations produce

$$h(z,u) - pzh(z,\sigma_1(u)) - qzh(z,\sigma_2,(u))\beta(z,\sigma_1(u))$$

$$= ze^{-u}[1 - h(z,\lambda)(p + q\beta(z,\lambda))] \qquad h(1,u) = 1, \quad (59)$$

where $\beta(\cdot,\cdot)$ is the gf for the CRI durations, defined in equation (3).

In order to use equation (59) for the first two moments, define

$$w_1(u) \equiv h_z(1,u) = e^{-u} \sum_{n \geq 1} E[W(n)] \frac{u^{n-1}}{(n-1)!} \text{ ,} \quad (60)$$

$$w_2(u) \equiv h_{zz}(1,u) = e^{-u} \sum_{n \geq 1} E[W^2(n)] \frac{u^{n-1}}{(n-1)!} - w_1(u). \quad (61)$$

Differentiating twice $h(z,u)$ in equation (59) and inserting these last definitions yield the equations

$$w_1(u) - pw_1(\sigma_1(u)) - qw_1(\sigma_2(u)) = 1 + q\phi(\sigma_1(u)) - e^{-u}[w_1(\lambda) + q\phi(\lambda)],\quad (62)$$

and

$$w_2(u) - pw_2(\sigma_1(u)) - qw_2(\sigma_2(u))$$
$$= 2qw_1(\sigma_2(u))\phi(\sigma_1(u)) + q\psi(\sigma_1(u)) + 2w_1(u) - 2 \qquad (63)$$
$$- e^{-u}[w_2(\lambda) + 2qw_1(\lambda)\phi(\lambda) + q\psi(\lambda)].$$

The function $\psi(u)$ is defined to equal $\beta_{zz}(1,u)$. It is computed very similarly to $\phi(u)$ (see Exercise 11).

Equation (63) appears not to be quite in the form of our earlier equations, but close enough for an easy second Corollary to Theorem 1 to close the gap:

Corollary: Let $f(z)$ be an analytic function satisfying the equation $f(z) - pf(\sigma_1(z)) - q f(\sigma_2(z)) = t(z)$, with a specified value for $f(0)$, and where $t(z)$ is an entire function satisfying the consistency condition $\int_{\lambda/p}^{\lambda/q} t(u)du = 0$, then the unique analytic solution for $f(z)$ is given by

$$f(z) = f(0) + \sum_{\sigma \in H}(p;q)^{\sigma}[t(\sigma(z)) - t(\sigma(0))]. \qquad \Box \qquad (64)$$

Now we can present the solutions to both equations (62) and (63). Define the operator **T**, similar to **S**:

$$\mathbf{T}(f;z) \equiv \sum_{\sigma \in H}(p;q)^{\sigma}[f(\sigma(z)) - f(\sigma(0))]. \qquad (65)$$

See Section 4.2.4 for the mechanics of computing **T**.

Next the boundary values $w_1(0)$ and $w_2(0)$ are required, and inspection of the definitions immediately reveals that these are 1 and 0, respectively, and thus

$$w_1(u) = 1 + q\mathbf{T}(\phi(\sigma_1(z)); u) - [w_1(\lambda) + q\phi(\lambda)]\mathbf{T}(e^{-z}; u) \qquad (66)$$

$$w_2(u) = \mathbf{T}[qw_1(\sigma_2(z))\phi(\sigma_1(z)) + q\psi(\sigma_1(z)) + 2w_1(z);u]$$
$$- [w_2(\lambda)+2qw_1(\lambda)\phi(\lambda) + q\psi(\lambda)]\mathbf{T}(e^{-z}; u). \qquad (67)$$

These are straightforward, if cumbersome to compute. The $w_i(\lambda)$ can be evaluated from equations (66)-(67), or directly from the integral condition in the Corollary above (if only the $w_i(\lambda)$ are desired, the latter course is simpler). One can then proceed: the moments are extracted from

$$E(W(n)) = (n-1)![u^{n-1}]e^u w_1(u),$$
$$E(W^2(n)) = (n-1)![u^{n-1}]e^u(w_1(u) + w_2(u)), \qquad (68)$$

and the conditioning removed through

$$E(W^k) = \sum_{n \geq 1}r_n E(W^k(n)). \qquad (69)$$

Actually the 'k' in equation (69) may be higher than 2, though the necessary equations were not worked out above. The next subsection presents a different approach to the determination of message delay.

4.2.3 Message Delay via Renewal Considerations

In Section 4.2.2 the message delay W was determined via conditioning on the top-of-stack population when the message was first transmitted. It turns out that there is a different mechanism for the analysis of this variable. The key observation is actually the same one: the evolutions of successive CRIs are independent, and thus concentrating on one CRI provides all the information that determines the distribution of all the descriptors of the transmission process. Other descriptors, besides L and W, could be the number of packets transmitted during a CRI, the top-of-stack occupancy that was computed in Section 4.2.2 (or the occupancy of any other level), maximum stack depth attained during a CRI, number of active users in a random slot and others.

Expected Message Delay

We start with the first moment; the same approach will be shown to support the evaluation of higher moments as well.

Theorem 2: Consider a single CRI; let C be the aggregate delay of all the messages handled during the CRI, and let M be the number of messages transmitted during a CRI; then:

$$E(W) = \frac{E(C)}{E(M)}. \tag{70}$$

Proof: This equality is a result of the CRI being realized by a regenerative process. We shall justify this equality in detail, for once; other applications of the same principle are to be found in this chapter (and others). The following definitions are required:

W_i - delay of the i-th packet, in the order of arrival,

M_k - the number of packets handled during the k-th CRI,

and we need also the following observations:

• (1) The M_k are mutually independent, and each has the same distribution; denote M_1 by M.

• (2) The W_i are not mutually independent; they are derived, however, from an irreducible and aperiodic Markov chain (the stack contents), and when that process is ergodic (that is, when $\lambda < \lambda_{max}$) they reach a limit, in distribution:

$$\lim_{i \to \infty} E\left(e^{-sW_i}\right) = E\left(e^{-sW_\infty}\right), \tag{71}$$

where W_∞ is a proper random variable. The existence of this variable is also deducible from the Renewal Key Theorem, see Cox (1962); the convergence of the transforms follows from Feller's Extended Continuity Theorem (Feller, 1971 Vol. II, §XIII.1 Theorem 2a).

• (3) The CRA dynamics imply that W_i and W_{i+M} are independent, for all $i \geq 1$, conditionally (on M).

• (4) Let $\{a_n\}$ be a real-valued sequence; if $\lim_{n \to \infty} a_n$ exists and equals a $(-\infty < a < \infty)$ then $\lim_{u \to 1^-} (1-u)\sum_{n \geq 1} u^n a_n$ exists and is equal to a.

Now we define

$$H(u,s) = (1-u)E \sum_{m \geq 1} u^m e^{-sW_m} \; ; \quad N_j \equiv \sum_{k=1}^{j} M_k , \tag{72}$$

and compute its value. Breaking down the summation on m by CRI,

$$H(u,s) = (1-u)E \sum_{k \geq 1} \sum_{m=N_{k-1}+1}^{N_k} u^m e^{-sW_m} .$$

Since all $M_k \sim M$, we may replace under the expectation operator $N_k - N_{k-1}$ by M,

$$H(u,s) = (1-u)E \sum_{k \geq 1} \sum_{m=1}^{M} u^{m+N_{k-1}} e^{-sW_{m+N_{k-1}}} ,$$

by observation (3) this equals

$$= (1-u)E \sum_{k \geq 1} u^{N_{k-1}} E \sum_{m=1}^{M} u^m e^{-sW_m} \tag{73}$$

$$= (1-u) \sum_{k \geq 1} [E(u^M)]^{k-1} E \sum_{m=1}^{M} u^m e^{-sW_m}$$

$$= \frac{1-u}{1-E(u^M)} E \sum_{m=1}^{M} u^m e^{-sW_m} .$$

Taking the limit on both sides as $u \to 1^-$, and using observations (4) and (2) for the left-hand side, we find

$$E(e^{-sW_\infty}) = \frac{1}{E(M)} E \sum_{m=1}^{M} e^{-sW_m} \tag{74}$$

now differentiation with respect to s, at $s = 0$ finally provides

$$E(W_\infty) = \frac{1}{E(M)} E\left[\sum_{m=1}^{M} E(W_m) \right] = \frac{E(C)}{E(M)} , \tag{75}$$

which is the equality required in equation (70). □

We proceed now to evaluate this last ratio. First we note that the denominator is simply given by

$$E(M) = \lambda \phi(\lambda), \tag{76}$$

itself a statement with the same flavor as (75). So, the entire effort hinges on obtaining $E(C)$. The same mechanism as in Section 4.2.2 is used again. Define

C_n - aggregate delay of packets in an n-CRI. Also define

$$c_n = E(C_n), \quad c(z) = e^{-z} \sum_{n \geq 1} c_n \frac{z^n}{n!}. \tag{77}$$

Now we find

$$E(C) = \sum_{n \geq 1} \text{Prob}(X = n) E(C_n) = \sum_{n \geq 1} e^{-\lambda} \frac{\lambda^n}{n!} c_n = c(\lambda),$$

so that

$$E(W) = \frac{c(\lambda)}{\lambda \phi(\lambda)}, \quad \lambda < \lambda_{\max}. \tag{78}$$

Again we consider the CRA dynamics to obtain

$$C_n = \begin{cases} 0 & n = 0 \\ 1 & n = 1 \\ n + C_{I+X_1} + (n-I)L_{I+X_1} + C_{n-I+X_2} & n \geq 2, \end{cases} \tag{79}$$

where I and X_i have the distributions $B(n,p)$ and $Poisson(\lambda)$, respectively, and they are all independent. Taking expectations of both sides the usual procedure provides:

$$c(z) - c(\sigma_1(z)) - c(\sigma_2(z)) = z + qz\,\phi(\sigma_1(z)) - e^{-z}[qz\,\phi(\lambda) + 2c(\lambda)(1+z) + zc\,'(\lambda)]$$

and the substitutions $z = \lambda/p$, $z = \lambda/q$ lead to a relation between $c(\lambda)$ and $c\,'(\lambda)$:

$$c\,'(\lambda) = 2c(\lambda)(K-1) - q\,\phi(\lambda) + A; \quad A = \frac{1/q - 1/p + \phi(\lambda/q) - (q/p)\phi(2\lambda)}{(1/q)e^{-\lambda/q} - (1/p)e^{-\lambda/p}} \tag{80}$$

so that:

$$\mathbf{R}c(z) = z + qz\,\phi(\sigma_1(z)) - e^{-z}[2c(\lambda)(1+Kz) + zA], \tag{81}$$

an equation the solution of which is provided by the Corollary of Section 4.2.1 (equation (34)).

We recognize $S(e^{-z}(1+Kz); u)$ as $(1 - \phi(u)/2\phi(\lambda)$ and $S(z; u) = 0$, hence

$$c(u) = u + \frac{c(\lambda)}{\phi(\lambda)}(\phi(u) - 1) + S(qz\,\phi(\sigma_1(z)) - zAe^{-z}; u) \tag{82}$$

which provides an immediate linear equation for $c(\lambda)$.

Substituting this in equation (78), we find

$$E(W) = 1 + \frac{1}{\lambda} S(qz\,\phi(\sigma_1(z)) - Aze^{-z}; \lambda). \tag{83}$$

Higher Moments of the Packet Delay

The same approach that yielded the expected value of W can yield its entire distribution. To this avail it is necessary to observe not the variable C_n as was done above, but its components. More precisely, define the random variables

$W_n(j)$ = The number of packets in an n–CRI that experience a delay of j slots,

$$W_n(z) \equiv \sum_{j\geq 1} W_n(j)z^j, \qquad W(z,u) \equiv e^{-u} \sum_{n\geq 0} W_n(z)\frac{u^n}{n!}, \qquad (84)$$

$$W_n(z) = E(W_n(z)), \qquad W(z,u) \equiv E(W(z,u)).$$

These $W_n(z)$ and $W(z,u)$ are *random generating functions*. The same argumentation leading to equation (70) would produce here

$$\text{Prob}(W{=}j) = \frac{[z^j]W(z,\lambda)}{E(M)}, \qquad (85)$$

and similarly moments can be recovered from $W(z,\lambda)$ by differentiation with respect to z, at $z=1$.

A recurrence relation for $W(z,u)$ can be obtained along the lines we have seen already. Using equation (58)

$$W_0(z) = 0, \qquad W_1(z) = z,$$

$$W_n(z) = nw(z\,;n) \qquad\qquad\qquad n \geq 2 \qquad\qquad (86)$$

$$+ E_{I,X_1,X_2}[W_{I+X_1}(z) - Iw(z\,;I+X_1) + W_{n-I+X_2}(z) - (n-I)w(z\,;n-I+X_2)].$$

The second and third lines of equation (86), are best considered for some particular $[z^j]$; thus $n[z^j]w(z;n)$ is, by its definition in equation (58), the expected number of the original n colliders that will be delayed j slots, and the following two pairs of terms are the contributions of the two subtrees sprouted by the CRA, where the original colliders are subtracted.

Proceeding along the familiar route of unconditioning the right-hand side of (86) and summing over n produces, using the function $h(z,u)$ defined in equation (58) as well,

$$W(z,u) - W(z,\sigma_1(u)) - W(z,\sigma_2(u))$$

$$= u[h(z,u) - ph(z,\sigma_1(u)) - qh(z,\sigma_2(u))] + ue^{-u}h(z,\lambda) \qquad (87)$$

$$- e^{-u}[2W(z,\lambda)(1+u) + uW_u(z,\lambda)].$$

The substitutions $u = \lambda/p$, λ/q produce, on eliminating $W(z,2\lambda)$,

$$W_u(z,\lambda) = 2W(z,\lambda)(K-1) + h(z,\lambda) + \lambda\frac{h(z,\lambda/q) - h(z,\lambda/p)}{\frac{\lambda}{q}e^{-\lambda/q} - \frac{\lambda}{p}e^{-\lambda/p}}. \qquad (88)$$

Now equation (87) has an immediate solution, using the S operator (the adjective does not refer to the amount of required computation). Note that the function $h(z,u)$ is required only at three different values of u, and these are obtainable from equation (59).

The moments of W are available from equation (85); thus

$$E(W) = \frac{d}{dz} \frac{W(z,\lambda)}{E(M)} \Big|_{z=1} = \frac{W_z(1,\lambda)}{\lambda\phi(\lambda)}, \tag{89}$$

and

$$E(W^2) = \frac{1}{\lambda\phi(\lambda)}[W_{zz}(1,\lambda) + W_z(1,\lambda)]. \tag{90}$$

4.2.4 Note on Computations

All the results of the last three subsections were expressed in terms of the summation operators S and T. Usually they are not easy to use except to obtain numerical results (see, though, equations (50) to (52)). Even this is not always simple, as the operators call in principle for infinite summation. Indeed, the proof of Theorem 1 implies that traversing a finite number of nodes, in the top of the tree generated by H is sufficient for any desired level of accuracy. (See Exercise 10 for a possible organization of such a computation.) However, as remarked in Exercise 19, it is not always easy to control the precision obtained by this traversal. Conversely, determining the portion of the tree required for a given precision is a non-trivial task, especially for $p \neq q$. This subsection presents an alternative procedure, that is especially useful with chained computations, as we have for example in equations (66, 67, 82), where the T and S operators are invoked to handle functions they were used to produce in an earlier pass.

Since the S and T operators are linear, and are only used on entire functions, which implies that they can be developed in power series around the origin - it would suffice if we could compute $S(u^k; z)$ and $T(u^k; z)$ for all k. We proceed to present a convenient scheme for this purpose.

According to the definitions of the operators

$$\begin{aligned} S(u^k; z) &= \sum_{\sigma \in H} [\sigma(z)^k - \sigma(0)^k - kz(p;q)^\sigma \sigma(0)^{k-1}], \\ T(u^k;z) &= \sum_{\sigma \in H} (p;q)^\sigma [\sigma(z)^k - \sigma(0)^k]. \end{aligned} \tag{91}$$

Writing $\sigma(z) = \sigma(0) + z(p;q)^\sigma$ (Exercise 4(c)), and defining

$$\xi_{j,l} = \sum_{\sigma \in H} \sigma(0)^j (p^l;q^l)^\sigma, \qquad l \geq 2, \ j \geq 0 \tag{92}$$

we see that equation (91) is equivalent to

$$S(u^k; z) = \sum_{l=2}^{k} \binom{k}{l}\xi_{k-l,l}z^l,$$

$$T(u^k; z) = \sum_{l=1}^{k} \binom{k}{l}\xi_{k-l,l+1}z^l. \tag{93}$$

The $\xi_{j,l}$ satisfy a convenient recursion. First, note that the definition (92) provides (see equation (25))

$$\xi_{0,l} = \sum_{\sigma \in H} (p^l; q^l)^\sigma = \frac{1}{1-p^l-q^l}, \qquad l \geq 2. \tag{94}$$

Then, for $j \geq 1$, using the first decomposition in (19), $H = \{\varepsilon\} \cup \{\sigma_1 H\} \cup \{\sigma_2 H\}$ and noting that $\varepsilon(0) = 0$, we find

$$\xi_{j,l} = \sum_{\sigma \in H} [\sigma_1(\sigma(0))^j p^l + \sigma_2(\sigma(0))^j q^l](p^l; q^l)^\sigma$$

$$= p^l \sum_{\sigma \in H} (\lambda + p\,\sigma(0))^j (p^l; q^l)^\sigma + q^l \sum_{\sigma \in H} (\lambda + q\,\sigma(0))^j (p^l; q^l)^\sigma, \tag{95}$$

and extracting $\sigma(0)^j$ from the right-hand side, that give $\xi_{j,l}$ there as well, we have the necessary recursion

$$\xi_{j,l} = \frac{1}{1-p^{l+j}-q^{l+j}} \sum_{r=0}^{j-1} \binom{j}{r}\lambda^{j-r}(p^{l+r}+q^{l+r})\xi_{r,l}, \qquad j \geq 1. \tag{96}$$

Since the $\xi_{j,l}$ are all positive, using this approach will prove usually more accurate than direct evaluation.

Exercises and Complements

1. (a) Referring to the CTM CRA, why does no user ever know that the stack is empty? How could this be known to a user that monitors the channel continuously (e.g. an administrator, or a scientist who studies the system)? [Hint: think of a counter that is changed by ±1 every slot during a CRI.]

(b) The CRI duration, as it was defined, is the time from an initial collision to the end of the slot when an outside observer, as in (a), would have known the stack to be empty. Define the *actual* CRI duration as the period that starts similarly, and ends when the stack actually empties. Show by an example how the two may differ. Is the difference bounded?

2. (a) Obtain equation (13) by the procedure outlined in the text.

(b) Obtain equation (13) directly from equation (1), by taking the expected value of both sides and substituting in equation (12). (The computation follows the steps leading to (11), but is somewhat shorter.)

(c) Can a similar approach be used to obtain the expected duration of the actual CRI duration, defined in Exercise 1(b)?

3. (a) Obtain equation (16) as outlined in the text, also for $p = \frac{1}{2}$ (use L'Hopital's rule).

(b) The following is rather a non-problem, designed to highlight the pitfalls of notational convenience. From equation (16) we have a differential equation; for simplicity consider the $p = \frac{1}{2}$ case:

$$\phi'(\lambda) = \phi(\lambda)\left(\frac{1}{1 - 2\lambda} - 1\right)$$

This is immediate to solve, as $\phi(\lambda) = A \dfrac{e^{-2\lambda}}{1 - 2\lambda}$, and the boundary condition $\phi(0) = 1$ yields $A = 1$. The condition $\phi'(0) = 0$ is satisfied as well. This holds for all $\lambda < \frac{1}{2}$, in contradiction with the claim following equation (39); or does it? Explain.

4. (a) Prove inequality (23), by induction on $|\sigma|$.

(b) Let $\mu(z) = \sup\limits_{u \in C_1} |t(u)|$, where $C_1 = \{u : |u| \le \max(|z|, \lambda/q)\}$ for any fixed z in C. Show $\mu(z) \le \max\limits_{\sigma \in H} |t(\sigma(z))|$.

(c) Prove: $\sigma(z) = \sigma(0) + (p;q)^\sigma z$.

5. Show that the three claims about H, listed as equations (28.1-3), hold.

6. Why can we use "max" in the definition (32) rather than "sup"? [Hint: $\delta(\cdot)$ is entire.]

7. Why is the discussion following the bound (33) necessary? Why cannot one just let there $n \to \infty$ and invoke the contraction condition to claim $\delta(\cdot) = 0$? [Hint: uniformity.]

8. Prove the Corollary (34). See the comment following equation (34) and use the boundary values.

9. Using the definition of the operator **S**, in equation (35), show that $S(af(\cdot) + b; z) = a\, S(f(\cdot); z)$.

10. In order to compute $\phi(\lambda)$, as given in equation (38) it is necessary to evaluate $S(e^{-z}(1+Kz); \lambda)$. Show

$$S(e^{-z}(1 + Kz); u) = \sum_{n \ge 2} [(1-nK)g_n + Kk_n]\,\frac{u^n}{u!},$$

where

$$g_n = (-1)^n \sum_{\sigma \in H} e^{-\sigma(0)}(p^n; q^n)^\sigma,$$

$$k_n = (-1)^n \sum_{\sigma \in H} e^{-\sigma(0)}\sigma(0)(p^n; q^n)^\sigma.$$

Use the result of Exercise 4(c).

11. In this exercise you are asked to compute the modified egf $\psi(u)$ for second moments of L_n. It is analogous to the function of $\phi(u)$ used for the first moments .
(a) In Exercise 2(a) you obtained $\beta_z(1, u)$, for $\phi(u)$; now differentiate once more to

get an equation for $\psi(u) = \beta_{zz}(1,u)$:

$$R\psi(u) = 2\phi(u) - 2 + 2\phi(\sigma_1(u))\phi(\sigma_2(u)) - e^{-u}\{2(1+u)\psi(\lambda) + u\,\psi'(\lambda)$$
$$+ 2\phi^2(\lambda)[(1 + u(2K-1)]\} \qquad \psi(0) = \psi'(0) = 0.$$

(b) Show $\psi(u) = e^{-u}\sum\limits_{n \geq 0} E(L_n^2)\dfrac{u^n}{n!} - \phi(u)$.

(c) Show that $\psi'(\lambda)$ can be expressed in terms of $\psi(\lambda)$, just as $\phi'(\lambda)$ in terms of $\phi(\lambda)$:

$$\psi'(\lambda) = 2(\psi(\lambda)-\phi^2(\lambda))(K-1) + \overline{K}$$

with

$$\overline{K} = 4\phi(\lambda)e^{-\lambda/pq}\frac{[\phi(\lambda/q) - \phi(\lambda/p)][\lambda/p - \lambda/q]}{\left[(\lambda/q)\,e^{-\lambda/q} - (\lambda/p)\,e^{-\lambda/p}\right]^2} \quad \text{and} \quad \overline{K}(p=\tfrac{1}{2}) = \frac{4\phi(\lambda)\phi'(2\lambda)}{(1-2\lambda)^2}$$

(d) Obtain the solution

$$\psi(z) = S(\Xi(u); z) + (\phi(z) - 1)S(\Xi(u); \lambda)$$

where

$$\Xi(u) \equiv 2\phi(u) - 2 + 2\phi(\sigma_1(u))\phi(\sigma_2(u)) - e^{-u}[2\phi^2(\lambda)(1 + uK) + u\overline{K}].$$

(e) Show that the variance of the unconditional CRI duration is given by

$$V(L) = \psi(\lambda) + \phi(\lambda)(1 - \phi(\lambda)),$$
$$\psi(\lambda) = \phi(\lambda)S(\Xi(u); \lambda).$$

12. The η_n^k were defined as level 0 expected occupancy counts. Define $\eta_{r,n}^k$ as the similar quantities for level r. What relation, similar to (41), do they satisfy?

13. Starting with equation (41) and definitions (42), obtain successively equations (43) to (45).

14. Show that Exercise 9 implies that the operators "differentiation with respect to u" and "S operating on z", as given by equation (35), commute when applied to an entire function $f(z,u)$.

15. Complete the details of computing equations (50) to (52). Argue why the value of q_1 is to be expected.

16. Comment about the following argument on relating R and Q, beside the fact that it leads to the correct result, equation (56):
"The arrivals of new packets to be transmitted are independent of each other, as well as of the component called Q_0 in the discussion preceding equation (54). Therefore, the number a packet sees besides itself when transmitted for the first time is Q. Hence $R = Q+1$ and (56) follows". [Hint: Q and R are measured over different sets of slots; there may be several new arrivals in a slot.]

17. (a) Show that the combination of equations (57) and (58) produces (59).
(b) Differentiating twice $h(z,u)$, introduce the definitions (60-61) to obtain

equations (62-63).

18. (a) Why is the consistency condition on $f(z)$ in Corollary (64) necessary? [Hint: integrate the equation on the range specified.]
(b) Prove equation (64). [Follow the proof of the first Corollary, Exercise 8.]

19. Solutions of the form (66)-(69) are quite opaque - one can get no idea from inspecting them how the quantities in question depend on the parameters. One needs at least numbers. Design a procedure to evaluate $E(W)$ and $V(W)$ for a range of p and λ values; if you have a machine available, test it. Fayolle et al. (1985) present a table of sample numerical results. Caution: while in principle rather simple, care must be exercised when series are truncated and the relevant portion of H defined. It is easy to get rather poor precision or consume a substantial computing time. Use either the scheme suggested in Exercise 10, or the one in Section 4.2.4.

20. Justify observation (4) (preceding equation (72)). [Hint: the existence of the limit means that for every $\varepsilon > 0$ there is an $N(\varepsilon)$ such that $|a_n - a| < \varepsilon$ for all $n > N(\varepsilon)$....]

21. Show that $E(M) = \lambda\phi(\lambda)$ using the argumentation that produced equation (75).

22. Justify equation (78) and compute to obtain equations (79)-(82).

23. In Theorem 2, Section 4.2.3, we showed $E(W) = E(C)/E(M)$. What is the interpretation of $E(C/M)$? When is it equal to $E(C)/E(M)$?

24. Show that the function $c(u)$ defined in equation (76) (or as the solution of (79)) coincides with $W_z(1,u)$, where $W(z,u)$ is defined in equation (84).
[Show this twice: from their interpretation in terms of the CRA processes, and from the equations they satisfy, which were arrived at differently.]

25. Why does equation (85) require $W(1,\lambda) = \lambda\phi(\lambda)$? Show that substituting $z = 1$ in equations (87)-(88) indeed provides this solution.

CHAPTER 5

Bin Packing Heuristics

> *– How do you seat four elephants in a car?*
> *– Two in the front seat, two in the back*[*] .

The Bin Packing (BP) problem is one of the more celebrated members of the class of problems commonly titled "combinatorial optimization". Other famous ones are machine scheduling, the knapsack problem, job assignment, the traveling salesman itinerary and many more. Practically all of these problems may be viewed as special cases of integer programming, but they display special structure and characteristics which have led to specialized algorithms and approaches. While the fame of the BP problem derives to no little extent from its being simple to present and relatively easy to analyze, the significance of many others of this class of problems derives from their commercial value in a business environment; hence the great interest in them. Karp (1986) gives a sweeping overview of the field.

Problem Statement

The standard BP problem considers a list of one-dimensional "pieces" $\{R_i, 1 \leq i \leq n\}$, with the size of R_i given by $X_i, 0 < X_i \leq b$. We are provided with an adequate number of bins, each of capacity b. The task is to pack the pieces into the bins so that:
  (a) The capacity of no bin is exceeded.
  (b) The minimal number of bins is used.

This problem has been shown to be NP-hard, the interpretation being that at our current level of knowledge, nothing essentially better than dynamic

---
[*] The oldest source for this chestnut appears to be a third century B.C. Greek manuscript.

programming is available to obtain the minimal packing. Coffman et al. (1984) give a very comprehensive survey of the known results about this problem. Fig. 5.1(a) presents an example of an optimal packing with 8 pieces.

In Chapter 1 it was suggested that there are two main criteria to judge an algorithm by: the quality of its result and how expensive (or efficient) is its operation. The algorithms of Chapter 3 produced "good" results - required to sort a list, they sorted it. The only question of interest there was the amount of resources consumed in the process. The same holds for the Collision Resolution Algorithm analyzed in Section 4.2. We are now presented with a problem coupled with the assurance that for any but trivial versions thereof, the task of solving it correctly is inordinately expensive. This immediately raises the interest in considering partial solutions and investigating their quality in comparison with the too-expensive-to-compute optimal one. Their quality, in this instance, will be judged by the number of bins they require.

One could argue that the above dichotomy is rather artificial, since we could ask similar questions about, say, the sorting algorithms and the time they require compared with the optimal time. This is true to some extent, although the fact that time can be traded-off there against space (see the Linear Probing sort of Section 3.3.3) complicates this argument. Still, one could consider the space × time integral ...

We proceed now to consider particular heuristics for the BP problem and their analysis. The number of bins required for n pieces, using algorithm L is denoted by $A_n(L)$. The number of bins required by the optimal packing will then be $A_n(OPT)$. The size of a bin, b, will be taken to be 1 in all analyses, thus fixing the linear scale. The sizes of the pieces will be assumed to be independently drawn from a population with the distribution $F_X(\cdot)$, and sometimes it will be

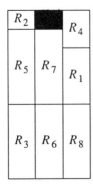

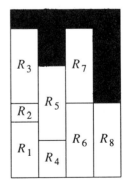

(a)   (b)

Fig. 5.1: Example of Optimal and Next Fit packings of eight pieces of sizes {3,1,4,2,4,4,4,4} into bins of size 9.

convenient to assume the existence of a density function $f_X(\cdot)$ as well.

An obvious relation, that every algorithm L has to satisfy, is

$$A_n(L) \geq A_n(OPT) \geq \sum_{i=1}^{n} X_i. \tag{1}$$

Over the years many heuristics have been fashioned for the BP problem, some of which are quite involved. We shall present just two, and of the simplest variety. It is only then possible to produce a reasonably detailed analysis. The more elaborate algorithms produce better packings mainly by considering certain pieces numerous times, or considering pieces in suitably constructed groups; whichever is the source of their relative success in packing the pieces well, it is precisely those factors that exacerbate the analysis, by generating many dependencies between successive operations. (See the interesting discussion, and relatively limited results in Bentley et al., 1984.)

5.1 The Next-Fit Bin Packing Algorithm

The Next Fit (NF) algorithm is probably the simplest heuristic (except the one-piece-to-a-bin possibility). Still, its analysis is not entirely trivial. It is defined as follows:

1) Set $k = 1, i = 1$.

2) Pack pieces $R_k, R_{k+1}, \cdots, R_m$ into the bin B_i, as long as $\sum_{l=k}^{m} X_l \leq 1$.

3) Set $k = m+1, i = i+1$ and repeat from step 2.

Figure 5.1(b) shows a sample output of this procedure.

There are a few points to make: first, once i is increased, the bin B_{i-1} is "discarded", and never reconsidered. This implies that occasionally we discard a bin that has a considerable unused capacity. Second, the only number the algorithm actually remembers is the level reached in the current bin (in the above version it also retains the position it has reached in the list, the index j. This variable is irrelevant for our analysis, since we shall assume the piece sizes are independent). Third, this paucity of state information indicates, and now from the analytic point of view, that the algorithm should be relatively tractable, since whatever it does at any given stage depends on the past to a very limited extent. Finally, this is an "online" algorithm; it operates with no knowledge of the "future", the pieces that are to be considered later. Thus, one should not expect it to achieve packings that are especially close the optimum.

The following analyses are adapted from Coffman et al. (1980), Hofri (1982 and 1984), and Karmarkar (1982).

As the algorithm operates, it gives rise to several processes:

$\{L_i; i \geq 1\}$ - the total size of pieces packed into B_i when it is "discarded". The complementary process, $W_i = 1 - L_i$, is the wasted space in bin B_i.

$\{N_i; i \geq 1\}$ - the number of pieces packed into B_i, when it is discarded.

$\{U_i; i \geq 1\}$ - the size of the first piece placed in B_i.

$\{T_n; n \geq 1\}$ - the level reached in bin number $A_n(NF)$, when the n-th piece is packed,

and of course the main process of interest, $A_n(NF)$, the number of bins required to pack n pieces. We begin by tackling this process indirectly, via the other ones.

5.1.1 Regularity and Convergence Properties

Our point of departure is the process $\{L_i\}$. The packing process under NF is such, that given the value of L_i (and the distribution of piece size), the evolution of all subsequent packing activity is independent of L_j, $1 \leq j < i$. In other words, $\{L_i\}$ is a first-order Markov chain. Hence the distributions of L_i and L_{i+1} are related via a kernel $K(x,y)$, which has the interpretation $K(x,y) = \text{Prob}(L_{i+1} \leq y \mid L_i = x)$:

$$F_{L_{i+1}}(y) \equiv \text{Prob}(L_{i+1} \leq y) = \int_0^1 K(x,y) dF_{L_i}(x). \tag{2}$$

Since L_1 may be viewed as following a bin with $L_0 = 1$, we have

$$F_{L_1}(y) = K(1,y). \tag{3}$$

Denote by S_n the sum of n independent samples of the piece size X; $L_i = x$ implies $U_{i+1} > 1-x$, and we obtain:

$$K(x,y) = \begin{cases} 0 & y \leq 1-x, \\ \sum_{n \geq 0} \text{Prob}(U_{i+1} + S_n \leq y, \, U_{i+1} + S_n + X > 1 \mid L_i = x) & y > 1-x. \end{cases} \tag{4}$$

The distribution of U_{i+1} is that of X conditioned on its being larger than $1 - L_i$:

$$F_{U_{i+1} \mid L_i}(u \mid x) = \begin{cases} 0 & u \leq 1-x, \\ \dfrac{F_X(u) - F_X(1-x)}{1 - F_X(1-x)} & 1-x < u \leq 1. \end{cases} \tag{5}$$

In Coffman et al. (1980) there is a detailed examination of $K(x,y)$, with the purpose of showing that it is a regular kernel. The discussion there establishes this fact under the requirement that $f_X(x) \equiv F_X'(x)$ is strictly positive on $[0, a]$, for some $a \leq 1$, but as remarked there the conclusion holds under much weaker conditions, and in particular the convergence of $F_{L_i}(\cdot)$ to a proper distribution is guaranteed as long as $F_X(\cdot)$ is not concentrated in a single point. Examples of such limiting distributions are given in Theorem 3 below and in Exercise 5.2-1.

The regularity of the kernel provides us with

Theorem 1: $\{L_i, i \geq 1\}$ is an ergodic Markov chain with a limit distribution $F_L(\cdot)$ satisfying

$$F_L(y) = \int_0^1 K(x,y) dF_L(x) = \lim_{i \to \infty} K^{(i)}(u,y), \qquad 0 \leq u, y \leq 1, \qquad (6)$$

where $K^{(i)}(x,y)$ is the i-step transition kernel, defined by

$$K^{(i+1)}(x,y) = \int_{u=0}^1 d_u K(x,u) K^{(i)}(u,y), \quad i \geq 1, \quad K^{(1)}(x,y) \equiv K(x,y). \quad \Box \quad (7)$$

Let $\bar{L} \equiv E(L)$; since $F_{L_i}(\cdot)$ converges of to $F_L(\cdot)$ at a geometrical rate (see Exercise 2), such is the convergence $E(L_i)$ to $\bar{L}$. From the latter follows the result (which is standard for Markov chains)

Theorem 2: There exists a constant α such that for all m

$$| m\bar{L} - \sum_{i=1}^m E(L_i) | < \alpha. \qquad \Box \qquad (8)$$

See Exercise 3 for a discussion of a proof.

The above nearly exhausts what can be said about the properties of this process without making any specific choice for the piece size distribution. Note, however, that the existence of the limit $F_L(\cdot)$ also implies the (equally fast) convergence $F_{U_i}(\cdot)$ to $F_U(\cdot)$, and similarly for the pmf of N_i, $p_{N_i}(\cdot)$.

5.1.2 Next Fit with $X \sim U(0,1)$ - Expected Values

The uniform distribution holds place of pride in the known analyses of the BP problem, and in particular when its support equals the bin size. Thus, in this subsection we assume $X \sim U(0,1)$, whence

$$F_X(x) = x, \qquad 0 \leq x \leq 1,$$
$$F_{S_n}(x) = \frac{x^n}{n!}, \qquad 0 \leq x \leq 1. \qquad (9)$$

It is arguably the simple form of $F_{S_n}(x)$ in this part of its support that is responsible for the tractability of this version. We shall indulge now in a few computational results.

First, the kernel for the chain $\{L_i\}$ and its limit:

Theorem 3: When $F_X(x) = x$, $0 \leq x \leq 1$, the kernel defined in equation (2) is given by

$$K(x,y) = \begin{cases} 0 & y \le 1-x, \\ 1 - \dfrac{1}{x}(1-y)e^{-(1-y)+x} & 1-x < y \le 1. \end{cases} \tag{10}$$

The limiting distribution for this kernel is

$$F_L(x) = x^3, \qquad 0 \le x \le 1,$$

$$\bar{L} = \frac{3}{4}, \quad \text{hence } A_n(NF) \sim \frac{2}{3} n. \tag{11}$$

Proof: Substituting from equation (9) in the second line of equation (5), we compute in detail; first

$$F_{U_{i+1}|L_i}(u \mid x) = \frac{1}{x}(x + u - 1), \qquad 1-x < u \le 1, \tag{12}$$

and using this in the second line of equation (4),

$$K(x,y) = \sum_{n \ge 0} \int_{u=1-x}^{y} f_{U|L}(u \mid x) \text{Prob}(S_n \le y-u, S_n + X > 1-u) du$$

$$= \sum_{n \ge 0} \int_{u=1-x}^{y} \int_{s=0}^{y-u} f_{U|L}(u \mid x) f_{S_n}(s) \text{Prob}(X > 1-u-s) ds \ du; \tag{13}$$

now, since $\text{Prob}(X > x) = 1-x$, and $f_{U|L}(u \mid x) = \dfrac{1}{x}$,

$$K(x,y) = \sum_{n \ge 0} \int_{u=1-x}^{y} \int_{s=0}^{y-u} \frac{1}{x} \frac{s^{n-1}}{(n-1)!} (u+s) ds \ du. \tag{14}$$

The $n=0$ term (that corresponds to the initial piece being the only one in the bin) has to be done separately; in such a case y is the limit on the size of U, and this term provides the contribution

$$\text{Prob}(U \le y, X+U>1) = \int_{u=1-x}^{y} \frac{1}{x} u \ du = \frac{y^2 - (1-x)^2}{2x}. \tag{15}$$

The rest, after exchanging the order of summation and integration (which we may do since the sums converge uniformly) yields equation (10). (See Exercise 4, for the proof of equation (11) as well.)   □

Now, the following is a straightforward result of Theorem 3 (see Exercise 5):

Theorem 4: When $F_X(x) = x$ $0 \le x \le 1$, we have

$$f_U(u) = \frac{3}{2}(2u - u^2), \qquad 0 \le u \le 1, \tag{16}$$

$$p_N(n) = 3 \frac{n^2 + 3n + 1}{(n+3)!}, \qquad n \ge 1, \tag{17}$$

and $E(U) = \dfrac{5}{8}$, $E(N) = \dfrac{3}{2}$.   □

The results concerning the expected values of L and N can be readily used to obtain asymptotic statements about $A_n(NF) = E[\mathbf{A}_n(NF)]$ (see Exercise 7), as given in equation (11). We shall show however, that one can do better: for $X \sim U(0,1)$ it is possible to compute the *distribution* of $\mathbf{A}_n(NF)$; this is done in Section 5.1.4.

5.1.3 Next Fit with $X \sim U(0,a)$ – Expected Values

We extend now the analysis of the process $\{L_i\}$ to the case where the support of $F_X(\cdot)$ may be shorter than the bin size, although still only for the uniform distribution, i.e. $X \sim U(0, a)$, $\frac{1}{2} \le a \le 1$. The situation when $a < \frac{1}{2}$ is computationally much more complicated, but of a similar nature. The following presentation is based on Karmarkar (1982), who introduced an interesting device to obtain $E(L)$ in this case. The regularity conditions discussed above apply here with no change, which is important, since the present approach only allows us to derive results at the limit $n \to \infty$.

Letting $a < 1$ destroys the simplicity of $F_{S_n}(\cdot)$ over the entire bin size, as in equation (9). Hence the kernel for the chain $\{L_i\}$ is rather unpleasant to work with, and instead we consider the chain $\{T_n\}$, the level in the *current* bin, as it changes when we place successive pieces. Now T_n denotes the level reached with the n-th piece. Since X has a probability density function, T_n will have one too (notice that T_1 has the same distribution as X). We write and solve an equation for the limiting distribution of T_n, and then show how the expected number of bins can be obtained from it. This result is in a sense less productive than a characterization of the chain $\{L_i\}$, from which information about $\{U_i\}$ and $\{N_i\}$ is readily forthcoming.

From the evolution of the packing process we can deduce the equation

$$f_{T_{n+1}}(u) = \int_{x=0}^{u} f_{T_n}(x)f_X(u-x)dx + \int_{x=1-u}^{1} f_{T_n}(x)f_X(u)dx, \qquad (18)$$

where the first term corresponds to the cases where the $n+1$-st piece would fit into the current bin, and the second one when it overflows and starts a new current bin. Let $n \to \infty$ in equation (18), with $f_{T_n}(\cdot) \to f_T(\cdot)$ and insert the value of $f_X(x)$, $1/a$ for $0 \le x \le a$, to obtain

$$f_T(u) = \begin{cases} \dfrac{1}{a} \displaystyle\int_{x=0}^{u} f_T(x)dx + \dfrac{1}{a} \displaystyle\int_{x=1-u}^{1} f_T(x)dx & u \le a, \\[4mm] \dfrac{1}{a} \displaystyle\int_{x=u-a}^{u} f_T(x)dx & u > a. \end{cases} \qquad (19)$$

The exceptional facility of handling the special case $a = 1$ is apparent in equation (19), which exists then only in a single region. Returning for the moment to equation (18), $a = 1$ transforms it to

$$f_{T_{n+1}}(u) = \int_0^u f_{T_n}(x)dx + \int_{1-u}^1 f_{T_n}(x)dx$$

$$= F_{T_n}(u) + 1 - F_{T_n}(1-u), \qquad a = 1. \tag{20}$$

We know that $f_{T_1}(x) = 1$ in $0 \le x \le 1$, and the recursion (20) admits then the surprisingly simple solution

$$f_{T_n}(x) = \begin{cases} 1 & n = 1 \\ 2x & n \ge 2 \end{cases} \quad 0 \le x \le 1; \quad E(T_n) = \begin{cases} 1/2 & n=1 \\ 2/3 & n \ge 2, \end{cases} \quad a = 1. \tag{21}$$

The limiting variable T has then obviously the density $f_T(x) = 2x$, $0 \le x \le 1$ and the expected value 2/3 as well.

Returning to the case $a < 1$, and rewriting equation (19) in terms of the limiting distribution function $F_T(\cdot)$ we get

$$aF_T'(u) = \begin{cases} F_T(u) + 1 - F_T(1-u) & u \le a, \\ F_T(u) - F_T(u-a) & u > a. \end{cases} \tag{22}$$

To handle these two equations together we decompose the unit interval into the three subintervals (remembering that $\frac{1}{2} \le a \le 1$):

$$[0,1] = I_1 \cup I_2 \cup I_3; \quad I_1 = [0, 1-a], \quad I_2 = [1-a, a], \quad I_3 = [a, 1].$$

First we note that $x \in I_2$ implies $1-x \in I_2$, i.e., only values of $F_T(\cdot)$ that are related by the first equation of (22) are involved in this interval. Hence we solve first for $F_T(x), x \in I_2$:

$$aF_T'(x) = F_T(x) + 1 - F_T(1-x), \quad x \in I_2. \tag{23}$$

This is a non-local differential equation, and the device we mentioned consists in converting it to a local one, except that we get not a single equation, but rather a *system* of simultaneous equations[1]. The length of I_2 is $l = 2a - 1$. Define now

$$\phi_1(x) = F_T(x+1-a)$$
$$\phi_2(x) = F_T(a-x) \qquad x \in [0, l]. \tag{24}$$

Equation (23) mixes the two functions ϕ_1 and ϕ_2. Using these functions it can be rewritten as

---

[1] For a *single* nonlocal equation of this type, the following "trick" is not essential, as we show later, with the slightly more complicated equation (39). Over the other subintervals there is no similar obvious reduction, and Karmarkar's device is quite handy.

$$a\phi_1'(x) = \phi_1(x) - \phi_2(x) + 1,$$
$$a\phi_2'(x) = \phi_1(x) - \phi_2(x) - 1.$$
(25)

How is such a system solved?

These are first-order equations with constant coefficients, and thus are a special case of the so called "normal form ordinary differential equation (ODE)". A standard way to handle such a system is to solve it algebraically for one of the functions in terms of the other, obtaining an ODE for one function, of a higher order. The set in equation (25) is of a particularly simple form. By subtracting the second equation from the first we find

$$a\phi_1'(x) - a\phi_2'(x) = 2,$$

and by differentiating the first and substituting from the last relation we get

$$a\phi_1''(x) = \phi_1'(x) - \phi_2'(x) = \frac{2}{a}.$$
(26)

Hence $\phi_1(x) = \dfrac{x^2}{a^2} + \alpha x + \beta$, and $\phi_2(x) = \dfrac{x^2}{a^2} + \gamma x + \delta$. Of these four constants we can forthwith determine three: first, resubstituting the solutions into the equations we find

$$\frac{2x}{a} + a\alpha = a\phi_1'(x) = \phi_1(x) - \phi_2(x) + 1 = (\alpha - \gamma)x + \beta - \delta + 1;$$

equating coefficients of x and the free terms we find $\gamma = \alpha - 2/a$, $\delta = \beta - a\alpha + 1$. A third relation is obtained by noting that for $x \in I_2$, $F_T(x) = \phi_1(x + a - 1)$ $= \phi_2(a - x)$, and substituting the solutions obtained above we get a value for α, $\alpha = (1 - a)/a^2$; hence $\gamma = (1 - 3a)/a^2$. The value of β (or δ) is to be determined once the function $F_T(\cdot)$ is known over the other subintervals; so for the time being we have, say from $\phi_1(\cdot)$:

$$F_T(x) = \frac{x^2}{a^2} + \frac{a-1}{a^2}x + \beta, \qquad x \in I_2.$$
(27)

We cannot write likewise separate equations for $F_T(\cdot)$ in I_1 and I_3, since equation (22) mixes these regions. Again following Karmarkar (1982) we define

$$\phi_1(x) = F_T(x)$$
$$\phi_2(x) = F_T(a+x)$$
$$\phi_3(x) = F_T(1-a-x) \qquad 0 \le x \le 1-a,$$
$$\phi_4(x) = F_T(1-x)$$
(28)

and substituting into equation (22), we obtain

$$a\phi_1'(x) = \phi_1(x) - \phi_4(x) + 1$$
$$a\phi_2'(x) = -\phi_1(x) + \phi_2(x)$$
$$a\phi_3'(x) = \phi_2(x) - \phi_3(x) - 1 \tag{29}$$
$$a\phi_4'(x) = \phi_3(x) - \phi_4(x).$$

Again, this is sparse enough a system to be easily reduced to an equation in one function, e.g. in $\phi_1(x)$:

$$a^4\phi_1^{[4]}(x) - 2a^2\phi_1''(x) = -2. \tag{30}$$

The homogeneous part of the equation has the solution $\alpha_1 x + \beta_1 + \gamma_1 e^{-\sqrt{2}x/a} + \delta_1 e^{\sqrt{2}x/a}$, and adding to this $\varepsilon_1 x^2$ as a particular solution of the inhomogeneous equation we obtain the complete solution

$$\phi_1(x) = \varepsilon_1 x^2 + \alpha_1 x + \beta_1 + \gamma_1 e^{-x\sqrt{2}/a} + \delta_1 e^{x\sqrt{2}/a}. \tag{31}$$

The same form holds for the other functions as well; only two of the functions, say $\phi_1(x)$ and $\phi_4(x)$, are needed in order to obtain $F_T(x)$ in I_1 and I_3. We are left still with 11 constants; since $\phi_4(x)$ is available, via equation (29), in terms of $\phi_1(x)$ and its derivative, only six remain. For these we have a plethora of relations to help in determining them:

$$F_T(0) = 0, \ F_T(1) = 1; \quad F_T(a^-) = F_T(a^+); \quad \phi_1(x) = \phi_3(1-a-x), \quad 0 \le x \le 1-a;$$

$$F_T((1-a)^-) = F_T((1-a)^+); \quad \phi_2(x-a) = \phi_4(1-x), \quad a \le x \le 1,$$

where the functional identities provide rich rewards (actually, the first four relations suffice). One ultimately obtains the desired distribution function, using the notation

$$h(x) = \frac{x^2 + (a-1)x}{2a^2}, \quad b = \frac{\sqrt{2}}{a}, \quad \sigma = \frac{1-a}{a\sqrt{2}}, \quad \theta = \log(1 + \sqrt{2}),$$

in the final form (see Exercise 10(a))

$$F_T(x) = \begin{cases} h(x) + \dfrac{\sigma}{2\cosh\sigma}\left(\sinh(bx - \sigma) + \sinh\sigma\right) & x \in I_1 \\[2ex] 2h(x) + \sigma\tanh\sigma & x \in I_2 \\[2ex] h(x) + \dfrac{1}{2} + \dfrac{\sigma}{2\cosh\sigma}[\sinh\sigma - \cosh(\theta + b(x-1) + \sigma)] & x \in I_3 \end{cases} \tag{32}$$

This gives then the limiting distribution of the level in the current bin, T. Trying to pack one more piece we can make do with the same bin if $T + X \le 1$, and have to start a new one when $T + X > 1$. Hence the limiting probability that a piece starts a new bin is

$$\delta \equiv \text{Prob}(X + T > 1) = \int\limits_{u=0}^{1} f_T(u)\text{Prob}(X > 1-u)\,du$$

$$= \int\limits_{1-a}^{1} f_T(u)\frac{a-1+u}{a}\,du = 1 - \frac{1}{a}\int\limits_{1-a}^{1} F_T(u)\,du, \tag{33}$$

and substituting from the second and third lines of the solution (32) we obtain (see Exercise 10(b)):

Theorem 5: The mean asymptotic rate of bin requirements of NF is given by

$$\delta = \frac{1}{12a^3}\left[15a^3 - 9a^2 + 3a - 1\right] + \frac{\sigma^2}{\sqrt{2}}\tanh\sigma, \tag{34}$$

whence $A_n(NF) \sim n\,\delta$.   □

Theorem 5 only provides the expected value of the required number of bins, and merely the asymptotically leading term, at that. If we limit ourselves to $a = 1$, the simplicity of equation (9) allows us to obtain the entire distribution of $A_n(NF)$, for any n.

5.1.4 The Distribution of $A_n(NF)$, when $X \sim U(0,1)$

In order to obtain $p_n(i) \equiv \text{Prob}[A_n(NF) = i]$ we use the same relation that produced equation (18),

$$A_n(NF) = A_{n-1}(NF) + \delta_n, \tag{35}$$

where

$$\delta_n = \begin{cases} 0 & \text{if } R_n \text{ was packed into bin number } A_{n-1}(NF), \\ 1 & \text{if } R_n \text{ overflowed into a new bin.} \end{cases}$$

The value δ defined in equation (33) is then simply $\lim\limits_{n\to\infty} E(\delta_n)$. Moreover, now we have to consider T_n together with $A_n(NF)$, that is, their joint distribution. Define

$$P_n(l,x) = \text{Prob}[A_n(NF) = l; T_n \le x], \qquad 1 \le l, \; 0 \le x \le 1$$

and the related density and marginal functions

$$p_n(l,x) = \frac{d}{dx}P_n(l,x), \quad p_n(l) = P_n(l,1), \quad F_{T_n}(x) = \sum_{l\ge 1}P_n(l,x),$$

the last two of which have already been used above. Taking the measure implied in equation (35) we find the recursion

(a) $p_n(l,x) = \int\limits_{s=0}^{x} p_{n-1}(l,s)f_X(x-s)ds + \int\limits_{s=1-x}^{1} f_X(x)p_{n-1}(l-1,s)ds$

$$(36)$$

$\quad\quad = f_X * p_{n-1}(l,x) + f_X(x)[p_{n-1}(l-1) - P_{n-1}(l-1,1-x)] , \quad\quad n \geq 2$

with the initial value

(b) $p_1(l,x) = \delta_{l,1}f_X(x).$

This relation greatly simplifies once we introduce the density of $X \sim U(0,1)$, to provide

$$p_n(l,x) = P_{n-1}(l,x) + p_{n-1}(l-1) - P_{n-1}(l-1,1-x) , \quad\quad n \geq 2. \quad (37)$$

This subsection treats exclusively the consequences of equation (37).

As usual when dealing with recursions we define gf's:

$$\beta_n(z,x) \equiv \sum_{l \geq 1} P_n(l,x)z^l , \quad n \geq 1; \quad\quad \beta_0(z,x) \equiv z,$$

$$\phi(u,z,x) \equiv \sum_{n \geq 0} \beta_n(z,x)u^n ; \quad\quad \phi(u,z,0) = z, \quad \phi_x(u,z,0) = uz,$$

$$(38)$$

so that equation (37) can be transformed into

$$\phi_x(u,z,x) = u\,\phi(u,z,x) + uz\,[\phi(u,z,1) - \phi(u,z,1-x)] , \quad\quad 0 \leq x \leq 1, \quad (39)$$

again a non-local differential equation, nearly identical with equation (22).

Because now we have a *single* relation across the entire range of x it is rather simpler to handle: differentiate (39) with respect to x to obtain

$$\phi_{xx}(u,z,x) = u\,\phi_x(u,z,x) + uz\,\phi_x(u,z,1-x). \quad (40)$$

Note that the u and z appear in equations (39) and (40) as mere parameters. Evaluating $\phi_x(u,z,1-x)$ in equation (39) and substituting into (40) provides a local equation:

$$\phi_{xx}(u,z,x) = u^2(1-z^2)\phi(u,z,x) + u^2z(1+z)\phi(u,z,1). \quad (41)$$

This is a second-order ODE of the form $g'' = ag + b$ which has the general solution $g = c_1 e^{x\sqrt{a}} + c_2 e^{-x\sqrt{a}} - b/a$, where c_i need still to be determined from initial conditions. For ϕ these conditions are given in equation (38), and the constants c_i are found then by substitution:

$$c_1 = \frac{z}{2} + \frac{z}{2s(z)} + \frac{z\,\phi(u,z,1)}{2(1-z)} , \quad\quad s(z) \equiv \sqrt{1-z^2},$$

$$(42)$$

$$c_2 = \frac{z}{2} - \frac{z}{2s(z)} + \frac{z\,\phi(u,z,1)}{2(1-z)} .$$

This provides an explicit expression for $\phi(u,z,x)$, involving $\phi(u,z,1)$; however, it is only the latter that we need for the distribution of A_n. On evaluating that solution at $x=1$ and solving for $\phi(u,z,1)$ we obtain (see Exercise 12)

$$\phi(u,z,1) = \frac{z(1-z)\left[e^{us(z)} + e^{-us(z)} + \frac{1}{s(z)}\left(e^{us(z)} - e^{-us(z)}\right)\right]}{2-z\left[e^{us(z)} + e^{-us(z)}\right]}. \qquad (43)$$

From the definition of $\phi(u,z,x)$ we see that $p_n(l) = [u^n z^l]\phi(u,z,1)$. Extricating this coefficient is rather tiresome. First the expression for $[u^n]\phi(u,z,1)$ is obtained by writing:

$$[u^n]\phi(u,z,1) = \frac{1}{2}z(1-z)[u^n]\left\{e^{us(z)} + e^{-us(z)}\right.$$
$$\left. + \frac{1}{s(z)}\left[e^{us(z)} - e^{-us(z)}\right]\right\}\sum_{i\ge 0}\left(\frac{z}{2}\right)^i\left(e^{us(z)} + e^{-us(z)}\right)^i.$$

Now

$$[u^j]\left(e^{us(z)} + e^{-us(z)}\right)^i = \sum_{k\ge 0}\binom{i}{k}[u^j]e^{us(z)(2k-i)} = \sum_{k\ge 0}\binom{i}{k}\frac{(2k-i)^j s(z)^j}{j!}.$$

So

$$[u^n]\phi(u,z,1) = \frac{z(1-z)}{2}\sum_{i\ge 0}2^{-i}z^i$$
$$\times\sum_{j=0}^{n}\frac{s(z)^{n-j-1}(1+s(z)) + (-s(z))^{n-j-1}(1-s(z))}{(n-j)!}\sum_{k\ge 0}\binom{i}{k}\frac{s(z)^j(2k-i)^j}{j!}. \qquad (44)$$

The summation over j can be carried out and yields:

$$[u^n]\phi(u,z,1) = \frac{z(1-z)}{2n!}s(z)^{n-1}\sum_{i\ge 0}2^{-i}z^i$$
$$\times\sum_{k\ge 0}\binom{i}{k}\left\{(2k-i+1)^n - (2k-i-1)^n + s(z)[(2k-i+1)^n + (2k-i-1)^n]\right\}. \qquad (45)$$

There are several ways one can take from this point. We do as follows: consider the summation over k,

$$\sum_{k\ge 0}\binom{i}{k}[(2k-i+1)^n - (2k-i-1)^n] = (1-(-1)^n)\sum_{k\ge 0}\binom{i}{k}(2k-i+1)^n,$$
$$\sum_{k\ge 0}\binom{i}{k}[(2k-i+1)^n + (2k-i-1)^n] = \tfrac{1}{2}(1+(-1)^n)\sum_{k\ge 0}\binom{i+1}{k}(2k-i-1)^n. \qquad (46)$$

Such combinations of powers of -1 naturally suggest the desirability of considering separately odd and even n. In both cases, equation (45) indicates that only even powers of $s(z)$ will contribute. Observe that

$$[z^{2j}]s^{2m}(z) = [z^{2j}](1-z^2)^m = \binom{m}{j}(-1)^j, \qquad (47)$$

and using this we find at some labor (see Exercise 13)

Theorem 6: The pmf of $\mathbf{A}_{2m}(NF)$ is given by

$$[u^{2m}z^l]\phi(u,z,1) = p_{2m}(l) = \frac{1}{(2m)!}\sum_{k\geq 0}\binom{m}{k}(-1)^k 2^{2k-l+1}$$

$$\times \sum_{j\geq 0}[\binom{l-2k}{j}(2j-l+2k)^{2m}-2\binom{l-2k-1}{j}(2j-l+2k+1)^{2m}].\quad\square$$

(48)

Note that the sum over k in equation (48) has no contribution for k larger than $K(l)\equiv\lfloor(l-1)/2\rfloor$. A similar expression holds for odd n, $n = 2m + 1$.

Evaluating the Moments of $A_n(NF)$

The probabilities $p_n(l)$ are given explicitly in equation (48) and its dual, for odd n; it is not easy to obtain the moments of $A_n(NF)$ from this expression. We show below an easier way, for the first two moments, and the same method could be used for higher ones as well. We drop the attribute (NF) in this discussion.

The first moment, A_n, can be obtained from $f_{T_n}(x)$, precisely as done in Section 5.1.3; we shall adopt however the same approach used later for the second moment; the starting point is equation (37). Integrated over $0\leq x\leq 1$ it yields

$$p_n(l) = \int_0^1 P_{n-1}(l,x)dx + p_{n-1}(l-1) - \int_0^1 P_{n-1}(l-1,x)dx\ ,\qquad n\geq 2.\quad(49)$$

Multiplying by l and summing for $l\geq 1$ we find, arranging terms for cancellation,

$$A_n = \sum_{l\geq 1}l\int_0^1 P_{n-1}(l,x)dx + \sum_{l\geq 1}(l-1)p_{n-1}(l-1) + \sum_{l\geq 1}p_{n-1}(l-1)$$

$$- \sum_{l\geq 1}(l-1)\int_0^1 P_{n-1}(l-1,x)dx - \sum_{l\geq 1}\int_0^1 P_{n-1}(l-1,x)dx\ ,\qquad n\geq 2,$$

(50)

hence

$$A_n = A_{n-1} + 1 - \int_0^1 F_{T_{n-1}}(x)dx = A_{n-1} + E(T_{n-1})\ ,\qquad n\geq 2.\quad(51)$$

Since $E(T_{n-1})$ is known from equation (21) we immediately find $A_n = A_{n-1} + \frac{2}{3}$ for $n > 1$, and so we obtain

Theorem 7: The expected value of $A_n(NF)$, for $X\sim U(0,1)$ is given by

$$A_n = \begin{cases} 1 & n=1, \\ \dfrac{2}{3}n + \dfrac{1}{6} & n\geq 2. \end{cases}\qquad\square\quad(52)$$

Instead of computing the second moment on its own, we compute directly what is really of interest, the variance of $A_n(NF)$, which we denote by V_n. Squaring equation (35), taking the expected value of both sides, and subtracting A_n^2 we find

$$V_n = E(A_{n-1}^2) + E(\delta_n^2) + 2E(A_{n-1}\delta_n) - (A_{n-1}+E(\delta_n))^2$$
$$= V_{n-1} + E(\delta_n)[1-E(\delta_n)-2A_{n-1}] + 2E(A_{n-1}\delta_n), \tag{53}$$

where we have used the fact that since δ_n only takes the values 0 and 1, $E(\delta_n^2) = E(\delta_n)$. This is a recursion that starts at $V_1 = 0$, but the last term in the right-hand side of equation (53) is not known yet. Writing it explicitly we have

$$\gamma_{n-1} \equiv E(A_{n-1}\delta_n) = \sum_{l \geq 1} l \int_0^1 p_{n-1}(l,x)\mathrm{Prob}(X > 1-x)dx. \tag{54}$$

This requires a computation like the one that led to A_n, except that now we multiply equation (37) by $\mathrm{Prob}(X > 1-x) = x$ before integrating x out; again multiplying by l and summing for $l \geq 1$ we find

$$\gamma_n = \sum_{l \geq 1} l \int_0^1 x P_{n-1}(l,x)dx + \frac{1}{2}\sum_{l \geq 1}(l-1)p_{n-1}(l-1) + \frac{1}{2}\sum_{l \geq 1} p_{n-1}(l-1)$$
$$+ \sum_{l \geq 1} l \int_0^1 (1-x)P_{n-1}(l-1,1-x)dx - \sum_{l \geq 1} l \int_0^1 P_{n-1}(l-1,1-x)dx,$$

and effects similar to those that produced equation (50) yield, with integration by parts:

$$\gamma_n = \gamma_{n-1} + \{\frac{1}{2}[A_{n-1} - E(T_{n-1}^2) + 2E(T_{n-1})]\} - \sum_{l \geq 1} l \int_0^1 x^2 p_{n-1}(l,x)dx, \tag{55}$$

where again we have a last term the value of which is not known; however, the computations leading to equation (55) suggest that when equation (37) is now treated with lx^2 before integrating x out we would get the same cancellations as in equation (50). Denoting the rightmost term in (55) by θ_{n-1} we shall find (see Exercise 15)

$$\theta_n = \gamma_{n-1} - \theta_{n-1} + \{E(T_{n-1}) - E(T_{n-1}^2) + \frac{1}{3}[A_{n-1} + E(T_{n-1}^3)]\}. \tag{56}$$

The functions in braces in equations (55) and (56) are by now known functions of n. Denote them by $f_1(n)$ and $f_2(n)$, respectively, and then equations (55) and (56) can be rewritten as the pair of equations

$$\gamma_n = \gamma_{n-1} - \theta_{n-1} + f_1(n)$$
$$\theta_n = \gamma_{n-1} - \theta_{n-1} + f_2(n)$$

which have an immediate solution: subtract the second from the first to find

$$\gamma_n - \theta_n = f_1(n) - f_2(n),$$

hence

$$\gamma_n = f_1(n-1) - f_2(n-1) + f_1(n), \qquad n \geq 2, \tag{57}$$

with $\gamma_1 = E(A_1\delta_1) = E(\delta_1) = 1/2$. Similarly $\theta_1 = 1/3$; now to complete the computation of $f_i(n)$ we find first

$$E(T_n) = \begin{cases} 1/2 & n=1 \\ 2/3 & n \geq 2, \end{cases} \qquad E(T_n^2) = \begin{cases} 1/3 & n=1 \\ 1/2 & n \geq 2, \end{cases}$$

$$E(T_n^3) = \begin{cases} 1/4 & n=1 \\ 2/5 & n \geq 2. \end{cases} \tag{58}$$

Computing directly the first few terms also gives $f_1(1) - f_2(1) = \gamma_1 - \theta_1 = 1/6$, which yields $\gamma_2 = 1$, and the rest can be computed directly, producing

$$\gamma_n = \begin{cases} 1/2 & n=1 \\ 1 & n=2 \\ 17/12 & n=3 \\ (20n+4)/45 & n \geq 4. \end{cases} \tag{59}$$

and substituting into (53) provides finally

Theorem 8: The variance of A_n (NF), for $X \sim U(0,1)$ is given by

$$V_n = \begin{cases} 0 & n=1 \\ 1/4 & n=2 \\ 17/36 & n=3 \\ (32n-13)/180 & n \geq 4. \end{cases} \tag{60} \qquad \square$$

The linearity of V_n in n need not be surprising, since we should expect the centralized and normalized A_n to approach a normal (Gaussian) distribution, when n increases; this is so since the contributions of large subsets of the n pieces are nearly independent.

Thus in a very special case we could compute a rather complete characterization of an algorithm, albeit a simple one. In the next section we shall consider a somewhat different algorithm, and find the analysis quite transformed as well.

Exercises and Complements

1. Argue why $\{N_i\}$ is not a Markov chain, unlike $\{L_i\}$ and $\{U_i\}$.

2. Show that $F_{L_i}(x)$ converges to its limit $F_L(x)$ geometrically in i, uniformly in x. Specifically, you have to show that there exist an integer k and a positive number $h < 1$ such that

$$|F_{L_i}(x) - F_L(x)| < ah^i, \qquad i > k, \quad 0 \leq x \leq 1$$

for some $a > 0$.
[This will follow if the kernel iterates converge in such a manner. Loève (1977) shows that this follows if the "Markov measure" Δ_n, defined through

$$\Delta_n = \sup_{x,y} \sup_z \Delta_n(x,y,z), \qquad \Delta_n(x,y,z) \equiv |K^{(n)}(x,z) - K^{(n)}(z,y)|,$$

satisfies a "contraction condition" $\Delta_{n_1} < 1$ for some $n_1 \geq 1$. Then the convergence above holds with $h \leq (\Delta_{n_1})^{1/n_1}$. In our case you can show by considering the interpretation of $K(x,y)$ that $\Delta_1 = 1$, $\Delta_n < 1$ for $n \geq 2$.]

3. Prove Theorem 2.
[Hint: rewrite equation (8) as $\sum_{i=1}^{m} E(L_i) = m\bar{L} + \sum_{i=1}^{m}(E(L_i) - \bar{L})$, and show that there exists an $\alpha^* < \infty$ equal to $\sum_{i \geq 1}(E(L_i) - \bar{L})$, using the results of Exercise 2.]

4. Complete the proof of Theorem 3:
(a) Start with the evaluation of the right-hand side of equation (14). (Prove that the change of order of summation and integration is valid.)
(b) Show that equations (10) and (11) satisfy equation (6).
[The more interesting part is finding $F_L(\cdot)$ in the first place. This is done by substituting (10) in (6) to obtain an integral equation for $F_L(\cdot)$:

$$F_L(y) = \int_{x=1-y}^{1} \left[1 - \frac{1-y}{x} e^{x+y-1}\right] dF_L(x). \tag{4-1}$$

The arguments used to show the regularity of $K(x,y)$ also imply that $F_L(\cdot)$ has a density, $f_L(\cdot)$, and differentiation of equation (4-1) yields

$$f_L(y) = y e^{y-1} \int_{x=1-y}^{1} \frac{e^x}{x} f_L(x) dx. \tag{4-2}$$

This equation suggests simplification by substitution $g(x) = e^{-x} f_L(x)/x$, and $g(\cdot)$ then has to satisfy

$$g(y) = \int_{x=1-y}^{1} e^{-(1-2x)} g(x) dx. \tag{4-3}$$

The integral equation can be converted to a differential one: differentiate (4-3) twice, using the first derivative to resubstitute for the integral, providing $g''(y) + 2g'(y) + g(y) = 0$, a homogeneous linear ODE with constant coefficients; the characteristic equation has the double root -1, that is readily shown to imply $g(y) = cye^{-y}$, and normalization furnishes the value of c. Note that it appears you have a second order ODE with a single condition on it: the normalization of $f_L(\cdot)$; this, however, is not the case. Why?]

5. Prove Theorem 4 (equations (16) and (17)).
[First compute $f_U(\cdot)$, since it is available directly by conditioning on L in equation (5), and then for N obtain the following expression and compute its value: $P_N(n) = \int_{u=0}^{1} f_U(u) \int_{s=0}^{1-u} \mathrm{Prob}(S_{n-1} = s, X > 1-u-s) ds\, du.$]

6. Show, for $X \sim U(0,1)$,

$$E(z^{N_i+1} \mid L_i = x) = 1 + \frac{1}{x}(e^{xz} - 1)(1 - \frac{1}{z}).$$

Use this relation and $F_L(\cdot)$ to obtain the limiting pgf of $\{N_i\}$.

7. Show the relation between the limiting values of $E(L), E(N)$ and an asymptotic estimates for $A_n(NF)$:

$$A_n(NF) \sim nE(X) / (3/4) = \frac{2}{3}n, \quad \text{or} \quad A_n(NF) \sim \frac{n}{E(N)}$$

which comes to the same value, of course.

8. Extract from equations (18) or (19) the Markov kernel for the chain $\{T_n\}$. Redo Exercise 2 for this kernel, showing that $F_{T_n}(x) \to F_T(x)$ exponentially in n and uniformly in x.

9. Verify that equations (24)-(25) are equivalent to equation (23).

10. (a) Show that equations (27)-(29), with the boundary conditions there lead to equation (32).
[Use $\phi_1(\cdot)$ for $F_T(\cdot)$ in I_1, and $\phi_4(\cdot)$ in I_3.]
(b) Obtain δ as given in equation (34), and show that it is a monotonic increasing function of a. We can also define η, the "efficiency" of the packing, as the ratio of the expected total size of the pieces, $nE(X) = na/2$, to the expected bin space requirement, A_n. Hence asymptotically $\eta = a/2\delta$. Show that this quantity has a local minimum at $a \approx 0.8414$. Can you "explain" this fact? The request for explanation is not trivial; one would expect (at least, it appears easier to explain why) the packing efficiency should be a continuous monotonic function of a, just as δ is.
[The computations are simple but tedious. Retain the expressions for the density $f_T(x)$ in terms of the hyperbolic functions. Use the identities $\sinh x - \sinh y = 2\cosh(x+y)/2 \cdot \sinh(x-y)/2$; $\cosh(x+y) = \cosh x \cosh y - \sinh x \sinh y$, and notice that $\sinh\theta = 1$; $\cosh\theta = \sqrt{2}$.]

11. Obtain equation (18) from (36) and the definition of $f_{T_n}(\cdot)$ as the marginal of the probability function $p_n(\cdot,\cdot)$.

12. Obtain the explicit solution for $\phi(u,z,x)$ from equation (41) and the discussion following it. Solve it for $\phi(u,z,1)$ to obtain equation (43).

13. (a) Obtain equation (48). This is probably easiest by considering separately also even and odd l, and showing they produce the same expression. It can be done directly, though, by splitting the sum over i to its odd and even contributions.
(b) Obtain $p_{2m+1}(l)$, which is similar to equation (48) as well.

14. (Hofri, 1982) Starting from equation (36), it is rather easy to obtain an equation for an *approximation* of $p_n(l)$. The idea is that for a value of n which is not "too small" A_n and T_n should be nearly independent, and hence $p_n(l,x)$ $\approx \hat{p}_n(l) f_{T_n}(x)$. Integrating over $0 \le x \le 1$ in equation (36), obtain

$$\hat{p}_n(l) = \hat{p}_{n-1}(l)c_{n-1} + \hat{p}_{n-1}(l-1)(1-c_{n-1}), \quad \text{for } c_n \equiv \int_0^1 f_X(x) \int_{u=0}^{1-x} f_{T_n}(u)du \ dx,$$

and $\hat{\beta}_n(z) \equiv \sum_{l \ge 1} \hat{p}_n(l)z^l$ then satisfies $\hat{\beta}_n(z) = \hat{\beta}_{n-1}(z)[c_{n-1} + z(1-c_{n-1})]$. This recursion can be continued down to

$$\hat{\beta}_n(z) = \beta_a(z) \prod_{j=a}^{n-1} [c_j + z(1-c_j)]$$

where $\beta_a(z) \equiv \beta_a(z,1)$ is obtained from the exact recursion

$$\beta_{n,x}(z,x) = \beta_{n-1}(z,x)f_X(0)$$

$$+ \int_0^x f_X'(x-s)\beta_{n-1}(z,s)ds + zf_X(x)[\beta_{n-1}(z) - \beta_{n-1}(z,1-x)].$$

For the two densities $f_X(x)=1$ and $f_X(x)=2x$, $0 \le x \le 1$ compute $p_{10}(l)$ by the above method, taking $a=3$. To obtain c_j use equation (18). Compute the estimates of A_n and V_n from these approximate functions. Explain the pattern of deviations that appears.

15. Obtain equations (54) to (57), to verify the value of V_n. In a similar way obtain $E[(A_n - A_n)^3]$.

16. Using the expressions for A_n and V_n, equations (52) and (60), estimate $\text{Prob}(A_n(NF) > 0.8n)$, from Chebyshev's inequality (relation (C.3)) and the Central Limit Theorem.

5.2 The Next-Fit-Decreasing Bin Packing Algorithm

The Next-Fit-Decreasing algorithm (NFD) is a variation of the NF algorithm: the pieces are first sorted by size, in non-increasing order, to create a new list $L=\{X_i, 1 \le i \le n\}$ where $X_1 \ge X_2 \ge \cdots \ge X_n$, and then NF is performed on this list L. At first blush this procedure may appear a strange one: not only does it destroy the convenience of on-line operation, and requires additional processing, but also it is not obvious that it improves the packing. We can offer the following observations:

1) It has been shown, see Coffman et al. (1984), that the worst-case-behavior of NFD is better than NF (1.691... times the optimum, compared with 2).

2) We shall show that for $X \sim U(0,1)$, NFD also packs better than NF on the average, with $A_n(NFD) = E[A_n(NFD)] \approx 0.6449n < A_n(NF) \approx 0.666n$.

3) Contrariwise, in Exercise 1 we bring a family of two-valued piece-size distributions under which NF outperforms NFD, on the average, for large n at least, and for certain parameters by a substantial margin, up to some 20%.

How does one evaluate $A_n(NFD)$? The situation appears much harder then before: once the pieces are sorted, their sizes are no longer independent. Nothing like the convenient Markov chain $\{L_i\}$ of Section 5.1.1 is available here. Indeed, under *no* non-trivial distributional assumptions can we compute precisely any of the moments of $A_n(NFD)$, for an n, as done in Section 5.1.4.

It will turn out, however, that if we are willing to make do with asymptotic results only, then NFD is actually *easier* to handle than NF. Of course, it is the sorting that does it, by separating out large and small pieces, with the latter, in a suitably defined limit - that we elaborate upon below - providing a negligible contribution. We shall present two analyses, rather different in their approach to this limiting process, and hence also in their capabilities; both however use the following construction:

Divide the unit interval (which necessarily contains the support of the piece size distribution) into the subintervals I_k where $I_k = (\frac{1}{k+1}, \frac{1}{k}]$. This also induces a partition of the n pieces into subsets W_k such that

$$W_k = \{R_i \mid X_i \in I_k\}, \qquad I_k = (\frac{1}{k+1}, \frac{1}{k}], \qquad k \geq 1. \tag{1}$$

Once sorted, these subsets will be packed in order. Exactly k pieces from W_k can be accommodated in one bin. There will be bins that contain pieces from two or more sets, but as n increases the fraction of such bins in $A_n(NFD)$ decreases. Quantifying this last phrase is the main task of the analysis. Finally, define P_k as the probability $\text{Prob}(X \in I_k)$ and N_k as $|W_k|$; thus each N_k has a marginal binomial distribution $B(n, P_k)$.

5.2.1 Direct Evaluation of Bin Requirements (Csirik et al., 1986)

The first method we consider uses one further observation about the variables defined above:

If we employ only a *finite* number of intervals, with the last one, $I_r = [0, 1/r]$, then the r random variables N_k, $1 \leq k \leq r$, have a joint multinomial distribution

$$\text{Prob}(N = n) = \binom{n}{n_1, \cdots, n_r} P_1^{n_1} \cdots P_r^{n_r}, \qquad \forall n_1, n_2, \cdots, n_r \mid \sum_{k=1}^{r} n_k = n, \tag{2}$$

and the corresponding pgf is

$$g_N(z) = E\left[\prod_{k=1}^{r} z_k^{N_k}\right] = \sum_{n_1, \cdots, n_r} z_1^{n_1} \cdots z_r^{n_r} \text{Prob}(N = n) = \left(\sum_{k=1}^{r} P_k z_k\right)^n. \quad (3)$$

A pgf of the form $f^n(z)$ suggests a sum of i.i.d. random variables. The suitable random variables become apparent if we evaluate $g_N(z)$ at the point $z_r \equiv (z_k = u^{1/k}, 1 \le k \le r)$, for some $u \ne 0$, to find

$$g_N(z_r) = \left[\sum_{k=1}^{r} u^{1/k} P_k\right]^n. \quad (4)$$

Now observe that this is precisely the pgf of $\sum_{j=1}^{n} y_{jr}$, evaluated at u, where the y_{jr} are i.i.d. random variables defined through $\text{Prob}(y_{jr} = 1/k) = P_k$, $1 \le k \le r$. The usefulness of this observation is clarified when we compute $g_N(z_r)$ differently:

$$g_N(z_r) = \sum_n u^{n_1} u^{n_2/2} \cdots u^{n_r/r} \text{Prob}(N = n)$$

$$= \sum_n u^{\sum n_k/k} \text{Prob}(N = n); \quad (5)$$

hence we see that the two random variables

$$\sum_{j=1}^{n} y_{jr}, \text{ and } S_{1,r} \equiv \sum_{k=1}^{r} \frac{N_k}{k} \quad (6)$$

are identically distributed. The important advantage that accrues from this is the replacement of a sum of dependent random variables by an identically distributed sum of independent ones, which is rather easier to handle.

Similarly, if we consider the sum $S_{2,r} \equiv \sum_{k=1}^{r-1} N_k/k$, without N_r, we find, by precisely the same argument, that its distribution coincides with that of another sum of n i.i.d. random variables, $\sum_{j=1}^{n} z_{jr}$, with the z_{jr} having the distribution $\text{Prob}(z_{jr} = 1/k) = P_k$, $1 \le k \le r-1$, and also $\text{Prob}(z_{jr} = 0) = P_r$.

Now obviously these variables $S_{1,r}$ and $S_{2,r}$ were not chosen haphazardly. Observe that since the pieces in W_k can be packed exactly k to a bin, $\lceil N_k/k \rceil$ is an upper limit on the number of bins the set W_k accounts for, and going through $1 \le k \le r$ we find

$$A_n(NFD) \le \sum_{k=1}^{r} \left\lceil \frac{N_k}{k} \right\rceil \le \sum_{k=1}^{r} \frac{N_k}{k} + r = S_{1,r} + r. \quad (7)$$

Similarly, $\lfloor N_k/k \rfloor$ bounds from below the bin requirements of W_k, $1 \le k \le r-1$. The pieces in W_r can be packed r (at least) to a bin as well, but we shall conveniently disregard in the lower bound, for simplicity (and as will be shown later also for reasons of symmetry in the calculations), the contribution of W_r:

$$\mathbf{A}_n(NFD) \geq \sum_{k=1}^{r-1} \left\lfloor \frac{N_k}{k} \right\rfloor \geq \sum_{k=1}^{r-1} \frac{N_k}{k} - (r-1) = S_{2,r} - (r-1). \tag{8}$$

These sums bracket $\mathbf{A}_n(NFD)$, and will now be used to obtain the limit $A_n(NFD)/n$, as $n \to \infty$. Note first that for all $1 \leq j \leq n$

$$E(y_{jr}) = \sum_{j=1}^{r} \frac{P_k}{k}, \quad E(z_{jr}) = \sum_{k=1}^{r-1} \frac{P_k}{k}, \quad 1 \leq j \leq n, \tag{9}$$

and then, bounding $A_n(NFD)/n$ we have

$$\sum_{k=1}^{r-1} \frac{P_k}{k} - \frac{(r-1)}{n} \leq \frac{A_n(NFD)}{n} \leq \sum_{k=1}^{r} \frac{P_k}{k} + \frac{r}{n}. \tag{10}$$

If $f_X(x)$ is continuous at $x = 0$ (in particular, when 0 is not an atom of this distribution, which amounts to saying that "pieces" of size zero are disallowed), $P_r \to 0$ when $r \to \infty$. Thus we let n and r go together to infinity. In order to have an orderly convergence we take $r = o(n)$, such as $r = n^s$, $0 < s < 1$; we have

$$\frac{A_n(NFD)}{n} \to \sum_{k \geq 1} \frac{P_k}{k}. \tag{11}$$

This holds for *any* piece size distribution, continuous at $x = 0$.

Now, reverting to our convenient "yardstick" measure, where $X \sim U(0,1)$, the P_k equal $1/k(k+1)$, $k \geq 1$, and

$$\lim_{n \to \infty} \frac{A_n(NFD)}{n} = \sum_{k \geq 1} \frac{1}{k^2(k+1)} = \sum_{k \geq 1} \frac{1}{k^2} - 1 = \frac{\pi^2}{6} - 1 \approx 0.6449. \tag{12}$$

See Exercise 2 for $X \sim U(0,a)$, $0 < a \leq 1$.

The result in equation (12) was also independently arrived at by Lee and Lee (1984). They call "HARMONIC"[2] a packing algorithm that proceeds as described in the derivation of the lower bound, equation (8). Their treatment is mainly oriented to worst-case results, and $\lim A_n(NFD)/n$ was a by-product.

The structure of the above approximation, with both r and n growing to infinity together is not conducive to obtaining a finer asymptotic expansion, let alone a complete one. In Section 5.2.2 we shall show that a somewhat different approach can yield an estimate of the next term, but this seems to be the extent of what is so far known for $A_n(NFD)$.

What one can do, however, in the present context is to obtain the *limit* of *all* the central moments of $\mathbf{A}_n(NFD)$. Furthermore, since we can characterize the evolution of $\mathbf{A}_n$ by a sum of *independent*, uniformly bounded random variables, the road is open to use inequality (C.6), so as to bound the probabilities of deviations that are $O(n)$. We show in detail this latter estimate.

---

[2] So dubbed because of the construction of the intervals I_k.

Deviations from the Expected Value

The purpose now is to estimate the probability

$$p_t = \text{Prob}[\, | A_n(NFD) - A_n(NFD) | \geq nt \,], \quad t > 0. \tag{13}$$

This probability is clearly the sum of two terms

$$p_t = \text{Prob}[A_n(NFD) - A_n(NFD) \leq -nt] \\ + \text{Prob}[A_n(NFD) - A_n(NFD) \geq nt]. \tag{14}$$

Each of the terms in equation (14) is to be handled separately, but we do it in parallel. We shall use equations (7) and (8) repeatedly.

The two terms of equation (14), using equations (8) and (7), respectively, have the following upper bounds

$$\text{Prob}[A_n(NFD) \leq A_n(NFD) - nt] \leq \text{Prob}[\sum_{j=1}^{n} z_{jr} - (r-1) \leq A_n(NFD) - nt],$$

$$\text{Prob}[A_n(NFD) \geq A_n(NFD) + nt] \leq \text{Prob}[\sum_{j=1}^{n} y_{jr} + r \geq A_n(NFD) + nt]. \tag{15}$$

The two right-hand sides equal, respectively, adding and subtracting the same quantities on both sides,

$$\text{Prob}[\sum_{j=1}^{n} z_{jr} - E(\sum_{j=1}^{n} z_{jr}) \leq A_n(NFD) - E(\sum_{j=1}^{n} z_{jr}) + (r-1) - nt],$$

$$\text{Prob}[\sum_{j=1}^{n} y_{jr} - E(\sum_{j=1}^{n} y_{jr}) \geq A_n(NFD) - E(\sum_{j=1}^{n} y_{jr}) - r + nt]. \tag{16}$$

Using the relation between the expected values of both sides in equations (7) and (8), to replace the expected value $A_n(NFD)$ in the above bounds, these probabilities have in turn the respective upper bounds

$$\text{Prob}[\sum_{j=1}^{n} z_{jr} - E(\sum_{j=1}^{n} z_{jr}) \leq \sum_{k=1}^{r} \frac{nP_k}{k} + r - n\sum_{k=1}^{r-1} \frac{P_k}{k} + (r-1) - nt],$$

$$\text{Prob}[\sum_{j=1}^{n} y_{jr} - E(\sum_{j=1}^{n} y_{jr}) \geq \sum_{k=1}^{r-1} \frac{nP_k}{k} - (r-1) - n\sum_{k=1}^{r} \frac{P_k}{k} - r + nt]. \tag{17}$$

Rearranging on the right, the following bounds are obtained:

$$\text{Prob}[\sum_{j=1}^{n} z_{jr} - E(\sum_{j=1}^{n} z_{jr}) \leq n\frac{P_r}{r} + 2r - 1 - nt],$$

$$\text{Prob}[\sum_{j=1}^{n} y_{jr} - E(\sum_{j=1}^{n} y_{jr}) \geq -n\frac{P_r}{r} - (2r-1) + nt]. \tag{18}$$

Both y_{jr} and z_{jr} are bounded by 0 and 1, so the above probabilities can be bounded (from above) by the inequalities discussed in Section 2.6.2. Using equation (2.6-13), $\exp[-2n\left(t - \dfrac{P_r}{r} - \dfrac{2r-1}{n}\right)^2]$ serves to bound each of them. For this bound to be useful for large n, all that is needed is that r will increase when n does, but more slowly, that is, $r = o(n)$. For $X \sim U(0,a), P_r = 1/ar$, and then $r = \log n$ or $n^{1/3}$ are adequate, providing in the latter case

$$\text{Prob}(\,|\mathbf{A}_n(NFD) - A_n(NFD)| \geq nt\,)$$

$$\leq 2\exp\left(-2n\,[t + \frac{1}{n^{1/3}}(2 + \frac{1}{a})]^2\right), \qquad X \sim U(0,a), \tag{19}$$

which decreases exponentially fast to zero when n increases. See Exercise 3.

In Exercise 4 you are asked to show that similar manipulations provide a Central Limit Theorem for $\mathbf{A}_n(NFD)$:

$$\lim_{n \to \infty} \text{Prob}\left\{ \frac{\mathbf{A}_n(NFD) - A_n(NFD)}{n\,\sigma} \leq x \right\} = \phi(x) \equiv \frac{1}{\sqrt{2\pi}} \int_{-\infty}^{x} e^{-u^2/2}du \tag{20}$$

where

$$\sigma^2 = \lim_{r \to \infty} V(z_{jr}) = \lim_{r \to \infty} V(y_{jr}) = \sum_{k \geq 1} \frac{P_k}{k^2} - \left(\sum_{k \geq 1} \frac{P_k}{k}\right)^2. \tag{21}$$

5.2.2 Asymptotic Bounds on Moments

The same "harmonic" construction that was used above to evaluate $\lim_{n \to \infty} A_n(NFD)/n$, and similarly the limit for the variance, can be used slightly differently. Viewing the packing in terms of processing successively the sets W_k, we see that the computational difficulty involves those bins into which pieces from distinct successive sets are packed. In the last section this was resolved by following the packing for a relatively small number of sets $(r = o(n))$, and using this number as the accuracy bound on the estimates of $\mathbf{A}_n(NFD)$. (Note that the difference between the upper and lower bound, in equations (7) and (8), is in excess of $2r$.)

Now we use a different tack, following Hofri and Kamhi (1986). The packing process is modified, to produce a slightly different packing algorithm - Next-Fit-Decreasing-by-Group (NFDG). Under NFDG each set W_k, which is not empty, starts a fresh bin, and the number of bins it requires is therefore exactly $\lceil N_k/k \rceil$. This process leaves occasionally unused space in the last of such a set of bins, a space that NFD might have used. The entire burden of the analysis consists in estimating the differences that thus arise between $A(n) \equiv \mathbf{A}_n(NFD)$ and $B(n) \equiv \mathbf{A}_n(NFDG)$.

Since we are not truncating the packing processes at any point, n is the only quantity we let increase, and thus we can obtain asymptotic estimates. Such an approach cannot possibly yield the exact value of $E[A(n)]$; it can come, however, rather close: thus, for uniformly distributed piece size we shall estimate $E[A(n)]$ to within a small number times $\log n$.

To estimate the above differences we must look more closely than heretofore at the variables N_k. Define

$$N_k = |W_k| = \begin{cases} 0 & W_k = \varnothing, \\ kr_k + l_k & N_k > 0: \ r_k \ge 0, \ 1 \le l_k \le k. \end{cases} \tag{22}$$

Note that l_k is nearly, but not quite N_k modulo k; it is simply the number of pieces NFDG places in the last bin used for W_k. We also need variables best called "actual bin space requirements" of NFD and NFDG: define $T(n)$, similar to the T_n of Section 5.1, as the level reached at bin $A(n)$ once the last piece was packed in it, then

$$A'(n) \equiv \begin{cases} 0 & A(n) = 0, \\ A(n) - 1 + T(n) & A(n) > 0, \end{cases} \tag{23}$$

is the actual space requirement of NFD. $B'(n)$ is similarly defined for NFDG.

The first line in equation (23) is trivial in the sense that it corresponds to an empty list, but later you will see the convenience it provides (as a base for the induction proofs asked for in Exercise 6).

The above definitions provide the immediate bounds

$$A'(n) \le A(n) = \lceil A'(n) \rceil < A'(n) + 1. \tag{24}$$

The following notational device is convenient in developing our bounds, and in particular for the proofs: Since the computations to be done consist of tracking the difference $B(n) - A(n)$ as it evolves during the entire packing process, we use the symbols $A_k(n), A'_k(n), B_k(n), B'_k(n)$ to denote the values reached by the nonsubscripted variables once the packing of W_k has been completed.

We finally introduce the crucial definition, that allows us to estimate the difference $B(n) - A(n)$:

$$G(n) \equiv \sum_{k \ge 1} g_k(n), \quad g_k(n) \equiv \begin{cases} 0 & N_k = 0, \\ \dfrac{N_k+1}{k} = r_k + \dfrac{l_k+1}{k} & N_k > 0, \end{cases} \tag{25}$$

and $G'(n) \equiv \sum_{k \ge 1} g'_k(n)$, where

$$g'_k(n) \equiv \begin{cases} 0 & N_k = 0, \\ \dfrac{N_k}{k} - \dfrac{1}{k+1} - \dfrac{l_k}{k(k+1)} = r_k + \dfrac{l_k-1}{k+1} & N_k > 0. \end{cases} \tag{26}$$

The reader may well ask what is the motivation for this particular definition. The line of reasoning can be put thus: we do not know how to compute $A(n)$ directly, so we approach it via $B(n)$. The differences between these two arise when the process passes from one set W_k to the next, so we follow the evolution of $A_k(n)$ and $B_k(n)$ (or, equivalently, of the primed variables). Let $a_k \equiv A_k(n) - A_{k-1}(n)$, $b_k \equiv B_k(n) - B_{k-1}(n)$, etc. It is easy to visualize situations (i.e. values for the N_k), where $b_k - a_k = 1$, or $b_k' - a_k' \approx 1$ *infinitely often* when n increases. Since $A(n) = O(n)$, this wont do; we need a more refined approach. It does not appear easy to bound the effect of such sequences via their low probabilities. We must therefore monitor the evolution via a related process that generates smaller errors. It appeared reasonable, when one observes the way differences between NFD and NFDG arise, to attempt to hold these errors to $O(1/k)$ at the stage of packing W_k. It is evident that with such an error at each group, the best we could do is to obtain an estimate to within some $\Sigma 1/k = O(\log n)$. This is why we juggle the components of N_k, i.e. r_k and l_k as above, while still allowing for a proof of the bounds in relation (27) below.

Indeed, the above definitions provide the key relation:

Theorem $G'(n) \le A'(n) \le G(n)$, $n \ge 0$.   (27)

For $n > 0$ the inequalities are strict (the proof is outlined in Exercise 6).   □

Once we have the bounds in (27), we can combine them with those in relation (24) to obtain

$$G'(n) \le A(n) < G(n) + 1,$$ (28)

on which the actual estimates are based. The quality of the entire analysis rests on the closeness of the bounds in equation (28).

We proceed now to evaluate moments for $G(n)$, $G'(n)$ and their difference

$$H(n) \equiv G(n) - G'(n); \text{ also } H_k(n) \equiv G_k(n) - G_k'(n),$$ (29)

with

$$h_k(n) \equiv g_k(n) - g_k'(n) = \begin{cases} 0 & N_k = 0, \\ \dfrac{l_k + 2k + 1}{k(k+1)} & N_k > 0. \end{cases}$$

The expected value $E[A(n)]$ will be simply estimated by

$$E[G'(n)] \le E[A(n)] < E[G(n)] + 1,$$ (30)

but for the variance things are somewhat complicated.

To tackle it, introduce the difference $X(n) \equiv G(n) - A(n)$, in terms of which we can write

$$V[A(n)] = V[G(n) - X(n)] = V[G(n)] + V[X(n)] - 2\mathrm{cov}[G(n), X(n)].$$ (31)

It is convenient to use the bound $|\mathrm{cov}[G(n), X(n)]| \le (V[G(n)]V[X(n)])^{\frac{1}{2}}$.

The inequality always holds, since their ratio is the correlation coefficient, known to be bounded by one, in absolute value. We have now the rather loose bounds

$$V[G(n)] - 2\big(V[G(n)]V[X(n)]\big)^{\frac{1}{2}}$$

$$\leq V[A(n)] \leq V[G(n)] + V[X(n)] + 2\big(V[G(n)]V[X(n)]\big)^{\frac{1}{2}} \quad (32)$$

Actually, a little reflection concerning the evolution of the packing process should convince the reader that $\mathrm{cov}[G(n), X(n)]$ is small compared with the other terms, and is often negative, which implies that the upper bound above is usually tighter than the lower one. This is rather better than the converse. Since $V[X(n)]$ does not have a readily computable representation, we use another rather liberal bound

$$V[X(n)] = V[G(n) - A(n)] < E[(G(n) - A(n))^2]$$

$$\leq E[(G(n) - G'(n))^2] = E[H^2(n)]. \quad (33)$$

Using the notation, $D^2(n) = E[H^2(n)]/V[G(n)]$ we finally can write

$$1 - 2D(n) \leq \frac{V[A(n)]}{V[G(n)]} \leq \big(1 + D(n)\big)^2. \quad (34)$$

Inspection of equation (29) suggests that we should expect $H(n)$ to be $O(\log n)$, and thus $D(n) = O(n^{-\frac{1}{2}}\log n) = o(1)$; i.e.

$$\frac{V[A(n)]}{V[G(n)]} \underset{n \to \infty}{\to} 1. \quad (35)$$

So the bounds in equation (32) should agree in their leading term (in n).

The explicit evaluation of the bounds calls for the computation of the moments of $G(n)$ and $G'(n)$, using the following definitions:

$$P_k \equiv \mathrm{Prob}(\text{a piece belongs to } W_k) = \mathrm{Prob}\Big(\frac{1}{k+1} < X_i \leq \frac{1}{k}\Big),$$

$$P_k(m) \equiv \mathrm{Prob}(N_k = m) = \binom{n}{m} P_k^m (1 - P_k)^{n-m}, \qquad k \geq 1, \qquad 0 \leq m \leq n$$

$$P_{k_1 k_2}(m_1, m_2) \equiv \mathrm{Prob}(N_{k_1} = m_1, N_{k_2} = m_2), \qquad k_1 \neq k_2$$

$$= \binom{n}{m_1, m_2} P_{k_1}^{m_1} P_{k_2}^{m_2} (1 - P_{k_1} - P_{k_2})^{n - m_1 - m_2}, \qquad 0 \leq m_1 + m_2 \leq n.$$

For the computations we use the following abbreviations for several sums over these probabilities:

$$d_1 \equiv \sum_{k \geq 1} \frac{P_k}{k}; \quad d_2 \equiv \sum_{k \geq 1} \frac{P_k^2}{k^2}; \quad d_3 \equiv \sum_{k \geq 1} \frac{P_k}{k^2}. \quad (36)$$

All the other quantities depend on n:

$$d_4(n) \equiv \sum_{k \geq 1} \frac{P_k (1 - P_k)^{n-1}}{k}; \quad d_5(n) \equiv \sum_{k \geq 1} \frac{P_k (1 - P_k)^{n-1}}{k^2}; \quad (37)$$

$$d_6(n) \equiv \sum_{k \geq 1} \frac{1}{k} \sum_{m=1}^{n} P_k(m) = \sum_{k \geq 1} \frac{1}{k}(1 - (1 - P_k)^n) = \sum_{k \geq 1} \frac{P_k}{k} \sum_{t=0}^{n-1} (1 - P_k)^t;$$

$$d_7(n) \equiv \sum_{k \geq 1} \frac{1}{k} \sum_{m=1}^{n} m P_k(m) = n d_1.$$
(38)

Note the reduction of $d_7(n)$; a few of the other sums will be thus reducible to simpler ones as well (see Exercise 8).

$$d_8(n) \equiv \sum_{k \geq 1} \frac{1}{k^2} \sum_{m=1}^{n} P_k(m) = \sum_{k \geq 1} \frac{P_k}{k^2} \sum_{t=0}^{n-1} (1 - P_k)^t;$$
(39)

$$d_9(n) \equiv \sum_{k \geq 1} \frac{1}{k^2} \sum_{m=1}^{n} m P_k(m) = n d_3;$$

$$d_{10}(n) \equiv \sum_{k \geq 1} \frac{1}{k^2} \sum_{m=1}^{n} m^2 P_k(m) = n(n-1)d_2 + n d_3;$$
(40)

$$d_{11}(n) \equiv \sum_{\substack{k_1,k_2 \geq 1 \\ k_1 \neq k_2}} \frac{1}{k_1 k_2} \sum_{m_1=1}^{n} \sum_{m_2=1}^{n-m_1} m_1 m_2 P_{k_1,k_2}(m_1,m_2) = n(n-1)(d_1^2 - d_2);$$
(41)

$$d_{12}(n) \equiv \sum_{\substack{k_1,k_2 \geq 1 \\ k_1 \neq k_2}} \frac{1}{k_1 k_2} \sum_{m_1=1}^{n} \sum_{m_2=1}^{n-m_1} m_2 P_{k_1,k_2}(m_1,m_2)$$

$$= n d_1 d_6(n-1) - n d_3 + n d_5(n);$$
(42)

$$d_{13}(n) \equiv \sum_{\substack{k_1,k_2 \geq 1 \\ k_1 \neq k_2}} \frac{1}{k_1 k_2} \sum_{m_1=1}^{n} \sum_{m_2=1}^{n-m_1} P_{k_1,k_2}(m_1,m_2).$$
(43)

Now we can get expressions for the moments of the required variables. First $G(n)$:

$$E[G(n)] = \sum_{k \geq 1} E\left[\frac{N_k+1}{k}\right] = \sum_{k \geq 1} \sum_{m=1}^{n} \frac{m+1}{k} P_k(m) = d_6(n) + d_7(n). \quad (44)$$

The variable $G'(n)$ is knottier. The notation $l_k(m)$ is used below for the value of l_k as defined in equation (22) when $N_k = m$.

$$E[G'(n)] = \sum_{k \geq 1} E\left[\frac{N_k}{k} - \frac{l_k+k}{k(k+1)}\right] = \sum_{k \geq 1} \sum_{m=1}^{n} P_k(m)\left[\frac{m-1}{k} - \frac{l_k(m)-1}{k(k+1)}\right]$$

$$= d_7(n) - d_6(n) - \sum_{k \geq 1} \sum_{m=1}^{n} P_k(m) \frac{l_k(m)-1}{k(k+1)}.$$
(45)

The remaining sum in equation (45) forms a multisection of $d_7(n)$ which is not easy to evaluate even for simple P_k (e.g. - those obtained from a uniform distribution). However, it is clearly bounded from above by $d_6(n)$, and we shall find that this bound suffices.

The bounds in equation (30) can now be stated explicitly:

$$d_7(n) - 2d_6(n) \le E[A(n)] \le d_7(n) + d_6(n) + 1. \tag{46}$$

Turning to the variance, we need $V[G(n)]$ and $E[H^2(n)]$ in order to evaluate $E[D^2(n)]$.

$$V[G(n)] = E[G^2(n)] - E^2[G(n)]$$

$$= \sum_{\substack{k_1,k_2 \ge 1 \\ k_1 \ne k_2}} \frac{1}{k_1 k_2} \sum_{m_1=1}^{n} \sum_{m_2=1}^{n-m_1} (m_1+1)(m_2+1)P_{k_1,k_2}(m_1,m_2)$$

$$+ \sum_{k \ge 1} \frac{1}{k^2} \sum_{m=1}^{n} (m+1)^2 P_k(m) - (d_6(n)+d_7(n))^2 \tag{47}$$

$$= d_{11}(n) + 2d_{12}(n) + d_{13}(n) + d_{10}(n) + 2d_9(n)$$

$$+ d_8(n) - [d_7(n) + d_6(n)]^2$$

$$= n(d_3 - d_1^2) + 2nd_5(n) - d_6^2(n)$$

$$\tag{48}$$

$$- 2nd_1[d_6(n) - d_6(n-1)] + d_{13}(n) + d_8(n).$$

Observe that the difference in the brackets in equation (48) equals $d_4(n)$. The sum $d_{13}(n) + d_8(n)$ can be shown to satisfy (see Exercise 10)

$$\frac{\pi^2}{6} + d_6^2(n) - d_1^2 < d_{13}(n) + d_8(n) < \frac{\pi^2}{6} + d_6^2(n). \tag{49}$$

Furthermore, since $d_4(n) \ge d_5(n)$ trivially, we obtain

$$n(d_3 - d_1^2) - 2nd_1 d_4(n) < V[G(n)] < n(d_3 - d_1^2) + \frac{\pi^2}{6} + 2nd_4(n). \tag{50}$$

Finally, for $E[H^2(n)]$, a rough estimate that will be seen to be adequate for our purposes is easily obtained as follows:

Since $1 \le l_k \le k$, observe from equation (9) that $2/k \le h_k(n) < 3/k$, for $N_k > 0$, and h_k vanishes when $N_k = 0$. Using the abbreviation χ_k for the indicator function of the last event, $\chi_{\{N_k > 0\}}$, let us compute

$$E\left[\sum_{k \ge 1} \frac{\chi_k}{k}\right]^2 = \sum_{\substack{k_1, k_2 \ge 1 \\ k_1 \ne k_2}} \frac{1}{k_1 k_2} \sum_{m_1=1}^{n} \sum_{m_2=1}^{n-m_1} P_{k_1,k_2}(m_1, m_2)$$

$$+ \sum_{k \ge 1} \frac{1}{k^2} \sum_{m=1}^{n} P_k(m) = d_{13}(n) + d_8(n). \tag{51}$$

This is the quantity that was bounded in equation (49), hence

$$4\left[\frac{\pi^2}{6} + d_6^2(n) - d_1^2\right] < E[H^2(n)] < 9\left[\frac{\pi^2}{6} + d_6^2(n)\right]. \tag{52}$$

Equations (34), (50) and (52) provide the desired bounds on $V[A(n)]$. In Exercise 9 you are asked to show that for $X \sim U(0,1)$ the leading terms of the bounds in relations (46) and (50) coincide with the limiting values in equations (11) and (21); and in Exercises 10 and 11 you are asked to estimate the moments for two specific values of n.

This concludes our treatment of the bin packing problem. More elaborate heuristics, that are known to provide better packings can be considered. Their analysis, however, is markedly more difficult. Thus consider the First Fit heuristic (the bins are ordered according to time of first use, no bin is discarded, and with each piece the entire set of bins used so far is scanned, to find the first with enough space yet to receive the piece; if none exists a fresh bin is inducted into service): It is not difficult to show, under rather mild assumptions on the piece size distribution, that $A_n(FF)/\sum_{i=1}^{n} X_i \to 1$, as n increases. Otherwise, the best result so far only *bounds* the *order* of the leading term in the asymptotic expression for the expected wasted space when pieces uniformly distributed on (0,1] are packed (Bentley et al., 1984). Further analyses, under varying assumptions on piece sizes and packing methods, in one or more dimensions, may be found is Csirik et al. (1986), Frederickson (1980), Hofri (1980), Karp et al. (1984) and Loulou (1984).

Exercises and Complements

1. Consider packing in bins of size 1 pieces that can be of the sizes 0.6 and 0.4 only, and they assume these sizes independently with probabilities p and q ($=1-p$) respectively. Show that under these assumptions $A_n(NF) < A_n(NFD)$ for all values of p and large n. Also show that the advantage of NF is maximal when p is close to $p = \frac{1}{2}$.
[$A_n(NFD)$ is immediate, and for $A_n(NF)$, use the requirement to prove for large n

only, to compute it through $E(L)$, which evaluates to $(3p^2+5q-2q^3)/5(q+p^2)$.]

2. Evaluate $\lim_{n\to\infty} A_n(NFD)/n$ for $X \sim U(0,a)$, $0 < a \leq 1$. Show from your result that the ratio of the number of bins used to total bin space actually used, $\lim A_n(NFD)/n(a/2)$, is monotone decreasing in a. Compare with Exercise 5.1-10(b).

[Answer: $\frac{1}{a}(\pi^2/6 - (1-a)/k_0 - \Sigma_{k=1}^{k_0}1/k^2)$, where k_0 is that integer that satisfies $1/(k_0+1) < a \leq 1/k_0$.]

3. The bound on $O(n)$ deviations obtained following equation (18) is valid for *all* values of n. What is the optimal choice of r, for some given distribution of piece size and n? (Optimal in the sense that it will provide the tightest bound). Compute this optimal choice explicitly for $X \sim U(0,a)$.

4. In this exercise you will prove the Central Limit Theorem for $A_n(NFD)$, equation (20). Proceed through the following steps, that are similar to those leading to equation (19); note that the latter is however an asymptotic result, whereas here you are asked to go to the limit. It will clarify the procedure if you use the asymptotic expression $n\alpha$ for $A_n(NFD)$. α depends on the distribution of X and is given by equation (11).

(a) Show an upper bound,

$$\text{Prob}\left[\frac{A_n(NFD)-\alpha n}{\delta n \sigma} \leq x\right] \leq \text{Prob}\left[\frac{\Sigma_{k=1}^{r-1}N_k/k - (r-1) - n\alpha}{\delta n \sigma} \leq x\right]$$

$$= \text{Prob}\left[\frac{\Sigma_{j=1}^{n}[z_{jr}-E(z_{jr})]}{\sqrt{nV(z_{jr})}} \leq \left[\frac{x\sigma+r-1}{\sqrt{nV(z_{jr})}} + \frac{\sqrt{n}\,\Sigma_{k\geq r}P_k/k}{\sqrt{V(z_{jr})}} \xrightarrow[r=o(n)]{n\to\infty} x\right]\right].$$

For what range of r (as a function of n) does this limit hold?

(b) Show a lower bound of a similar form, via the y_{jr}. Show that both $V(z_{jr})$ and $V(y_{jr})$ converge to the same σ as $r\to\infty$, and show that this is the limiting variance of $A_n(NFD)/n$ as well.

(c) Now use the CLT, (see e.g. Loève, 1977 Vol. I, p. 321) to obtain equation (20).

5. In Exercise 4 you obtained a general expression for the limiting variance of $A_n(NFD)$. Obtain an explicit result when $X \sim U(0,1)$. Compare the limiting estimate it provides for the probability $\text{Prob}[A_n(NFD) \geq 1.1A_n(NFD)]$ with the one obtained from relation (19).

6. Prove the Theorem of relation (27).

[Prove separately the two inequalities. Proceed by induction over k, showing $A_k'(n) \leq G_k(n)$, etc., as $A'(n) = \lim_{k\to\infty} A_k'(n)$. The proof proceeds by assuming that all the pieces in W_k take their maximal possible size, $1/k$ (when proving the right-hand side, and the converse, $1/(k+1)$, for the other side). The proof is fairly long, as it has to consider the several possible cases for the number of pieces from W_k that are packed under NFD to the last bin used for W_{k-1}. See Appendix A in Hofri and Kamhi (1986).]

7. Following equation (32) it is claimed that $cov[G(n), X(n)]$ should be relatively small and often negative. Why is this so?

8. Justify the equalities obtained in the definitions (38)-(43).

9. Show that the leading terms, in n, for $E(A(n))$ and $V(A(n))$ as given by equations (46), and (50) with (52), respectively, are precisely those obtained in Section 5.2.1 (equations (11) and (21) there).

10. For $X \sim U(0,1)$ show that the $d_i(n)$ defined in equations (36)-(39) assume the following values:

$$d_1 \approx 0.6449341, \quad d_2 \approx 0.2579457, \quad d_3 \approx 0.5571228,$$

$$d_4(n) \leq \frac{1}{2(n-1)} + \frac{0.2213}{(n-1)^{3/2}} + O(n^{-5/2}).$$

$$d_5(n) \leq 0.55688654 \cdot \frac{1}{(n-1)^{3/2}} + \frac{1}{2(n-1)^2} + O(n^{-5/2})$$

$$d_6(n) = \frac{1}{2}\log(n-1) + 1.0776534 + \frac{1}{4(n-1)} + O(n^{-2}).$$

$$d_8(n) \approx 2.83327.$$

Prove relation (49).

[Guidance: For this distribution $P_k = 1/k(k+1)$. $d_1 = \Sigma_{k\geq 1} 1/k^2(k+1) = \pi^2/6 - 1 \approx 0.6449341$. $d_2 = \Sigma_{k\geq 1} 1/k^4(k+1)^2 = 4\zeta(2) - 2\zeta(3) + \zeta(4) - 5 \approx 0.2579457$. $d_3 = \Sigma_{k\geq 1} 1/k^3(k+1) = \zeta(3) - \zeta(2) + 1 \approx 0.5571228$. $d_4(n) = \Sigma_{k\geq 1} [k^2(k+1)]^{-1} \times \left(1 - 1/k(k+1)\right)^{n-1}$. The expression for $d_4(n)$ does not seem to have a simpler form, but a reasonable bound for it obtains by noting that $(1- 1/t)^t$ is monotonic increasing in t, and is bounded by $1/e$, hence $d_4(n) < \Sigma_{k\geq 1} [k^2(k+1)]^{-1} \times e^{-(n-1)/k(k+1)} < \int_{x\geq 0} x^{-2}(x+1)^{-1} e^{-(n-1)/x(x+1)} dx$. Substituting in the integrand $u = 1/x(x+1)$, the integral transforms into $\frac{1}{2}\int_{u\geq 0} \left(1 + \sqrt{u/(u+4)}\right) e^{-(n-1)u} du$. The first term is immediate, and the second one equals a form of Whittaker's function $W_{-\frac{1}{2},\frac{1}{2}}(4(n-1))$, which can be shown (see Abramowitz and Stegun (1964), pp. 505, 508) to rapidly approach for increasing n the value $\frac{1}{4}\Gamma(3/2)(n-1)^{-3/2}$. Thus $d_4(n) = \frac{1}{2}(n-1)^{-1} + 0.2213(n-1)^{-3/2} + O(n^{-5/2})$. Show that this bound is at most a few percent off for $n \geq 10$. Similarly,

$$d_5(n) = \sum_{k \geq 1} \frac{1}{k^3(k+1)} \left(1 - \frac{1}{k(k+1)}\right)^{n-1} < \int_{x \geq 0} \frac{e^{(n-1)/x(x+1)}}{x^3(x+1)} \, dx$$

$$= \int_{u \geq 0} \left(u/2 + \frac{1}{2}\sqrt{u} \sqrt{u+4} - \sqrt{u/(u+4)}\right) e^{-u(n-1)} du$$

$$< \left(1 - \frac{1}{2}\Gamma(3/2)\right)(n-1)^{-3/2} + \frac{1}{2}(n-1)^{-2} + O(n^{-5/2}).$$

The numerical value of the coefficient of the leading term is 0.55688654.
The evaluations of $d_6(n)$ and $d_8(n)$ clearly result from those of $d_4(n)$ and $d_5(n)$ respectively:

$$d_6(n) = \sum_{k \geq 1} \frac{1}{k^2(k+1)} \sum_{t=0}^{n-1} \left(1 - \frac{1}{k(k+1)}\right)^t = \sum_{k \geq 1} \frac{1}{k^2(k+1)} + \sum_{t=2}^{n} d_4(t).$$

To improve the approximation (for rather small values of n) the first few terms in the second sum could be handled explicitly. Doing it for two terms yields: $d_6(n) = \zeta(4) - 5\zeta(3) + 22\zeta(2) - 30 + \sum_{t=4}^{n} d_4(t)$ and the last sum could now be replaced by: $\frac{1}{2} \sum_{j=3}^{n-1} \left[j^{-1} + \frac{1}{2}\Gamma(3/2)j^{-3/2}\right] \approx \frac{1}{2}[\gamma - 3/2 + \log(n-1) + 1/2(n-1) + \frac{1}{2}\Gamma(3/2)\left(\zeta(3/2) - 1 - 1/\sqrt{8}\right)] \approx \frac{1}{2}[\log(n-1) + 1/2(n-1) - 0.3658696...].$
Finally then, $d_6(n) = \frac{1}{2}\log(n-1) + \frac{1}{4}(n-1)^{-1} + 1.0776534 + O(n^{-2})$.
The value of $d_8(n)$ is handled analogously, except that since the leading term in $d_5(n)$ is $O(n^{-3/2})$ we can save some of the care required for $d_6(n)$. $d_8(n) = \sum_{k \geq 1} P_k/k^2 + \sum_{t=2}^{n} d_5(t)$. Replacing the later sum by the corresponding infinite sum produces $d_8(n) < d_3 + \left(1 - \frac{1}{2}\Gamma(3/2)\right)\zeta(3/2) + \frac{1}{2}\zeta(2) = 2.83327$.
Note that the bound $d_{13}(n) < d_6^2(n)$ is quite acceptable for this distribution, as it only contributes to terms of order lower than the leading one (and produces an overestimate of rather less than 20% for $n > 100$).]

11. Use the values obtained in Exercise 10 to estimate $E[A(n)]$ and $V[A(n)]$ for $n = 100$ and $n = 10^6$.
[Guidance: The lower bound for $V[G(n)]$ is $\underline{V[G(n)]} \equiv n(d_3 - d_1^2) - 2nd_1 d_4(n) \geq 0.1411829n + 1 - \pi^2/6 - 0.28545/\sqrt{n}$, and the upper bound $\overline{V[G(n)]} \equiv n(d_3 - d_1^2) + \pi^2/6 + 2nd_4(n) \leq 0.1411829n + 1 + \pi^2/6 + 0.28545/\sqrt{n}$. The bounds on $E[H^2(n)]$ were set at $4(d_8(n) + d_{13}(n)) < E[H^2(n)] < 9(d_8(n) + d_{13}(n))$; they do not appear easy to improve upon in a material way, and thus $\dfrac{4(d_8(n) + d_{13}(n))}{\underline{V[G(n)]}}$

$< D(n)^2 < \dfrac{9(d_8(n) + d_{13}(n))}{\underline{V[G(n)]}} \equiv \overline{D}(n)^2.$
Hence we can state $\underline{V[G(n)]}(1 - 2\overline{D}(n)) < V[A(n)] < \overline{V[G(n)]}(1 + \overline{D}(n))^2$. The upper and lower bounds have the same leading terms in n, but for finite values of n the range can be appreciable.
For $n = 100$ and $n = 10^6$ proceed as follows. First the mean: $E[G(n)] - E[H(n)] <$

$E[A(n)] < E[G(n)] + 1$. Since $E[G(n)] \approx (\pi^2/6 - 1)\, n + \frac{1}{2} \log(n-1) + 1/4(n-1) + 1.0777$, we obtain now $E[G(100)] \approx 67.871$. $E[H(100)] < 3d_6(100) \approx 10.1333$. So: $57.74 < E(A(100)) < 68.9$. For the variance: $\overline{V[G(100)]} = 16.791$, $\underline{V[G(100)]} = 13.445$, $\overline{D(100)}^2 = 8.738$, and hence $0 < V[A(100)] < 262.79$. Note the poor lower bound for the variance. Here $E(A) \approx 4\sqrt{V(A)}$, taking the upper limit for $V(A)$.

Now considering the much larger n, 10^6; the corresponding figures would be: $644921. < E(A) < 644942$. $\underline{V(G)} = 141182.3$, $\overline{V(G)} = 141185.5$, $125604. < V(A) < 157666.$, $(\overline{D} = 0.056767)$ with $E(A) \approx 1600\sqrt{V(A)}$, implying the much smaller (relative) likely variations of $A(10^6)$.]

12. When the bounds in (32) - and (34) - were formulated, we deleted from the left-hand side the term $V[X(n)]$. Why was this necessary?
[Relations (33) supply the hint.]

13. For $X \sim U(0,a)$, $a \le 1$, determine the leading terms in the bounds (46) and (50), and show that they provide, using the definition of k_0 as given in Exercise 2:

$$d_1(a) = \frac{1}{a}\left[\frac{\pi^2}{6} - \frac{1-a}{k_0} - \sum_{k=1}^{k_0} \frac{1}{k^2} \right]$$

$$d_3(a) = \frac{1}{a}\left[\frac{a+k_0-1}{k_0^2} + \zeta(3) - \frac{\pi^2}{6} + \sum_{k=2}^{k_0} \frac{k-1}{k} \right]$$

So that the leading terms are

$$E(A(n)) \approx \frac{n}{a}\left[\frac{\pi^2}{6} - \frac{1-a}{k_0} - \sum_{k=1}^{k_0} \frac{1}{k^2} \right]$$

$$V(A(n)) \approx \frac{n}{a}\left\{ \zeta(3) - \frac{\pi^2}{6} + \frac{a+k_0-1}{k_0^2} + \sum_{k=2}^{k_0} \frac{k-1}{k^3} - \frac{1}{a}\left[\frac{\pi^2}{6} - \frac{1-a}{k_0} - \sum_{k=1}^{k_0} \frac{1}{k^2} \right]^2 \right\}.$$

Appendix A

Binomial Coefficients

The binomial coefficients are probably the most important combinatorial numbers (except the natural numbers as such, that is). Thus the following rather short collection of relations they satisfy should prove useful when reading the text, and for reference value when tackling the exercises. Together with their ubiquity comes the fact that they can be assembled to form a seemingly uncountable number of identities. Riordan (1968) writes with fascination (and exasperation) on the chameleon-like properties of these identities. The only claim I can make for this particular collection is that here are those relations I found useful in my work.

1. Expansion and conversion

$$\binom{r-1}{k-1} + \binom{r-1}{k} = \binom{r}{k} \tag{1.1}$$

$$\binom{-r}{k}(-1)^k = \binom{r+k-1}{k}; \quad \binom{r}{k} = \frac{r}{k}\binom{r-1}{k-1} \tag{1.2}$$

$$\binom{r}{m}\binom{m}{k} = \binom{r}{k}\binom{r-k}{m-k} \tag{1.3}$$

2. Summations with a single coefficient

$$\sum_{k=0}^{n}\binom{r+k}{r} = \binom{r+n+1}{n}; \quad \sum_{i=0}^{m}\binom{i+n}{t} = \binom{m+n+1}{t+1} - \binom{n}{t+1} \tag{2.1}$$

$$\sum_{k=m}^{n}\binom{k}{m} = \binom{n+1}{m+1} \tag{2.2}$$

$$\sum_{k=0}^{n} \binom{k+a}{k} z^k = \sum_{i=0}^{a} z^{a-i} \frac{\binom{a}{i}-\binom{a+n+1}{i} z^{n+1}}{(1-z)^{i+a+1}} , \quad \text{realistic for moderate } a \tag{2.3}$$

$$\sum_{k\geq 0} \binom{k+a}{k} z^k = \frac{1}{(1-z)^{a+1}} ; \quad \sum_{k\geq 0} \binom{s+k}{u} z^k = \frac{z^{u-s}}{(1-z)^{u+1}} , \quad \text{integers } u\geq s \tag{2.4}$$

$$\sum_{k\geq 0} \binom{r-tk}{k} z^k = \frac{x^{r+1}}{(t+1)x-t} , \quad \text{where } z=x^{t+1}-x^t , \quad |z| < |t^t(t+1)^{-(t+1)}| \tag{2.5}$$

$$\sum_{k\geq 0} \binom{r-tk}{k} \frac{r}{r-tk} z^k = x^r , \quad \text{iff } r\neq tk; \quad z=x^{t+1}-x^t, \quad |z| < |t^t(t+1)^{-(t+1)}| \tag{2.6}$$

3. Summations with two binomial coefficients

$$\sum_{k} \binom{r}{k}\binom{s}{n-k} = \binom{r+s}{n} , \quad n \text{ integer (Vandermonde's convolution).} \tag{3.1}$$

$$\sum_{k} \binom{n+\alpha}{k}\binom{n+\beta}{n-k} t^k = (t-1)^n P_n^{(\alpha,\beta)}\left(\frac{t+1}{t-1}\right) \tag{3.2}$$

$P^{(\alpha,\beta)}$ – Jacobi polynomial, Gradshtein & Rej'ik, § 8.96, $\alpha, \beta > -1$.

$$\sum_{k} \binom{r}{k}\binom{s}{n+k} = \binom{r+s}{r+n} \quad \text{integer } n, \quad \text{integer } r\geq 0. \tag{3.3}$$

$$\sum_{k=0}^{r} \binom{r-k}{m}\binom{s+k}{n} = \binom{r+s+1}{m+n+1} , \quad n\geq s\geq 0, \ m\geq 0, \ r\geq 0. \tag{3.4}$$

$$\sum_{k} \binom{r}{k}\binom{s+k}{n}(-1)^k = (-1)^r \binom{s}{n-r} \quad \text{integer } n, \quad \text{integer } r\geq 0. \tag{3.5}$$

$$\sum_{k} \binom{r-k}{m}\binom{s}{k-t}(-1)^k = (-1)^t \binom{r-t-s}{r-t-m} , \quad \text{integers } r, m, t. \tag{3.6}$$

$$\sum_{k} \binom{r-tk}{k}\binom{s-t(n-k)}{n-k} \frac{r}{r-tk} = \binom{r+s-tn}{n} , \quad \text{integer } n\geq 0. \tag{3.7}$$

$$\sum_{k\geq 0} \binom{r+tk}{k}\binom{s-tk}{n-k} = \sum_{k\geq 0} \binom{p-k}{n-k} t^k = \begin{cases} t^{p+1}(t-1)^{n-p-1} & p<n \\ (1-t^{n+1})/(1-t) & p=n \quad p\equiv r+s \\ \text{cf. (2.3)} & p>n \end{cases} \tag{3.8}$$

4. Inverse relations

$$a_n = \sum_k (-1)^k \binom{n}{k} b_k , \qquad\qquad b_n = \sum_k (-1)^k \binom{n}{k} a_k \qquad\qquad (4.1)$$

$$a_n = \sum_k (-1)^k \binom{n}{k}\binom{s+tk}{n} b_k , \quad \binom{s+tn}{n} b_n = \sum_k (-1)^k \frac{s+tk-k}{s+tn-k}\binom{s+tn-k}{n-k} a_k \quad (4.2)$$

$$a_n = \sum_{k=0}^{\lfloor n/2 \rfloor} \binom{n}{k} b_{n-2k} , \qquad\qquad b_n = \sum_{k=0}^{\lfloor n/2 \rfloor} (-1)^k \frac{n}{n-k}\binom{n-k}{k} a_{n-2k} \qquad (4.3)$$

5. Asymptotic values (from Stirling approximation)

$$\Gamma(n+1) = n! = \sqrt{2\pi n}\, n^{n+\frac{1}{2}} e^{-n}\left(1 + \frac{1}{12n} + \frac{1}{288n^2} + O(n^{-3})\right) \qquad (5.1)$$

$$\binom{n}{k} = \left(\frac{n}{2\pi k(n-k)}\right)^{\frac{1}{2}}\left(\frac{n}{k}\right)^k \left(\frac{n}{n-k}\right)^{n-k}$$
$$\times\left[1 + \frac{1}{12}\left(\frac{1}{n} - \frac{1}{k} - \frac{1}{n-k}\right) + \frac{1}{288}\left(\frac{1}{n} - \frac{1}{k} - \frac{1}{n-k}\right)^2 + O\left(\frac{1}{kn(n-k)}\right)\right] \qquad (5.2)$$

$$\text{If } j = \frac{n}{2} - k = o(n), \qquad \binom{n}{k} = \left(\frac{2}{n\pi}\right)^{\frac{1}{2}} 2^n e^{-\frac{2j^2}{n} + O(j^3/n^2)} \qquad (5.3)$$

$$\binom{n}{s+t} \sim \binom{n}{s}\left(\frac{n-s}{s}\right)^t \quad \text{uniformly in } t \text{ and } s,\, t^2 = o(s),\, t^2 = o(n-s), \text{ large } n. \quad (5.4)$$

Appendix B

Stirling Numbers

The Stirling numbers of the first and second type were defined in Section 3.1 via equations (8) and (9) respectively, repeated below for completeness, as equations (1.1) and (1.2). Most of the following formulas and properties have been collected from Knuth (1968) and Abramowitz and Stegun (1964).

1. Generating functions: Lower index

$$n!\binom{x}{n} = \sum_{k=0}^{n} \left[{n \atop k}\right](-1)^{n-k} x^k \tag{1.1}$$

$$x^n = \sum_{k=0}^{n} \left\langle{n \atop k}\right\rangle k! \binom{x}{k} \tag{1.2}$$

Upper index

$$[\log(1+x)]^m = m! \sum_{n \geq m} \left[{n \atop m}\right](-1)^{n-m} \frac{x^n}{n!} \tag{1.3}$$

$$(e^x - 1)^m = m! \sum_{n \geq m} \left\langle{n \atop m}\right\rangle \frac{x^n}{n!} \tag{1.4}$$

$$\prod_{j=1}^{m} x(1-jx)^{-1} = \sum_{n \geq m} \left\langle{n \atop m}\right\rangle x^n, \quad mx < 1 \tag{1.5}$$

2. Addition formulas

$$\left[{n \atop m}\right] = (n-1)\left[{n-1 \atop m}\right] + \left[{n-1 \atop m-1}\right], \quad n \geq 1 \tag{2.1}$$

$$\left\langle {n \atop m} \right\rangle = m \left\langle {n-1 \atop m} \right\rangle + \left\langle {n-1 \atop m-1} \right\rangle, \qquad n \geq 1 \tag{2.2}$$

3. Inverse and orthogonal relations (Cf. Part 5)

$$a_n = \sum_k (-1)^{n-k} \left[{n \atop k}\right] b_k , \qquad b_n = \sum_k \left\langle {n \atop k} \right\rangle a_k \tag{3.1}$$

$$\sum_k \left[{n \atop k}\right] \left\langle {k \atop m} \right\rangle (-1)^k = (-1)^n \delta_{mn} ; \qquad \sum_k \left\langle {n \atop k} \right\rangle \left[{k \atop m}\right] (-1)^k = (-1)^n \delta_{mn} \tag{3.2}$$

$$\sum_k \left\langle {n+1 \atop k+1} \right\rangle \left[{k \atop m}\right] (-1)^k = (-1)^m \binom{n}{m} \tag{3.3}$$

$$\sum_k \left\langle {k \atop m} \right\rangle \left[{n+1 \atop k+1}\right] (-1)^k = (-1)^m \frac{n!}{m!} , \qquad n \geq m, \quad \text{otherwise } 0. \tag{3.4}$$

4. Special values

$$\binom{m}{n} = \left[{m \atop n}\right] = \left\langle {m \atop n} \right\rangle = 0, \quad n > m; \qquad \binom{n}{n} = \left[{n \atop n}\right] = \left\langle {n \atop n} \right\rangle = 1 \tag{4.1}$$

$$\left[{n \atop n-1}\right] = \left\langle {n \atop n-1} \right\rangle = \binom{n}{2} \tag{4.2}$$

$$\left[{n \atop 0}\right] = \left\langle {n \atop 0} \right\rangle = 0; \quad \left[{n \atop 1}\right] = (n-1)!; \quad \left\langle {n \atop 1} \right\rangle = 1; \quad \left\langle {n \atop 2} \right\rangle = 2^{n-1}-1, \quad n > 0. \tag{4.3}$$

5. Expansion formulas

$$\sum_k \left[{n \atop k}\right] \binom{k}{m} = \left[{n+1 \atop m+1}\right]; \qquad \sum_k \left[{n+1 \atop k+1}\right] \binom{k}{m} (-1)^k = \left[{n \atop m}\right] (-1)^m \tag{5.1}$$

$$\sum_k \left\langle {k \atop m} \right\rangle \binom{n}{k} = \left\langle {n+1 \atop m+1} \right\rangle; \qquad \sum_k \left\langle {k+1 \atop m+1} \right\rangle \binom{n}{k} (-1)^k = \left\langle {n \atop m} \right\rangle (-1)^n \tag{5.2}$$

$$\sum_{k \leq n} \left[{k \atop m}\right] \frac{n!}{k!} = \left[{n+1 \atop m+1}\right] \tag{5.3}$$

$$\sum_{k \leq n} \left\langle {k \atop m} \right\rangle (m+1)^{n-k} = \left\langle {n+1 \atop m+1} \right\rangle \tag{5.4}$$

$$\sum_k \binom{n}{k} k^m (-1)^k = (-1)^n n! \left\langle {m \atop n} \right\rangle \tag{5.5}$$

$$\sum_{m=1}^n (-1)^m \left[{n \atop m}\right] = 0, \quad n \geq 2; \qquad \sum_{m=0}^n \left[{n \atop m}\right] = n! \tag{5.6}$$

$$\sum_{k=m}^{n} \begin{bmatrix} n+1 \\ k+1 \end{bmatrix} (-n)^{k-m} = \begin{bmatrix} n \\ m \end{bmatrix} \tag{5.7}$$

$$\sum_{m=1}^{n} (-1)^m (m-1)! \left\langle {n \atop m} \right\rangle = 0, \quad n \geq 2 ; \qquad \sum_{m=0}^{n} (-1)^{n-m} m! \left\langle {n \atop m} \right\rangle = 1 \tag{5.8}$$

$$\sum_{k} \binom{m-n}{m+k}\binom{m+n}{n+k}\left\langle {m+k \atop k} \right\rangle = \begin{bmatrix} n \\ n-m \end{bmatrix}, \quad n \geq m \tag{5.9}$$

$$\sum_{k} \binom{m-n}{n+k}\binom{m+n}{n+k}\begin{bmatrix} m+k \\ k \end{bmatrix} = \left\langle {n \atop n-m} \right\rangle, \quad n \geq m \tag{5.10}$$

$$\sum_{k=m-r}^{n-r} \binom{n}{k}\begin{bmatrix} n-k \\ r \end{bmatrix}\begin{bmatrix} k \\ m-r \end{bmatrix} = \binom{m}{r}\begin{bmatrix} n \\ m \end{bmatrix}, \quad n \geq m \geq r \tag{5.11}$$

$$\sum_{k=m-r}^{n-r} \binom{n}{k}\left\langle {n-k \atop r} \right\rangle\left\langle {k \atop m-r} \right\rangle = \binom{m}{r}\left\langle {n \atop m} \right\rangle, \quad n \geq m \geq r \tag{5.12}$$

6. Asymptotics

$$\begin{bmatrix} n \\ m \end{bmatrix} \sim \frac{(n-1)!}{(m-1)!} (\gamma + \log n)^{m-1}, \quad m = o(\log n) \tag{6.1}$$

$$\left\langle {n+m \atop m} \right\rangle \sim \frac{m^{2n}}{2^n n!}, \quad n = o(\sqrt{m}) \tag{6.2}$$

$$\lim_{n \to \infty} \frac{\begin{bmatrix} n+1 \\ m \end{bmatrix}}{n \begin{bmatrix} n \\ m \end{bmatrix}} = 1 \tag{6.3}$$

$$\lim_{m \to \infty} \frac{\begin{bmatrix} n+m \\ m \end{bmatrix}}{m^{2n}} = \frac{(-1)^n}{2^n n!} \tag{6.4}$$

$$\lim_{n \to \infty} m^{-n} \left\langle {n \atop m} \right\rangle = \frac{1}{m!} \tag{6.5}$$

$$\lim_{n \to \infty} \frac{\left\langle {n+1 \atop m} \right\rangle}{\left\langle {n \atop m} \right\rangle} = m. \tag{6.6}$$

Appendix C

Inequalities

The apologia introduced in Appendix A holds here as well: Inequalities are ubiquitous, numerous and useful. These are the ones I keep meeting and using. First are listed bounds on probabilities, and then "analytic" ones.

Markov:
$$\frac{E\,|X\,|^r - a^r}{\text{a.s. sup}\,|X\,|^r} \le \text{Prob}\,\{\,|X\,|\ge a\,\} \le E\,[\,(\frac{|X\,|}{a})^n\,], \quad n > 0. \tag{1}$$

(This is the best possible bound when the only information is that X is nonnegative and with finite mean.)

Bienaymè–Chebyshev: $\text{Prob}\,\{\,|X\,|>t\,\} \le t^{-2}E\,(X^2).$ (2)

This is the same as the right-hand side of (1) for $n=2$.

Chebyshev-Cantelli: $\text{Prob}\{X - \mu \ge t\,\} \le \dfrac{\sigma^2}{\sigma^2 + t^2}.$ (3)

Both (1) and (2) are special cases of the following, more general inequality (Loève, (1977) vol I, p. 159): Let X be an arbitrary rv and g on R be a nonnegative Borel function. If g is even and nondecreasing on $[0, +\infty)$ then, for every $a \ge 0$

Loève: $\dfrac{Eg\,(X) - g\,(a)}{\text{a.s. sup}\,g\,(X)} \le \text{Prob}[\,|X\,|\ge a\,] \le \dfrac{Eg\,(X)}{g\,(a)}.$ (4)

If g is nondecreasing on all of R, then the middle term is replaced by $\text{Prob}[\,X \ge a\,]$, where a is an arbitrary real number. □

Let $X_1, X_2, \cdots, X_n$ be independent rv's with finite second moments, and let S_k be the sum of the first k X_i's. Then, for any $\varepsilon > 0$

Kolmogorov: $\mathrm{Prob}\big(\max\limits_{1\le k\le n} |S_k - E(S_k)| \ge \varepsilon\big) \le \dfrac{\sigma_n^2}{\varepsilon^2}$, $\qquad \sigma_n^2 \equiv V(S_n).$ $\qquad\square$ (5)

Let X_i $1\le i \le n$ be independent bounded rv's $0\le X_i \le 1$, $\mu = E(S = \Sigma X_i)/n$, then, for $0 < t < 1-\mu$:

Hoeffding: $\mathrm{Prob}(S - n\mu \ge nt\,) \le \big[\big(\dfrac{\mu}{\mu+t}\big)^{\mu+t} \big(\dfrac{1-\mu}{1-\mu-t}\big)^{1-\mu-t}\big]^n$

(6)

$$\le \exp(-nt^2 g(\mu)),$$

where $g(\mu) = \begin{cases} \dfrac{1}{1-2\mu}\log(\dfrac{1-\mu}{\mu}) & 0 < \mu < \dfrac{1}{2} \\[2ex] \dfrac{1}{2\mu(1-\mu)} & \dfrac{1}{2} \le \mu < 1. \end{cases}$ $\quad g(\mu) \ge 2,\ \ \forall\,\mu$

Since $g(\mu) \ge 2$, $\forall\,\mu$, a milder and easier to use bound is obtained by replacing $g(\mu)$ in (6) by 2.

For $t > 1 - \mu$ the first bound in the right-hand-side in (6) is 0, and for $t = 1 - \mu$ it equals μ^n. Hoeffding (1963) also gives expressions for the cases when the bounds on the random variables are not all the same (Theorem 2 in section 2.6.2), and for certain forms of dependence. $\square$

The combinatorial **Bonferroni** inequalities are easily adapted to probability measures (Comtet (1974), pp. 192-3). Let $\mathsf{A} = \{A_i, 1\le i \le n\}$ be a set of events in some probability space Ω, associated with a measure P, and define the probabilities S_k as the sum of probabilities of occurrence of the intersections of all k-strong subsets of these events:

$$S_k = \sum_{1\le i_1 < i_2 < \cdots < i_k \le n} P(A_{i_1} A_{i_2} \cdots A_{i_k}) \qquad S_0 \equiv P(\Omega)$$

then the sum $\sum_{k=1}^{n}(-1)^{k-1}S_k$ satisfies the *alternating inequalities*

Bonferroni: $(-1)^k \big[P\big(\bigcup\limits_{i=1}^{n} A_i\big) + \sum\limits_{j=1}^{k}(-1)^j S_j \big] \ge 0$, $\quad 1\le k \le n$

(7)

$(-1)^{k+1}\big[P\big(\bigcap\limits_{i=1}^{n} \bar{A}_i\big) + \sum\limits_{j=0}^{k}(-1)^{j+1}S_j\big] \ge 0$, $\quad 1\le k \le n.$

For $k = 1$ the above reduces to **Boole**'s inequality, which is rarely useful for estimation, but good for proofs of convergence etc. $\square$

Jensen: $E[u(X)] \ge u(E[X])$, $\qquad$ when $u(\cdot)$ is a convex function. $\qquad\square$ (8)

If $a_1 \ge a_2 \ge \cdots \ge a_n$ and $b_1 \ge b_2 \ge \cdots \ge b_n$, then

Chebyshev: $n\sum\limits_{k=1}^{n} a_k b_k \ge \big(\sum\limits_{k=1}^{n} a_k\big)\big(\sum\limits_{k=1}^{n} b_k\big)$ $\qquad\square$

(9)

If $p > 1$, $q > 1$ and $p^{-1} + q^{-1} = 1$, then

Holder: $\displaystyle\sum_{k=1}^{n} |a_k b_k| \le \left(\sum_{k=1}^{n} |a_k|^p\right)^{1/p} \left(\sum_{k=1}^{n} |b_k|^q\right)^{1/q}.$ (10)

The **Cauchy-Schwartz** inequality is obtained for $p=q=2$. The analogue holds for integrals. ☐

If $p>1$ and a_k, b_k are positive for all k,

Minkowski: $\displaystyle\left(\sum_{k=1}^{n} (a_k + b_k)^p\right)^{1/p} \le \left(\sum_{k=1}^{n} a_k^p\right)^{1/p} + \left(\sum_{k=1}^{n} b_k^p\right)^{1/p}.$ (11)

The analogue holds for integrals. ☐

The Three Means: Let A, G and H denote the arithmetic, geometric and harmonic means of the sequence of real numbers $\{a_i, 1 \le i \le n\}$:

$$A = \sum a_i/n, \quad G = \left[\prod a_i\right]^{1/n}, \quad H = \left(\sum a_i^{-1}/n\right)^{-1}, \quad \text{then} \quad A \ge G \ge H. \quad \square \quad (12)$$

References

The following publications cover material which is useful for most of the chapters:

D.H. Greene, D.E. Knuth: *Mathematics for the Analysis of Algorithms.* 2nd Edition, Birkhaüser, 1982.

R. Kemp: *Fundamentals of the Average Case Analysis of Particular Algorithms.* Wiley-Teubner, 1984.

D.E. Knuth: *The Art of Computer Programming.* Addison-Wesley, Vol.I 1968, 2nd Ed. 1973; Vol.II 1969, 2nd Ed. 1981; Vol.III 1973.

R. Sedgewick: Mathematical Analysis of Combinatorial Algorithms. Included, as chapters 7-12 in G. Louchard and G. Latouche (Eds.), *Probability Theory and Computer Science.* Academic Press, 1983.
   A very terse survey of existing analyses rather than an independent text.

Further Books

M. Abramowitz, I. Stegun: *Handbook of Mathematical Functions.* Dover, 1964.

R. Bellman, R.E. Kalaba, J.A. Locket: *Numerical Inversion of the Laplace Transform: Applications to Biology, Economics, Engineering and Physics.* American Elsevier, 1966.

E.K. Blum: *Numerical Analysis and Computation: Theory and Practice.* Addison-Wesley, 1972.

B. Bollobas: *Graph Theory: An Introductory Course.* Springer-Verlag, 1979.
   Chapter VII is an introduction to the basic concepts of random graphs.

N. G. de Bruijn: *Asymptotic Methods in Analysis.* Dover, 1981.

L. Comtet: *Advanced Combinatorics.* D. Reidel Publ. Co. 1974.
   A veritable cyclopaedia of all lore combinatoric. Generating function oriented, very terse, but miraculously manages to insert a great many insights.

E. T. Copson: *Asymptotic Expansions.* Cambridge Univ. Press, 1965.
   Largely orthogonal to de Bruijn's, mainly integral estimation.
D. R. Cox: *Renewal Theory.* Methuen, 1962.
D. R. Cox, H. D. Miller: *The Theory of Stochastic Processes.* Chapman and Hall,
   1965.
B. Davies: *Integral Transforms and Their Applications.* Springer-Verlag, 1978.
   A lovely, lively survey of the major integral transforms and their properties.
   Beware of the typos.
G. Doetsch: *Guide to the Applications of the Laplace Transform.* D. Van
   Nostrand, 1971.
   THE reference on this transform, by the same author, *Handbuch der
   Laplace-Transformation,* Vols I-III, Birkhaüser, 1950-56, has not yet
   apparently (1986) been translated into English.
A. Erdélyi (Ed.): *Higher Transcendental Functions.* Vols I-III (Bateman
   Manuscript Project) McGraw Hill 1953.
A. Erdélyi (Ed.): *Tables of Integral Transforms.* Vols I-II (Bateman Manuscript
   Project) McGraw Hill 1954.
W. Feller: *An Introduction to Probability Theory and Its Applications.* J. Wiley.
   Vol. I, 3rd Ed. 1973, Vol. II, 2nd. Ed. 1971
George S. Fishman: *Principles of Discrete Event Simulation* 2nd Ed, J. Wiley,
   1978.
George E. Forsythe, Michael A. Malcolm, Cleve, B. Moller: *Computer Methods
   for Mathematical Computations.* Prentice-Hall 1977.
F. R. Gantmacher: *Theory of Matrices,* vol II, Chelsea, New York 1959.
R. M. Garey, D. S. Johnson: *Computers and Intractability* W.H. Freeman Co., San
   Francisco, 1979.
G. H. Gonnet: *Handbook of Algorithms and Data Structures.* Addison-Wesley,
   1984.
   Algorithms, implementation comments and main results of probabilistic
   analysis, as far as known.
I. P. Goulden, D. M. Jackson: *Combinatorial Enumeration.* J. Wiley, 1983.
   A very comprehensive coverage of the applications of gf's (ordinary and
   exponential) in combinatorics. Numerous exercises, with detailed solutions.
I. S. Gradshtein, I. M. Rej'ik: *Sums, Products and Integral Tables.* $(\sum \prod \int)$ 5th.
   Ed., Verlag Harri Deutsch, Thun 1981.
   This is the only translation of the 5th edition now available in English (the
   above edition is bilingual, with German). It is the best source for definite and
   indefinite integrals, but contains much material on special functions as well.
P. Henrici: *Applied and Computational Complex Analysis* J. Wiley, 3 Vols., 1974,
   1977, 1986.
S. Karlin: *A First Course in Stochastic Processes.* Academic Press, 1966.
J. G. Kemeny, J. L. Snell, A. W. Knapp: *Denumerable Markov Chains.* Springer-
   Verlag, 1976.
V. F. Kolchin, B. A. Sevast'yanov, V. P. Chistyakov: *Random Allocations.* V. H.

Winston, 1978.

M. Loève: *Probability Theory.* 4th Ed. Springer-Verlag, 1977.

K. Mehlhorn: *Data Structures and Algorithms.* Vols.1-3, Springer-Verlag, 1984.

Z. Nehari: *Conformal Mappings.* Dover, 1982 (Republication of the 1952 edition).

The first three chapters give a well paced survey of the concepts and techniques of complex function theory that we use. For a more complete coverage Whittaker and Watson or Henrici are the recommended sources.

E. Parzen: *Stochastic Processes.* Holden-Day, 1962.

Chapter 6 provides a clear exposition of the general properties of Markov chains, suitable for our needs. More comprehensive treatments may be found in Karlin and in Kemeny *et al.*

J. Riordan: *An Introduction to Combinatorial Analysis.* J. Wiley, 1958

J. Riordan: *Combinatorial Identities.* J. Wiley, 1968 (Reprinted with corrections by the Robert E. Krieger Pub. Co., 1979)

N. J. A. Sloane: *A Handbook of Integer Sequences* Academic Press, 1973.

G. Szegö : *Orthogonal Polynomials* Amer. Math. Soc. 3rd. Ed., 1967.

E. T. Whittaker, G. N. Watson: *A Course of Modern Analysis.* 4th Ed., Cambridge Univ. Press, 1927.

Still the standard reference for complex function theory and properties of the principal transcendental functions.

Papers cited in the text.

E. A. Bender: Central and Local Limit Theorems Applied to Asymptotic Enumeration. Jour. of Combinatorial Theory (A) **15,** 91-111 (1973)

E. A. Bender: Asymptotic Methods in Enumeration. SIAM Review, **16,** #4, 485-515 (1974)

E. A. Bender: An Asymptotic Expansion for the Coefficients of Some Formal Power Series. J. London Math. Soc. **9,** 451-458 (1975)

J. L. Bentley, D.S. Johnson, F. T. Leighton, C. C. McGeoch, L. A. McGeoch: Some Unexpected Expected Behavior Results for Bin Packing. Proceedings of STOC 1984, 279-288.

N. A. Brigham: A General Asymptotic Formula for Partition Functions. Proc. Amer. Math. Soc. **1,** 182-191 (1950)

N. G. de Bruijn, D. E. Knuth, S. O. Rice: The Average Height of Planted Plane Trees. In *Graph Theory and Computing* R-C. Read (ed.), Academic Press New York 1972 15-22.

J. I. Capetanakis: Tree Algorithms for Packet Broadcast Channels. IEEE Trans. Inf. Th. IT- **25** 505-515 (1979)

J. I. Capetanakis: Generalized TDMA: The Multiaccessing Tree Protocol. IEEE Trans. Comm. COM- **27** 1476-1487 (1979a)

L. Carlitz: The Coefficients in an Asymptotic Expansion. Proc. Amer. Math. Soc.

16, 248-252 (1965)

E. G. Coffman Jr., M. Hofri, Kimming, So., A.C. Yao: A Stochastic Model of Bin Packing. Inf. and Control, **44,** 105-115, (1980).

E. G. Coffman Jr., Garey M. R., Johnson D. S.: "Approximation Algorithms for Bin-Packing - An Updated Survey" In *Algorithm Design for Computer System Design* G. Ausiello, M. Lucertini, and P. Serafini (eds.) Springer-Verlag, New York, l984, 49-106.
Currently, this is the most comprehensive reference concerning a problem that has become the paradigm for combinatorial optimization heuristics. Not only stochastic results but also (mostly, actually) worst-case bounds.

E. G. Coffman Jr., G. S. Leuker, A. H. G. Rinnooy Kan: An Introduction to the Probabilistic Analysis of Sequencing and Packing Heuristics. TT, Econometric Institute, Erasmus University (1985).

E. G. Coffman Jr., T. T. Kadota, F. T. Leighton, L. A. Shepp: Stochastic Analysis of Storage Fragmentation. In O.J. Boxma, J.W. Cohen, H.C. Tijms (Eds.), *Proceedings of the International Seminar on Teletraffic Analysis and Computer Performance Evaluation,* held at the Centre for Mathematics and Computer Science, June 2-6 Amsterdam, The Netherlands. Elsevier Science Publishers B. V. (North-Holland), 275-295, 1986.

J. Csirik, J. B. G. Frenk, G. Galambos, A. H. G. Rinnooy Kan: A Probabilistic Analysis of the Dual Bin Packing Problem.
Preprint, 1986.

J. Csirik, J. B. G. Frenk, A. M. Frieze, G. Galambos, A. H. G. Rinnooy Kan: A Probabilistic Analysis of the Next-Fit-Decreasing Bin Packing Heuristic.
Preprint, 1986.

G. Fayolle, E. Gelenbe, J. Labetoulle: Stability and Optimal Control of the Packet Switching Broadcast Channel. JACM, **24** 375-386, 1977.

G. Fayolle, M. Hofri: On the Capacity of a Collision Channel Under Stack-Based Collision Resolution Algorithms. Technion, Haifa Israel TR #237. March 1982.

G. Fayolle, Philippe Flajolet, M. Hofri: On a Functional Equation Arising in the Evaluation of a Protocol for Multiaccess Broadcast Collision Channel. Adv. Appl. Probab. **18,** 441-472 (1986).

G. Fayolle, P. Flajolet, M. Hofri, P. Jacquet: Analysis of a Stack Algorithm for Random Multiple Access Communication. IEEE Trans. on Inf. Th., **IT-31** #2, 244-254, (1985).

P. Flajolet: Combinatorial Aspects of Continued Fractions. Discrete Mathem. **32** 125-161 (1980).

P. Flajolet: *Mathematical Methods in the Analysis of Algorithms and Data Structures.* Lecture notes for *A Graduate Course in Computation Theory,* Fall 1984.

P. Flajolet, A. Odlyzko: The Average Height of Binary Trees and Other Simple Trees. J. of Comp. & System Sc. **25** #2 171-213 (1982).

J. Franco: Sensitivity of Probabilistic results on Algorithms for NP-Complete

Problems to Input Distributions. SIGACT News **17** #1 40-59 (Summer 1985).

J. Franco, M. Paull: Probabilistic Analysis of the Davis-Putnam Procedure for Solving the Satisfiability Problem. Discr. Appl. Math. **5** 77-87 (1983).

G. N. Frederickson: Probabilistic Analysis for One- and Two-Dimensional Bin Packing Algorithms. Infor. Proc. Lett. **11**, 156-161 (1980).

K. Geihs, H. Kobayashi: Bounds on Buffer Overflow Probabilities in Communications Systems. Perf. Evaluation **2**, #3, 149-160 (1982).

A. Goldberg: Average Case Complexity of the Satisfiability Problem. In: Proc. 4th. Workshop on Automatic Deduction (Austin Texas, 1979).

G. H. Gonnet, J. I. Munro: The Analysis of Linear Probing Sort by the Use of a New Mathematical Transform. J. of Algorithms, **5**, 451-470 (1984).

B. Harris, L Schoenfeld: Asymptotic Expansions for the Coefficients of Analytic Functions. Illinois J. Math. **12**, 264-277 (1968)

W. K. Hayman: A Generalization of Stirling's Formula. J. Reine und Angew. Math. **196**, 67-95 (1956).

W. Hoeffding: Probability Inequalities for Sums of Bounded Random Variables. J. Am. Stat. Ass. **58**, 13-30 (1963).

M. Hofri: Two Dimensional Packing: Expected Performance of Simple Level Algorithms. Inf. and Control, **45**, 1-17, (1980).

M. Hofri: Stack Algorithms for Collision-Detecting Channels and Their Analysis: A Limited Survey. In F. Baccelli, G. Fayolle (Eds.): *Modelling and Performance Evaluation Methodology.* Proceedings of the International Seminar, Paris, January 1983. Published as Vol. 60 in the Lecture Notes in Control and Information Sciences Series by Springer-Verlag. 71-88.

M. Hofri: A Probabilistic Analysis of the Next-Fit Bin Packing Algorithm. J. of Algorithms, **5**, 547-556, (1984). (A somewhat expanded version exists as TR#242 of the Department of Computer Science, The Technion, Haifa, May 1982).

M. Hofri: A Feedback-less Distributed Broadcast Algorithm for Multihop Radio Networks with Time-Varying Structure. TR #451, Department of Computer Science, The Technion-IIT, Haifa 32000, Israel. March 1987.

M. Hofri, S. Kamhi: A Stochastic Analysis of the NFD Bin-Packing Algorithm. J. on Algorithms, **7**, 489-509, (1986).

M. Hofri, A.G. Konheim: The Analysis of a Finite Quasi-Symmetric ALOHA Network with Reservation. W. Bux, H. Rudin. (Eds.) Proc. "Performance of Computer-Communications Systems", North-Holland Amsterdam 1984, 505-525.

N. Karmarkar: Probabilistic Analysis of some Bin-Packing Problems. In Proceedings of the 23rd. FOCS 107-111 (1982)

R. M. Karp: Combinatorics, Complexity and Randomness. Comm. of the ACM, **29**, #2, 98-109, (1986).
    A Turing award lecture, surveying aspects of algorithms and probabilistic analysis from a point of view markedly different than this text (the focus is

entirely on combinatorial optimization).

R. M. Karp, M. Luby, A. Marchetti-Spaccamela: A Probabilistic Analysis of Multidimensional Bin Packing Problems. In Proceedings of STOC 1984, 289-298.

J. C. Lagarias, A. M. Odlyzko, D. B. Zagier: On the Capacity of Disjointly Shared Networks. Computer Networks, **10**, 275-285 (1985).

S. L. Lam: Multiple Access Protocols. Chapter 4 in *Computer Communications* Vol.I, W. Chou (Editor), Prentice-Hall Englewood Cliffs, NJ, 1982.

C. C. Lee, D. T. Lee: A Simple On-Line Bin-Packing Algorithm. Dept. of EE and CS Northwestern University, Evanston Ill. 60201, (1984)

R. Loulou: Tight Bounds and Probabilistic Analysis of Two Heuristics for Parallel Processor Scheduling. Math of Oper. Research, **9**, #1, 142-150 (1984).

A. Meir, J. W. Moon: On the Altitude of Nodes in Random Trees. Can. J. of Math. **30**, 997-1015 (1978).

A. M. Odlyzko: Periodic Oscillations of Coefficients of Power Series that Satisfy Functional Equations. Adv. in Math. **44**, #2 180-205 (1982).

A. M. Odlyzko, L. B. Richmond: Asymptotic Expansions for the Coefficients of Analytic Generating Functions.
Bell Labs Preprint, 1984.

V. R. Pratt: Shellsort and Sorting Networks. Ph.D. Thesis, Computer Science Dept., Stanford University, 1972.

H. Prodinger: On the Number of Combinations without a Fixed Distance. Jour. of Comb. Th. (A) **35**, 362-365 (1983).

J.M. Robson: Worst Case Fragmentation of First Fit and Best Fit Storage Allocation Strategies. *The Comp. J.,* **20** 242-244 (1978).

R. Sedgewick: The Analysis of Quicksort Programs. Acta Inform. **7**, 327-355 (1977).

D. L. Shell: A High-Speed Sorting Procedure. Comm. of the ACM **2** 30-32, (July 1959).

B. S. Tsybakov, V. A. Mikhailov: Free Synchronous Packet Access in a Broadcast Channel with Feedback. Prob. of Inf. Trans.(English Translation) **14** #4 259-280 (1978)

B. S. Tsybakov, N. D. Vvedenskaya: Random Multiple-Access Stack Algorithm. Prob. of Inf. Trans. (English Translation) **16** #3 230-243 (1980)

E. M. Wright: Asymptotic Relations Between Enumeration Functions in Graph Theory. Proc. London Math. Soc.(3) **20**, 558-72 (1970).

A. C.-C. Yao: An Analysis of $(h,k,1)$-Shellsort. J. of Algorithms, **1**. 14-50 (1980).

Sh. Zaks: Lexicographic Generation of Ordered Trees, Theo. Comp. Science, **10** 63-82 (1980).

NOTATION INDEX and numerical constants

Note: The list below contains mainly generic symbols, or such that appear at numerous places. Symbols that are only used near to where they are defined probably need not be here. Page numbers, when given, refer to place of definition.

Operators

$\binom{n}{k}$ - binomial coefficient, $n!/(k!(n-k)!)$.

$[z^n]f(z)$ - the coefficient of z^n in $f(z)$.

$\left[\begin{smallmatrix} n \\ k \end{smallmatrix}\right]$ - Stirling number of the first kind

$\left\langle\begin{smallmatrix} n \\ k \end{smallmatrix}\right\rangle$ - Stirling number of the second kind

$\lfloor x \rfloor$ - Floor function, the largest integer not exceeding x.

$\lceil x \rceil$ - Ceiling function, the smallest integer not less than x.

For an integer x, $x = \lfloor x \rfloor = \lceil x \rceil$

$\{x\}$ - x modulo $1 = x - \lfloor x \rfloor$

$\{x^k\}$ - expression in x, containing only powers of x not less than k.

$f'(x), f''(x), f^{[r]}(x)$ - Derivatives of the function $f(\cdot)$ at the point x.

$n^{\underline{l}} - n(n-1)\cdots(n-l+1) = n!/l!$, n, l integers.

$\displaystyle\oint_C - \frac{1}{2\pi i}\int_C$, an integral taken along the contour C in a counterclockwise sense.

$\displaystyle\int_{(c)} - \frac{1}{2\pi i}\int_{c-i\infty}^{c+i\infty}$

D - Differentiation operator.

$E(X)$ - Expected value of the random variable X.

$\mathrm{Re}(z), \mathrm{Im}(z)$ - Real and imaginary components of the complex number z.

$\mathrm{Res}(f(z); z_o)$ - Residue of the function $f(z)$ at $z = z_o$

U - Evaluation at 1. 68

$V(X)$ - Variance of the random variable X.

Z - Evaluation at 0. 68

$\Omega, \Theta, \sim, O, o$ - Asymptotic notation 12,13

$\sim$ - When used in $X \sim F(\cdot)$, the random variable X has the distribution function $F(\cdot)$.

Special Symbols and Functions

2^A - the power-set of the set A.

$A(n,k)$ - Eulerian numbers 118

$A_r(\cdot)$ - Eulerian polynomial of order r 7

$A_n(L)$ - the number of bins algorithm L requires to pack n pieces 186

B_k - k'th Bell number; k'th Bernoulli number.

$B_k(\cdot)$ - k'th Bernoulli polynomial 18

C - Generic symbol for the complex plane.

C - A contour (closed curve) in the complex plane.

e - Base of natural logarithm, 2.71828 18285

F_n - n'th Fibonacci number 43

$G(V,E)$ - A graph with a set of vertices V and a set of edges E.

H_n - The n'th harmonic number, equalls $\sum_{i=1}^{n} i^{-1}$.

I_k - The set of integers not less than k.

L_n - The duration of an order n CRI, l_n - its expected value.

$L_f(\cdot)$ - Laplace transform of the function $f(\cdot)$.

$L_X(\cdot)$ - Laplace-Stieltjes transform (LST) of the random variable X.

$\log n$ - Natural logarithm, to base e.

$M_f(\cdot)$ - Mellin transform of the function $f(\cdot)$.

N_n - The set of the first n natural numbers.

R - The continuum of real numbers;

    The number of steps a Markov chain takes before absorption

$S(A)$ - The set of all permutations of the set A (the symmetric group).

γ - Euler constant, 0.57721 56649 p.116

$\Gamma(x)$ - The common gamma function, equals $(x-1)!$ when x is integer; $\Gamma(\frac{1}{2}) = \pi^{\frac{1}{2}}$.

δ_{ij} - Kronecker's delta; one when $i = j$ and zero otherwise.

$\zeta(s)$ - Riemann zeta function, equals $\sum_{i \geq 1} i^{-s}$

    Special values: $\zeta(3/2) = 2.61237\ 534869$, $\zeta(2) = \pi^2/6$, $\zeta(3) = 1.20205\ 69032$

π - 3.14159 26536

$\varnothing$ - The empty set.

$\phi_S(\cdot)$ - Generating function for the set S.

χ_E - Indicator function of the event E.

INDEX

Italicized entries are acronyms; normally only their expansion is given. Italicized page numbers denote occurrence of the term in an exercise. Authors are only indexed to text entries. Multiple-authored works create only first-author index entries.

summation asymptotics 13*ff*
symmetric group *118*,120
sympathetic asymptotics 82*ff*
Szegö G. 158,159

transition probability kernel
  (of a Markov chain) 188*ff*
transition probability matrix
  (of a Markov chain) 100
trees
  binary 30,33
  k-ary 33,*41*
  labeled *97*
  ordered *41*
  plane *41*
Tsybakov B.S. *40*,162
Turing machine algorithm 5
  analysis 6*ff*

union operation 61,66

Vandermonde convolution 220

Wald's identity 106,107,*110,111*
Watson's lemma 45
weight 53
Whittaker E.T. 32,*41*,50,77
Whittaker's function *216*
word counting *72*
worst-case analysis 2
Wright E.M. 84

Yao A.C.-C. 129,134

z transform 25
Zaks Sh. *41*